Mergers in India

About the Author

Dr. Paramjeet Kaur is an Associate Professor of Economics at Sri Guru Gobind Singh College of Commerce, University of Delhi. She received her postgraduate and M.Phil degrees from Delhi School of Economics and PhD from Faculty of Management Studies, University of Delhi. Her areas of specialisation are economic theory of a firm, macroeconomic theory and statistical methods.

Mergers in India

Exploiting Financial Synergies

PARAMJEET KAUR

ACADEMIC FOUNDATION
NEW DELHI

www.academicfoundation.com

First published in 2012
by

ACADEMIC FOUNDATION
4772-73 / 23 Bharat Ram Road, (23 Ansari Road),
Darya Ganj, New Delhi - 110 002 (India).
Phones : 23245001 / 02 / 03 / 04.
Fax : +91-11-23245005.
E-mail : books@academicfoundation.com
www.academicfoundation.com

Cataloging in Publication Data--DK
Courtesy: D.K. Agencies (P) Ltd. <docinfo@dkagencies.com>

Paramjeet Kaur.
Mergers in India : exploiting financial synergies / Paramjeet Kaur.
p. cm.
Includes bibliographical references (p.).
ISBN 13: 9788171889112
ISBN 10: 8171889115

1. Consolidation and merger of corporations--India. 2. India--Economic policy--1991- I. Title.

DDC 338.830954 23

Typeset by Italics India, New Delhi.
Printed and bound in India.

Dedicated to my father

Late S. Arjan Singh ji

Contents

List of Tables and Figures

Tables

Figures

Acknowledgments

No words can suffice my deep gratitude to Prof. Raghav Gaiha, Faculty of Management Studies (University of Delhi), for the valuable directions provided for the econometric analysis carried in this book. I shall always remain indebted to his invaluable guidance, intellectual stimulation and patience with which he read drafts of various chapters of my book. I owe a great deal to Prof. Simrit Kaur, Faculty of Management Studies, for her inspiring guidance, encouragement and incessant support in completing this book.

I am obliged to Ms Harpreet Kaur for rendering her unfailing help in reading the preliminary drafts. I must acknowledge Mr Rajeev Ranjan, Accounts Manager, at Prowess Database-CMIE, for providing all possible assistance in collecting relevant material required for the analysis. My graititude also extends towards the library staff of Institute of Economic Growth, Faculty of Management Studies, Ratan Tata (Delhi School of Economics) and World Bank for assisting me in finding the required material.

My heartfelt thanks are also due to my family members as without their support the book could not have taken the present shape.

— Paramjeet Kaur

Foreword

Takeovers and mergers are as old as capitalism itself. In the Anglo-Saxon countries, they are an increasingly important part of the corporate landscape, as well as of activity on the stock market. They also raise international regulatory concerns, normally due to differences in regulatory philosophy, policies and practices between the European community and the US. However, their role is much more salient in developed rather than developing countries. Within developed countries their role is far more important in the UK and US than in France, Japan or Germany. The Anglo-Saxon practice involves the concept of involuntary takeovers whereby one large corporation may acquire control of another corporation through the device of a 'so-called' takeover bid. This involves the offer to buy the shares of the potential victim at a higher price than its current market price—over the heads of the board of directors or managers of the victim corporation. Strangely enough, the introduction of the takeover bid is a relatively recent phenomenon. It started in the UK in the 1950s and spread to the US in the 1960s and onwards. The reasons for this late introduction of the takeover mechanism even in developed capitalist countries such as the UK or US are not far to seek. There needs to be a certain separation between ownership and control of corporations before a takeover bid can become a method of acquiring control over another corporation. If share ownership is not widespread, and the shares are mainly family-owned, it will be difficult to mount a takeover bid if the family does not wish to sell. It was not until the 1950s and 1960s that the environment became conducive for the operation of a market for corporate control. Until now, most other developed countries have not met the condition of the diffusion of share ownership, nor the additional requirement of the availability of accurate accounting information about individual corporations. Outside Anglo-Saxon countries, corporations tend to be family-controlled or controlled by big-block shareholders, neither of which encourage the establishment of an Anglo-Saxon-type market for corporate control.

A very important question in this context is whether the absence of a market for corporate control helps or harms the non-Anglo-Saxon developed countries (NADs). A great deal of research has been done on this subject in the last 50 years for developed countries, which by and large suggests that not having a market for corporate control is not a great handicap for the NADs. Research on Anglo-Saxon developed countries shows that a market for corporate control seldom increases efficiency of resource allocation or distribution. Selection in the market for corporate control, for example, takes place on the basis not just of performance (in terms of either profitability or Tobin's queue) but also on the basis of size. The large firms are more likely to take over small firms, and often the inefficient take over the efficient. A large unprofitable company has a greater chance of survival than a small profitable one. Takeovers are also regarded as encouraging short-termism and speculation. In view of these and other results of the research on takeovers, the continental European countries and Japan are in no great hurry to follow the Anglo-Saxon countries. It is possible, however, that the NAD countries may be obliged by the terms of current globalisation to follow nonetheless, as there may be the development of a universal market for corporate control. Some signs of this are visible in the form of larger incidents of cross-border takeovers than were seen before. The question is what implications do these phenomena have for developing countries? Should they establish a market for corporate control? Should they continue to participate in a globalised system which has free flow of foreign capital or should they ask for dispensation under the rules of special and differential treatment for developing countries, which is an important accepted part of international jurisprudence.

The book by Dr. Paramjeet Kaur on Indian mergers addresses precisely these questions. It is a path-breaking and a brilliant piece of analysis for a developing country. The author is to be congratulated both on the rigour of her research as well as its fruitful application of research results to policy in the real world. Written originally as a PhD thesis at the Faculty of

Management Studies, Delhi University under the supervision of Prof. Raghav Gaiha, this book will be welcome by scholars of takeovers and mergers all over the world. The book provides new data on corporate mergers in the pharmaceutical industry where India has done particularly well. India's cheap, highly skilled labour gives it a natural advantage in pharmaceuticals in much the same way that it helps it in the information technology industry. India is certainly the top country in the developing world in the production of and research on pharmaceuticals. Dr. Kaur describes the process of reorganisation of the industry through corporate mergers as by and large voluntary. They have not involved the use of the involuntary takeover device, contrary to acquisitions and mergers in the US and the UK. Her verdict is that the voluntary mergers have been successful in preparing the industry to compete in the world markets and have not led to significant anti-trust issues.

Dr. Kaur's book provides a state of the art econometric analysis of the characteristics of merging firms: those of acquiring and acquired firms; acquired and non-acquired firms; acquiring and non-acquiring firms. She considers carefully the efficiency implications of these results. In the light of her findings, her conclusion is unequivocal and entirely plausible. Contrary to previous authors, including the present writer, she suggests that there is a case for a market for corporate control to be permitted to evolve in India. She argues that in India mergers & acquisitions (M&As) largely took place with the mutual interest of those who sold and of those who acquired, i.e., the activity was friendly and synergistic in nature. In order to be an acquiring firm, along with large size, a firm needed to be more efficient as well. Apart from attaining economies of scale, bigger size and higher market share through consolidation, acquiring firms were primarily aiming to exploit financial synergies by merging with highly debt-burdened firms. In short, Dr. Kaur's findings are in conformity with studies examining friendly takeovers which are undertaken to attain synergistic benefits.

This is an important book on the increasingly important subject of corporate amalgamations and stock market developments in emerging countries. The book sets a new standard for rigorous scholarship and policy-oriented economic analysis. It also suggests an agenda for future research which is bound to be taken up by students of takeovers and mergers in developing countries around the world. Dr. Kaur deserves full praise for a pioneering contribution.

—Ajit Singh*

* Emeritus Professor of Economics, University of Cambridge, Life Fellow, Queens' College, and Senior Research Fellow, Judge Business School, Cambridge.

Preface

The controlled and restrictive regime adopted by India after its independence was found to be deficient in providing sufficient incentive to increase productivity, minimise cost and enhance efficiency. The most important limitation was that it restricted free and fair competition. The limitations and inefficiencies cropping from the restrictive regime became evident by the 1970s. However, no major step was taken to change the policy framework until the balance of payments crisis in 1990-91. This marked a radical change from an inward-looking to outward-looking policy framework that brought the onset of economic reforms, called the 'New Economic Policy' of 1991-92. With the objective to instill greater competition and hence improve growth capabilities, the main focus of the reform measures was on an open and less restricted regime in both the domestic and external sectors. The New Economic Policy made possible the decisions regarding price, scale, investment, location and product-composition to be market-based rather than policy-driven.

Industrial sector reforms, in particular, included abolition of industrial licensing, opening of many areas for private sector's participation erstwhile reserved for the public sector, and abolition of Monopolies and Restrictive Trade Practices Act (1969). A number of steps were also taken to regularise the stock market activities, by establishing the Securities and Exchange Board of India (SEBI) as a watchdog of the capital market. Companies were made free to enter the capital market and decide their own prices within the SEBI's norms for their offer documents. Indian companies were allowed to list on foreign exchanges and were permitted to raise funds from abroad through a set of guidelines.

Worldwide changes in the policy environment, the need to survive in the wake of intense competitive pressure thus created, essentially required a large-scale restructuring and consolidation process. Progressive liberalised policies facilitated as well as necessitated the restructuring operations in the Indian corporate world. As a means to have quick expansion and as a corrective measure to its pre-reform policies, the corporate sector reshaped itself through mergers and acquisitions (M&As). Later, to ensure an orderly takeover of a company, SEBI issued guidelines for substantial acquisition of shares and takeovers in 1994 referred as the 'Takeover Code'. This led to the development of market for corporate control in India.

This phenomenon is of key importance—especially in view of its effects on the industrial growth—through its effects on the level of concentration, competition and consequent effects on the average size and profitability of firms and hence, on the economic growth. In addition to this, it is also imperative to know the nature of selection of firms in the M&A activity and whether the market for corporate control provides some degree of stock market discipline for unprofitable firms or does it encourage a large unprofitable firm to immune itself to takeover by increasing its size rather than profitability? Although the phenomenon of M&As has accelerated in volume and value—especially, over the past 15 years—it has not received adequate attention in research. Envisaging the effects that M&As can have on the economic health of the economy, our book seeks to analyse some key issues relating to M&As with special reference to the drugs and pharmaceutical industry (D&P) during the post-reform period. Question of pooling of firms in different industries does not arise as the analysis is based on an industry-specific study. So far the validity of pooling firms over a period of time is concerned, it is not expected to introduce biases as the entire period during which the M&A activity is being examined, corresponds to the post-liberalisation period. Further, it has been witnessed that the financial characteristics of firms across different types of mergers also vary. However, the book focusses on horizontal mergers only. The analysis is based on the accounting measures calculated from the annual reports of the respective companies.

The main objective of our book is to explore the factors that determine the probability of a firm going for a merger (Chapter 8) and probability of a firm becoming a merger target (Chapter 9). Using a specially designed size-matched sample, the book also compares the pre-merger characteristics of acquiring and acquired firms (Chapter 6) and also differentiates the merging from non-merging firms (Chapter 7). An analysis of the pattern of M&A activity in the post-reform period based on the review of Indian studies on M&As in India is carried out in Chapter 5. Using a number of self-explanatory diagrams, the book also analyses the trends in cross-border M&As and establishes their relation with the gross national income and openness of a country (Chapter 4). Apart from this, the changes in the macro policy regime and their effects on growth acceleration (Chapter 1), and on saving, investment and the emerging market for 'open-offers' (Chapter 2) are also explored.

The point of departure of our book is that it focusses on the effect of factors other than the size of the firm. Empirically, size of the firm in the merger activity has dominated to such an extent that other characteristics of firm have been neglected. The study is designed to redress the balance. By considering a similarly-sized control group, it investigates the effect of variables other than the size of a firm. Some of the results of our analysis are dramatically different from those of the earlier studies.

Contrary to the contention that growth of the market that allows mergers, acquisitions and takeovers is more likely to harm the economy and should therefore be discouraged, our analysis shows that in India M&As largely took place with the mutual interest of those who sold and of those who acquired i.e., the activity was friendly and synergistic in nature. The analysis shows that bigness is neither a necessary nor a sufficient condition for a firm in adopting merger strategy to grow externally. Further, when the finding that acquiring firms are less leveraged, is substantiated with the fact that acquired firms are debt-saddled, it brings in the possibility of gaining financial synergies that acquiring firms could foresee while making acquisitions. What finally emerges from the analysis is that despite acquired firms being small, unprofitable and highly leveraged, they are attractive targets for acquiring companies. All this resonates with the objective of exploiting mutual synergies, as opposed to taking advantage of low stock market valuations. Concerning the contention that M&As increase concentration, it is noted that in D&P industry, the industrial concentration fell till the year 2000 and rose thereafter. Even if a rise in concentration leads to the emergence of a few dominant firms, this is not a sufficient ground for a case against the development of market for mergers, acquisitions and takeovers. Rather, this calls for an effective regulation of the Competition Law. In the course of the analysis it is suggested that there is a case for market for corporate control to evolve.

— Paramjeet Kaur

1 Economic Reforms

An Appraisal

Introduction

The main objectives of the comprehensive planning followed to implement our development strategy were self-reliance, technological independence, and public sector dominance. It heavily relied upon pervasive government controls and regulations on the private sector such as, industrial licensing on capacity expansion, restrictions on foreign investment, quantitative restrictions on imports and exports along with import licensing and heavy import duties. The main criticism of this regime was that the incentive structure to which the industrial sector responded was determined by the government and not by the free interplay of forces of demand and supply in the market. With the emergence of uneconomic units, high production cost and low productivity in many industries, non-competitiveness, technological backwardness and low quality of goods produced, the need for policy shift became evident by the mid-1970s.

However, changes in the restrictive policies with main focus on the external sector were announced during the mid-1980s, particularly during 1985-1988 (Panagariya, 2004). A more comprehensive and systematic change in the policy regime was undertaken in response to a severe balance of payments (BoP) crisis that occurred in 1990-91. It was only in 1991, that the process of economic reforms[1] was started in India. These reforms stressed the need for domestic and external liberalisation. Domestic liberalisation means setting the private sector free from government's price and quantity controls, reducing the public sector dominance and giving a

1. These reforms were implemented under the guiding philosophy of structural adjustments and stabilisation policy of the World Bank and International Monetary Fund (IMF).

larger role to the private sector in production. External liberalisation aims at removal of price and quantity restrictions on trade, resulting in greater integration of the Indian economy with the world economy. The basic rationale behind the policy of liberalisation and privatisation was to infuse greater competition in the economy from the domestic as well as the world economy.

The process of economic reforms included stabilisation and structural adjustment policies. The former included only short-term measures to have immediate impact on the BoP crisis faced at that particular point of time, for example, devaluation of the Indian rupee in two successive steps, tightening of quantitative restrictions on imports, cutting down of fiscal deficit through reduction in government expenditure and tax reforms, and heavy loans from IMF. All these measures aimed at controlling the demand side of the economy.

The structural measures were all long-term and market-oriented measures, with an aim to foster allocative efficiency and thus growth of the economy on a sustainable basis. These measures encompassed almost all sectors of the economy and affected the supply side of the economy. Hence they are also called supply–side policies. The policies relating to industrial sector, trade sector, foreign investment, financial and public sector were the main focus areas targeted through these measures.

This chapter attempts to review the economic reforms and their effects on the general performance of the Indian economy. It has seven sections: Section 1.1 discusses the main components of regulatory regime adopted during the 1950s. Section 1.2 presents a theoretical perspective on assessing the potential benefits from both the internal and external liberalisation measures. In Section 1.3 mild reforms introduced during the mid-1980s are covered. Section 1.4 briefly discusses the major industrial and trade policy reforms adopted since 1991, while Section 1.5 reviews the effects of these reforms on the general performance of the economy. On the basis of the assertions made by various authors regarding the role of economic reforms followed in 1980s and 1990s, Section 1.6 analyses the ongoing debate on the timing of growth acceleration in India. Section 1.7 contains some concluding observations.

1.1 Nature of Policy Regime in India

The *modus operandi* adopted to implement the development strategy, followed soon after Independence, was comprehensive planning with self-reliance and technological independence as the major goals. The inward-looking comprehensive planning heavily relied upon restrictive policy regime. Targets regarding production, investment, imports, exports and prices were all fixed by the government and not by the market. Private sector was excluded from certain industries with a dominant role assigned to the public sector. Restrictions on capital markets were also abundant. A brief overview of the main sources of controls is given below (Mohammad and Whalley, 1984):

- Industrial licensing: Prior approval for creating capacity in plant machinery, structure and capital equipment.
- Investment targets for public and private sector fixed by the Planning Commission.
- Control on large firms by Monopolies and Restrictive Trade Practices (MRTP) Act[2] and foreign companies through Foreign Exchange Regulation Act (FERA).
- Depending upon the priorities set by the Planning Commission, foreign participation was permitted in specific industries. It was fully banned in consumer goods industry.
- Public sector was allowed in industries such as power, iron and steel, heavy plant machinery, airport, railways, coal, shipbuilding and communication.
- Agencies set up by the government regulated the system of subsidies and allocation of loans, and ceiling on amounts of loans to small-scale units, export firms and agriculture.
- Control on lending rates of commercial banks depending upon the purpose and duration of loan.
- Controls on the pricing policy of certain goods such as food grains, sugar, cement, steel, automobile and goods produced by public sector

---

2. It was passed in 1969, to curb concentration of economic power, control the growth of monopolies and prevent various trade practices detrimental to public interest. A company with assets at least worth Rs 200 million, operating in one or more lines of production was defined as MRTP company. This limit was raised to Rs 1 billion or more, in 1985.

enterprises e.g., power, irrigation, air transport, post and telegraph, road and sea transport, fertilisers and heavy electrical equipments.

- Import licensing governed by many factors, such as type of importers (public or private), commodities to be imported and production target fixed for the industry by the Planning Commission.
- Import tariff ranged from 450 per cent to 75 per cent depending upon the type of goods (consumer or capital goods and degree of processing involved).
- Stringent controls on foreign exchange and quantity restrictions also existed along with import licensing and import tariffs.
- Quantity controls on exports and ban on certain items for exports.

All these controls restricted the competition from the domestic and external sectors and gave protection to many high-cost firms. The MRTP Act limited the expansion of capacity by firms and instead encouraged other private entrepreneurs to set up new units. It resulted in a number of small units—especially in paper, cement and fertiliser industries. Dominance of public sector also led to many operational inefficiencies leading to over-staffing, underutilised capacity and thereby losses. The economic costs of such inward-oriented policy have been documented by several studies (Krueger, 1974; Bhagwati and Srinivasan, 1980; Desai, 1981; Bhagwati, 1982).

Apart from certain inefficiencies and losses, a major consequence of these control measures was corruption. Those in charge of these controls, heavily exploited needy people and demanded heavy amounts to get a decision in their favour. Those, who managed to obtain economic rent, also developed vested interests in the continuation of these controls. Several studies subsequently analysed the effects of these activities through coining of terms, such as 'premium-seeking' or 'rent-seeking' (whereby claimants compete for premium fetching import licence), 'revenue-seeking' (whereby an economic agent tries to get a slice of the tariff revenue resulting from the adoption of a protectionist tariff) and 'tariff-seeking' (lobbies seek protectionist trade tariff). Bhagwati (1982) describes all these activities as directly unproductive profit seeking (DUP) activities because these represent ways of making a profit without being productive for the economy. Activities, such as tariff-seeking, lobbying, tariff evasion, avoidance of controls, and premium-seeking for a given licence, are all privately profitable activities and divert resources from production to non-production activities (Srinivasan, 1987). Few attempted to measure the rents and revenues generated by these controls and regulatory measures.

Krueger (1974) pioneered the attempt to measure the cost of rent-seeking created in a system, full of price and quantity controls in India. Taking value of rents so created as an approximation of the measure of the annual welfare cost of rent-seeking, she estimated the losses to be 7 per cent of GNP per annum in 1964. Later, Mohammad and Whalley (1984) re-examined her work and found the estimates to be largely underestimated, as her work was confined to only quantity restrictions on imports. They extended the analysis to include foreign trade controls, capital market control, controls in goods and labour market and produced the estimates within a range of 30 to 45 per cent of GNP per year during 1980-81 (Table 1.1). They found price controls and rationing in goods and financial markets to be the main source of rent-seeking rather than the quantity restrictions put on foreign trade. They also suggested that welfare losses induced by rent-seeking arising from quotas were likely to be higher than those originating from the imposition of tariffs. The share of rent-seeking costs arising from the 'price controls in goods market' was found to be the highest (between 16-20 per cent) followed by 'capital market controls'. The controls, sourcing from 'import licences and export incentives' and 'labour market', did not contribute much to these costs.

Table 1.1

Estimates of Costs of Rent-seeking in India, 1980-81

Source	*Rs Billion (in %)*
Import licences and export incentives	40 (4%)
Capital market controls	85-170 (8%-16%)
Goods market (price) controls	170-210 (16%-20%)
Labour market controls	30 (3%)
Total	325-450 (30%-45%)
Indian GNP 1980/81	1042

Note : Figures in parenthesis represent rent-seeking costs as a per cent of GNP.

Source: Mohammad and Whalley (1984).

In the next section, we present theoretically, a clear picture of these costs and demonstrate the role of liberalisation measures in an economy in removing the inefficiencies and thereby, allowing it to attain higher welfare.

1.2 Analytical Framework—Liberalisation Measures: Internal and External

As stated earlier, liberalisation measures can be both domestic and external. The former measures remove rigidities in the system and allow resources to move freely within the economy according to market signals. Through external measures, an economy can improve upon the domestic availability of goods, resources and also efficiency in the use of resources (through, say, import of technology, knowledge, and better organisational techniques). An unprotected regime forces firms to remain competitive and employ cost-minimising techniques to survive in the market. Further, by participating in the world trade through imports and exports, domestic producers can improve upon the quality of their product to make it internationally competitive. In order to obtain full efficiency benefits (both economic and allocative efficiency), it is necessary that an economy should adopt both internal and external liberalisation measures simultaneously, as demonstrated through Figure 1.1.

Within a simple analytical framework of a two-goods economy, using production possibility frontier (PPF) and a set of social indifference curves (SICs), this section explains the effects of lifting of economic controls and regulations on the internal and external sectors of an economy (Srinivasan, 1987). A PPF gives all possible combinations of goods and services that an economy can produce, assuming full and efficient utilisation of given resources. A social indifference curve shows all combinations of goods that result in equal levels of social welfare.

Given a closed economy, its consumption as well as production possibility are represented by a PPF in Figure 1.1, denoted by XX_1. Given a set of SICs, an economy would attain maximum welfare by producing and consuming at a point like A, given by the tangency of the PPF, the highest possible social indifference curve (SIC_1) and the price line (PQ) which denotes the domestic price ratio. With the opening of the economy (external liberalisation) and consequent trade possibilities, given by the price line P_1Q_1 (the price line at which goods can now be exchanged in the world market), the economy can move to a higher SIC shown by SIC_2, merely by trading along P_1Q_{-1} and consuming at C (assuming production is kept at the previous level A). The gains to the society from only free trading are given by a shift from SIC_1 to SIC_2. On the other hand, if resources are also allowed to be reallocated (domestic liberalisation), the economy would instead produce at B and then by trading along P_2Q_2,[3] it can consume at D, thereby attain even higher social welfare by reaching at SIC_3.

Figure 1.1

Domestic and External Liberalisation: A Theoretical Framework

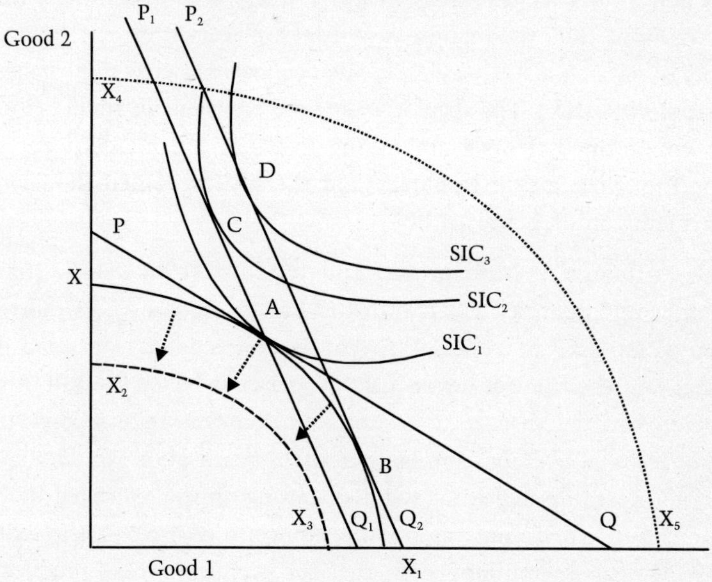

Source: Adapted from Srinivasan (1987).

The total gains associated with freedom in production (through allocation of resources) and consumption (through free trading in the world market) are given by the shift from SIC_1 to SIC_3 or a movement from A to D. These gains are decomposed as consumption gains and production

3. It is parallel to P_1Q_1, and shows the relative price ratio at which goods can be exchanged in the world market.

gains. The movement from point A to C (or a shift from SIC_1 to SIC_2) is termed as consumption gains where as the movement from C to D and the associated shift from SIC_2 to SIC_3 gives the production gains. It is important to note that the total gains from external liberalisation can be realised only if internal liberalisation is also followed. It is the domestic liberalised policies that would allow flexibility in resources and thereby, reallocation of resources from A to B.

It is worth pointing out here, that an economy produces at a point on the PPF if given resources are fully and efficiently utilised i.e., the marginal product from the resource in all its uses is the same. Such a possibility exists in an economy, which is free from all kinds of restrictions and controls and allows its resources to move freely according to the market signals. Without this, production would take place within the production possibility shown by a PPF, say X_2X_3 (also called restricted PPF) instead of its potential PPF—XX_1. The regulatory regime prevalent in India before the reforms constrained firms from taking free and independent decisions regarding the allocation of resources and thereby, prevented the economy from producing on its potential PPF.

The estimates of Mohammad and Whalley (1984) show that the various price and quantity controls in the Indian economy cost more than one-third of its GNP in 1980-1981. The Indian economy operated below its frontier i.e., the frontier lay at least 30 per cent below the PPF it could have operated in the absence of controls on domestic transactions. In the absence of internal liberalisation, an external liberalisation would allow the economy to obtain limited gains while operating on the restricted PPF. It is in the long run when controls on the domestic as well as the external sector are abolished simultaneously, that the economy would produce at B (a point lying on the potential PPF) and consume at D. Thus, in order to take full advantage of the reform process, it is necessary that both domestic and external liberalised policies should be adopted simultaneously, otherwise limited benefits can be obtained. Once the economy moves from a point inside the PPF to a point on it (i.e., a shift from the restricted PPF to the PPF with full and efficient utilisation of resources), further growth (shown by a rightward shift from XX_1 to X_4X_5) is possible only through capital accumulation, technical advancement and improvement in total factor productivity.

1.3 Reforms of the Mid-1980s

The pattern of industrialisation that emerged from the controlled regime brought to notice various deficiencies in the policies followed. The corporate sector started demanding relaxation of restrictions on industrial and trade sectors. In view of this, reform process began in 1980s with major changes however, being announced from 1985-1988. Unlike the 1990s reforms, the reforms during the mid-1980s were introduced quietly, therefore also described as 'liberalisation by stealth'. Expansion in open general licence (OGL) list, decline in the share of canalised imports,[4] certain export incentives to expand the products available to exporters, duty free imports of capital goods in certain export industries, delicensing of certain industries, increase in the asset ceiling of small-scale industries investment, increase in the asset limit of MRTP firms from Rs 200 million to Rs 1,000 million, decontrol of cement (eliminated black market and increased competition from new entrants), introduction of modified value added tax (MODVAT), depreciation of real exchange rate by 30 per cent (from 1985-86 to 1989-90) are few of the measures adopted since 1985-86 (Panagariya, 2004).

The reforms of the mid-1980s, though half-hearted, were significant and exhibited a noticeable impact on growth and other indicators.[5] The imports to GDP ratio increased from 5 per cent in 1980-81 to 6 per cent in 1989-90 and industrial growth increased from 4.5 per cent in 1985-86 to 10.5 per cent in 1989-90. The average annual growth of 9.2 per cent during 1988-1991 mainly resulted from increased productivity rather than through increase in private investment as a proportion of GDP (Joshi and Little, 1996). External debt to GDP increased from 17.7 per cent in 1984-85 to 24.5 per cent in 1989-90 whereas debt-service ratio went up from 80 to 87 per cent during the same period. On the internal front, combined current government (Central and state) expenditure increased from 18.6 per cent in the first half of 1980s to 23 per cent in the second half of the1980s. All these factors led to a rise in the fiscal deficit from 8 per cent during 1980-1985 to 10.1 per cent during 1985-1990.

---

4. Canalisation refers to monopoly rights of the government for the import of certain items such as oil and lubricants, non-petroleum items.

5. For details, see Panagariya (2003, 2004).

Reforms of the 1990s were bolder in their announcement and deeper in their coverage. They clearly represented a shift in the conventional thinking of regulated and controlled economy to an open and less restricted economy.

1.4 Industrial and Trade Policy Reforms of the 1990s

India's reform process in its early stages mainly focussed on industrial and trade policies.

Industrial Policy Reforms

The basic thrust behind the industrial sector reforms (called New Industrial Policy) was the realisation of the negative impact of pervasive government regulation on industrial and overall health of the economy. To improve the competitive environment and efficient utilisation of resources, it was necessary that private investment should respond freely to market signals. This necessitated deregulating and liberalising the domestic economy from the government controls.

The abolition of industrial licensing was the first and foremost step undertaken by the Indian government in 1991-92. Industrial licensing had plagued the Indian industry with many inefficiencies. It had deteriorated the competitive environment by restricting the entry of new firms and limiting their size and capacity. Restrictions on capacity expansion ensured that the Indian industry remained fragmented with uneconomic plant sizes, unable to exploit economies of scale. The withdrawal of industrial licensing, restrictions on capacity, location, size, mergers and acquisitions (M&As) implied that the corporate entrepreneurs were saved from the clutches of bureaucracy. On the grounds of health, safety and environment, only five industries required licences: (a) arms and ammunition, explosives and allied items of defence equipments, defence aircrafts and warships; (b) atomic substances; (c) narcotics and psychotropic substances and hazardous chemicals; (d) distillation and brewing of alcoholic drinks; and (e) cigarettes/cigars and manufactured tobacco substitutes.

The second major step was the abolition of the MRTP Act, under which special permission was needed for any investment activity by large business houses. This law had been introduced to regulate and control the growth of big private houses and thus discourage the concentration of economic power. However, in practice, it simply acted as a barrier to entry of new firms and restricted competition. Under the new regime no prior approval regarding the establishment of new undertaking or any kind of expansion is required. The Competition Act, 2002 that attempts to regulate anti-competitive behaviour has replaced this act. The core essence of the law is that it is not dominance *per se* but the abuse of dominance that is undesirable for the economy.

The next major breakthrough in industrial sector reform was opening up of areas for private participation, which earlier were reserved only for the public sector. The list of industries reserved for the public sector was pruned from 18 to 8 (which later reduced to 3, *viz.*, defence aircrafts and war ships, atomic energy generation and railway transport). Private investment was allowed in iron and steel, telecommunication, air transport, electricity generation and shipbuilding. Considerable progress has been made in opening the services sector—especially banking (allowing private and foreign banks in banking sector), insurance (establishment of Insurance Regulatory Development Authority in 1999) and telecommunication (National Telecommunication Policy in 1994 and New Telecom Policy in 1999 opened the cellular, basic and value added services) to private as well as foreign investors (Panagariya, 2004). Steps were also taken to divest part of the equity of selected public sector enterprises and to give greater autonomy to public sector management to operate on commercial lines.

Dereservation of many of the items for production in the small-scale industries[6] (SSIs) was another major step to promote competition within the domestic economy. The control was exercised not only by barring the large firms in the reserved area but also by restricting the expansion of firms beyond the maximum permissible limit of investment. The reforms in this area have been inadequate and the progress thus, has been slow. The 1997-98 budget dereserved 14 items, such as ice-cream, biscuits,

6. In 1950 an undertaking with fixed capital investment of less than Rs 5 lakh was defined as small-scale enterprise. The limit increased to Rs 7.5,10, 20, 35 and Rs 60 lakh in 1966, 1975, 1980, 1985 and 1990, respectively. During 1997, the government increased the limit from Rs 60 lakh to Rs 3 crore that was reduced to Rs 1 crore in the year 2000 (GOI, various issues).

synthetic syrup, vinegar, and a variety of automobile parts. Another item, 'agricultural equipments' was dereserved in 1998-99. Textile Policy (2000) dereserved the garment sector. On June 29, 2001, further 14 items were dereserved that included leather goods, shoes and toys. Despite the dereservation of 85 items in 2004, the list of reserved item stood at 605 in 2005. To facilitate technology upgradation and enhance competitiveness, the limit for investment was increased from Rs 1 crore to Rs 5 crore in respect of 7 items (GOI, 2004-05).

Banks and financial institutions, which financed a large part of industrial investment, followed a mandatory practice of including a convertibility clause in their lending operations. This mandatory clause of converting part of loans into equity by financial institutions (though never exercised) has been removed as it was considered an unwarranted takeover threat for firms.

Competition Act, 2002

After the initiation of the more liberalised policy regime in 1991, the MRTP Act was found to be inappropriate for handling the problems arising in the new scenario. With a shift in focus from curbing monopolies to promotion of free and fair competition, the Competition Act, 2002 (implemented by Competition Commission of India, CCI) was passed in the parliament, to replace the MRTP Act.[7] The new Act is much more industry-friendly, comprehensive in coverage, simpler in language, flexible and proactive in its approach. An important distinguishing feature of this Act is that it is based on the behaviour or conduct approach rather than the size or structure approach[8] followed earlier.

With the basic objective of promoting competition to raise consumer welfare and to ensure a level playing field to the participants in the market, the new Act primarily deals with three areas:

1. *Restrictive anti-competitive agreements*: The Act seeks to focus on the agreements amongst the enterprises, which have adverse effects

7. In this context, a committee, under the chairmanship of SVS Raghavan, was set up in 1999, to frame a set of regulations, called Competition Law. The latter aimed at providing necessary powers to the commission to enforce and implement the Competition Policy.

8. For details, see Chakravarthy (2004).

on competition. The rule of reason rather than the rule of law (as in the MRTP Act) would be used to determine whether the agreement is anti-competitive or promotes competition.

2. *Abuse of dominance*: It is not dominance *per se* rather the abuse of dominance that is considered detrimental. Abuse includes agreements, charging or paying unfair prices, territory sharing agreements, cartel, and restrictions on quantity, markets and technical development.
3. *Regulations of mergers and combinations beyond a certain size*:[9] The Act seeks to regulate the combinations with the threshold limit of Rs1,000 crore (US $208 million on 2004 exchange rate) or Rs 3,000 crore (US $625 million) in terms of aggregate value of assets or turnover, respectively, of the combining parties. Keeping in view the relatively small size of Indian firms in the global markets, the Act did not favour monitoring of all mergers.

The Competition Act, 2002 also provides for a competition fund that is to be utilised for promotion of competition advocacy i.e., creating awareness about competition issues among the consumers. For its effective implementation, it has been suggested the CCI—the competition watchdog or a regulator to look at competition in the Indian market—should be better resourced and should be provided with greater autonomy in taking decisions.

Recent Amendments in M&As Regulations

Addressing over the concerns of several corporate groups over competition law's intrusive nature, the CCI has relaxed several of its earlier proposals, which would take effect from June 1, 2011.

- The CCI has listed a number of transactions[10] where companies going in for M&As will have to submit details only through Form I, and if the CCI finds necessary, it will call for more information in Form II.[11]

9. For further details, see Aggarwal (2004).
10. For details, see CCI's website.
11. Form I, which is expected to cover 90-95 per cent of transactions, is much simpler than the Form II. The latter is to be filled for those transactions which could raise legitimate concerns on competition.

- The merger notification fee has been slashed from Rs 40 lakh to Rs 50,000 for Form I and from Rs 40 lakh to Rs 10 lakh for Form II.
- Those M&A deals that create combined assets of Rs 1,500 crore or turnover of Rs 4,500 crore would require CCI's approval before concluding the deal. Also, for transactions where the assets of a business group cross Rs 6,000 or its turnover exceeds Rs 18,000 crore post acquisition, CCI's approval would be required.
- To lessen compliance burden on companies that are in acquisition mode, it is specified that once the viability of a transaction is verified, it would not be required to go through the notification process for subsequent transactions.
- Acquisition of shares or voting rights through bonus issues, stock splits, consolidation of face value of shares or rights issues will be exempted, if it does not lead to acquisition of control.
- If an acquirer already has 50 per cent stake in a firm, then his further acquisition will trigger the competition law only if the acquisition leads to transfer from joint control to single control.
- An acquisition of less than 15 per cent voting right, if it is in the usual course of business or purely an investment, will be exempted from seeking permission by the CCI. Also, a stock market intermediary acquiring shares on behalf of its clients will also be exempted from reporting requirements.
- In case of overseas companies that have Indian subsidiaries, only those transactions that, according to CCI, are expected to have adverse effects on competition in India would be required to go for second round of scrutiny.
- To speed up the procedure of approval, CCI assures to clear the proposals, which are expected to increase efficiencies due to 'economies of scale', combined production plants, integrating procurement and pooling of research and development resources, within a period of one month of their filing. The cases that require second round of investigations would be cleared within six to seven months.
- In order to guide companies and facilitate the process, the CCI also plans to provide the consultation process on its website.

Through these amendments CCI has ensured that its objective is not to hinder the process of growth of companies, foreign direct investments and thereby economic growth of the country. Rather, it intends to promote competitiveness in the market by putting restraint on those M&A deals that end up creating monopolies or abuse of dominance, harmful to consumers and small producers.

Trade Policy Reforms

The process of external liberalisation was started along with domestic liberalisation. To give some breathing period to domestic companies to adjust to the increasing pressures, external sector reforms were followed at a gradual pace. The trade policy of India was heavily dependent on the quantitative restrictions (QRs) in the form of import quotas, import licences and high tariffs. The protection given to domestic firms made them complacent and also distorted resource allocation.

After the initiation of economic reforms, a consistent policy of gradual removal of restriction on imports was followed. 'Tariff line-wise import policy' was first announced on 31st March 1996, when import of 6,161 tariff lines out of 10,202 were made free. Consequent to the improvement in BoP crisis, import restrictions were gradually removed.[12] Import of intermediate inputs and capital goods was made free. On grounds of health, safety and moral conduct, at present QRs are being maintained on just 5 per cent of tariff lines. Along with the removal of import licensing, it became important to reduce the tariff rates to allow imports to move freely.[13] India's import duties before the reforms were among the highest in the world with duty rates above 200 per cent being common. The peak tariff rates were brought down to 85 per cent in 1993-94, 50 per cent in 1995-96, 25 per cent in 2003-04, and further to 15 per cent in 2005-06.

As part of the stabilisation policy, controls on exchange rates were also lifted. The rupee exchange rate was devalued twice in July 1991, to manage

---

12. Import restrictions on 488 tariff lines were removed in 1996-97, 391 in 1997-98, 894 in 1998-99 and 714 in 1999-2000. The process of removal of QRs was completed in 2001 with the removal of QRs on 715 items.

13. To minimise rent-seeking on the part of bureaucrats and turn quota rents into tariff revenue, tariff rates in 1980s were increased substantially. In 1990-91, the highest tariff rate was 355 per cent with a simple average of all tariffs at 113 per cent (Panagariya, 2004).

the BoP crisis experienced at that point of time. After the partial convertibility of rupee on trade account that was announced in 1992-93, it was subsequently broadened towards full current account convertibility by August 1994. This eased restrictions on accessibility to foreign currency. A number of measures were also taken for a move towards capital account convertibility. At present, the government follows the policy of (managed) flexible exchange rates, allowing the demand and supply condition to determine the exchange rate movement so as to maintain necessary competitiveness.

With a view to exploiting the relationship between domestic and foreign industry through technology transfer, market expertise, modern managerial techniques, the government became more receptive to foreign direct investment[14] (FDI). The industrial approval system was abolished in all industries, leaving 18 environmentally sensitive industries. In 34 high priority industries, FDI up to 51 per cent was approved. The trading companies engaged primarily in export activities were also allowed up to 51 per cent equity. To attract the multinational corporations (MNCs) in infrastructure sector, 100 per cent equity was permitted under automatic route in power generation, construction, roads, highways, ports and maintenance of roads. FDI up to 100 per cent was permitted in airports with FDI up to 74 per cent requiring prior approval. In budget 2002-03, 100 per cent FDI was also permitted under automatic route in advertising, film, tea plantation, and manufacturing activities in special economic zones (SEZs). With regard to services, FDI up to 74 per cent for internet service providers, up to 100 per cent in e-commerce and information technology units set up exclusively for export units and automatic approval route for foreign equity in software was permitted. FDI up to 26 per cent (subject to licensing) was also permitted in the defence sector.

The Foreign Exchange Regulation Act (FERA) of 1973 was amended and consequently restrictions placed on foreign companies by FERA were

14. Foreign investment flows comprise FDI and portfolio investment. The former supplements domestic investment and benefits industry through technological up-gradation, access to global skill and practices. The latter is short-term, volatile, often speculative, and capable of being pulled out at short notice, thereby endangering the financial health of the country. In India, since 1996-97 FDI dominated over portfolio flows, however, the trend reversed in 2003-04.

lifted. Later, the Foreign Exchange Management Act (FEMA) of 1999 replaced it. Foreign companies were allowed in mining, banking, telecommunications, highways, construction and management. A Foreign Investment Promotion Board (FIPB) was set up to consider all other proposals that do not qualify for the automatic clearance route. A number of measures were taken to promote portfolio investment by non-resident Indians (NRIs) as well as financial institutional investors (FIIs). To avoid crowding out of NRIs by FII investment, the aggregate ceiling for investment by NRIs was made separate and exclusive of the investment ceiling available for FIIs.

1.5 Macroeconomic Effects of Reforms

The process of structural reforms in India has led to the transformation of a controlled, protected and regulated economy to a relatively liberal and deregulated economy. It has given all sectors, especially the corporate sector, a reorientation towards market-driven signals and has made the system more competitive.

As far as the effects of stabilisation measures are concerned, performance in the first two years of economic reforms was appreciable. The rate of growth of gross domestic product (GDP), which had collapsed to 0.8 per cent in 1991-92, increased to 5.5 per cent by the mid-1990s and later to 6 per cent within the next two to three years. The foreign reserves were built to respectable levels, rate of inflation declined from 13.7 per cent to 8 per cent, current account deficit decreased from 3.2 per cent of GDP to 0.4 per cent. Thus, the government was able to manage the crisis through its stabilisation policy measures.

With respect to the structural measures, the effects in terms of main macroeconomic indicators are also remarkable. In particular, the effects on corporate restructuring are still being assessed and an in-depth analysis is yet to be carried out.

Economic growth is the principal yardstick of macroeconomic performance. After averaging 3.6 per cent per annum growth from 1950-51 to 1980-81, it increased to 6 per cent from 1992-93 to 2000-01. The acceleration was higher in the early years of reforms than in later years after 1998-99 (Table 1.2). Despite the deceleration of growth since 1997-

1998, India has the distinction of being one of the fastest growing economies of the world.[15] Growth rate of per capita GDP was less than 1 per cent until 1980. During the following two decades, it grew at an average of 3.7 per cent, with 4.75 per cent per annum growth during the five years following the crisis year 1991-92. During 1990s,[16] excluding the 1991-92 crisis year, per capita GDP recorded 4.2 per cent growth rate.

As far as sectoral performances are concerned (Table 1.2), it is observed that the industrial sector grew at a higher rate in 1980s, whereas both agriculture and services improved their performances in the post-reform period. On average, during the period 1990-91 to 2000-01 agriculture, industry and services grew at rates of 2.9, 5.9 and 7.6 per cent, respectively. The services grew consistently at a rate greater than 7.5 per cent whereas the growth rates of agriculture and industry varied across the period. These sectors grew at an average rate of 4.6 and 7.6 per cent, respectively, during 1992-93 to 1996-97. However, during the next four years, the corresponding rates fell to -1.2 and 4.9 per cent, respectively.

The industrial sector liberalisation being the most important and prominent feature of economic reforms, the fall in the average growth of the industrial sector is disappointing. Its effect could also be seen through a fall in the share of industry in GDP from 27.6 per cent in 1990 to 26.9 per cent in 2000.[17] Consequently, the decline in the share of GDP originating from agriculture from 31.3 per cent to 24.9 per cent was completely absorbed by a rise in the share of services from 41.1 to 48.2 per cent.[18]

The savings rate[19] defined as share of gross domestic savings in GDP at current market prices, generally remained high after reforms. After reaching its peak of 25.1 per cent in 1995-96, it declined for a few years

15. During the Tenth Five-Year Plan, 2002-2007, India grew at an average annual growth of 7.6 per cent, as against the target of 8 per cent (GOI, 2006-07).

16. Since 2002-03, per capita income is growing at an average annual of 7.2 per cent (GOI, 2007-08).

17. The shares of agriculture, services and industry in GDP were 18.5, 55.1, and 26.4 per cent, respectively during 2002-03 to 2006-07 (GOI, 2006-07).

18. This was in contrast to China where out of the 12-percentage fall in the share of agriculture in its GDP from 1990 to 2000, 10 per cent was absorbed by industrial sector and proportion of services increased marginally by 2 per cent (Panagariya, 2004).

19. Details discussed in Chapter 2.

Table 1.2

Performance of the Indian Economy, 1990-2001

	1990-91 to 2000-01	*1992-93 to 2000-01*	*1992-93 to 1996-97*	*1997-98 to 2000-01*
GDP (average growth rate)	5.61 (32.7)	6.1 (20.9)	6.68 (16.9)	5.35 (22.6)
Per capita GDP (average growth rate)	3.68	4.17	4.75	3.42
Investment (average growth rate)	6.93 (136.3)	8.31 (92.08)	9.63 (90.89)	6.68 (99.8)
Fixed capital formation (average growth rate)	6.68 (85.9)	7.39 (75.7)	8.47 (84.62)	6.03 (53.32)
Public investment (average growth rate)	3.14 (238.39)	4.12 (180.7)	2.28 (343.53)	6.43 (113.75)
Private investment (average growth rate)	8.75 (136.32)	10.21 (92.2)	13.01 (82.03)	6.71 (114.12)
Investment as per cent of GDP	22.87	22.85	23.34	22.22
Saving as per cent of GDP	23.20	23.15	23.50	22.80
Services: Share in GDP	44.30	44.92	43.04	47.28
(average growth rate)	7.6 (24.9)	8.1 (19.6)	7.55 (24.4)	8.82 (12.4)
Industry: Share in GDP	27.10	27.12	27.11	27.13
(average growth rate)	5.9 (56.7)	6.39 (44.3)	7.61 (42.6)	4.86 (26.7)
Agriculture: Share in GDP	32.15	30.40	32.42	27.88
(average growth rate)	2.87 (132.2)	3.12 (125.1)	4.64 (80.8)	-1.23 (297.8)

Notes: Figures in brackets are coefficient of variation (in per cent).

Source: Rakshit (2003).

(Table 1.3). The investment rate, gross domestic capital formation (GDCF) as share of GDP at current market prices, also witnessed a similar trend and recorded its maximum at 26.9 per cent in the same year and declined after that till recently. The fall in public investment as a ratio of gross domestic investment did not affect the GDCF because the rise in private investment more than offset the fall in public investment. This indicates that the private sector responded positively to changes in the industrial policy regime.

Table 1.3

Savings and Investment (as per cent of GDP at current market prices)

Year	GDCF*	Public Invest-ment	Private Invest-ment	GDS	Public Savings	Private Savings	Household Savings	Corporate Savings	Saving-Invest-ment Gap
Average 1985-90	22.7	10.1	14.14	20.4	2.4	18.0	16.0	2.0	-2.3
1990-91	26.3	9.3	14.7	23.1	2.1	22.0	19.3	2.7	-3.2
1991-92	22.6	8.8	13.1	22.0	2.0	20.1	17.0	3.1	-.6
1992-93	23.6	8.6	15.2	22.8	2.6	20.2	17.5	2.7	-2.8
1993-94	23.1	8.2	13.0	22.5	0.6	22.9	18.4	3.5	-.6
1994-95	26.0	8.7	14.7	24.8	2.7	23.2	19.7	3.5	-2.2
1995-96	26.9	7.7	18.9	25.1	2.0	23.1	18.2	4.9	-2.8
1996-97	24.5	6.9	14.7	23.2	2.7	22.5	17.0	4.5	-2.3
1997-98	24.6	7.0	16.0	23.1	2.3	22.8	17.6	4.2	-2.5
1998-99	22.7	6.6	14.8	22.7	-2.0	25.2	18.9	3.7	-2.1
1999-00	25.3	6.9	16.7	24.2	-2.0	22.6	20.9	4.4	-2.1
2000-01	24.4	6.3	16.3	23.5	-2.3	25.2	22.6	4.1	-0.4
2001-02	22.6	6.2	16.0	23.4	-2.7	26.2	22.6	3.6	0.8
2002-03	25.3	6.2	18.5	26.5	-.7	27.2	23.1	4.1	1.2
2003-04	28	6.3	19.4	29.7	1.2	28.5	23.8	4.7	1.7

Note: * It includes errors and omissions.

Source: GOI, 2004-05, 2005-06 and 2006-07.

The years 2002-03 and 2003-04 marked a departure from the falling trend. The saving and investment rates are estimated to be 29.7 per cent and 28 per cent, respectively, for the fiscal year 2003-04. The improvement in the former is due to a reduction in public dissavings and improvement in private savings (comprising both household and private corporate savings) and, in the latter, it is mainly due to a rise in private investment. The savings-investments gap on account of relatively low savings generated by the public sector *vis-à-vis* its investment requirement, was negative till 2000-01. It is only since 2001-02, that the gap (because of large saving-investment surplus in private sector) recorded a positive sign and was positive 1.7 in 2003-04.

India's BoP situation improved remarkably. The ratio of exports rose from 7.3 per cent in 1990 to 14 per cent in 2000 whereas imports showed lesser responsiveness to liberalisation measures. The proportion of trade in goods and services to GDP approximately doubled from 17.2 per cent to 30.6 per cent (Panagariya, 2004). Though current account deficit (as a per cent of GDP at market prices) fell considerably since 1990, it averaged 1 per cent of GDP till 2001-02. The capital account of India has emerged much stronger after liberalisation—especially since 1993-94. From 1993-94 to 2000-01, net capital inflows averaged about US $9 billion per year. A sharp increase in exports on account of global recovery accompanied by robust inflows of workers' remittances resulted in current account surplus for three successive years since 2001-02. This along with an expanding capital account led to an increase in the level of exchange reserves. During 2004-05, India experienced an all time high reserve accumulation with the total at US $128.9 billion on February 4, 2005. India's external debt situation improved significantly. The external debt to GDP ratio declined from 28.7 per cent in 1991 to 21 per cent in 2001 and 17.8 per cent in 2004. The short-term debt as a percentage of foreign reserves declined from 146.5 in 1990 to 8.2 per cent in 2002. The debt-service ratio from a peak of 35.3 per cent of current receipts in 1991 reduced to half in recent years. The import cover of foreign exchange reserves (in months) increased from a level of 2.5 in 1990-91 to 8.8 in 2000-01 and further to 17 in 2003-04 (GOI, 2004-05). The World Bank also classified India as a 'less-indebted' country in 2002.

The levels of FDI are on an increase but still at a low level. The annual flows increased from a meagre amount of US $3 billion in 1991-92 to a sum of US $3.6 billion in 1997-98. After experiencing a declining trend for two years on account of a host of factors,[20] FDI inflows reached a peak of US $3.9 billion in 2001-02, surpassing the previous high of 1997-1998. India's share of FDI in the total for all developing countries increased from 0.5 per cent in 1992 to 2 per cent during the same period. As a result, India was ranked as the 13th emerging market economy (UNCTAD, 1999). China is the highest recipient of FDI inflows among the developing economies of Asia. In the year 2004, China received some US $60 billion, about 12 times of the amount that flowed in India. It has been argued that it is not the 'deregulation' but the procedural system that stands in the way

20. The main factors were political instability in the country, poor domestic industrial environment and Southeast Asian financial crisis.

of free flow of investment into our country. The procedural simplifications require urgent attention to encourage greater FDI flows.

In the post-reform period, fiscal deficit (FD) was kept below 5 per cent till 1997-98 but after that it remained above 5 per cent till 2002-03, and, in 2004-05, it is provisionally estimated at 4.5 per cent. Now with the operationalisation of Fiscal Responsibility and Budget Management (FRBM) Act, 2003, from July 2004, and introduction of value added tax (VAT) from April 1, 2005, it is estimated to fall further. Despite a fall in capital expenditure from 4.4 per cent in 1990-91 to 2.2 per cent in 2000-01, the inability to reduce FDI is due to the consistent rise in revenue expenditure as a percentage of total expenditure of government. The rising interest payments, expenditure on subsidies, pay and allowances coupled with a near stagnant tax-GDP ratio contributed to worsening of revenue expenditure.

The performance of Indian economy in the sphere of poverty elimination is quite impressive. The number of poor persons fell from 320 million in early 1990s to 260 million and poverty ratio by 10 percentage points from 36 per cent to 26 per cent during 1993-94 to 1999-2000.

In conclusion, most of the macroeconomic indicators responded positively to structural policies in the early years of economic reforms. But after 1996-97, growth flattened because of some external and internal factors. In recent years the economy is again showing signs of recovery.

1.6 Debate on Growth Acceleration

In view of the fact that in recent years substantial research work has been directed towards establishing the role of economic reforms in accelerating the growth as well as finding a structural break in the growth rates, in this section we present a brief review of this work followed by our own econometric work and analysis. The average annual growth of approximately 6 per cent from 1992-93 to 2002-03 highlights an important fact when the growth during the whole period is subdivided between two periods 1992-93 to 1996-97 and 1997-98 to 2002-03 (Ahluwalia, 2002). The average annual growth of 6.7 per cent in the former period falls to 5.25 per cent during the latter period (see Table 1.8, comparison 5). Industrial growth came down from 8 per cent in the first five years of reform to 4.5

per cent during 1997-98 to 2002-03 (Table 1.2). Further, there was a steady fall in public savings from 2.7 per cent of GDP in 1996-97 to –2.7 per cent in 2001-02 (Table 1.3), along with a rising fiscal deficit in the second half of 1990s, which was not used for financing public investment (Ahluwalia, 2002). This led to a debate on the effectiveness of reforms in bringing a structural change in the average growth of the economy.

As opposed to the common view that acceleration in average growth is credited to policy reforms initiated in 1991, Delong (2004) argues that acceleration began in the early or mid-1980s. He does however, concede that the rapid growth in the second half of the 1980s could not be sustained without the second wave of reforms of 1990s. Rodrik (2004) joins Delong (2004) in stating that liberalisation reforms undertaken in 1990s cannot be accepted as a turning point in taking off the Indian economy from the 'Hindu rate of growth' of 3 per cent per annum. They strongly emphasise that mild reforms undertaken during Rajiv Gandhi's period, indicated an attitudinal change of officials over the change in policies. The credibility of this change encouraged entrepreneurial activities and thus had a greater bearing on growth than the specific policy reforms followed during 1990s.[21]

Panagariya (2004), on the other hand, documents that Delong (2004) and Rodrik (2004) overstate the growth and understate the reforms during 1980s. He proceeds with Delong and Rodrik's view that the 1980s reforms played a significant role in spurring the growth in 1980s, and also accepts that reforms of the 1980s though ad hoc and limited in scope, served as necessary groundwork for the more comprehensive reforms of 1990s. But the latter, according to Panagariya, were more systematic, systemic and deeper in coverage, encompassing both internal and external sectors. He argues that the growth during 1980s was fragile and sporadic[22] and therefore, was unsustainable whereas that of 1990s was more stable, less variable and sustainable. He is emphatic that the high growth during 1988-1991 (7.6 per cent per annum, Table 1.4) is key to the high average growth

---

21. Pursell (1992), Virmani (1997) and Desai (1999) also share the view that trade and industrial liberalisation reforms undertaken in 1980s, caused acceleration in growth (Panagariya, 2004).

22. It is because growth in 1980s exhibited significantly higher variance than growth in 1990s (Panagariya, 2004).

exhibited during 1980s, without which the latter would have been significantly lower.

In order to address the issue of shift in growth rates, Panagariya analyses the average annual GDP growth pattern during 1981-82 to 2002-2003. He presents the estimates by dividing the whole period between the two sub-periods, termed as pre-reform (1981-82 to 1991-92) and post-reform period (1992-93 to 2002-03). The former period registered an average annual growth of 5.3 per cent whereas in the latter, it was 5.9 per cent. An important point to which Panagariya draws attention is that if the growth is considered from 1980-81 to until 1987-88 only, the average falls to 4.8 per cent. Further, he argues if the period is taken from 1978-79 to 1987-88 the average falls to 4.1 per cent and with this he concludes that if India was still on Hindu rate of growth before the reforms of the 1990s. He also points to the volatility of growth paths in the 1980s and 1990s by applying standard F-test and unequivocally concludes in favour of high growth fragility in the 1980s.

Another group of researchers (Joshi and Little, 1994; Ahluwalia, 2002; and Srinivasan and Tendulkar, 2003) also hold the view that the growth of 1980s is not explicitly attributable to the policy reforms. Rather, it resulted from the fiscal expansion financed through external and internal borrowing during that period. Earlier, Joshi and Little (1999) also addressed the issue of shift in the growth rate by analysing growth experiences from 1960-61 to 1989-90. They divided the 30-year period into two sub-periods, from 1960-61 to 1975-76 and 1976-77 to 1989-90. The average growth rate during these two periods was 3.4 per cent and 4.7 per cent, respectively. They termed the former as the 'low-growth' and latter as the 'high-growth' period.

Rakshit (2003) documents that the Indian economy, after a quick recovery in the early years of post-reform period up to 1996, has again entered into a prolonged phase of deceleration. Decomposing the post-reform period into two sub-periods, *viz.*, 1992-1997 and 1997-2001, Rakshit views that the seeds of deceleration are traceable since 1995-96 but became visible through GDP growth only from 1997-98.[23] Differences in

23. Both industry and services registered a fall during 1995-96, yet the economy registered some increase in the growth of GDP in 1996-97, on account of a rise in household consumption that resulted from an increase in the agricultural income and increase in remittances from US (Rakshit, 2003).

the various indicators during the two sub-periods can be easily glanced from Table 1.2. The average growth of industry fell from 7.6 to 4.9 per cent and that of agricultural growth from 4.6 to -2.2 per cent (with wide variation, as depicted by the high value of coefficient of variation). Also the average annual growth of investment fell from 9.6 to 6.7 per cent on account of a drastic fall in the growth of private investment during the two sub-periods. Further, growth in public investment also fell during 1995-1998 with some revival in the late 1990s.

Rakshit points out that the sources of deceleration lie within the domestic economy. In his view, slow down in the yearly average growth rate of investment and financial distress, are the two major weaknesses of structural policy that contributed to the deceleration in recent years. The declining trends in both public and private investments became visible when both were at their peaks in 1994-95. The average annual growth of public investment fell from 7 per cent to 2.5 per cent between 1992-1995 and 1995-2001 whereas private investment fell by 8 percentage points during the same period. The fall in public investment particularly hit the agricultural infrastructure that in turn adversely affected agricultural and GDP growth thereby. Regarding the financial constraints[24] that held back the business activity in the economy, Rakshit identifies a rise in the share of bank credit to government at the expense of non-food commercial credit[25] and a fall in the capital raised through primary issues after the mid-1990s clearly suggest the same. He views the overall performance of the economy in 1990s as worse than that in 1980s—especially in core areas like GDP growth, unemployment and capacity utilisation.

Bardhan (2003) highlights the issue of lack of political consensus on reforms as one of the major causes of reform being halting and hesitant. He argues that with growing powers of regional government and regional parties, national coordination on macro policies, such as fiscal consolidation and reduction in subsidies will become a formidable task. High revenue deficit, large public dissavings (because of high fiscal deficit and public enterprise losses), creaking infrastructure bottlenecks, lack of

24. Also see, Ahluwalia (2002).

25. Non-food commercial credit decreased from 80.6 per cent in 1995-96 to 48.3 per cent in 2000-01 (Rakshit, 2003).

orientation of reforms towards human development (e.g., education, health and child nutrition) are few other reasons that restrict the further growth.

Balakrishnan (2005) in his recent work does not provide any support for the acceleration in the rate of growth during the post-reform period. At the same time, he argues against the conclusion that reforms failed. Estimating the two regression lines by fitting a linear trend from 1980-81 to 1989-90 and 1990-91 to 1999-2000, he finds that the trend rates of growth of 5.4 and 6.3 per cent, respectively, for the two periods were not statistically different. He identifies the declining budgetary support to capital formation and missing monetary policy as the two main factors that have failed to provide a significant step up to the rate of growth of the economy in the post-1990s reform period.

As a contribution to this debate, our analysis[26] investigates the following issues:

a) Whether the pre- and post-reform growth rates are structurally different.

b) The timing of structural break in growth of GDP.

c) Examination of Panagariya's (over) emphasis on growth volatility during the 1980s.

d) Testing Rakshit's contention regarding growth deceleration since the mid-1990s.

Firstly, using a semi-logarithmic specification, a non-linear (quadratic) trend is fitted to the series of GDP[27] for the period 1980-81 to 2003-04 (Table 1.4) as specified below.

$$\ln(GDP)_t = \alpha + \beta_1 t + \beta_2 t^2 \qquad (1)$$

where t is time, taking value 1 (for the first year i.e., 1980-81) to 24. The average annual trend growth has time varying element in it, and is given by $\beta_1 + 2\beta_2 t$. The coefficient β_2 multiplied by 2 gives the change in the average rate of growth over time. It gives the rate of acceleration (if the sign is positive) or deceleration (if the sign is negative) in the average growth.

---

26. The whole analysis was carried out, using 'Stata 8: statistical data analysis' package.
27. For sources of data, refer to Annexure IV.

Table 1.4

GDP and Annual Growth Rates of GDP, 1980-81 to 2004-05
(GDP measured at 1993-94 prices)

Year	GDP (Rs '000 crore)	Growth Rate (in %)	Year	GDP (Rs '000 crore)	Growth Rate (in %)
1980-81	402.128	7.17	1992-93	737.792	5.12
1981-82	425.073	5.97	1993-94	782.345	5.90
1982-83	438.079	3.06	1994-95	838.031	7.25
1983-84	472.742	7.68	1995-96	899.563	7.34
1984-85	492.077	4.31	1996-97	970.083	7.84
1985-86	513.99	4.45	1997-98	1016.595	4.79
1986-87	536.257	4.33	1998-99	1082.748	6.51
1987-88	556.778	3.83	1999-00	1148.368	6.06
1988-89	615.098	10.47	2000-01	1198.592	4.37
1989-90	656.331	6.70	2001-02	1267.945	5.79
1990-91	692.871	5.57	2002-03(P)	1318.362	3.98
1991-92	702.863	2.30	2003-04(Q)	1430.548	8.51

Note : P : Provisional estimates; Q : Quick estimates.
Source: GOI, 2004-05.

The estimated results obtained from the equation (1) are (with t ratios in parentheses) as follows:

$$\ln\widehat{GDP} = \underset{(1099.09)^{*}}{12.849} + \underset{(23.13)^{*}}{.05t} + \underset{(2.73)^{*}}{.00023t^2} \qquad (2)$$

$$DW = 2.24$$

* significant at 1 per cent level

Since the coefficients, β_1 and β_2 are positive and statistically significant at the 1 per cent level, GDP (at constant prices) is following a positive and accelerating trend. This is also illustrated in the curve formed by GDP in Figure 1.2. The interpretation is that over the entire period of 24 years ranging from 1980-81 to 2003-04, the real GDP (measured at 1993-94 prices) grows at an average rate of 5 per cent per annum, with acceleration over time.

Figure 1.2

Trends in Gross Domestic Product (measured at 1993-94 prices)

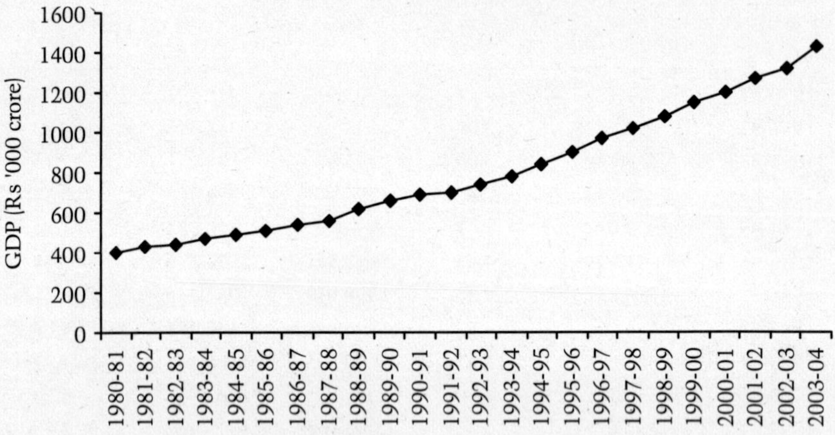

In the rest of this section, we primarily assess the relative effectiveness of economic reforms of the late 1980s and the 1990s, in accelerating growth in the Indian economy.

In order to demonstrate the role of policy reforms of the 1990s in bringing acceleration in growth rate, our analysis separately covers the two sub-periods naming: pre-1991 and post-1991 reform period. The post 1991 reform period comprises 12 years, beginning from 1992-93 up to 2003-04. It must be recognised here that the policy reforms initiated in July 1991 were driven by the crisis faced during 1991-92. The effect of reforms on various indicators of economic growth should therefore be analysed from 1992-93 onwards[28] instead of 1990-91. The pre-1991 reform period of equal length is considered (beginning from 1980-81 up to 1991-92) to compare the average trend growth rate in the two periods. To put it in another way, the underlying exercise compares whether trend growth rates in the two periods are significantly different or not.

---

28. Panagariya (2004) and Ahluwalia (2002), among others considered the post-reform period beginning from 1992-93 whereas Balakrishnan (2005) considered from 1990-1991 onwards.

To carry out this analysis we estimated trend growth rates for the two periods separately. A different version of non-linear[29] trend equation [given in equation (1)'] was used for the purpose.

$$\ln (GDP)_t = \alpha + \beta_1 t, \text{ for pre-reform period} \quad (1)'$$

and

$$\ln (GDP)_t = \alpha' + \beta'_1 t, \text{ for post-reform period}$$

Adding the disturbance term to above equations, we obtain:

$$\ln (GDP)_t = \alpha + \beta_1 t + u_t, \quad (3)$$

$$\ln (GDP)_t = \alpha' + \beta'_1 t + u'_t, \quad (3)'$$

The estimated regression results (with t ratios in parentheses) obtained are:

Pre-reform period: 1980-81 to 1991-92

$$\ln(\widehat{GDP})_t = \underset{(1087.95)^*}{12.84} + \underset{(32.96)^*}{.053t}, \quad t = 1 \ldots\ldots\ldots\ldots 12. \quad (4)$$

DW = 2.5

Post-reform period: 1992-93 to 2003-04

$$\ln(\widehat{GDP})_t = \underset{(540.64)^*}{12.758} + \underset{(47.11)^*}{.059t}, \quad t = 13 \ldots\ldots\ldots\ldots 24. \quad (5)$$

DW = .84

Or

$$\ln(\widehat{GDP})_t = \underset{(1459.25)^*}{13.467} + \underset{(47.11)^*}{.059t}, \quad t = 1 \ldots\ldots\ldots\ldots 12. \quad (5)'$$

DW = .84

* significant at 1 per cent level

29. It is important to emphasise here that non-linear trend, as given in equation (1), was fitted for both the periods separately. For the pre-reform period, β_2 was found to be significant whereas for the post-reform, it was non-significant. Therefore to test the structural difference in the trend growth rates during the two periods, we preferred using trend equation as specified in equation (1)' for both the periods.

Comparing (4) and (5), we find that the trend growth rate in the post-1991 reform period is 5.9 per cent and is higher than that of the pre-1991 reform period. Now, in order to investigate the issue of a structural difference in the trend equations for the two periods, we tested the null hypothesis where the set of coefficients in the pre-1991 reform period [equation (4)] is equal to the set of coefficients in the post-1991 reform period [equation (5)]. Assuming the two equations to be structurally the same we test the null hypothesis (jointly),

$$\alpha = \alpha' \qquad \beta_1 = \beta'_1$$

To perform the above exercise, we can either use the 'dummy variable approach' or the 'chow test'. The former is preferred over the latter because of its distinct advantages.[30] To find the difference in the coefficients of intercept as well as slope in the pre- and post-1991 reform periods, using 'dummy variable approach', we introduced both additive (D) and multiplicative (D multiplied by t) dummies to equation (3) and estimated the following expanded regression equation by pooling all 24 observations.

$$\ln(GDP)_t = \alpha + \alpha_1 D_i + \beta_1 t + \beta_2 (D_i t) + u_i, \qquad t = 1 \ldots\ldots 24 \qquad (6)$$

where $D_i = 0$ for all observations for the pre-reform period (i.e., 1980-81 to 1991-92) and 1 for observations from the post-reform period i.e., 1992-93 to 2003-04.

From this it follows

$$E\,(GDP_t / D_i = 0) = \alpha + \beta_1 t \qquad \text{for pre-reform period} \qquad (7)$$

and

$$E\,(GDP_t / D_i = 1) = (\alpha + \alpha_1) + (\beta_1 + \beta_2) t \quad \text{for post-reform period} \quad (8)$$

$$= \gamma_1 + \gamma_2 t$$

It is important to note here that equations (3) and (3)' are same as equations (7) and (8) respectively, with $\alpha' = \gamma_1 = (\alpha + \alpha_1)$ and

30. The 'chow test' does not explicitly tell us whether the two regression equations are different on account of differences in the coefficients of the slope and/or of the intercept. The dummy variable approach indicates the source(s) of the difference along with. Also, for chow test three regressions are required to be run whereas for dummy variable approach only one regression is required.

$\beta'_1 = \gamma_2 = (\beta_1 + \beta_2)$. The coefficient α_1 is the differential intercept (it tells by how much the value of the intercept in post-1991 reform differs from that of the pre-1991 reform period) and β_2 is the differential slope coefficient (indicating the difference in the slopes of regression lines) for the period for which D_i=1 i.e., post-1991 reform period. The signs of these coefficients indicate the direction of change in the intercept and slope during the post-1991 reform period. The results obtained by estimating equation (6) using GDP data are given as:

$$\ln(\widehat{GDP})_t = 12.84 - .084D + .0528t + .0062Dt \; ; \quad t=1 \,.....24. \quad (9)$$

$$(1212.1)^* \quad (-2.89)^* \quad (36.72)^* \quad (3.05)^*$$

$$DW = 2.24$$

Since in the above regression the t test on both the differential intercept and differential slope coefficients are statistically significant at the 1 per cent, we infer that the regressions for the two periods are different i.e., trend growth equation for the post-1991 reform period is structurally different from that of the pre-1991 reform period.[31] The estimated annual trend growth rate of 5.9 per cent in equation (5) during the post-1991 reform period is significantly different from the annual growth of 5.3 per cent estimated for the pre-1991 reform period in equation (4).[32]

Further, putting the value of dummy variable, D_i=0 for pre-reform and D_i=1 for post-reform in equation (9) we can also obtain the two regressions as:

$$\ln(GDP)_t = 12.84 + .053t \qquad \text{for pre-reform period} \qquad (10)$$

$$(t = 1 .... 12)$$

$$\ln(GDP)_t = (12.84 - .084) + (.0528 + .0062)t$$

$$= 12.756 + .059t \qquad \text{for post-reform period} \qquad (11)$$

$$(t = 13 .... 24)$$

31. If the two regression lines (4) and (5) are plotted on a graph, the line for the post-1991 reform period as in equation (5), would be steeper and will lie above that of the pre-1991 reform period's estimated line in equation (4).

32. The chow test was also computed for which we combined all the 24 observations i.e., estimated one trend equation over the entire period as ln (GDP) = 12.8+. 056. The F-statistic used to test the hypothesis was found to be equal to 4.75 which is significant at 5 per cent level, indicating a structural difference in the two regressions, estimated in equation (4) and (5) above. Therefore trend growth must be estimated separately for the two periods. See Pindyck and Rubinfeld (1998), for details.

The test of the stability of the entire regression, using F-statistic,[33] in equation (9) was also performed by testing the null hypothesis that coefficients of both the additive and multiplicative dummies are simultaneously equal to zero, i.e.,

$$\alpha_1 = \beta_2 = 0$$

As the value of F-statistic obtained was 8.55, which is statistically significant at 1 per cent level, we reject the null hypothesis and conclude that the trend growth equation for the post-1991 reform period is statistically different from that of the pre-1991 reform period. The estimated regression equation for the post-1991 reform period has shifted upward with a higher slope. The exercise performed above refutes Balakrishnan's (2005) assertion that there is no significant pick up in the average annual growth rate in the post-reform period.

Turning our attention to the timing of the turnaround in the growth rate, both additive and multiplicative dummies beginning from the mid-1980s up to the mid-1990s were considered. This is to test, whether the turnaround in growth occurred in response to the mild reforms of the mid-1980s (Delong, 2004 and Rodrik, 2004) or it began only after the onset of the more comprehensive policy reforms of the 1990s (Panagariya, 2004). After fitting a semi-logarithmic trend equation over the entire period from 1980-81 to 2003-04 [equation (12)], we re-estimated the equation with a number of alternative dummy variables (both additive and multiplicative) in various years from the mid-1980s to 1990s, beginning from 1984-85 onwards, to search for the timing of the turnaround (see Table 1.5).

The estimated regression equation using GDP data for the period, 1980-81 to 2003-04 is

$$\ln(\widehat{GDP})_t = \underset{(1526.7)^*}{12.82} + \underset{(94.5)^*}{.0555t} \qquad t = 1,\ldots\ldots,24 \qquad (12)$$

$$DW = .9$$

From Table 1.5, it is found that the sign of the coefficient of the multiplicative dummy (D*t) is positive indicating that acceleration in

33. The appropriate F-statistic is $[(R^2_{UR}-R^2_R)/q] \,/\, [(1-R^2_{UR})/(N-k)]$ (Pindyck and Rubinfeld, 1998).

Table 1.5

Search for Structural Break in Growth of GDP, 1980-81 to 2003-04

Dependent Variable: ln(GDP)

Dummy Variable	*Intercept*	*Additive Dummy (D)*	*Time*	*Multiplicative Dummy (D*t)*	R^2	*DW*
D_1 =1 beginning 1984-85	12.85 (586.6)	-0.47 (-19.2)	.052 (6.46)	.005 (.637)	.99	2.22
D_2=1 beginning 1985-86	12.8 (712.6)	-.054 (-2.52)	.051 (9.42)	.006 (1.06)	.99	2.3
D_3=1 beginning 1986-87	12.85 (809.0)	-.061 (-3.11)	.050 (12.28)	.007 (1.74)*	.99	2.3
D_4=1 beginning 1987-88	12.86 (886.13)	-.06 (-2.52)	.050 (15.05)	. 01 (3.11)***	.99	2.24
D_5=1 beginning 1988-89	12.86 (999.6)	-.06 (-2.85)	.050 (18.59)	.01 (3.47) ***	.99	2.09
D_6 =1 beginning 1989-90	12.85 (999.1)	-.056 (-2.5)	-.050 (22.95)	.007 (2.77) ***	.99	2.24
D_7=1 beginning 1990-91	12.84 (1050.1)	-.065 (-2.65)	-.052 (26.58)	.006 (2.45) **	.99	2.24
D_8=1 beginning 1991-92	12.84 (1183.7)	-.084 (-3.33)	.054 (33.57)	.006 (2.74) ***	.99	2.13
D_9=1 beginning 1992-93	12.84 (1212.1)	-.08 (-2.89)	.053 (36.7)	.006 (3.05) ***	.99	2.24
D_{10}=1 beginning 1993-94	12.84 (1275)	-.07 (-2.14)	.052 (42.2)	.006 (2.90) ***	.99	2.27
D_{11}=1 beginning 1994-95	12.85 (1406.6)	-.042 (-2.15)	.052 (48.53)	.005 (2.31) **	.99	2.42
D_{12}=1 beginning 1995-96	12.84 (1520.7)	-.007 (-.18)	.052 (56.35)	.003 (2.34)	.99	2.64
D_{13}=1 beginning 1996-97	12.84 (1522)	.025 (.48)	.053 (60.7)	.001 (.39)	.99	2.5
D_{14}=1 beginning 1997-98	12.84 (1384)	.025 (.35)	.054 (59.5)	.000 (.11)	.99	2.4
D_{15}=1 beginning 1998-99	12.83 (1372)	.05 (.51)	.054 (62.85)	-.001 (-.23)	.99	2.14
D_{16}=1 beginning 1999-00	12.83 (1344.6)	.048 (.34)	.055 (65.47)	-.001 (-.21)	.99	2.02

Note : *** significant at 1 per cent; ** significant at 5 per cent; *significant at 10 per cent.

Source: Calculations based on growth estimates given in Table 1.4.

growth occurred from 1984-85 onwards. However, it became significant at 10 per cent level from 1986-87 and at 5 per cent (or lower) from 1987-88 onwards. The significant rise in average or trend rate of growth is evident in all the regressions using dummies up to 1994-95.

For the dummies beginning from the years 1995-96, 1996-97 and 1997-98, we find that the sign of the multiplicative dummy is non-significant. The significant change in the trend growth fails to appear beyond 1994-95. The clear message that emerges from the results in Table 1.5 is that the turnaround or significant break in trend rate became visible from mid-1980s (1986-87/1987-88), validating the view of Delong (2004) and Rodrik (2004), among others. However, it is also indicated that the structural break continued till the mid-1990s. The economy experienced accelerated growth from the mid-1980s up to the mid-1990s.

Two additional comments on Panagariya's analysis regarding the growth experience during the 1980s are necessary. Firstly, he accepts that average growth during the 1980s was essentially higher than the average growth during the 1970s. However, he also argues that high growth in the former period is discernible only because of 'crucial high' ('super high') growth of 7.6 per cent during 1988-1991, without which the growth of '1980s' (1981-82 to 1987-88) is unimpressive and significantly lower than growth in the post-1991 reform period. Secondly, he also contrasts the growth experience of the '1980s' (1980-81 to 1991-92) from the '1990s'[34] by arguing that growth in the former period was fragile and unsustainable because the variance of growth rates during '1980s' was found to be significantly higher (using F-statistic to test equality of sample variances) than that of growth during the '1990s'.

With regard to Panagariya's (2004) first contention, it may be useful to consider the average growth rates for various selected periods in Table 1.6. For the first three decades of our planning era, the average annual growth remained below 4 per cent, averaging at 3.5 per cent during 1951-52 to 1979-80. It was during the fourth decade (i.e., 1980s) that a noticeable spurt in the average growth is clearly observed. To follow Panagariya's suggestion, even if the growth during 1988-1991 is excluded, the average crosses the 5 per cent mark. An average growth of 5.1 per cent per annum during 1980-81 to 1987-88 is unquestionably remarkable—especially, when compared with the 3 per cent average during the preceding decade. It is also comparable to an average growth of 5.9 per cent in the 1990s.

---

34. Panagariya (2004) defined the period '1980s' from 1980-81 to 1991-92 and '1990s' from 1992-93 to 2002-03.

In fact, the manner in which Panagariya arrives at an average of 4.8 per cent growth during the 1980s (excluding high growth period of the late 1980s) and finds it to be strictly lying below the average growth rate of 4.9 per cent (achieved during the Fifth Five-Year Plan: 1974-1979) is arguable. Further, using this as a basis for inferring that the average growth during the 1980s as being no different from the growth attained during the earlier periods (i.e., comparable to the 1970s or not comparable to growth rate in the 1990s) is also questionable.

It is important to stress here that, while finding an average for the 1980s (excluding high growth period of late 1980s) the growth attained during 1980-81 has been ignored without any justification. In order to find this average if we calculate the average of 1980s (excluding high growth period) from 1980-81 to 1987-88 (instead of 1981-82 to 1987-88), the average growth is 5.1 per cent (Table 1.6). Since this is strictly higher than average annual growth of 4.9 per cent attained during the Fifth Five-Year Plan (using Panagariya's reasoning), it may be concluded that the average growth of 1980s is different from that attained in the earlier period.

Table 1.6

Average Annual Growth during Selected Periods (in per cent)

1951-52 to 1959-60	*1960-61 to 1969-70*	*1970-71 to 1979-80*	*1951-52 to 1979-80*	*1980-81 to 1989-90*	*1980-81 to 1987-88*	*1980-81 to 1990-91*	*1980-81 to 1991-92*	*1992-93 to 2002-03*
3.6	3.95	2.95	3.5	5.8	5.1	5.78	5.4	5.9

Source: Calculations based on growth estimates given in GOI, 2004-05.

Scrutinising the validity of Panagariya's second conclusion, let us consider the argument used by him to support his first contention. If the growth rates in GDP experienced during the three years i.e., 1988-1991 can make the average growth of 1980s higher, then it is important to draw attention to the fact that the conclusion regarding the fragility of growth during 1980s is also simply based on only one year's growth rate i.e., 1988-1989. If average growth of only this period is omitted from the period '1980s' (defined by Panagariya) then the F-statistic fails to be significant, regardless of whether the growth rate of 2.3 per cent during the 'crisis year' i.e., 1991-92 (Table 1.4), is included or not.

In Table 1.7 we recalculate the F-statistic for all the periods considered by Panagariya (after excluding growth rate of only 1988-89) with respect to the growth in '1990s' (as defined by him) and find that the F-statistic fails to be significant even at the 10 per cent level of significance. It is only when the average growth during the 1980s is considered from 1977-78 onwards, that the F-statistic is significant. These results can also be confirmed from Table 1.8 where we present the comparisons of averages and variances of growth rates during the selected periods. If the period '1980s' is not accepted to be a high growth period because of the presence of 'crucial growth period' of 1988-1991, then it would be justified to question the acceptance of the 'fragility' of growth during '1980s' which is simply based on one year's growth estimates.

Table 1.7

Testing of Equality of Variances of Average Annual Growth Estimates during '1980s' and '1990s'

Period	*Variance*	*Variance*[a]	*F-statistic*	*F-statistic*[a]	*F-critical value*[a]*: 5%*
1981-82 to 1991-92	6.1	3.41	4.1	2.14	$F_{(9,10)} = 3.02$
1980-81 to 1990-91	4.6	2.39	3.1	2.50	$F_{(9,10)} = 3.02$
1981-82 to 1990-91	4.8	2.20	3.3	2.38	$F_{(8,10)} = 3.07$
1977-78 to 1990-91	12.5	10.96	8.5	6.87	$F_{(12,10)} = 2.91$
1992-93 to 2002-03	2.59[b]				

Notes: [a] Calculations for each period are made after excluding the growth rate of 1988-89.

[b] Panagariya (2004) calculates this value as 2.5 (The difference in calculation is on account of growth estimates considered by Panagariya for 2001-02 and 2002-03 are based on provisional and quick estimates).

Source: Column 2 and 4 are taken from Panagariya (2004).

Column 3 and 5 are calculated using growth estimates shown in Table 1.4.

When the pre-1991 reform period i.e., 1980-81 to 1991-92 (or 1990-1991) is compared to the post-1991 reform period i.e., 1992-93 to 2003-04, we find that the variability of the latter period is significantly lower and average growth is higher, though non-significantly (see comparison 1 and 2 in Table 1.8). But when the variability in growth during 1980-81 to 1986-1987 is compared to the period 1988-89 to 2003-04[35] (see comparison 3 in Table 1.8), we find the variance in growth is higher for the latter period,

35. Here we compare the variability in growth in '1980s' (excluding the high growth period i.e., from 1988-1991) and growth in '1990s' (including the high growth period).

Table 1.8

Comparisons of Means and Variances of Growth Rates between Selected Periods

S. No.		*Period 1*	*Period 2*	*F-statistic*	*t- statistic*
1		*1980-81 to 1991-92*	*1992-93 to 2003-04*		
	Average	5.4	6.12		-.89
	Variance	5.8	2.01	2.89**	
2		*1980-81 to 1990-91*	*1992-93 to 2003-04*		
	Average	5.8	6.12		-.45
	Variance	4.58	2.01	2.27*	
3		*1980-81 to 1987-88*	*1988-89 to 2003-04*		
	Average	5.1	6.09		-1.17
	Variance	2.7	4.33	.63	
4		*1980-81 to 1987-88*	*1988-89 to 2003-04@*		
	Average	5.1	6.4		-1.78*
	Variance	2.7	2.9	.95	
5		*1992-93 to 1996-97*	*1997-98 to 2002-03*		
	Average	6.7	5.25		2.23**
	Variance	2.29	2.02	1.26	
6		*1992-93 to 1996-97*	*1997-98 to 2003-04*		
	Average	6.7	5.7		1.22
	Variance	2.29	2.37	.54	

Notes: @ Calculations are made ignoring the growth estimates of 'crisis year', i.e., 1991-92.
* Significant at 10 per cent; ** Significant at 5 per cent.

Source: Calculations based on growth estimates given in Table 1.4.

though the F-statistic is non-significant. Further, even if the 'crisis year' i.e., 1991-92[36] is excluded from the latter period (see comparison 4 in Table 1.8), the above result remains unaltered. Does this mean it is the high growth period of 1980s that is causing the variability in growth and making it fragile? The validity of both the conclusions remains questionable.

In order to assess the argument of Rakshit (2003) regarding the deceleration in growth since the mid-1990s, we used dummies, beginning from 1998-99 and 1999-2000. An important result that emerges from Table

36. The inclusion of this year can be objectionable because the growth during this period was only 2.3 per cent, as argued by Panagariya (2004).

1.5, is that beyond 1997-98, the sign of the multiplicative dummy becomes non-significantly negative. This validates Rakshit's assertion of a decline in the trend rate of growth, though it is not significant. The claim is also verified by comparing the average growth rates. Rakshit's claim is also verified by comparing the average growth rates during the two sub-periods: (i) 1992-93 to 1996-97, and (ii) 1997-98 to 2002-03 given in Table 1.8 (see comparison 5). The average annual growth of 6.7 per cent during 1992-93 to 1996-97 is higher and statistically significant at 5 per cent than the average annual growth of 5.25 per cent during 1997-98 to 2002-03. Further the average annual growth of the latter remains higher than the former period if the growth estimates of 2003-04 and beyond are also included. However the difference in averages fails to be significant (comparison 6).

The deceleration phase of the late 1990s seems to be a transitory phenomenon. From the provisional, quick and advance growth estimates for the economy during the last three years in a row i.e., 2003-2006, it can be inferred that the recovery period is already underway (Figure 1.3a).

Table 1.9

Sectoral Average Growth Rates during Selected Periods

Period	*Agriculture*	*Industry*	*Services*
1980-81 to 1985-86	5.84	5.65	6.07
1986-87 to 1990-91	4.22	7.98	7.06
1992-93 to 1996-97	4.62	8.04	7.58
1997-98 to 2001-02	2.06	4.62	8.12
2002-03 to 2005-06*	2.5	7.6	9.5

Note: * Includes provisional, quick and advanced estimates for 2003-04, 2004-05, and 2005-06, respectively.

Source: Compiled from GOI (2004-05) and CSO (2006).

The GDP is estimated to grow respectively at 8.5 and 7.5 per cent during 2003-04 and 2004-05. Even in the first half of the fiscal year 2005-2006, despite a low performance of agriculture, the economy registered a strong growth of 8.1 per cent with robust performance by industry (9.4%) and services (12%) and is also projected to grow at the same rate during rest of the year (advance estimates of CSO, 2006). After witnessing a downfall during the late 1990s, industry has been exhibiting a rising trend since

2001-02, while average growth rates of services with some variability has been on the rise since the beginning of 1991 reforms (Table 1.9 and Figure 1.3b). Further, industry and services are estimated to grow at an average annual rate of 7 and 8.6 per cent, respectively, during 2002-2005 (GOI, 2004-05). The deterioration in the performance of agriculture since 1980-1981 is evident from Table 1.9.

Figure 1.3

Average Annual Growth Rate of GDP, Industry and Services (%)

(a)

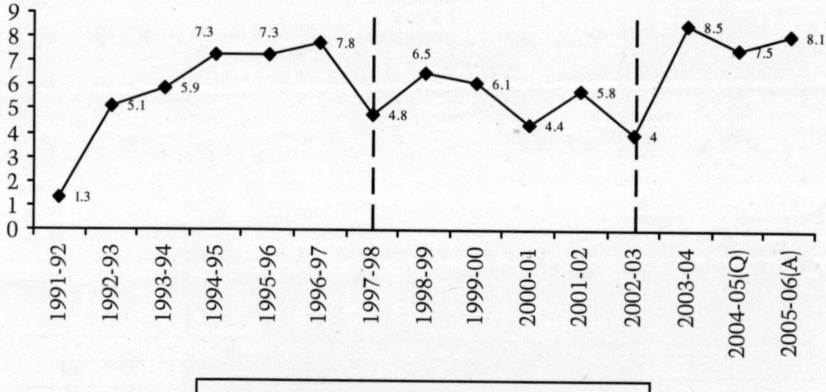

(b)

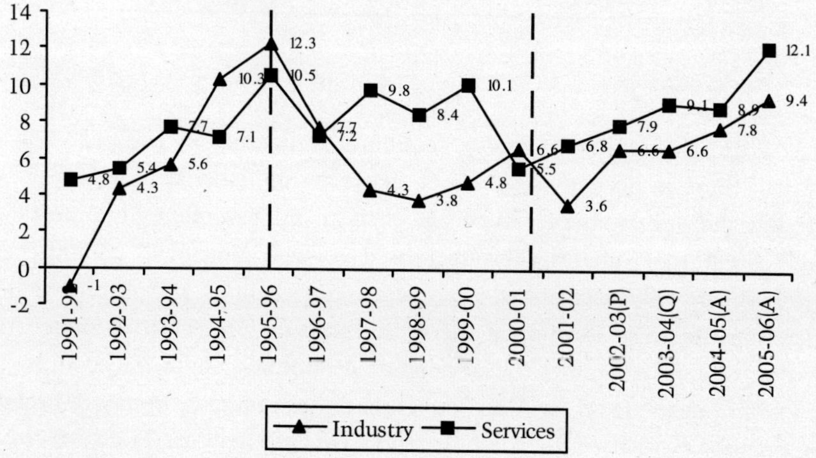

Also, despite a fall in public investment, the gross domestic capital formation (GDCF) also showed a rising trend on account of increased private investment that more than compensated for the fall in the former component (Figure 1.4). The saving-investment gap has turned positive since 2001 and is estimated to be 1.8 in 2003-04. On the external front, with revival of growth in the industry and increased export competitiveness, exports grew at an average rate of more than 20 per cent during 2002-2005. On the basis of this evidence, it is difficult to accept the proposition that the economy has entered into a prolonged deceleration.

Figure 1.4

Percentage Share of Investment in GDP (at market prices)

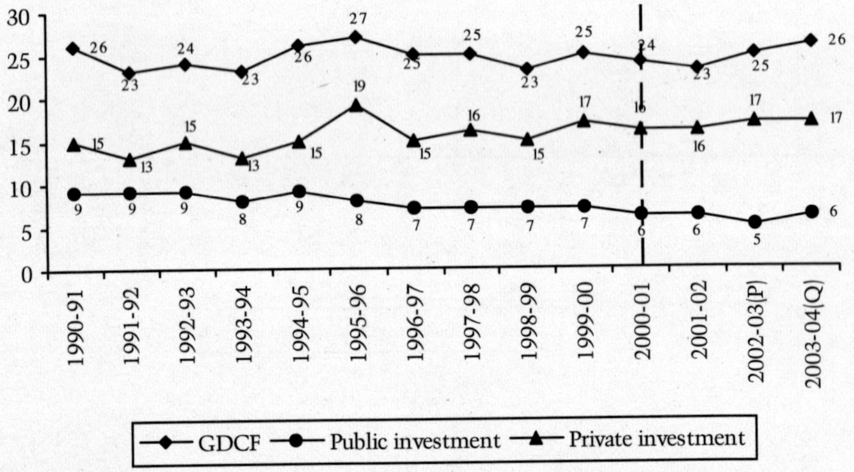

1.7 Conclusion

From the review of major economic indicators in the post-reform period, there is no denying the fact that reforms ushered in a new era of growth and development. There has been an improvement in domestic as well as external spheres. The liberalised policies adopted as part of these reforms not only accelerated the overall growth rates and improved BoP situation but also developed the confidence of foreign investors in the Indian economy. Among the developing economies, India is becoming an important destination for FDI. The potential of Indian economy to become an engine of growth for the whole world is being realised. From 55th place in the world in 2004, India has moved up to 50th rank in the Growth Competitiveness Index (World Economic Forum, 2005-06).

The average annual growth of 3.6 per cent experienced during 1950-1980 increased to 5 per cent during 1980s and it even crossed the 6.5 per cent mark during the first five years of the 1990s reforms. High growth of services contributed the most in average GDP growth. The reform process largely neglected the agricultural sector. Moreover, the decline in public sector investment has particularly affected the infrastructure in agriculture, which is crucial for achieving high growth in this sector. The dependence of agriculture on factors beyond human control and poor infrastructure make its average growth to remain variable and fluctuate by high margins. There has been an improvement in income and in human development indicators since 1991. However, despite this India continues to lag behind many emerging economies. Though Human Development Index (HDI) has increased from 0.439 in 1992 to 0.595 for the year 2002, yet India's ranking remains low.

Assessing the relative effectiveness of reforms of the late 1980s and the 1990s, in accelerating growth, our results, broadly speaking, are consistent with the view that reforms of the mid-1980s had a palpable impact on the average growth levels. Indian economy experienced a structural break in the average growth rates during this period. As against the finding that the average growth in the 1990s is not a considerable improvement over the 1980s, it is suggested that the more comprehensive reforms followed since 1991-92 provided a significant step-up to growth rates. Analysing the trend growth rates during the pre-1991 reform and the post-1991 reform period, it is clearly established that the trend growth rates of the two periods are structurally different. Our analysis also demonstrates that the issues of average growth 'not crossing the 5 per cent mark' and its 'variability' during 1980s are sensitive to the data used. Whether Indian economy entered a prolonged deceleration phase in the late 1990s, is not corroborated by our analysis. There are strong signs that the Indian economy is heading towards a 'high growth' period.

In order to keep the Indian economy growing on a higher, stable and sustainable path, it is important that there should not be any halt in the reform process. Apart from reforms in agriculture, if the reforms in some key areas, such as labour reforms—giving freedom to firms regarding hiring and firing of workers, end of reservation in small-scale industries, reforms in banking sector, procedural simplification to encourage greater FDI flows, lowering of tariff rates, improvement in infrastructure and reduction of government's debt continue attaining long-term annual growth for GDP in the vicinity of 7 per cent may no longer be a distant dream.

2 Stock Market Reforms and Takeover Market

An Analysis

This chapter, primarily, focusses on stock market reforms and the development of market for corporate control. It is divided in four sections. The first section discusses the stock market reforms and their effects on the financing of corporate growth and the real economy. Section 2.2 is devoted to the analysis of 'takeover market' since the establishment of the 'Takeover Code' in 1997. On the basis of the experience during 1997-2007, Section 2.3 evaluates the need for such a market in India. Finally, Section 2.4 concludes with some observations.

2.1 Stock Market Reforms and Effects

Stock Market Reforms

In India stock market reforms occurred almost simultaneously along with the process of liberalisation. To regulate the functioning of capital and stock market and to ensure transparency, Securities and Exchange Board of India (SEBI) was set up in 1992 as a watchdog of capital market. SEBI's original mandate was to provide a fair and honest stock market and to regulate the activities of stockbrokers, merchant banks and bankers to an issue, brokerage firms, registrars and portfolio managers. Over a period of 15 years, a number of amendments have been made to increase SEBI's punitive powers and to control irregularities experienced by the stock market. A bill named, SEBI (Amendment) Act, 2002, gave SEBI comprehensive powers to regulate the stock market and protect the interest of small investors. Talks are underway to merge jurisdiction of Department of Company Affairs and Company Law Board with the SEBI to bring greater efficiency in the system. If given sweeping powers, SEBI will be able to prosecute the corporate sector and provide greater security to small investors.

The first step taken to reform stock market was dissolution of office of Controller of Capital Issues (CCI) and consequent repeal of 'Capital Issues (Control) Act'[1] of 1947 in May 1992. Under this act, the government controlled the timing, composition, quantum and pricing of new shares issues. This reform was a major step moving from direct government control to procedural regulation of the capital market. SEBI was given substantial powers under the SEBI Act, to regulate the activities of various players in the capital market. Companies were now free to enter the capital market and set their own prices after meeting SEBI's norms for their offer documents. In 1993, Indian companies were allowed to list on foreign exchanges[2] through a set of guidelines. Conditions going for initial public offerings (IPOs) were also relaxed in the year 2000. As a step towards market modernisation, SEBI also introduced online trading and dematerialised trading to save time in transacting shares. Companies were allowed to buyback their own shares, subject to relaxed regulation laid down by SEBI. As a step towards external liberalisation, financial institutional investors (FIIs) were allowed to invest in all types of securities traded in the primary and secondary market with full repatriation benefits. The restriction on value of trading or lock-in period was removed. Similarly, Indian companies were permitted to raise funds from abroad.

In continuation of the reform process, a number of policy developments are still being initiated by SEBI. The recommendations of the committee, constituted to analyse the application of sectoral foreign direct investment (FDI) limits upon FII investments, which submitted its report in June 2004, are under consideration. Another policy effort, in the form of a committee to evaluate mechanisms to encourage FII flows while curbing speculative tendencies, is underway. In April 2004, SEBI set up the Securities Market Infrastructure Leveraging Expert (SMILE) Committee to report on primary market infrastructure and mutual fund industry. SEBI has also approved the establishment of a 'Central Listing Authority' to centralise the listing function. To improve the debt market, Clearing Corporation of India limited

1. This was in response to Narsimham Committee Report submitted in 1991, which argued against the tight control exercised by the government, and number of restrictions placed by the CCI on the operation of the capital market.

2. In 1998, Infosys became the first Indian registered company to list on American exchange, NASDAQ.

(CCIL) in 2001 and Negotiated Dealing System (NDS) in 2002 were set up. SEBI has also developed a database about market participants and investors, called the MAPIN to give a unique identification number (UIN) to participants in the capital market (GOI, 2004-05).

Growth of Stock Market

The stock market had existed for long in India. However, the corporate sector was not much dependent on it for its financing. Hence, it remained quite dormant till the early 1980s. The pattern of demand for capital has undergone a significant change during the last two decades and has improved stock market activity spectacularly. As far as the period from 1980s to 1990s is concerned, there was an expansion in the stock market activity, *albeit* at a slow pace. The capitalisation ratio[3] increased from 4 to 13.4 per cent, turnover ratio[4] increased from 1.5 to 6 per cent and the number of listed companies moved up from 2,265 to 5,698 during this period. Till 1990s, the institutional term-lending was the primary source of industrial finance in India. FIIs raised money through government guaranteed bonds at low rates of interest and, in turn, lent funds at concessional rates of interest to the corporate sector. Such easy and cheap availability of credit not only discouraged corporates to raise capital from equity market but also helped them in undertaking risky projects (RBI, 2000-01).

With the onset of economic reforms and establishment of SEBI, the growth in the stock market was remarkably high during the 1990s. The capitalisation and turnover ratio increased to 45 per cent and 10 per cent, respectively, in the mid-1990s. As of March 31, 2000, Bombay Stock Exchange's (BSE) market capitalisation stood at Rs 9,128.42 billion (US $209.3 billion) or 52 per cent of 1999 GDP and its turnover ratio was 75 per cent. NSE's market capitalisation was Rs10,204.26 billion (US $233.9 billion) or 82 per cent of 1999 GDP; its turnover ratio was approximately 82 per cent. The ratio of market capitalisation to assets of scheduled commercial banks[5] increased from 28 per cent in the early 1990s to 85 per

---

3. It is measured as market capitalisation to gross domestic product at current market prices.
4. It is measured as value of shares traded to market capitalisation.
5. It is a tentative measure of the significance of stock market relative to the banking system.

cent in the mid-1990s (RBI, 2000-01). In terms of other indicators, such as number of stock exchanges and number of listed companies also, there was an explosive growth in the stock market. After witnessing a fall in these indicators in the late 1990s, the stock market again gained momentum in 2004-05. However, it could not reach its level of the mid-1990s.

Stock Market Reforms and Corporate Financing

Now, a more pertinent question that needs to be addressed is: How far is the corporate sector growth financing dependent on the stock market and overtime, how has the corporate sector's dependence on the stock market changed?

Singh (1995), on the basis of a sample of 100 largest listed manufacturing companies that existed from 1980-1990, demonstrated that Indian corporates during the 1980s financed 40 per cent of its growth of net assets[6] from internal sources i.e., retained earnings, and 60 per cent from external source.[7] Of the latter, one-third are financed from equity and two-thirds from debt, implying 2:1 as the debt/equity (D/E) ratio. In view of the imperfection in stock market volatility in share prices, presence of family-controlled firms and lack of protection for minority shareholder, a large recourse to stock markets finance was found to be surprising. Before proceeding, some comments are necessary.

First, Cobham and Subramaniam (1995) argued that Singh's (1995) methodology, used to measure the contribution of internal and external finance in the growth of net assets of firms, overstated the contribution of equity finance to Indian corporate growth and market. Using the alternative methodology,[8] they found a relatively smaller contribution of equity.

Second, Singh's result was based on top 100 listed companies in manufacturing, which cannot be generalised for all Indian firms. In a cross-sectional study (GOI, 2000-01) on a sample of 1,730 firms for the year 2001, it was found that there are large variations across the size

6. For definition see Annexure 1.
7. Detailed discussion on internal and external finance is included as text in Chapter 8.
8. For details, see Singh (1998).

distribution of firms.[9] The results show (Table 2.1) that the smaller firms have much higher debt-equity ratio than the larger firms. This suggests that larger firms' dependence on equity market is much more than that of the smaller firms. This could also be one of the reasons for the difference in estimates obtained by Cobham and Subramaniam and Singh, as the former used the data relating to the corporate sector as a whole rather than to the individual firms, used by the latter.

Table 2.1

Debt Financing across Size Deciles, 2001

	All	*Large*	*2*	*3*	*4*	*5*	*6*	*7*	*8*	*9*	*Small*
D/E ratio	0.9	0.76	1.06	1.42	1.44	1.08	1.2	2.82	2.52	2.61	—
Sources of borrowing:											
Institutions (%)	23	17	34	42	33	26	36	29	27	35	31
Corporate bonds (%)	21	25	15	10	10	11	6	7	4	2	11

Source: GOI (2001-02).

Thirdly, turning to the sources of debt financing, marked differences in the financing pattern of debt are also evident. Specifically, the larger firms are less reliant on institutional borrowing than the smaller ones (Table 2.1). Among all the firms, the largest one-tenth of the firms have least dependence on institutions (17 per cent) and maximum on corporate bonds (25 per cent) for their financing requirements. However, moving down towards smaller firm's dependence on bond market funding declines sharply. This also supports the finding that, other things remaining the same, the larger the firm the more important is the security market for its financing requirement. Thus, one of the reasons for large recourse to stock market, reported by Singh (1995), could also be due to the selection of 100 largest firms examined in his study.

Leaving aside the difference in estimates, there is no denying the fact that the contribution of stock market to corporate sector growth has increased tremendously. A number of reasons can be cited to explain the

9. The universe of firms is sorted by value added and is divided into ten equal groups.

large amount of finance raised from the stock market in the late 1980s and early 1990s.

First, there was a share price boom in Indian stock market that persisted till the mid-1990s. The Bombay Stock Index (BSI) rose from 396.4 in 1985 to 1040.7 in 1990, 4000 by 1994, but after that the market remained dull for a few years. The BSI fell to 3060 in 1995, 3100 in September 1998 and immediately after the 11 September 2001 attack, it came down to 2918.

Second, in this period because of high cost of credit (due to the high interest rate regime and lack of availability of credit by development financial institutions and commercial banks to meet the private corporate sector needs), firms came to rely more on internal resources and equity finance (see Tables 2.5 and 2.6). The high cost and lack of availability of credit undermined the ability of Indian firms to protect their market and helped foreign suppliers over Indian firms. The problem was much more acute for small and medium firms, which were already facing an intense competitive pressure from the more liberalised domestic market.

Third, the Reserve Bank of India (RBI) tried to mobilise household savings through capital market expansion by giving various fiscal incentives that helped the stock market boom.

Fourth, booming stock market was further encouraged by the entry of foreign investors. The consequent fall in the cost of equity (defined as reciprocal of price-earning P/E) and freedom in pricing and quantum of shares, implied that a large amount of finance was raised through the stock market. As a result the debt-equity ratio of private sector firms also came down (Table 2.2).

Table 2.2

Debt-Equity Ratio, 1990-91 to 1996-97

Year	*1990-91*	*1991-92*	*1992-93*	*1993-94*	*1994-95*	*1995-96*	*1996-97*
CMIE	1.95	2.04	1.97	1.59	1.28	1.23	1.32
RBI Data	1.18	1.08	1.07	0.89	0.74	N.A.	N.A.

Source: CMIE[1] and RBI[2], various issues.

This phase lasted only till the mid-1990s. After that the market slumped because of a number of internal and external factors, such as the deceleration in industrial sector growth, East Asian crisis, number of security scams, price rigging in the Indian stock market leading to loss of confidence of investors, Indo-Pak tension, and the worldwide recession in 2002-03.

The boom that occurred in the early 1990s could not be sustained; P/E ratio started falling in the mid-1990s and thus, raised the cost of equity. From the data shown in Table 2.3 and Figure 2.1, we find the cost of equity was higher on average in late 1990s than in early 1990s. A detailed analysis of P/E ratio further indicates that the drop in P/E ratio was much sharper for second-rung stock[10] in the country (GOI, 2001-02). This shows that there was a sharper increase in the cost of capital as one moves from the largest stock in the country to the second tier of stocks.

Table 2.3

P/E Ratio Sensex, April 1992 to December 2004

Time Period	*Apr-1992*	*Dec-1992*	*Apr-1993*	*Dec-1993*	*Apr-1994*	*Dec-1994*	*Apr-1995*	*Dec-1995*	*Apr-1996*	*Dec-1996*	*Apr-1997*
P/E Ratio Sensex	52.6	31.4	27.4	40	46.4	34.5	27.8	16	14.8	13	16
Time Period	*Dec-1997*	*Apr-1998*	*Dec-1998*	*Apr-1999*	*Dec-1999*	*Apr-2000*	*Dec-2000*	*End Yr 2001*	*End Yr 2002*	*End Yr 2003*	*End Yr 2004*
P/E Ratio Sensex	12	13	20	25	19	16	14	15.6	14.6	18.9	17.1

Source: GOI, various issues.

In order to comment on the rate of drop in P/E ratios, we fitted a semi-logarithmic trend, specified in equation (1), to the data series of P/E for the period April 1992 to December 2000, covering 18 observations.

$$\ln(P/E)_t = \alpha + \beta_1 T + \beta_2 T^2 \qquad (1)$$

where T is time, taking values 1 (for the initial period i.e., April 1992) to 18. Here, the average annual trend growth has time varying element and β_2 indicates the change in the average rate of growth over time. The sign of

10. It includes the members of Nifty junior and portrays the behaviour of smaller companies.

Figure 2.1

Trends in P/E Ratio Sensex

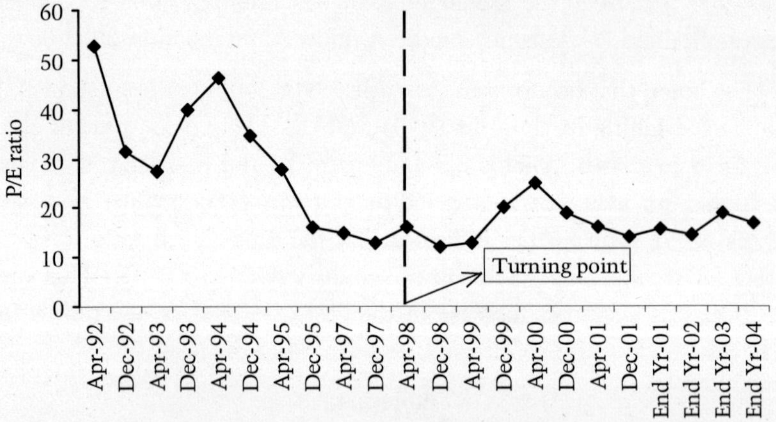

β_2 gives acceleration or deceleration in the average growth. The estimated results obtained from the regression (equation 2) signify that, over the period 1992 to 2000, P/E fell at a diminishing rate.[11] The t-ratios corresponding to the coefficients of T and T^2 imply that both the average fall and the rate of fall are significant at the 1 and 5 per cent level, respectively.

$$\widehat{P/E} = 51.7 - 5.07T + .18T^2 \quad (2)$$

t ratio (8.55) (-3.46)* (2.38)**

* denotes significant at 1 per cent level, and

** significant at 5 per cent level.

A disaggregative picture of the financing pattern of corporate sector since 1993-94, shown in Table 2.4, further lends support to the fact that there was loss in public confidence in the stock market and low level of resource mobilisation observed during the mid-1990s.

11. The turning point, according to the estimated trend equation occurred in April 1998.

Table 2.4

Capital Raised through Public and Rights Issues, 1993-94 to 2001-02

Year	Public			Rights		Total		
	No.	Amount (Rs billion)	Amount per Issue (Rs crore)	No.	Amount (Rs billion)	No.	Amount (Rs billion)	Amount per Issue (Rs crore)
1993-94	773 (68)	154.4 (63)	19.98	370 (32)	89.2 (37)	1143	243.7	21.32
1994-95	1342 (81)	210.44 (76)	15.68	324 (19)	65.76 (24)	1666	276.4	16.59
1995-96	1428 (83)	142.39 (68)	9.97	298 (17)	65.64 (32)	1726	208.03	12.05
1996-97	751 (85)	115.56 (81)	15.38	131 (15)	27.19 (19)	882	142.75	16.18
Average (1993-1997)	(79)	(72)		(21)	(28)	(100)	(100)	
1997-98	62 (56)	28.61 (63)	46.14	49 (44)	17.08 (37)	111	45.69	41.16
1998-99	32 (55)	50.19 (90)	156.84	26 (45)	5.68 (10)	58	55.87	96.32
Average (1997-1999)	(56)	(76)		(44)	(24)	(100)	(100)	
1999-2000	65 (70)	62.57 (80)	96.26	28 (30)	15.6 (20)	93	78.17	84.05
2000-01	124 (82)	53.78 (88)	43.37	27 (18)	7.29 (12)	151	61.07	40.44
2001-02		65.02 (86)			10.41(14)		75.43	

Note: Figures in parentheses are percentages of the respective yearly totals.
Source: Based on data available in GOI and RBI[1], various issues.

Equity capital[12] can be raised either by public offerings[13] i.e., either by the direct offering to public or through rights issues. From the data it is observed that there was a decline in the number of public issues as well as the amount raised through it, after 1995-96. But the decline is much sharper for the number of issues than for the amount raised. During 1995-1996 to 2000-01, the number of issues declined by 11.5 times whereas the amount raised declined by only 2.6 times. This implies that there was an increase in the amount raised per public issue in late 1990s. Despite a decline in the number of issues, investors responded favourably and overwhelmingly to these issues. On average, during 1993-1997, roughly 80 per cent of the total issues and 72 per cent of total amount raised were in the form of public offerings. The corresponding figure fell to 56 for the

12. For its definition, see Chapter 8.
13. Public offerings are classified into two categories, *viz.*, Public and Rights issues. The former includes Initial Public Offerings (IPOs), where a company goes public for the first time and Seasoned Equity Offerings (SEOs), where a listed company sells shares to the public. Rights issues are issues where a company sells additional shares to the existing shareholders.

former and rose to 76 for the latter, during 1997-1999. This signals growing investors' preference and awareness for quality of issues, which are seen as marked improvement because of introduction of stringent entry point norms by SEBI (GOI, 2001-02).

After the degeneration of stock market boom in the late 1990s, the debt market again picked up and became an important source of finance not only because of loss of interest in the primary market but also because of government's policy of soft interest regime.[14] The bank rate (BR) and prime lending rate (PLR) started falling since 1995-96. The downward trend in interest rates is clearly visible from the Figures 2.2 and 2.3 and is also validated from the non-linear trend equations fitted to the corresponding data series given in Tables 2.5 and 2.6. From the estimated equations (3) and (4), it can be observed that both BR and PLR registered a significant fall. The rate of reduction diminishes, however, it is not significant.

$$\widehat{BR} = 14.06 - 1.12T + .031T^2 \qquad (3)$$
$$\text{t ratio} \quad (17.42) \quad (-3.62)^{*} \quad (1.22)$$

$$\widehat{PLR} = 17.07 - 1.05T + .04\,T^2 \qquad (4)$$
$$\text{t ratio} \quad (21.39) \quad (-3.42)^{*} \quad (1.64)$$

Table 2.5

Prime Lending Rates of Scheduled Commercial Banks, 1991-92 to 2005-06 (in per cent)

Item	*1991-92*	*1993-94*	*1994-95*	*1995-96*	*1996-97*	*1997-98*	*1998-99*	*1999-2000*	*2000-01*	*2001-02*	*2002-03*	*2003-04***	*2004-05***	*2005-06***
PLR	19*	14*	15	16.5	14.5	14	12	12	11.5	11.5	11.25	10.6	10.6	10.5

Note: ** PLR relates to average of five major public sector banks;
* Minimum lending rate.
Source: GOI, various issues.

14. An administrative interest regime existed during 1975-76 to 1994-95. During 1975-76 to 1980-81, RBI prescribed both the minimum lending rate and the ceiling rate. During 1981-82 to 1987-88, RBI prescribed only the ceiling rate. From 1988-89 to 1994-95, RBI switched to minimum lending rate. With effect from October, 1994 lending rate was deregulated in respect of loans above Rs 2 lakh and also PLR was introduced in 1994. With effect from April 19, 2001, PLR has been converted to a benchmark rate for banks rather than a minimum lending rate (GOI, various issues).

Table 2.6

Bank Rate, 1994-95 to January 2006 (in per cent)

Item	*1994-1995*	*1995-1996*	*1996-1997*	*1997-1998*	*Jan.-1998*	*Oct.-1999*	*Jan.-1999*	*Jan.-2000*	*Mar.-2001*	*Jan.-2002*	*Jan.-2003*	*Jan.-2004*	*Jan.-2005*	*Jan.-2006*
Bank rate	12	12	12	11	11	10	9	8	7	6.5	6.25	6	6	6

Source: GOI, various issues.

Figure 2.2

Trends in Prime Lending Rates of Scheduled Commercial Banks

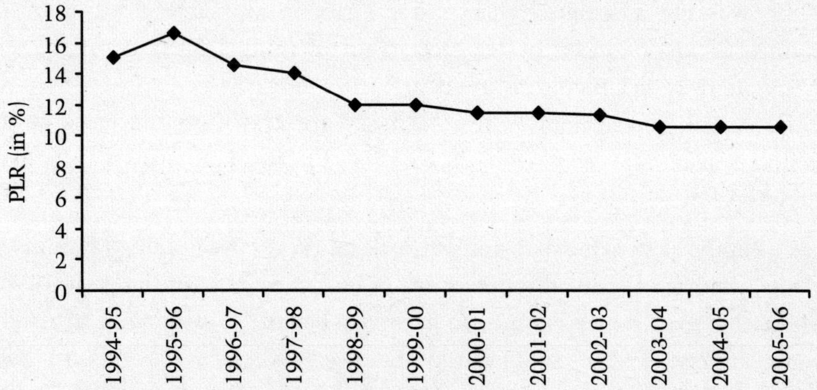

Figure 2.3

Trends in Bank Rates during 1994-2006

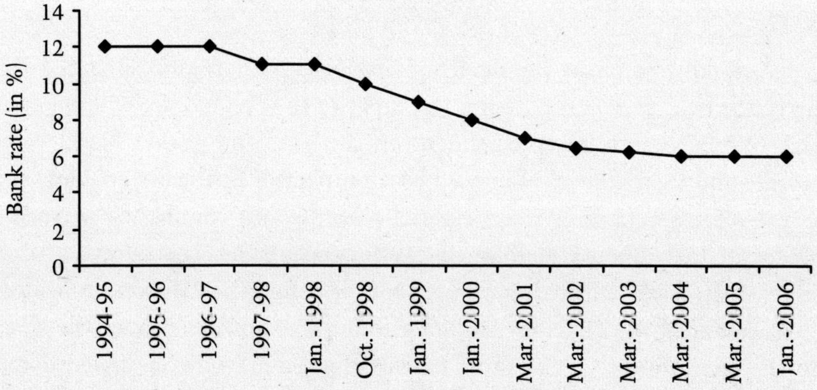

After remaining sluggish for few years, there has been a rebound in stock market in the year 2004.The volume of public issues increased by approximately five times and recorded highest-ever level of public equity in India's history (GOI, 2004-05).

Stock Market Reforms and the Real Economy

As far as the effects of stock market expansion on real economy i.e., the proportion of savings and investment, is concerned, we extend the analysis to post-reform years.

Regarding the effects of stock market reforms on savings, one of the main findings was that the expansion in stock market financing during the 1980s was not associated with either a rise in aggregate gross domestic savings or an increase in the proportion of financial savings (Nagaraj, 1996). It only led to portfolio substitution from bank deposits towards stock market instrument. These findings are drawn on the basis of the comparison of data from 1978-79 to 1984-85. Two points need to be paid attention here.

Firstly, although expansion in stock market started taking place in the 1980s, the market gained momentum in real sense only in the early 1990s, when the process of economic reforms began. It was only after the establishment of SEBI, as an autonomous supervisory and regulatory body for the Indian capital market, in 1992 that boosted public confidence and brought rapid growth in the stock market. Therefore, the issues pertaining to the effects of stock market development on savings should focus on the data obtained even after 1984-85 as well and should cover the post-reform years.

Secondly, as far as the determinants of gross domestic savings (GDS) are concerned, they depend upon the capacity to save and the willingness to save. While the former is dependent on the level and growth of per capita income and the latter is influenced by a number of financial variables, such as rate of interest, growth in financial sector and confidence in various modes or instruments of financial savings available. The effects of these determinants get reflected in a much longer period than the one considered by Nagaraj (1996). Therefore, in order to draw conclusions about the effects on the quantum of GDS and its constituents, our study has relied upon a longer period data.

A detailed analysis of the magnitude and composition of gross domestic savings over a period, 1980-81 up to 2002-03, does not support Nagaraj's findings. The following observations, based on Tables 2.7 and 2.11, are pertinent.

1. A secular but a slow increase in the gross domestic savings marks the period 1980-81 to 2002-03. When the trend in gross domestic savings during this period is decomposed in various blocks of years, as shown in Table 2.7, it is found that from 1980-81 to 1984-85 and 1985-86 to 1992-93, the ratio of GDSs as the percentage of GDP at market prices increased from 19.4 to 21.5. Further, the ratio increased from 23.9 to 25.1 during 1993-1999 to 1999-2003. This rise could be attributed to the structural reforms along with the stock market reforms that resulted in growth of GDP and increased public confidence in the financial sector. The fall in GDSs registered during the late 1970s to early years of 1980s (as reported by Nagaraj, 1996) should not be attributed to either structural reforms or stock market reforms.

Table 2.7

Trends in Gross Domestic Savings
(as per cent of GDP at current market prices)

Item	*1970-71 to 1974-75*	*1975-76 to 1979-80*	*1980-81 to 1984-85*	*1985-86 to 1992-93*	*1993-94 to 1998-99*	*1999-2000 to 2002-03**
1. Household sector	12.0	15.2	14.1	17.1	18.6	22.54
1.1. Financial saving	4.0	5.7	6.7	8.4	10.6	10.8
1.2. Saving in physical assets	8.0	9.5	7.4	8.8	8.0	11.8
2. Private Corporate sector	1.7	1.5	1.6	2.4	4.1	4
3. Public sector	3.0	4.5	3.7	2.0	1.2	-1.5
4. Gross domestic savings	16.6	21.2	19.4	21.5	23.9	25.06

Note: * Includes quick estimates of 2002-03.
Source: RBI[2], 2000-01 and 2003-04; GOI, 2004-05.

2. It is the increase in the proportion of household and private sector savings in GDP that have contributed to rise in the GDSs, the contribution of public sector savings has declined continuously in the post-reform era (Figure 2.4). Decomposing total savings among its

three contributors, *viz.*, households, private corporate sector and public sector, it is found that both the household and private corporate sectors contributed to the increase in the amount of total savings (Figure 2.5). This shows that both these sectors responded favourably to the financial sector and other reforms but the extent of rise differed between the periods. Household sector was more responsive from mid-1980s to the early years of reforms whereas corporate sector showed greater responsiveness during the post-reform years. The share of public sector in total savings is negative (since 1998-99) and the amount of dissavings increased till 2001-02 (Figures 2.4 and 2.5).

Figure 2.4

Percentage Share of Household, Private and Public Sectors in GDSs

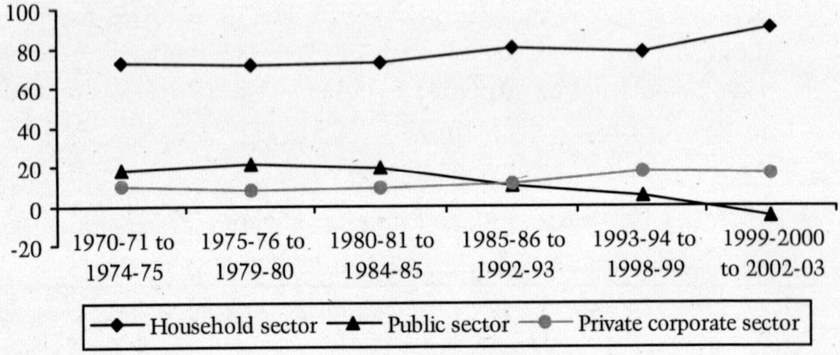

Figure 2.5

Share of Household, Private and Public Sector Savings in GDSs (as per cent of GDP at market prices)

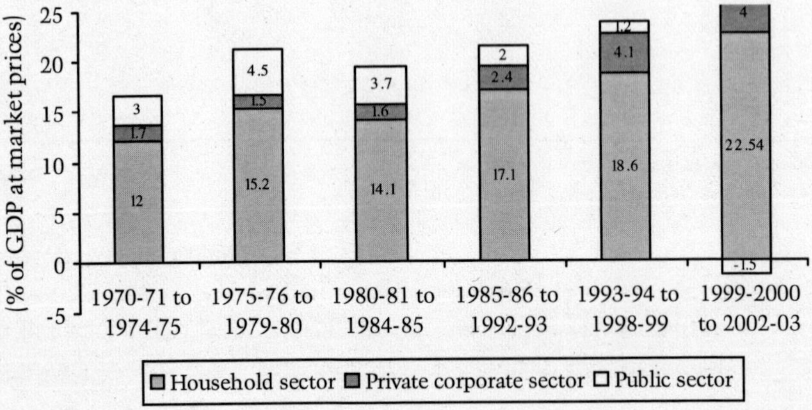

To further corroborate these observations, regression analysis was conducted to find the trend rate of growth of GDS and its two constituents (household and private corporate savings) for various selected periods during 1970-71 to 2003-04. Besides fitting two specifications of non-linear trend [equations (5) and (6)], dummy variables (both additive and multiplicative, to check the stability of the saving function during various periods) are also used to find the structural shifts in the three forms of savings. The results are presented below in Tables 2.8, 2.9 and 2.10.

$$\ln(GDS)_t = \alpha + \beta_1 T + \beta_2 T^2 \quad (5)$$

$$\ln(GDS)_t = \alpha + \beta_1 T \quad (6)$$

From Table 2.8 it is evident that GDS, HH savings and private corporate savings followed a positive linear trend. Since the coefficient of T^2 is 0 for all three forms of savings (though, it is significant for only private corporate savings), the regression estimates were made by fitting equation (6) (See Table 2.9).

Table 2.8

Results of Non-linear Trend (Equation 5) Fitted to GDSs, HH Savings and Pvt. Corporate Savings, 1980-81 to 2003-04

	GD Savings		*HH Savings*		*Pvt. Corporate Savings*	
	Coefficient	*t ratio*	*Coefficient*	*t ratio*	*Coefficient*	*t ratio*
Intercept	8.65	186.2	8.27	184.2	6.26	49.8
T	0.146	23.8***	0.147	24.9***	0.133	8.02***
T^2	-0.00	-0.07	0.00	1.06	0.00	2.32**

Note: *** significant at 1 per cent; ** significant at 5 per cent.

Results as shown in Table 2.9 reveal that the first two forms of savings increased at annual trend rate of 14.5 and 15.3 per cent, respectively, and the third form increased at 17 per cent per annum during 1970-71 to 2003-2004. Decomposing the whole period into two sub-periods, *viz*., 1970-71 to 1984-85 and 1985-86 to 1999-2000, it is found that the trend growth is higher for all three forms of savings during the latter period, which is marked with the structural changes in the financial sector. The response of private corporate sector is particularly noticeable, as the annual trend growth rate of its savings rose from 12 to 22 per cent during the two sub-periods. Further, running the regressions separately for the 1970s, 1980s and 1990s (regressions 4, 5, and 6 in Table 2.9), it is observed that the trend growth for the HH savings is highest during the 1980s and for the private corporate sector during the 1990s. This validates the comments made above in observation 2.

Table 2.9

Results of Non-linear Trend (Equation 6) Fitted to GDSs, HH Savings and Pvt. Corporate Savings during Various Selected Periods

	GD Savings		*HH Savings*		*Pvt. Corporate Savings*	
	Coefficient	*t ratio*	*Coefficient*	*t ratio*	*Coefficient*	*t ratio*
1. *Period: 1970-71 to 2003-04*			(No. of observations = 34)			
Intercept	8.65	294.7	8.24	285.1	6.04	70.2
T	.145	99.3***	.153	106.5***	.17	39.7***
2. *Period: 1970-71 to 1984-85*			(No. of observations = 15)			
Intercept	8.7	205.5	8.33	190	6.39	94.3
T	.138	29.7***	.141	29.2***	.12	16.5***
3. *Period: 1985-86 to 1999-2000*			(No. of observations = 15)			
Intercept	10.76	282.6	10.51	269.2	8.26	94.4
T	.157	37.4***	.16	37.2***	.217	22.6***
4. *Period: 1970-71 to 1979-80*			(No. of observations = 10)			
Intercept	8.6	197.7	8.26	167	6.41	60.2
T	.158	22.5***	.157	19.7***	.118	6.9***
5. *Period: 1980-81 to 1989-90*			(No. of observations = 10)			
Intercept	10.0	301.5	9.6	216.6	7.49	99.1
T	.15	28***	.17	23.7***	.171	14.0***
6. *Period: 1990-91 to 1999-2000*			(No. of observations = 10)			
Intercept	11.63	252.9	11.4	279.6	9.5	88.1
T	.143	19.3***	.146	22.3***	.194	11.2***

Note: *** significant at 1 per cent.

The results obtained after the introduction of dummy variable (used for three periods; D=1 for observations beyond 1979-80, 1984-85 and 1989-90) shown in Table 2.10 further substantiate our observations. The statistical significance of the DT coefficient indicates a structural shift in the trend growth of HH savings in the period beginning from 1985-86. The private corporate sector indicates a structural shift in its saving function parameters, beginning from 1980-81 as well as from 1985-86. The shift is due to both the intercept and trend growth rate. The private corporate sector savings increased at a very high average annual growth during 1990s. However, no structural change is observable from the regressions. The shift in GDS is discernible beginning from only 1990-91, as the coefficient of the additive dummy (D) is significant at the 5 per cent.

Table 2.10

Results of Dummy Variable Fitted to GDSs, HH Savings and Pvt. Corporate Savings during Various Selected Periods

	GD Savings		*HH Savings*		*Pvt. Corporate Savings*	
	Coefficient	*t ratio*	*Coefficient*	*t ratio*	*Coefficient*	*t ratio*
1. Dummy Variable D=1 beginning from 1980-81						
Intercept	8.6	162.4	8.26	164.8	6.41	46.1
T	.157	18.5***	.157	19.4***	.119	5.3***
D	-.06	-.8	.159	-2.2**	-.80	-4.04***
DT	-.008	-.99	.002	.26	.068	2.96***
2. Dummy Variable D=1 beginning from 1985-86						
Intercept	8.7	191.6	8.33	204.9	6.4	58.8
T	.138	27.7***	.141	31.5***	.123	10.3***
D	-.07	-.68	-.11	-1.27	-.67	-2.8***
DT	.007	1.28	.014	2.56**	.06	4.1***
3. Dummy Variable D=1 beginning from 1990-91						
Intercept	8.7	260.3	8.33	240.7	6.3	78.4
T	.14	50.2***	.147	51.3***	.139	20.7***
D	.32	2.35**	.199	1.41	.43	1.3
DT	.007	-1.21	.002	-.35	.01	.8

Note: *** significant at 1 per cent ; ** significant at 5 per cent.

The other observations can be made by further decomposing the HH savings between financial and non-financial savings.

3. The impact of stock market reforms after the establishment of SEBI and consequential increased public confidence is clearly indicated by the trends in physical assets and financial savings, shown in Figure 2.6. Although financial savings show an upward trend since 1970s, the extent of rise was highest during 1993 to 1999. The most noticeable aspect of this period is that the proportion of financial

savings exceeded the physical assets savings' proportion in GDP (Table 2.7 and Figure 2.6). The effect of loss of public confidence in stock market in recent years is also reflected in the reversal of trends being shown by both the kinds of household savings (Figure 2.6). The savings in physical assets after registering a decline in the mid-1990s again picked up in the early 2000s and its share moved above that of financial savings in 2002-03.

Figure 2.6

Share of HH Savings, Financial Savings and Savings in Physical Assets in GDP (as per cent of GDP at current market prices)

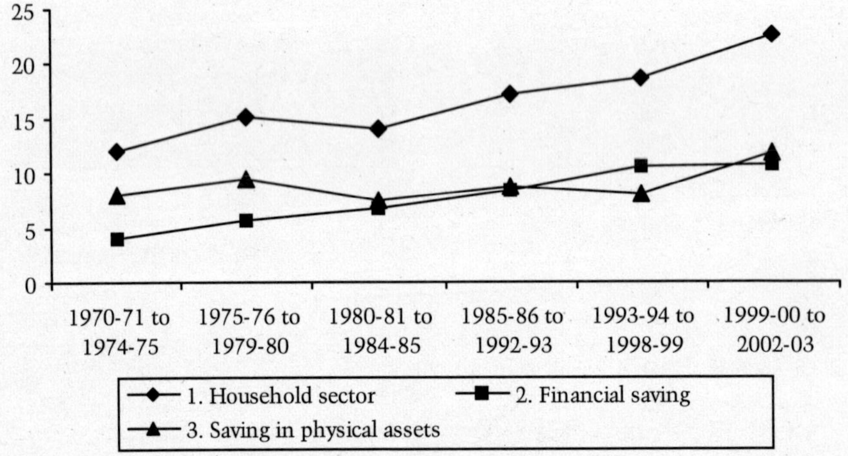

4. The effect of stock market boom witnessed in the late 1980s and early 1990s and the further loss of public confidence in stock market become very clear when the financial sector savings are decomposed among its constituents, as shown in Table 2.11.

It is observed that during 1985-86 to 1992-93, share of net deposits in total domestic savings after continuously rising till 1984-85, recorded a decline whereas savings in the form of shares and debentures remained constant till 1980 and thereafter registered a marked increase in its share. The fall in the share of net deposits from 11.3 per cent to 9.8 per cent during 1981-1985 to 1986-1993 and the rise in per cent of shares and debentures in total savings from 2.1 to 5.8 per cent during the same period, clearly indicates the portfolio substitution of households' financial savings from bank deposits to shares and equities, as noted by Nagaraj (1996). It must be pointed out here that this movement of household savings towards stock market did not merely represent a reallocation of households' funds from bank deposits to stock market instruments but it was also accompanied by a rise in the share of household savings in GDP from 14.1 per cent to 17.1 per cent. It was the booming stock market and increased public confidence in stock market that allured the households to invest in higher amounts. The reverse turn taken by the shares of net deposits and that of stock market instruments in the second half of the 1990s, is indicative of loss of public confidence in the stock market.

Table 2.11

Composition of Gross Domestic Savings, 1970-71 to 2002-03 (in per cent)

Item	*1970-71 to 1974-75*	*1975-76 to 1979-80*	*1980-81 to 1984-85*	*1985-86 to 1992-93*	*1993-94 to 1998-99*	*1999-2000 to 2002-03*
1. Household Sector	72.1	71.5	72.6	79.4	77.8	90.2
1.1 Financial saving	24.9	26.9	34.9	38.8	44.5	43.1
Currency	5.1	4.7	5.7	5.5	5.3	N.A.
Net deposits	8.1	10.0	11.3	9.8	16.3	N.A.
Shares & debentures	0.8	0.9	2.1	5.8	3.9	N.A.
Net claim on govt.	0.6	1.7	4.5	4.9	4.6	N.A.
Life insurance fund	2.9	2.7	3.2	3.9	4.9	N.A.
Provident & pension funds	7.4	6.9	8.0	9.0	9.6	N.A.
1.2 Saving in physical funds	48.4	44.6	37.8	40.6	33.3	47.1
2. Private Corporate Sector	10.1	7.3	8.4	10.9	17.1	16.0
3. Public Sector	17.9	21.2	19.0	9.7	5.1	-6.0
4. Gross Domestic Savings (1+2+3)	100.0	100.0	100.0	100.0	100.0	100.0

Note: N.A.- Not available; *Includes quick estimates of 2002-03.
Source: RBI[2], 2000-2001.

On the other hand, turning to the effects on gross fixed capital formation, there has been some rise in the corporate sector's GFCF as a proportion of GDP at market prices but the extent to which it can be ascribed to the expansion of stock market is debatable. The ratio of GFCF to GDP not only gets affected by cost and availability of finance but also by other pertinent factors, such as general economic conditions, agricultural sector growth affecting the industrial sector demand, optimism or pessimism on the part of investor and the world's economic conditions.

On the question of productivity of investment, two pieces of evidence are cited by Nagaraj (1996). First, smaller non-corporate firms, which did not have access to the stock market funds, were able to grow at a faster rate than large corporate firms. Second, there was a secular decline in the corporate profitability during 1980s. Whether this decline is due to decrease in efficiency or fall in profit margins is questionable. Testing this hypothesis on the basis of the results of 100 largest firms[15] in 1980s, Singh (1995) found that the decrease in profitability was due to fall in productivity of assets and not due to profit margins.[16]

Following the above discussion, the issues raised here are required to be further tested for the following reasons: (1) given large inter-firm differences, the results of 100 largest firms used by Singh (1995) cannot be generalised for all firms; (2) the fall in profitability witnessed by Nagaraj (1996) from 1980-1990 can not be accepted for the following decade i.e., 1990-2000 because of changed economic conditions in the form of structural reforms that led to increased competitive pressures from both the domestic and world corporations.

Basant (2000) in his work on corporate performance reports that profitability decreased in the first two years of economic reforms but picked up thereafter. In 1996-97 profitability again started declining. Price-cost margin was significantly different across industry groups, reflecting variation in the intensity and level of competitive pressure. Profitability rose significantly for iron and steel, drugs and pharmaceutical and automobiles. Further, even if we find some evidence of reduced profitability because of increased competitive pressure it cannot be taken as an indicator of inefficiency because real cost of capital had also fallen (resulting from the stock market boom) during this period. But as we have already seen that the boom lasted only till the mid-1990s. Further, in view of the stock

15. The rate of return on net assets (profit/net assets) was decomposed between profit margins (profit/sales) and productivity of investment (sales/net assets). Refer also to Chapter 6.

16. A fall in profit margin would have resulted from greater competition in the product market.

market volatility in India, the efficiency of stock market pricing signals is also reduced. So, further work in this area is necessary.

2.2 Analysis of the 'Takeover Market'

Once the process of economic liberalisation started in our country the financial community started urging for a market for corporate control (MCC) to maximise the benefits from the stock market development. MCC, also referred to as 'Takeover Market', is a market in which alternative managerial teams compete for the rights to manage corporate resources. In such markets competing management teams are the primary activists and stockholders (including institutions) act as intermediaries to value offers by competing management teams, including incumbent managers (Jensen, 1988). Stockholders simply choose the highest rupee value offer from a well functioning MCC and have no loyalty to incumbent managers. In this way competition among managerial teams for the right to manage resources limits divergence from the shareholders' wealth maximisation by managers and provides the mechanism through which economies of scale or other synergies available from combining or reorganising control and management of corporate resources are realised.

As referred earlier, in 1991 the government announced a New Industrial Policy (NIP) and abolished CCI, MRTP Act (1969) and FERA (1973). In 1992, after the establishment of SEBI, with powers vested in it to regulate the Indian capital market, the drift towards the establishment of MCC took place. In 1994, SEBI issued guidelines for substantial acquisition of shares and takeovers, widely referred to as the 'Takeover (T.O.) code.

Evolution of Takeover Code

The takeover is a set of regulations under the SEBI Act, which determines whether or not an acquisition of shares in a company amounts to an attempt to takeover.[17] The aim of the T.O. code was,

- To ensure orderly takeover of a company.

---

17. When an 'acquirer' takes over the control of the 'target company', it is termed as a Takeover. Outcome of a successful takeover is a booting out of the existing management in the target company by the acquirer. Also refer to Chapter 3.

- To ensure that the entire process of takeover is transparent and done in a fair manner.
- To ensure that an acquirer gives an opportunity to investors to exit if they feel that the change in control is not in the company's best interest.
- To create a level playing field between a potential acquirer and the existing promoter.

Before the T.O. code, the only way for a takeover was through the M&A[18] route, involving courts, which was very time-consuming. The code unleashed a kind of energy and desire that existed in the corporate sector but was not tapped before (The Economic Times, 2000).

The code was first established in 1994. Soon the experience demonstrated that the code had lacunae in dealing with the complexity of a situation. Hence, a committee chaired by Chief Justice of India P.N. Bhagwati, was appointed in November 1995 to review the T.O. code of 1994. On the basis of the committee's report, SEBI adopted a revised takeover code in February 1997, which was termed as Substantial Acquisition of Shares and Takeovers Regulations, 1997. Before 1990, an open offer was mandatory for acquiring 25 per cent stake in a company. In 1990, this threshold was reduced to 10 per cent of a company's capital. In case of MNCs related acquisitions, provisions of FERA (1973) were applied. In addition, the MRTP Act (1969) had powers to prevent an acquisition, if it was considered to lead to 'concentration of economic power to the common detriment'. The new code provided for the acquirer to make a public offer (or announcement)[19] for a minimum of 20 per cent of capital as soon as 10 per cent ownership and management control had been acquired.[20] In October 1998, again some new amendments[21] were made

---

18. The Companies Act, 1956, regulated mergers and certain other forms of corporate restructurings.
19. A public announcement is an announcement made in the newspapers by the acquirer, primarily disclosing his intention to acquire shares of the target company from existing shareholders, by means of an 'open-offer'.
20. Acquisition by those owning more than 51 per cent ownership were outside the purview of code.

and the threshold limit for applicability of code was raised from 10 per cent to acquisition of 15 per cent. The threshold limit of 2 per cent per annum for creeping acquisition was raised to 5 per cent. The code underwent another revision in October 2000, after the hostile attempt of Arun Bajoria to takeover 'Bombay Dyeing'.

After the amendments, SEBI made clear that it is not against hostile takeovers[22] but it is against *clandestine takeovers*. In order to protect the interests of companies—especially, professionally-managed companies where there is no clear promoter—it was made mandatory for an acquirer[23] to disclose his holdings to the target company[24] as well as exchange offices at the acquisition of 5, 10 and 14 per cent of shares or voting rights of the target company. When the limit reached 15 per cent, the acquirer required making an open-offer of at least additional 20 per cent of the voting capital of the target company from the shareholders. For failure to carry out these obligations as well as for non-compliance of other provisions, the Regulations laid down several penalties for non-compliance. In order to give a chance to the existing promoters to save their companies, several relaxations were given, for example; limit for creeping acquisition was increased from 2 to 5 per cent, allotment through preferential route was allowed, limit for buy-back was raised and competitive bids[25] were also allowed (The Economic Times, November 14, 2000). In order to provide flexibility to corporate restructuring, the code is reviewed from time to time, depending on the economic conditions of the market and representations received from investors and corporate sector.

---

21. For details of the Bhagwati Committee report, the 'Substantial Acquisition of Shares and Takeovers Regulations, 1997' and subsequent amendments, and public announcements, refer to SEBI's website *http://www.sebi.gov.in*.

22. An acquisition is considered to be hostile if it is without the tacit approval of existing management. The T.O. code does not differentiate between friendly and hostile acquisitions (The Economic Times, November 22, 2000).

23. An acquirer [including persons acting in concert (PAC) with him] means any individual/company/any other legal entity, which intends to acquire or acquires substantial quantity of shares or voting rights of target company or acquires or agrees to acquire control over the target company (see SEBI's website).

24. A target company is a listed company i.e., a company whose shares are listed on any stock exchange and whose shares or voting rights are acquired/being acquired or whose control is taken over/being taken over by an acquirer.

25. It is an offer made by a person, other than the acquirer who made the first public announcement.

Recent Indian Experience regarding Open Offers

Indian corporate sector restructured itself swiftly since it got its T.O. code. Although, few offers were made in 1995-96, the takeover market started functioning in the real sense only after 1997, when SEBI published its revised T.O. code. In February 1998, the Government of India took another measure to promote corporate takeovers by allowing financial institutions to lend money to fund takeovers. By the spring of 1998, these reforms already had a dramatic impact and a wave of takeovers swept across India's corporate sector. Since then, Indian corporate sector witnessed an important takeover market where many companies experienced a change in the controlling management team.

SEBI, in its exhaustive study of all 'open-offers' completed in 2000, suggested that the takeover code served its purpose and facilitated speedy corporate restructuring (The Economic Times, June 2, 2000). During 1997-2000, close to 700 companies acquired shares through open offers or through routes, that granted them an exemption from the code. An important aspect of this phenomenon revealed in the study was that out of the total value of Rs11,600 crore of shares acquired during this period, Rs 9,500 crore (82 per cent) worth shares, spread over 510 companies, did not require the T.O. code, while 18 per cent were acquired through the latter route. This shows that most of the action took place outside the purview of SEBI's T.O. code. Further, in 1997-98, 73 per cent of the total companies using open-offer route were of foreigners. This per cent rose to 88 in 1999-2000. The MNCs used this route mainly for the purpose of delisting from the Indian stock market.

The disaggregated data giving the number, value and objective of 'open offers' that required T.O. code during 1997-2010 are shown in Tables 2.12 and 2.13. The following features can be noted:

1. The number as well as value of open offers increased continuously from 1997-98 to 2002-03. The activity slowed down in the following two years and again rose till 2008-09. After reaching its peak at 88 in number and Rs 6,400 crore in value in 2002-03, the activity touched new heights at 113 and Rs 13,768 crore respectively, during 2008-09 (Figure 2.7).

Figure 2.7

Number and Value of Open Offers, 1997-2010

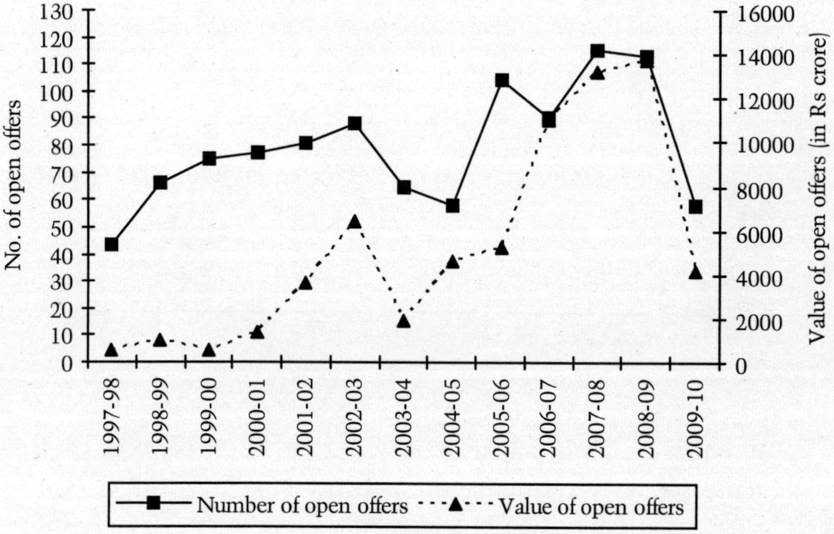

Table 2.12

Number and Objective of Open Offers (Selected Years), 1997-2010

Objective of Open Offers	*1997-98*	*1998-99*	*1999-2000*	*2002-03*	*2003-04*	*2004-05*	*2006-07*	*2008-09*	*Total*
Management change	20	29	43	47	38	33	62	86	666 (64)
Stake consolidation	10	25	9	39	16	12	17	14	222 (22)
Substantial acquisition	13	12	23	2	11	13	11	13	145 (14)
Total	43 (4)	66 (6)	75 (7)	88 (9)	65 (6)	58 (6)	90 (9)	113 (11)	1033 (100)

Note: Figures in brackets are percentages of 14-year totals.
Source: Calculations are based on data available at SEBI website.

2. In value as well as numbers, the objective management change dominated during the period under consideration. The other objectives i.e., stake consolidation and substantial acquisition of shares ranked second and third, respectively. On an average during 1997-2010, 63 per cent of the companies used the open offer route

Table 2.13

Value and Objective of Open Offers (Selected Years), 1997-2010

(Rs crore)

Objective of Open Offers	*1997-98*	*1998-99*	*1999-2000*	*2002-03*	*2003-04*	*2004-05*	*2007-08*	*2008-09*	*Total*
Management change	143	100	329	3816	548	3477	3785	11841	38969(58)
Stake consolidation	340	587	71	2571	262	165	8969	1147	21404(32)
Substantial acquisition	96	327	130	1	1048	964	480	780	7033(10)
Total	579 (1)	1014 (2)	530 (1)	6388 (9)	1858 (3)	4606 (7)	13234 (20)	13768 (20)	67406 (100)

Note: Figures in parentheses are percentages of 14-year totals.
Source: Calculations based on data available at SEBI website.

to effect the change in management control, 22 per cent used the route for stake consolidation and the remaining 15 per cent for substantial acquisition of shares.[26] In value terms, 53, 31, and 17 per cent of shares were intended with respect to the three objectives (Table 2.14).

3. A careful examination of the data gives a different picture when it is observed during the various sub-periods such as, 1997-1999 (the years immediately following the revised T.O. code), 1999-2005, 2005-2008 and 2008-2010. (Table 2.14). During 1997-2099, of the Rs 1,600 crore worth of open offers, approximately 60 per cent, were made with an intention to consolidate the holdings in the company, while approximately, 17 per cent were with the objective of management change. However, in terms of number of offers, only 31 per cent of the companies used this route for stake consolidation and 45 per cent for change of management control. The average for the third objective, substantial acquisition of shares was 24 per cent in terms of number and size of offer. The proportion for 'consolidation of stakeholding' being relatively very large in value terms, shows that the lesser number of larger corporate houses made open offers

26. The average is calculated from the average percentage figures for each year.

to consolidate their holdings and a large number of smaller companies faced a change in the management through this route during 1997-1999. The consolidation of their stakes by large corporate houses is a clear reflection of the fact that the companies started securing their positions to avoid takeover attempt (Figure 2.8 and Figure 2.9).

Table 2.14

Average Number and Value of Open Offers during Various Sub-Periods

	Average 1997-1999 (in %)		*Average 1999-2005 (in %)*		*Average 2005-2008 (in %)*		*Average 2008-2010 (in %)*		*Average 1997-2010 (in %)*	
Objective of Open Offers	*Number of Offers*	*Value of Offers*	*Number of Offers*	*Value of Offers*	*Number of Offers*	*Value of Offers*	*Number of Offers*	*Value of Offers*	*Number of Offers*	*Value of Offers*
Management change	45	17	64	60	66	48	74	73	63	53
Stake consolidation	31	58	23	22	18	36	15	19	22	31
Substantial acquisition	24	24	13	18	16	16	11	8	15	17
Total	100	100	100	100	100	100	100	100	100	100

Note: Each average is calculated as average of percentage figures for each year.

Source: Calculations based on data available at SEBI's website.

4. During 1999-2005, in terms of both the number and the value of offer, the averages for the three objectives, *viz*., change of management; stake consolidation, and substantial acquisition of shares, were roughly 63, 22 and 15 per cent, respectively. This shows that the objective, change of management, in number as well as value terms, dominated the takeover market during 1999-2005 (Table 2.14). During 2000-01, 90 per cent of the open-offers in number and 84 per cent in value targeted change in management and the rest aimed at stake consolidation. These figures changed to approximately, 60 per cent (in both number and value terms) for the former and 40 per cent for the latter objective, during 2002-03 (see Tables 2.12 and 2.13).

Figure 2.8

Distribution of Total Number of Open Offers based on Various Objectives (in %)

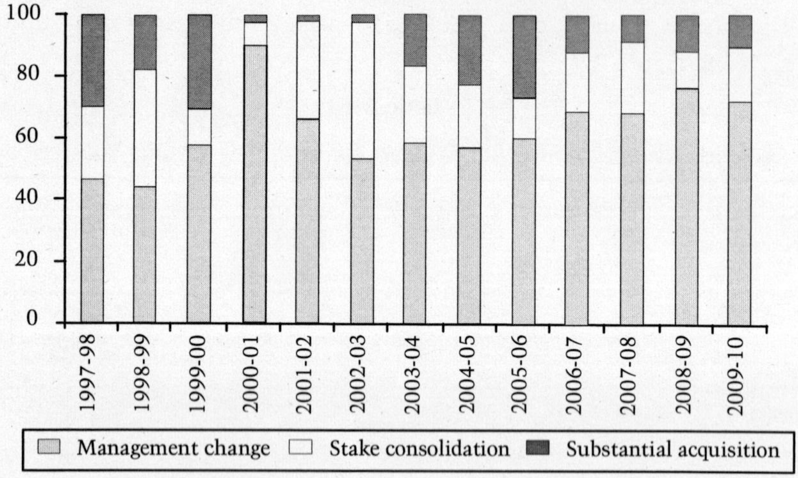

5. The importance of the objective, change of management rose tremendously in terms of both the number and value of offer, during 1997-2010. From 45 and 17 per cent in number and value of offer respectively, during 1997-1999, approximately three-fourths of the total offers (in both number and value) were made in order to change the management of the company.
6. The objective, substantial acquisition of shares in terms of both offer size and number of offers, was more common during 1997-1999 than during 1999-2010. However, during the whole period the substantial acquisition of shares as an objective behind the open offers was least desired by the corporates and therefore, remained a low-key affair. From 24 per cent in both the value and the number of offer in the former period, the magnitude fell to 11 per cent in number and 8 per cent in value of offer during 2008-2010.
7. During April 2008 to March 2009, management control was the overriding objective of open offers. Out of the 113 open offers made during this period, 76 per cent were made with a purpose to bring a change in management control, 12 per cent each were intended at

the other two objectives i.e., stake consolidation and substantial acquisition of shares. In value terms, the corresponding figures are 86, 8 and 7 per cent, respectively.

Figure 2.9

Distribution of Total Value of Open Offers based on Various Objectives (in %)

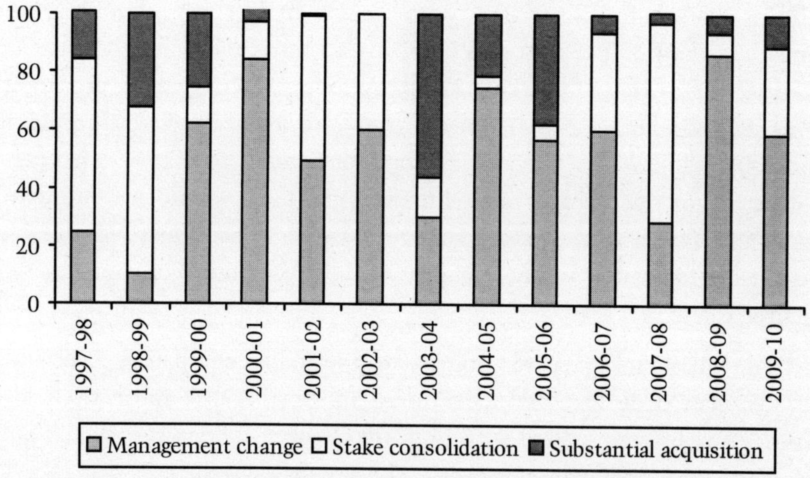

A fear of hostile takeovers spread among Indian corporates in the mid-2000.[27] The acquisition of large blocks of shares in Bombay Dyeing and Ballarpur Industries by Arun Bajoria made many promoter-held companies—especially, those trading below their book values—to feel the pinch. This takeover attempt captivated the stock markets, shareholders, creditors and financial institutions. There was hectic activity in the form of buy-back,[28] open offers, rights issues and preferential allotment on takeover

27. The bearish sentiments in the stock market set the stage for a few hostile bids by corporate raiders seeking to exploit the poor valuation and unlock value for shareholder. As several companies traded below their book value and the stock prices did not reflect the true intrinsic value, the market was in its prime for hostile bids. The first major takeover battle was by Renaissance Estates (represented by Abhishek Dalmia) for GESCO Corporation (a sister company of Great Eastern Shipping Company).

28. In buy-back, a company extinguishes the shares it buys back and thereby reduces the capital of the company. In an open offer shares revert to the promoter and capital of the company remains unaffected.

front. Many top Indian groups including industrial conglomerate Mahindra & Mahindra, Tata and Birla groups, despite being leaders in the truck, chemical, and cement markets respectively, considered themselves vulnerable. With the market down, acquisition was also looked upon as an attractive strategy. It was the low shareholdings of promoters and the depressed price of stocks that made companies ripe cases for takeovers and thus, feel unsafe.[29] This period also witnessed consolidation drive i.e., the trend of promoters hiking their own stakes. In fact any promoter, who owned less than 20 per cent of a company's share capital, found himself a potential target in the market. As many as in 17 companies promoters increased their holdings that ranged from 2 to 44 per cent, during April-June 2001 (Table 2.15). The rise in promoters' stake, from 2 to 26 per cent, in a period of one year in Tata Engineering and Locomotive Company (Telco) and Tata Iron and Steel Company (Tisco), is particularly noticeable. It is a clear indication of vulnerability of the Tata group[30] of companies to takeover threat.

The hostile takeover was not new to the Indian companies. Ever since the Takeover code became operational in April 1997, more than 900 takeover cases were reported with SEBI till October 2000, out of which only 8 were attempts of hostile takeovers. The Bombay Dyeing case was the 9th one. Till 2000-01, Indian corporate sector had experienced around 15 cases of hostile attempts. However, the success rate of hostile takeovers was very poor. Takeover bids by Autoriders Group on Saurashtra Cement, Sterlite on Indal, Peacock Chemicals on AEC India and on Indo Gulf Industries by HB Leasing, are few other cases of unsuccessful hostile bids. The lop-sided nature of takeover laws that protect existing management is one of the main causes of hostile takeovers not being materialised in India. This is not to say that none succeeded. In May 1998, India Cement mounted a hostile bid on Raasi Cements and eventually bought over Raasi for a consideration of Rs 100 crore (The Economic Times, October 22, 2000).

---

29. In response to the corporate sector's appeal and to slow down the hostile T.O. activity, SEBI enhanced the creeping acquisition limit to 10 per cent and also relaxed the buy-back norms till March 2002.

30. As a safeguard towards takeover, Tata group also merged its three power companies, namely, Tata Power, Tata Hydro and Andhra Valley, into a single entity, called Tata Electric Company -TEC. Later, in Oct. 2000, TEC also bought Gujarat Power Gen Energy Corp, to make itself India's biggest private power company.

Table 2.15

Rise in Promoters' Stake during April-June 2001

Company	*Rise in Promoters' Stake during April-June 2001 (in %)*	*Stake in July 2001 (in %)*
Hitech Drilling Engineers	44.4	81.6
Centurion Bank	2.3	43.2
GE Shipping	1.9	21.0
ITC Bhadrachalam	1.1	61.0
Tisco*	2	26.2
Telco*	2.5	26.0
Indian Rayon	2.5	26.5
Bombay Dyeing	5	41.0
EIH Ltd.	3.1	39.0
Bajaj Electricals	5	45.0

Note: * Rise in stake during 2000-01.
Source: The Economic Times, September 3, 2001.

During the year 2001, the trend that dominated capital market was overall reduction in the floating stock available with the public. Although, a beginning had already been made in 2000, 2001 saw a surge of open offers, buy-back, preferential allotment and rights issues because of decreasing valuation on the bourses. There were hardly any initial public offerings (IPOs) during this period. The bigger firms with sufficient cash reserves went for buy-back of shares or open offers, while relatively smaller firms consolidated their stake through preferential allotment of shares. It was observed that most of the open-offers were made by multinational companies (MNCs) whereas buy-backs were by Indian companies. The objective behind buy-backs was to provide an exit route to shareholders and to increase stakeholding to prevent any attempt of takeover. The objective behind open offer made by MNCs was to gain full control over their subsidiaries and de-list them from Indian bourses on account of cumbersome process of complying with listing requirements. According to an estimate, 95 companies in which promoters' holdings were in excess of 51 per cent, considered the delisting option to convert their Indian ventures into fully-owned subsidiaries, during this period (The Economics Times, January 1, 2002).

2.3 Need for a Takeover Market

International experience suggests that this market is an important vehicle through which the efficiency of utilisation of assets in the economy is enhanced. But Singh (1998), on the basis of evidence available from western countries, argued that such reforms are likely to harm the economy and should therefore be discouraged. Before accepting his (1998) prescription, the evidence available must be analysed in depth. It is not possible at this stage to attempt a rigorous econometric exercise as it is a recent phenomenon and the situation is still evolving. Nevertheless, some observations can be made.

After the initiation of economic reforms the firms had to face increasing competitive pressure from both the domestic companies and MNCs. M&As were used as a route to enhance efficiency. Takeover market was expected to provide an additional mechanism through which the stock market could promote a more efficient utilisation of capital resources. It institutionalises a threat of takeover, which may lead inefficient firms to perform better. Even if all firms are on the efficiency frontier, the amalgamation of firms through the act of takeover may lead to a better social allocation of resources via synergy (Singh, 1998). Contested takeovers, proxy contests are only means that can force the ineffective management to go out. Even the presence of threat of being taken over may stimulate existing management to perform better.

The foremost corporate objective should be to maximise long-term shareholder wealth. Indian companies, on the other hand, by and large neglected shareholders' interest and used the funds to create their own business empires in diverse fields (Banerjee, 2000). Due to generous attitude of financial institutions and government,[31] companies in India were allowed to mess up, despite holding very small percentage of equity.[32]

31. Ambani's and Sterlite's attempt to acquire the control of L&T and Indal, respectively, failed due to the support the existing management obtained from financial institutions (*The Economics Times*, November 10, 2000).

32. On an average, founding families generally held a small part of their shares. Instead, banks and fund companies (state financial institutions such as the Unit Trust of India and Industrial Development Bank of India) held big blocks (approximately 40 per cent). The rest, usually 40 per cent to 60 per cent was in the public hands.

For decades, companies paid negligible attention to share prices.[33] The financial institutions together with family nominees[34] dominated the corporate boards and hardly ever questioned the decisions of companies (*Dalal Street Investment Journal*, November 6-19, 2000). This brought irreparable loss to the thousands of other investors in the company. This situation undeniably required a change. It is the establishment of takeover market that made Indian companies—especially, promoter-controlled- to realise the importance of meeting the long-term expectations of the shareholders' wealth. In an era where management is divorced from ownership, owners of the company must have powers to discipline management. Earlier, Shareholders had no say in removing inefficient or incompetent management. Now, Takeover market has made shareholder realise his powers. SEBI made clear that the small investor is its first priority and also continues to revise the T.O. code from time to time for their benefit.

The important question is, whether the evolution of such a market is conducive to Indian industrialisation and faster economic growth. The review of the available evidence in developed countries—especially, USA and UK—suggests that the imperfections associated with such markets lowers its potential.

Analysing the experiences of companies in India, it is observed that most of the companies that received hostile takeover attempts were the companies with low stock market valuation e.g. takeover threat of Jute tycoon Arun Bajoria on Bombay Dyeing is a case of gross neglect of shareholders and destruction of long-term shareholder value. Looking at the company's performance in five years i.e., from 1995-96 to 1999-2000 (Table 2.16) it is found that the company's sales fell by 30 per cent, profit margins by 65 per cent and its market capitalisation fell by 200 per cent. This was a clear signal of the fact that capital market had lost interest in the company. Taking advantage of the low stock prices, Bajoria tried a takeover attempt on the company by buying a sizable number of its shares from the market.

---

33. Discussed as 'agency problem hypothesis' in Section 3.4 of Chapter 3.
34. For details, see Gupta (1989).

Further, it was also found that most of the friendly acquisitions took place with the objective of exploiting mutual synergies and the hostile ones were to take advantage of low stock market valuations. These hostile attempts were an eye-opener for Indian promoters—especially those who had low holdings. Even though the raiders' bids were unsuccessful, these raids were a blessing in disguise for minority shareholders, individuals and fund companies because they became hopeful of getting fair value of their shares.[35]

Table 2.16

Profit and Loss Statement of Bombay Dyeing and Manufacturing Company

	1995-96 (in Rs crore)	*1999-2000 (in Rs crore)*
Net sales	1184.20	870
Profit after tax	117.0	41.5
Net worth	650-700	650-750
Market capitalisation	1100	254

Source: Compiled from Banerjee (2000).

It is argued that the takeover mechanism in US is used as a device not to honour the implicit contracts of workers in the acquired firm with pre-acquisition management. Such abandonment of implicit contracts is harmful for the society, as it will discourage firm-specific accumulation of human capital by workers. In a country like ours, where labour reforms are still to take place, this argument does not have much relevance.

Grossman and Hart (1980) have pointed to the 'free rider'[36] problem that can render takeover mechanism inefficient. If the 'free rider' problem exists, the disciplinary or hostile take over bids will not materialise. It is important to mention here that low rate of success of hostile attempt in India is not because of the free rider problem but because of two other

---

35. The share price of loss-making Telco rose by more than 20 per cent in November 2000, as the Tata group started buying back shares in its 43 quoted companies.

36. It is argued that a shareholder, presuming that his action is unlikely to affect the takeover bid, may not accept a raider's offer with the expectation of price rise after the bid is materialised. If every shareholder thinks this way, Grossman and Hart argued that a hostile takeover may never be realised, Singh (1998).

reasons. Firstly, the Indian systems help the incumbent management. A large percentage of companies is being managed by families or their associates. This makes it difficult for hostile takeovers to be successful. However, in case of professionally managed companies, M&As help in unlocking the shareholder values. Secondly, in India financial institutions (FIs) play a critical role. The FIs either directly support the incumbent or indirectly help the existing management by remaining passive.

To summarise, it can be said that, if the takeover code: (i) is neither too harsh nor unduly protective, (ii) ensures rigorous standards of transparency, fairness and disclosures, (iii) allows investors to decide their own course of action; then establishment of takeover market can take the economy on a higher growth path. Additionally, it needs to be accepted that takeovers are a part of business strategy, and in this competitive world they are bound to take place, whenever favourable conditions crop up. The raider will not disturb the management unnecessarily, as this would involve many costs, such as hiring and firing, training and search for new managers. This in turn would weaken the company, destabilise the management and the very objective of the takeover game would be spoiled (Panandiker, 2000).

2.4 Conclusion

With the initiation of liberalisation (both internal and external) process, the Indian economy gathered momentum in all spheres of activities. The analysis reveals that the growth accelerated as a result of deregulation. The corporate sector restructured itself in response to the newly unleashed market forces. It strove hard to survive in the new intensely competitive environment both on the domestic and global front, by reducing cost and enhancing efficiency.

The stock market reforms boosted public confidence and contributed to the corporate sector growth. They also led to change in the corporate financing patterns that were clearly witnessed from the mid-1980s to the mid-1990s. On account of the high cost and unavailability of credit - especially to small and medium enterprises—and a boom in the stock markct, a largc amount of financc was raiscd through thc capital markct. Further, GDS as a proportion of GDP also registered a rise. It occurred on account of both the HH savings and private corporate sector savings. The rise in financial savings during the mid-1980s to the mid-1990s, noticeably, point to the increased public confidence in financial instruments.

The stock exchanges witnessed a robust trading activity after the T.O. code came into being in 1997. A large number of shares changed hands with the objectives of management change, stake consolidation or substantial acquisition of shares of a company. Management change remained the overriding feature of open offers. The number of hostile bids remained limited because of the presence of large number of promoter-held companies and the passivity of the financial institutions (the other major shareholder in most of the companies). But growth of 'takeover market' alerted the companies to threats of takeover. It shattered the improbable act of challenging the big companies. The incumbent managements were compelled to be watchful and take corrective measures to evade takeover threats. Now, even a small fish could think of challenging a big fish. The shareholder is powerful and wants his money to be better managed and not squandered away. It made companies to realise that enhancing shareholders' wealth is the only way to secure control over management. The reforms have also provoked India's financial institutions to become more active and responsible shareholders. They also started insisting on better governance and proper utilisation of their funds.

Although the economy has improved on every front, there is a long way to go. The government needs to continue the reform process, if its benefits are to be maintained in future, growth process is to be continued and competition in the product market is to be stimulated.

3 Corporate Restructuring, Mergers and Acquisitions

Theory and Evidence

Every firm or corporation structures its business operations to attain its desired objectives and remain successful. The extent to which it undertakes activities, such as expansion programmes, bring changes in capital structure, ownership and organisation structure, are all determined by the prevailing macroeconomic environment and regulatory framework. Any change in the latter would force the firm to restructure its business operations so as to remain competitive and synergistic in the corporate world. Restructuring or more specifically, corporate restructuring is a broad umbrella that embraces many activities. It includes many activities, such as relating to expansion or contraction of a firm's operations, abandoning of old strategies, relocation of facilities, closure or sale of facilities and change in the assets or financial structures that are outside the ordinary course of business. It requires a significant amount of reorientation, reorganisation and realignment of resources of the firm. The restructuring strategy adopted by a firm depends, *inter alia*, on its desired goals and its existing financial structure.

In order to explain different dimensions of corporate restructuring and control, this chapter is organised as follows. A brief description of the various forms of corporate restructuring is given in Section 3.1. Section 3.2 covers in detail, the meaning of 'merger' and 'acquisition'. Section 3.3 discusses various exogeneous factors affecting aggregate merger activity. The rationale of mergers from a firm's point of view, termed as 'motives' of mergers is discussed in Section 3.4. The empirical evidence on the effects of mergers on various economic dimensions, such as profitability, growth, share price return, concentration, and market share are analysed in Section 3.5. The nature of selection mechanism along with its evidence on the characteristics of acquiring and acquired firms and predictability of acquisitions are outlined in Section 3.6. Section 3.7 offers concluding observations.

3.1 Corporate Restructuring

Different forms of corporate activities can broadly be divided into four categories:

1. portfolio restructuring,
2. financial restructuring,
3. organisational restructuring, and
4. corporate control.

A brief explanation of each form of restructuring (as given in Figure 3.1) is as follows:

Portfolio Restructuring

Portfolio restructuring can take place through combining and uncombining assets. It is divided in two parts, *viz*.: (i) expansion, and (ii) sell-offs.

(i) Expansion: It covers activities that help firms to expand and grow through external means. Apart from being one of the prime objectives of a firm, growth is an essential ingredient of success. It can be attained through internal means i.e., by expanding the existing capacity or introducing new products or externally, by acquiring the other existing businesses. Mergers and acquisitions (M&As), tender offers, and joint ventures are different forms by which a firm can expand externally.

Merger: In simple terminology, a merger is a joining of two or more firms into one, where the assets and liabilities of all the firms are vested into one surviving firm. The surviving firm can be one of the existing firms or it can be a new entity. The former is defined as a merger through absorption where the surviving firm is called the merging entity and all other firms involved in merger are called merged firms. The latter is a merger through consolidation or an amalgamation where the newly formed entity is termed as an amalgamated entity and the firms forming the entity, are called the amalgamating firms.

Figure 3.1

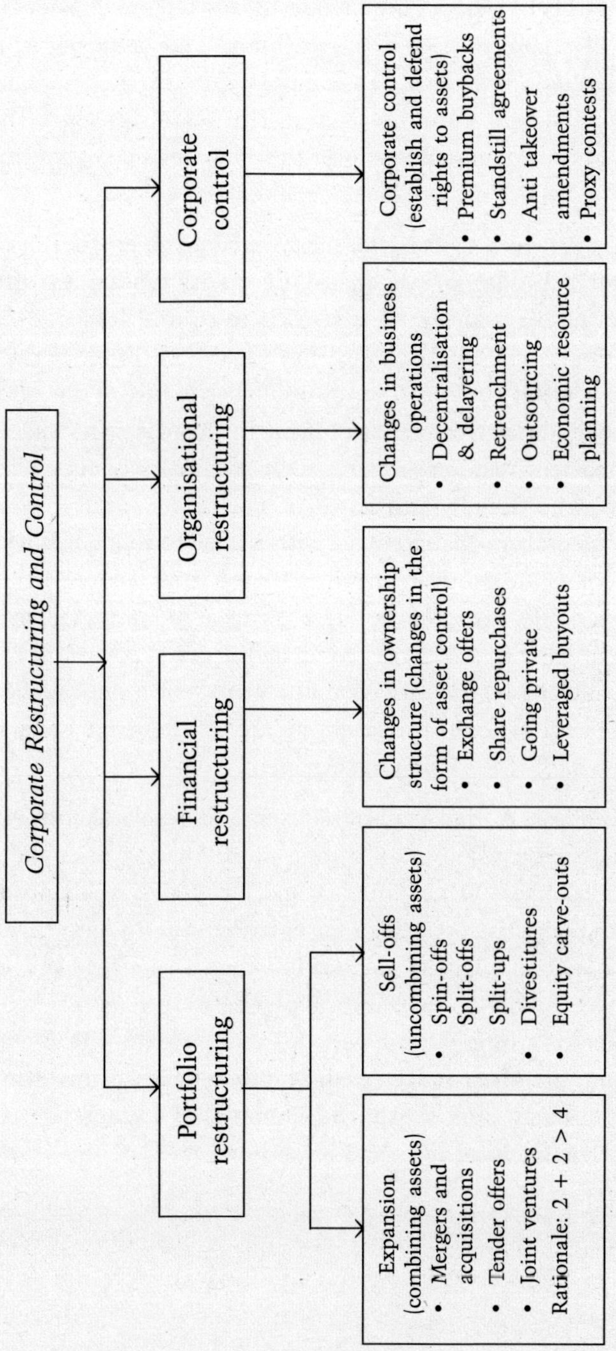

Source: Compilation based on Weston *et al.* (1990) and existing literature.

Acquisition: In general, acquisition means buying of assets (a plant or a division) of a company, to acquire a brand of a company or to acquire ownership rights in the assets of a company through share purchase. In the context of business combinations, acquisition essentially implies acquisition of controlling interest over the affairs of a company, through the purchase of a certain block of share capital.

Tender offer: In a tender offer (also called an 'open offer' in India) one firm (called a bidder or an acquiring firm) makes an offer to the shareholders of the company, it is seeking to control (called a target firm), to submit their shares in exchange for a specified price. If the acquiring firm is successful in attaining the controlling structure of this target firm, it is said to have taken over the latter firm. In this case, the target company retains its existence and experiences a change in its management control. Takeovers can be friendly/negotiated or hostile in nature. In case of the former, the incumbent management with a view to relinquishing control of the management to another party negotiates the takeover. In case of the hostile or open offer takeovers, a raider (party or group that plans to acquire controlling interest in the target company) acquires shares from the open market or financial institutions or mutual funds at a price higher than the prevailing market price. These takeovers are called hostile because they are against the will of the existing management.

Joint venture: A joint venture is used as a viable alternative to M&A strategy for the expansion of an organisation. Sharing risks and resources, cost reduction, access to new market and favourable regulatory treatment, are few of the objectives of a firm for entering into a joint venture. A joint venture is a form of business alliance in which an independent legal entity is formed by involving a fraction of the activities of two or more organisations for a limited time period. In accordance with the agreement, each company involved makes cash or other forms of investments. The agreement clearly spells out the sharing of ownership, operation responsibilities, financial risks and rewards.

(ii) Sell-offs: It involves uncombining assets. The rationale behind sell-offs is the expectation that slicing off a unit of business—especially that is performing poorly—may create value for a firm i.e., four minus two can be more than two.

Spin-offs and divestitures are two major types of sell-offs.

Spin-offs: When a parent company forms a new legal entity out of its existing business, it is a spin-off. The existing shareholders are given the shares of the new entity on a pro-rata basis and they continue to hold the same proportion of ownership in the new entity. It is important to note that a spin-off does not involve any cash transactions and only shares are transferred. The newly formed entity develops its own policies and takes decisions independently, for example, the information technology division of Wipro Ltd. was spun off as a separate company in the late 1980s.

The two variants of spin-offs are split-off and split-up. In case of the former, a portion of existing shareholders receives stock in a subsidiary, in exchange for parent company stock. The latter involves breaking up of the entire firm in a series of spin-offs so that the parent company no longer exists and the new offspring survives (Weston *et al.*, 1990).

Divestiture/demerger: A demerger or divestiture involves a sale of a portion or assets of a firm (could be a plant or a division or a unit) to an outside party. The selling firm is called a divesting firm and the portion sold is called a divestiture. The selling firm receives cash in exchange and also experiences a contraction in its existing business, whereas the buying firm, typically an existing firm, experiences an expansion in its business after the purchase. The selling firm's motive could be to get rid of unproductive, unprofitable or non-performing assets and use the cash received in exchange for streamlining the operation in more profitable ways. Equity carve-outs is a variation of divestiture. In it a portion of a firm is sold to an outside party through an equity offer. A new legal entity is created whose ownership lies with the group that bought the shares.

Financial Restructuring

This is the second group of restructuring in which the capital structure as well as ownership structure of the firm get affected. It can be done in the following four ways.

(i) Exchange offers: In this form of restructuring, debt or preferred stock is exchanged for ordinary stock, that results in increased leverage or common stock is exchanged for debt, resulting in decreased leverage.

(ii) Share repurchase or buy-back: A firm buy backs its shares outstanding, through an open-offer. This can also lead to a change in the control structure of the firm—especially, if the percentage of shares repurchased is substantial.

(iii) Going private: As the name suggests, in this form of restructuring a company turns from public limited to private limited. Members of the incumbent group, with the help of the funds received from a small group of investors, buy substantial part of the equity held by the public. By 'going private' a firm is no longer subject to compulsory obligations, such as holding shareholder meetings, providing periodical reports to investors and communicating with financial analysts. In recent times, Castrol India and Philips India have adopted this strategy to restructure themselves.

(iv) Leveraged buyouts (LBO):[1] In the above transactions, an outside investor can also arrange finance in the form of debt from a third party (typically a private company). When financing from the third party involves a substantial borrowing by the private company, such a transaction is termed as leveraged buyouts (LBOs). It entails a considerable dependence on debt. Whenever the members of incumbent management buy a company or a business unit, it is commonly called management buyouts (MBOs). The acquisition of Tetley Brand in the year 2000 by Tata Tea for £271 million was an LBO, which was financed through a debt worth £235 million (Chandra, 2004).

Organisational Restructuring

This form of restructuring, though important, may not necessarily take place in response to a change in the business environment. Rather, it also relates to day-to-day changes in the operations of the firm to cope with intense competition. Activities, such as changes in business strategies, reorganisation of working styles, decentralisation, retrenchment and so, are covered in it. Few of which are described below (Chandra, 2004).

- *Decentralisation and delayering*: It is practised to generate quicker response and empower people down the line in the organisation.
- *Downsizing*: Surplus manpower is retrenched to save on cost factor.

---

1. The fourth merger wave (1984-1989) in the US involved many acquisitions in the form of LBOs, see Table 3.1.

- *Outsourcing and sub-contracting*: Instead of employing manpower in the organisation, companies prefer to outsource their work to other firms. Through this, companies convert fixed cost into variable cost.
- *Enterprise resource planning*: To improve planning and control functions, many companies are using computer based, enterprise-wide integrated management information system.

Corporate Control

This group includes all the strategies that allow the incumbent management or promoter of the target firm to retain control over its operations and also put restrictions on the raiders to increase their controlling stake in the target company.[2]

(i) Premium buybacks/liability restructuring: It is a strategy in which the target company repurchases its share ownership at a premium, above the market price. This repurchase is made from the stockholder also called raider, who tries to acquire substantial shares of the target company.

(ii) Standstill agreement/greenmail: Such agreements are made with the raider or substantial stockholder, with the aim to put a limit on the per cent of holdings of a raider. An agreement is written between a target company and a raider where the latter agrees to refrain from making further investments in the target company in future. This is to put a limit on the controlling stake held by the raider over the target and thus, refrain him from making a hostile takeover. Such agreement can be made with or without premium buybacks.

(iii) Proxy contests: Proxy contexts occur when 'insurgent' group, also called 'dissidents', attempt to gain controlling seat on the existing board of directors to reduce the control of incumbent management.

(iv) Anti-takeover amendments: Amendments are made in the corporate by-laws to make acquisition of a company more difficult, expensive and thereafter, ward off a takeover attempt by raiders. Depending

2. Research work of the 1980s in the US focussed on the impact of takeover tactics on the shareholders' wealth. For details, see Jensen (1986a; 1988) and Jarrell *et al.* (1988).

upon the regulatory system, these laws vary from country to country. These include pre-offer as well as post-offer defences.

- *Super majority clause:* A high percentage, for example, 80 per cent of votes, is required to approve a merger.
- *Staggered board:* This is a pre-offer defence used to delay the change in the control over a number of years. The board consists of three equal groups of directors, out of which one group is elected every year. This prevents the acquiring firm from changing the entire board at its will.
- *Golden parachutes:* This is a post-takeover defence. In case a company is taken over and the existing management is terminated, the incumbent management is entitled to receive large termination benefits.
- *Poison pills*: In case of an event of a merger, the existing shareholders are given the right to buy the shares of the acquiring firms at a substantial discount. It is used to make the company a less attractive target for the acquiring firm. It is called so, because it is released when the raider takes sufficient bite of the target firm (Van Horne and Wachowicz, 1996).

Staggered board and poison pills are the two common defences employed by the American firms. As compared to the US companies, the Indian firms have relatively fewer anti-takeover defences.

In India, SEBI allows for the following defences (Chandra, 2004):

- *Make preferential allotment:* To avoid a takeover threat, a company is allowed to enhance its equity stake, through an allotment of preferential shares to the members of the promoter group.
- *Creeping acquisition:* A company under SEBI guidelines is allowed to raise its equity holding through creeping acquisition (between 2 to 5 per cent) without involving an open offer.
- *Sell the crown jewel:* To make itself less attractive, the target company can sell its valuable assets that have tempted the raider for a takeover attempt.
- *White knight:* A company may ask for support from its friends to ward off a takeover attempt.

Having discussed the various forms of restructuring, in the next section we give an exposition of an important form of portfolio restructuring, namely, merger and acquisition.

3.2 Merger and Acquisition

M&As represent the most important form of restructuring. These strategies are adopted by a business organisation to seek growth through external means. In comparison to the internal means of growth, it is considered to be a faster way of expanding businesses and entering into new product lines or new market areas.

Merger

A merger is said to occur when two or more companies combine to form a company, which could be an existing one or a new entity. The companies A and B can be involved in a merger in the following three ways.

(i) A + B = A, It is a case of B merging into A where B is the merged entity and A is the merging firm.[3]

(ii) A + B = B, Here A is merging into B where A is the merged entity and B the merging entity.

(iii) A + B = C, Here A and B combine to form a new entity C. Companies A and B are merged or amalgamating firms and C is a consolidated or an amalgamated firm.

Cases (i) and (ii) are merger through absorption because here, two or more companies are absorbed into an existing entity and all companies except one, lose their entities. In merger through absorption, the shareholders of the firms that cease to exist, get shareholding in the surviving company (merging) on the basis of the share exchange ratio incorporated in the scheme of merger, approved by voters of all the merging firms.

Case (iii) is merger through consolidation.[4] In this all companies dissolve to form a new entity. In 1986, four companies, namely, Hindustan

3. The terms merger and acquisition are used interchangeably in literature; therefore, a merging or surviving firm is also called an acquiring firm and a merged firm as an acquired firm.

4. Laws in India use amalgamation for such cases of merger. The newly formed company C is called an amalgamated company and companies A and B are amalgamating companies.

Computers Ltd., Hindustan Instruments Ltd., Indian Software Company Ltd. and India Reprographics Ltd. merged together to form an entirely new company, called HCL Ltd. GlaxoSmithKline Pharmaceuticals Ltd. formed from the merger of SmithKline Beecham Pharmaceutical (India) Ltd. and Glaxo Wellcome (India) Ltd. is another example of merger through consolidation or amalgamation that took place in the Indian drug and pharmaceutical industry in the year 2000-01.

Types of Mergers

Depending upon the similarity or (non-similarity) of the businesses in which the combining firms deal with, a merger may be classified into the following types.

1. *Horizontal*: A merger is said to be horizontal in nature when the firms involved in the merger are engaged in the same lines of business, for example, merger of two firms producing steel represent a horizontal merger. Availing the benefit of economies of scale and restructuring the competition (through elimination of a competitor) in an industry, are the two key benefits of such mergers. These mergers can lead to concentration of economic power. Hence, they are generally regulated by the government.
2. *Vertical:* Joining of firms engaged at different stages of production of the same product or service (having buyer and seller relation) is termed as a vertical merger. This can be forward or backward in nature. Joining of a firm with the source of raw material is backward and joining of a firm in the direction of the customer to market its product is a *forward* merger. Ensuring smooth supply of raw material and easy marketability of the product are the two main aims behind such mergers. Pharmaceutical firms entering into mergers with a biotechnology firm or a drug distributor firm are common forms of vertical mergers. Merger of a car manufacturing with sheet manufacturing firm or with the firm involved in the distribution of car is an example of backward and forward mergers respectively. Such mergers may also lead to concentration of economic power.
3. *Conglomerate:* A joining of firms engaged in unrelated lines of business is termed as a conglomerate merger. Diversification of risk (through lesser dependence on one market) expansion in debt

capacity, reduction in risk and having more stable income through entering into wider fields of products, are the main motives behind such mergers.

4. *Concentric:* Merger of firms that are related to each other either through basic technologies or production processes or markets is called a concentric merger. It, thereby leads to either product extension (broadening the product lines of firm) or market extension (expanding to other geographical areas).
5. *Reverse:* Conventionally, a healthy or a profit making company absorbs a weak company. As the name indicates, in the case of a reverse merger, a healthy company gets merged into a sick or a financially weak company. This takes place mainly to take advantage of the provision of income tax act, which permits a company to carry forward its losses to set off against its future profits.
6. *Cross-border mergers:* When the firms combining their businesses belong to different countries of the world, it is called a cross-border merger. Companies from the US, UK and Japan are very active in such mergers. After economic liberalisation, Indian firms are also active participants in the cross-border mergers.

Acquisition

Acquiring of the effective working control by one working company over another, through the purchase of controlling interest in the share capital of the latter, is termed as an acquisition or a takeover. It is important to mention that acquisition does not lead to dissolution of the company whose shares are acquired. Rather, it simply means that control of assets changes from one group to another.[5] The shares may be purchased either by means of cash or in exchange of shares of the acquiring company. The acquisition of controlling stake through purchase of shares where the incumbent management willingly agrees to relinquish control to another group is called a friendly or a negotiated takeover. These takeovers can also

5. In order to have complete effective working control, it is not necessary to own 51 per cent of the share capital of the acquired firm. Rather, ownership of 20 per cent or sometimes as low as 10 per cent for widely held company, can bring the change in the management, since the remaining share holders are scattered and ill-organised and are therefore, unlikely to challenge the control of the acquirer.

take place through an allotment of preferential equity share in exchange of ordinary shares of the target company. The terms and conditions are mutually agreeable to both the groups. These takeovers are also called synergistic, since the motivating force behind them is the possibility of benefits from combining the businesses of two firms after the acquisition.

If the purchase is made through the open market, which is against the wishes of the incumbent group, it is called a hostile acquisition or a hostile takeover. If the response of shareholders is favourable, the acquiring firm (raider) gains control and can replace the management of the target firm. These are generally disciplinary in nature because the underlying motive is often to correct the non-value maximising practices of managers of the target firms. In this case, to avoid a takeover attempt, the target firm can adopt anti-takeover techniques (discussed above) or offer large cash dividends to its shareholders.

Sometimes a profit-earning firm acquires shares in a financially weak[6] (not sick)[7] company in pursuance of a scheme of rehabilitation approved by public financial institutions or a scheduled bank (lead financial institution). Such a takeover is defined as bailout takeover, which is said to take place when a profitable company takes over a financially weak company. The purpose of this is to rehabilitate the latter. In such cases, the leading financial institutions evaluate the takeover bids by all acquirers and the decision is taken on the basis of the track record of acquirers and their financial position. In this case, it is the duty of the lead institution to ensure compliance with the SEBI takeover code. Taking into account the financial viability and requirement of funds, and also keeping in view the transparency and interests of the minority shareholders, the lead institution draws up the rehabilitation scheme.

The main difference between a merger and a takeover (or acquisition) is that in the former, at least one company loses its identity whereas in the latter, the acquiring firm gains only management control over the taken

---

6. A company is defined to be financially weak if its accumulated losses at the end of the previous financial year lead to erosion of net worth between 50 to 100 per cent of its net worth.

7. A company is deemed to be a sick company if it is registered for at least five years and has accumulated losses more than or equal to its net worth at the end of any financial year.

over firm. Later on, depending upon its objectives, the acquiring firm can either merge the acquired firm into itself (in that case it is same as a merger) or can operate it as a separate entity, having control over its managerial issues. Further, restructuring in the form of an acquisition takes much lesser time than a merger, as the procedure of a merger is much more cumbersome and time-consuming. An acquiring company, after getting approval in the general body meeting of the shareholders of both the companies involved in merger, has to seek permission from the High Court. In the case of acquisition, after getting acquired the 14 per cent of shares from the market, the acquiring company has to make an open offer to the remaining shareholders. This is to acquire 20 per cent of the total shares of the target company in the stipulated time period. The acquisition process generally, gets over in three to four months whereas for a merger it takes a year or more to complete the whole process.

The use of terms merger, acquisition and takeover in the literature has varied across researchers. Singh (1971) distinguished between merger and acquisition (used interchangeably with takeover) in the following way.

When company A (B) acquires more than 50 per cent of the equity of company B (A), B (A) is recorded as having been taken over or acquired by A (B). In this case of a takeover of company B (A) by company A (B), only one company B (A) is regarded as dying. This is the same as cases (i) and (ii) considered in our definition of merger, called, 'merger through absorption'. A merger between company A and B is deem to occur when the two companies amalgamate to form a new legal entity, say, company C. In this case, if A and B merge, both are regarded as dying. This is case (iii) of our definition, termed as amalgamation or consolidation. For his empirical work, Singh (1971) regarded the smaller of the two companies involved in merger as being essentially, an acquisition of the larger. He used merger, acquisition and takeover[8] interchangeably to mean 'merger', as defined above in our definition.

It is important to stress here that in our study, the terms merger, acquisition and takeover have been used interchangeably to mean 'merger' as defined in Section 3.2.

---

8. The term 'proxy contest' was used to cover the cases of 'change of management' after acquisition.

3.3 Factors underlying Mergers

To answer questions, such as; why do we witness more mergers in some periods than in others? why do mergers concentrate in few industries during a given time period? what motivates a firm to undertake a merger?, we turn to the issue of factors that cause merger activity. The factors causing merger activity can broadly be categorised into two heads: exogeneous factors and endogeneous or firm-specific factors (Section 3.4).

Exogeneous Factors

This section spells out the reasons for M&A activity occurring in waves i.e., periods with high activity followed by relatively inactive periods. A rich body of empirical literature for the US, UK, and many other European countries, has deepened our understanding of aggregate merger activity. A thorough research of merger movement, experienced predominantly in the UK and US, enabled researchers to identify an important fact i.e., mergers occurred in waves (Golbe and White, 1988). These waves in merger movements clearly highlight the macroeconomic aspects and industry-specific causes behind the merger movement. Table 3.1 offers insights into many noticeable features of merger movements, such as how mergers in the US differed in terms of accompanying developments that took place in the economy, industries in which merger movement was concentrated, and kinds of mergers. It is observed, the kind of merger activity that dominated during different phases and the industries in which merger activity located, differed across waves. This is because the phenomenon was also affected by the industry-specific conditions and the policy regime (regulatory environment) followed during that period.

The exogenous factors are better understood by dividing these into two broad groups, also shown in Figure 3.2.

(a) Macroeconomic factors, and

(b) Industry-specific factors.

(a) Macroeconomic Factors

These factors can further be subdivided as follows.

i) General Economic Environment

All merger movements had one common feature: All began with a general economic upturn, rising stock market, low rate of interest (lowering the cost of capital for financing acquisitions) and ended with recession and a downturn in the stock market. The accompanying innovations, such as emergence of railroads, motor vehicle transportation, radio, personal computers, internet, and cell phones, further accelerated the general economic and business upturn. These factors determine the timing when most of the firms consider restructuring of their businesses, either to take advantage of conducive business environment or to use it as a survival strategy.

One of the main reasons of M&A activity being concentrated in periods of high rates of growth and heightened business activity, is because only during this period firms find the business environment favourable to undertake new investment projects. Moreover, during this period competitive environment also changes. It alters the relationship among the existing firms, brings uncertainty regarding the future survival of firms, and thus forces firms to enter into new business strategies through the process of restructuring.

It was observed that the extent or the size of M&A activity during different waves was also affected by other complementary services that developed during the periods of expansion (see Table 3.1). The rise in railroad transportation and automobile transportation, advent of electricity during the first and second merger waves in the US brought expansion in markets, thereby giving rise to mass production and mass marketing techniques. All of this provided considerable impetus to the M&A activity. The third merger wave in the US was relatively small in size, since during this period, the economy was accompanied by neither any major technological change nor a change in the business environment. The highest merger activity occurred during the period 1967-1969. Each merger wave came to an end when the US economy turned down and entered into a period of recession.

Table 3.1

Historical Overview of Various Merger Movements in the US, 1895-1990s

Period	*Reasons of High Merger Activity*	*Kind of Activity*	*Motives of Merger*	*Industries involved in Merger Movements*	*Other Features*
First merger wave (1895-1904)	High growth period, technological and organisational innovations, development in business environment and advent of rail road transport	Horizontal mergers	To gain monopoly	Heavy manufacturing industry	Characterised as merging for 'monopoly'
Second merger wave (1922-1929)	Relaxed enforcement of laws, upturn in business, increase in automobile transportation, enhanced road transportation and improved communication (home radios)	Horizontal and vertical mergers (product and market extension)	To gain oligopolistic power, avoid bankruptcy in banks	Public utility, banking, food processing, chemical and mining	Radio facilitated advertising and growth of national brand
1940-1947*	Rapid growth of economy, government regulation and tax policies				
Third merger wave (conglomerate mergers movement) (1965-1969)	Strict enforcement of Clayton Act (1914), booming economy, instability in sales in few industry, excess capacity in many industries, low growth prospects in railway equipment, textiles and tobacco	Conglomerate mergers (product extension), beginning of hostile takeovers of medium-sized companies	Diversification to avoid sales and profit instability and uncertainty regarding future profits	Aerospace, industrial machinery, and auto parts, electrical industries, natural resource industries and tobacco	Mergers by declining and matured firms, during 1967-68 merger activity at highest ever level

contd...

...contd...

Period	*Reasons of High Merger Activity*	*Kind of Activity*	*Motives of Merger*	*Industries involved in Merger Movements*	*Other Features*
1976-onwards*	Greater contribution of services sector, deregulation in financial sector, broadcasting and health services and relaxation of anti-trust regulations	Horizontal and conglomerate mergers	Defence against sales and profit instability	Service industry, banking, finance and insurance, wholesale, retail, broadcasting, health care and natural resources	Beginning of hostile takeovers
Fourth merger wave (1984-1989)	Recovery from recession of 1982-83, anti-takeover defences, financial innovation (junk bonds), emergence of takeover specialists, aggressive use of debt, strong economy and low interest rate	Hostile takeovers and LBO, unsuccessful conglomerates of 1960s spun-off, carved-out and sold off, Horizontal mergers in new and deregulated industries	To takeover inefficient corporations that failed to provide shareholders' wealth maximisation	Oil and gas, banking, finance, food processing, mining and minerals	Shareholders of target companies benefited, use of aggressive takeover tactics of raiders, use of anti-takeover tactics by targets, (staggered terms of board, super majority provisions poison pills)
Mergers in 1990s	Heightened economic activity, rising stock prices, low interest rates, innovation in information systems (computer, internet, e-commerce, mobile phones) and deregulations in many industries	Friendly and equity-financed takeovers, strategically motivated takeovers	To take advantage of economies of scale, to compete globally	Transportation, telecommunication, financial services, energy sector, health care, drugs & pharmaceutical	Change in the method of financing from debt to equity because of failure of LBOs of 1980s

Note: * Not named as 'merger wave' because these periods did not have sufficient number of M&A to constitute a merger wave. In this period growth in the economy was not accompanied by any major change in technology or business environment.

Source: Based on works by Weston and Mansinghka (1971), Weston *et al.* (1990), Mueller (1995), Jensen (1988), Gaughan (1994) and Carroll (2002).

Figure 3.2

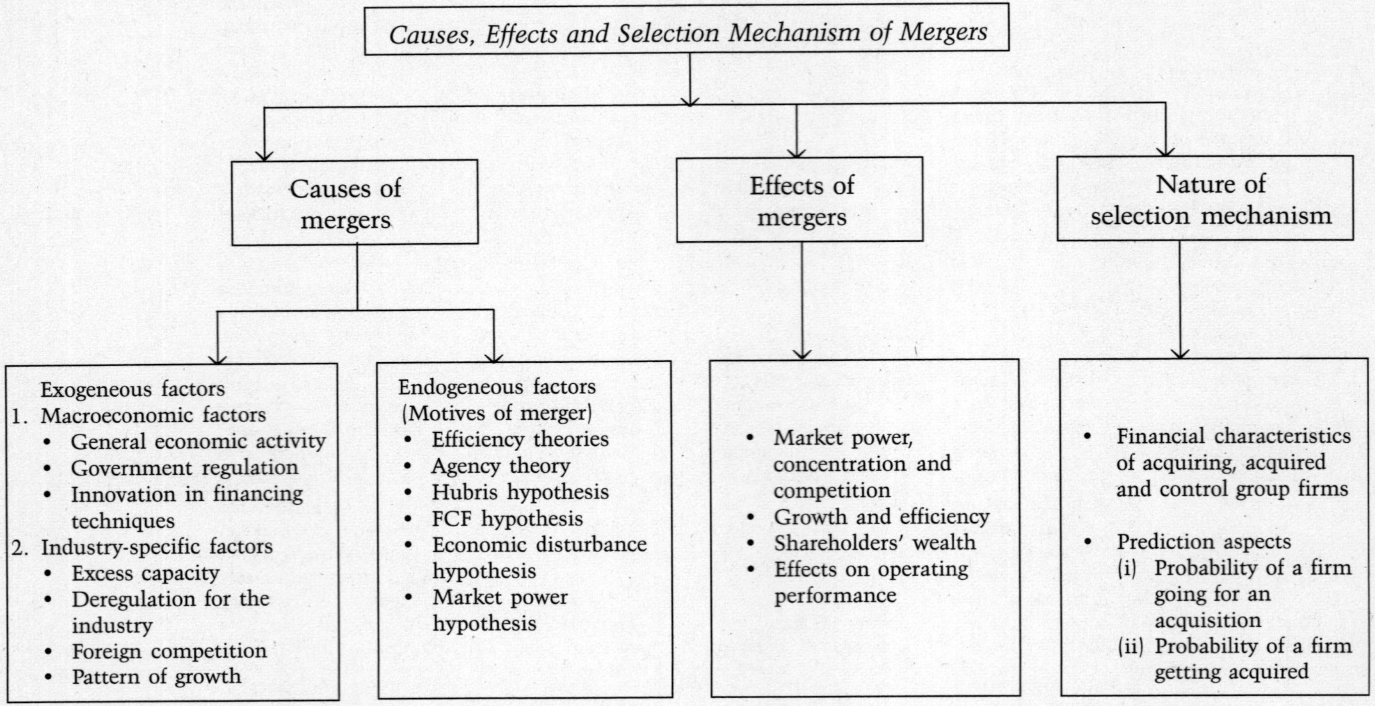

Source: Compilation based on existing literature.

ii) Government Regulation

The regulatory framework of the country is an important factor determining the M&A activity. Any relaxation in artificial constraints imposed by the government always brings new investment opportunities and thus, encourages restructuring. The prevailing regulatory environment in the US economy also governed the general merger activities as well as the types of mergers. During the first merger wave, the government's liberal attitude drove corporations to involve in horizontal and vertical mergers in large numbers. During the 1960s merger wave, because of restrictions put in the form of the Clayton Act[9] on horizontal mergers, firms entered in conglomerate mergers[10] (in particular, product extension). It is widely recognised that government's anti-trust policies helped to shape the conglomerate merger movement. As a result of these regulatory changes, a marked decline occurred in the horizontal merger in the 1950s and a corresponding increase in conglomerate mergers in the 1960s (Stigler, 1966). It was again in the late 1970s and the early 1980s, because of increase in international competitiveness and relaxation on anti-trust regulations, firms entered into a number of horizontal mergers in the US (Table 3.1). Higher merger activity in response to changes in regulation was also recorded in countries, such as the UK, France, Sweden and Italy. In order to meet the American challenge and make firms capable of facing increased competition from foreign firms, governments of many European countries adopted an encouraging policy to promote mergers of the domestic firms.

iii) Innovation in Takeover Financing

Since the 1980s, this has become an important factor leading to a high level of M&A activity in the western world. It is widely recognised that aggressive use of debt through 'junk bonds financing' and 'strip financing' facilitated the fourth merger wave (1984-1989) in the US (Jensen, 1988). Because of this, the fourth merger wave is marked by large-

---

9. During 1950s the Clayton Act of 1914 was amended and federal government was empowered to declare those mergers illegal that tended to increase concentration. This Act prohibited a corporation from acquiring the stock of another corporation if the competition were to be substantially lessened. The Act referred to acquisition of stock and not assets (Weston *et al.*, 1990).

10. This merger movement of 1960s was also named as 'Conglomerate wave'.

scale hostile battles, use of aggressive takeover tactics and restructuring in the form of leveraged buy-outs (Table 3.1). Consequent to this, the fourth merger wave also witnessed the use of defensive strategies, such as super majority provisions, staggered terms of board, and poison pills defences to restrict hostile bidders. The development in financing techniques permitted small firms to obtain resources from the market and paved way for even smaller firms to undertake large-sized acquisitions. Out of the 100 largest acquisition transactions recorded through 1983, 65 occurred after 1982 and only 11 took place prior to 1979. That is why, the decade of the 1980s was also called as decade of 'mega mergers'. The development of innovations in financing the M&A activity removed size as a deterrent to competition in the market for corporate control.

(b) Industry-specific Factors

An important feature noticed in the empirical studies is that mergers are not distributed across all industries. Rather they cluster by industry. It is observed from Table 3.1 that each merger wave was concentrated in a few industries. This led researchers to believe that, besides general economic activity and policy regulations, there are industry-specific factors that cause merger activity. Industry-specific factors include those factors that bring a change in the structure of the industry or the policy regime that governs the industry. These factors include capacity utilisation, level of growth of the industry, deregulation, competition from foreign firms and instability in the supply and demand conditions within the industry. It has been widely recognised in literature that these factors affect the strategies adopted by firms regarding expansion in production and growth. Any factor that affects the structure of industry, say, a sudden change in demand and supply conditions, deregulation of industry and change in input prices is termed as 'industrial shock' in the theory.

i) Change in Regulatory Regime for the Industry

Deregulation in finance industry in the 1970s and in broadcasting and health care during the early 1980s, led to the concentration of merger in these industries during the merger movement that took place in the late 1970s and early 1980s in the US. A rise in acquisitions in broadcasting industry in the 1984 in US is a typical example of relaxed policy regime that governed the ownership of television and radio stations. Similarly, restructuring in health services, airlines and transportations, oil and gas industries during the early 1980s, were also caused by deregulation in those industries. Financial services, transportation and broadcasting together accounted for 20 per cent of all M&As from 1981 to 1984 (Jensen, 1988).

ii) Excess Capacity and Decreasing Growth

Whenever an industry's capacity is underutilised or it is a declining industry, it does not pay to expand internally. Under such conditions, M&As or external expansion is the best way to survive. This has been confirmed empirically in several studies. A substantial rise in foreign competition during the 1980s caused many sectors of the US economy to experience slow growth and over-capacity. Major changes in energy sector—especially oil and gas that required restructuring and retrenchment, were achieved through merger and takeover activity. Exit through these means was found to be cheaper than the bankruptcy, particularly in an industry that was already burdened with excess capacity. Oil and gas industry ranked first in the takeover activity and accounted for 26.3 per cent of the total takeover activity during 1981 to 1984, in the US (Jensen, 1988).

Recently, several studies notably, Mitchell and Mulherin (1996); Andrade and Stafford (1999); and Andrade *et al.* (2001) focussed on industry-clustering aspect of M&A activity. They found that the inter-industry variation in the rate of restructuring was directly related to the magnitude of 'economic shocks' borne by the sample industries. Jensen (1993) also suggested that the oil price shock of the 1970s, causing changes in input costs, led to takeover activity in many industries during that period. Palepu (1986) observed industry-shock to be a significant determinant of firm's acquisition. He reports that a firm belonging to an industry that is subject to an economic shock, has a greater probability of being taken over than the other firms.

The above discussion documents the existence of 'macroeconomic' and 'industry-specific' factors that cause waves in the overall M&A activity i.e., periods of high and low activity. Since the ultimate unit that is involved in M&A activity is a firm, it is important to find what drives or what motivates a firm towards this activity. Unless a firm is motivated to undertake M&As, no set of factors can explain the existence of this activity. The factors that explain the M&As from the perspective of a firm are covered under 'motives of merger', also called 'firm-specific' or endogeneous factors. The driving forces for a firm, explained by the theories of merger in the literature, are reviewed in the following section.

3.4 Firm-specific Factors: Motives of Merger

Several hypotheses, such as replacing inefficient management, exploiting synergies, pursuing self-interest of managers and using free cash available to a firm, have been advanced in the literature as motives of M&As. There is no consensus on the primary motives of merger in the industrial organisation literature. The theories, often documented as explanations of M&A activity, can be divided in three broad categories (Weston *et al.*, 1990; Mueller, 1995). They are:

1. greater efficiency related theories;
2. profit related motives: Agency problem and managerialism, free cash flow, economic disturbance and Hubris hypothesis; and
3. market power based explanations.

1. Efficiency theories: Firms combine their assets and merge with others to obtain synergistic gains. But the question relates to the origin of these synergistic benefits. Efficiency theories are optimistic explanations of the potentials of merger for social and private gains. There are several efficiency theories, which explain different classes of merger.

(a) Differential managerial efficiency or managerial synergy: If two firms have differential management efficiency levels, and when the firm with a relatively higher efficiency level acquires the other, efficiency will improve after the merger. This results in private as well as social gain. But if this process were carried to its extreme, it would result in one firm with highest managerial efficiency.

Another formulation is that at any point of time, there are many firms, which do not operate to their full potential level. Such firms are more likely to be acquired by other firms (engaged in similar kinds of business activity). It is assumed that acquiring firms have excess managerial know-how to improve the performance of the acquired firm.

(b) Inefficient management theory: Another formulation of efficiency theory is inefficient management theory i.e., when the firm is unable to

manage its assets up to its own potential (inefficiency is taken in an absolute sense unlike differential efficiency theory). This theory better explains the rationale for unrelated or conglomerate merger whereas differential management efficiency theory explains horizontal mergers, as the firm involved has superior management in the same product line. Manne (1965), who originally advanced this view, called it 'market for control' hypothesis. Even inefficiency theory is open to many arguments. Firstly, it presumes that the shareholders of the acquired firm cannot replace inefficient management and entering into a merger is the only option to improve their management. This implies that merger is a disciplinary action required on the acquired firm—an implausible argument. Proponents have argued that a merger does not imply inefficiency of shareholders to replace management. Rather, it implies a scarcity of able managers. Secondly, an acquiring firm can operate the acquired firm as a subsidiary if replacement of management is the sole motive. Thirdly, evidence should reflect that the acquired firm's management is replaced after merger. This does not appear to be the case (Weston *et al.*, 1990). Lynch (1971) in a study of 28 conglomerate firms showed that these companies acquired firms with capable managers who could be retained after the merger. Markham (1973), in a study of 30 large acquisitions reported that the top management was retained in 60 per cent of the cases examined.

(c) Operating synergy: The principal reason for a firm going for a merger is its expectation of some synergistic gain that makes the value of the combined entity (V_{AB}) greater than the sum of the independent values (V_A and V_B) of the two merged firms, A and B (i.e., 2 + 2 > 4). Depending upon the type and the underlying motive, benefits can be reaped by firms in many forms after undertaking a merger.

(d) Economies of scale and scope: Economies of scale are the advantages in terms of low cost of production on account of increase in the scale of operation that results from the merger of two or more firms. The fall in cost of production could be due to the lower requirement of factor inputs per unit of output (called real economies) or due to the possibility of getting factor inputs at lower prices because of bulk transaction (called pecuniary economies). The former, in turn may be linked to economies in transport, storage, marketing and distribution activities, inventory

requirement, research and development (R&D) programmes and managerial skills. Indivisibility (more intensive utilisation of plant) of various factors is an important source of such economies—especially in industries where heavy investments in plant and equipment are made—as the cost gets spread over larger number of units of output. Obtaining cheaper and larger finances, both debt and equity, result from the pecuniary economies. Debt can be obtained at lower rates and unit cost of larger issue of equity capital falls because of the fixed transaction cost involved in such transactions.

Such economies generally arise in horizontal mergers, as both the merging firms are involved in the same product line. In case of vertical mergers, benefits arise from smoother production process, reflecting better coordination of activities, lower inventory requirement and wider marketing network strength. These economies can also occur in conglomerate merger leading to product or market extension. Diversification of activities leads to fall in overhead expenses and reduced riskiness of investment, thereby, reduced cost of capital. The justification for conglomerate merger is also provided through financial synergy. Economies of scale in flotation and transaction cost of security are also available in conglomerate mergers. Increased debt capacity of combined firm provides tax savings on income. A company can also obtain economies of scale by widening the scope of activities through the skill and assets it possesses after merger. Complementarities of resources of two merging firm can be an important source of obtaining synergistic benefits. A firm, weak in marketing but strong in R&D, can merge with a firm weak in R&D but strong in marketing to get this advantage. If a profit-making firm combines its business with a loss-making firm through accumulated losses and/or unabsorbed depreciation, it can obtain tax advantage.

(e) Undervaluation: Undervaluation of the target company is also attributed as one of the important motives of M&As. A firm is undervalued if the market value of its assets is lower than the replacement cost. It is reflected in the low value of the q-ratio, defined as ratio of market value of the firm's shares to the replacement cost of the assets. Undervaluation could be due to poor performance of the firm indicating inefficient management. If the acquiring or raider firm with inside information, places higher value on the assets of the firm, it can acquire additional capacity by

buying undervalued firms. During the late 1970s and the early 1980s in the US, inflation and depressed stock prices caused a fall in q-ratio ranging between 0.5 and 0.6 and that in return led to high rate of acquisition. Undervaluation of a firm is an important motivating factor to consider a firm for merger. However, undervaluation *per se* cannot explain the M&A activity, there has to be a reason for the acquiring firm to add to its capacity (Weston *et al.*, 1998).

2. Agency problem hypothesis (principal-agent relationship): In the modern world corporation, agency problem or principal-agent relationship arises because of the separation of ownership (stockholder) and control (managers), and the divergence of interest between them. The main motive of shareholders is to increase their wealth through maximisation of the price of shares, whereas the management's prime objective is to maximise their personal utility function that includes higher income perquisites, luxurious offices, company cars and so on. The managers, being the decision or control agents, take decisions regarding the use of resources that benefit them personally, the cost being borne by the owners or shareholders. Further, in a company with widely spread ownership, there is no sufficient incentive for individual shareholder to monitor the behaviour of managers. It is the lack of a monitoring mechanism on the part of shareholders that gives power to managers to utilise funds in their interest, and this brings in the agency problem. Presuming a high positive correlation between corporate managerial efficiency and share price, it has been argued that the stock market acts as an external monitor of the decisions taken by managers (Fama and Jensen, 1983). Low stock prices, that can make firm a takeover target, exert pressure on managers to use the funds in the direction of the shareholders' wealth maximisation. So, Manne (1965) and Fama and Jensen (1983) suggested that the agency problem arising from the separation of ownership and control is considerably reduced because of the existence of market for corporate control. This is one aspect of merger theory where threat of takeover is a solution to the agency problem.

(a) Managerialism: As opposed to this view, 'managerial hypothesis' considers mergers as a manifestation of the agency problem rather than a solution (Mueller, 1969). This hypothesis posits that M&A activity is primarily motivated by the self-interest of the managers, even if it does not

bring any increase in shareholders' wealth. It is argued that managers of the modern world's corporation often adopt merger strategy in order to grow bigger as: first, their compensation and rewards are directly linked to the growth in the size (measured in sales or assets) of the firm or resources under their control and, second, mergers are the fastest way to grow relative to the internal expansion growth strategy. Further, it is observed that merger as a growth strategy with latter reason is often adopted by mature firms or firms in the slow growing or declining industries that do not have sufficient opportunities to grow. The underlying argument is that it is the separation of ownership and control along with the absence of internal checks and control (on account of widely scattered shareholders) that induces managers to undertake merger, even if it results in greater inefficiency.

(b) Hubris hypothesis: Hubris means 'animal spirit'. Roll (1986) holds the view that takeover is a result of hubris on the part of bidders and that takeover mechanism does not control the agency problem. His hypothesis is based upon evidence available in the US: firstly, most of the increases in share price returns accrue to the target firm shareholders, and, secondly, returns to the acquiring firms continuously declined from low positive to zero to even negative from the 1960s to 1970s to 1980s, respectively.[11] He emphasised that managers in their over-exuberance and over-optimism overbid for their merger target and in this process transfer the gain to the target shareholders. It is believed that in such cases, the post-merger performance of acquiring firms does not improve because managers systematically overestimate their ability to improve the acquired firm's performance.

Free cash flow (FCF) hypothesis: The Agency theory was widely discussed and accepted in the economic literature. However, the agency cost arising from the conflict between the shareholders and managers over the pay out of FCF was highlighted by Jensen (1986a). According to him, agency cost arising from the conflict between managers and shareholders over the disbursal of FCF is one of the major causes of takeover activity. FCF is the cash flow in excess of the amounts required to fund all the projects that have positive net present value when discounted at the

11. For details, see Jensen and Ruback (1983).

applicable cost of capital (Jensen 1986b; 1988). This FCF must be paid to the shareholders to maximise their long-term wealth. But if paid, it will reduce the resources under the control of managers and reduce their power. FCF theory predicts that a firm with large cash flows is more likely to undertake mergers and takeovers, even with negative returns or there is greater probability for such firms to undertake diversification programmes. Such takeovers take place in industries with excess capacity, low growth opportunities and industries requiring retrenchment or in declining industries.

(c) Economic disturbance hypothesis: Put forward by Michael Gort (1969), this hypothesis emphasises the difference in expectations of buying (acquiring) and selling (acquired) firms on the future profit levels, as a cause of merger activity. High merger coincides with the periods when stock prices change rapidly, as during such periods divergences in expectation are most likely to occur.

3. *Market power hypothesis:* It is advocated that companies merge to increase their market share and thus increase their monopoly power and earn monopoly profits. The obvious question that comes to mind is: what are the gains to the firm from increasing market share i.e., how does the firm obtain synergies? If increase in market share implies increase in the size of the firm, the economies of scale argument (discussed earlier) applies. In fact, an increasing market share implies an increase in the size of the firm relative to the other firms in the industry. This increases the ranking of the firm (on the basis of its size measured in sales or assets) in the industry. But again, the issue is that, what gains would the firm obtain by increasing the relative size in the industry? It has been argued that increased market share brings 'undue concentration'[12] in the industry, which in turn increases the possibility of monopoly profits through tacit collusion of other existing firms in the industry.

Evidence on motives of merger: Among the early empirical investigations on the motives of merger, we have studies for industrialised countries of Europe and US. 'The economies of scale' as motive behind merger was consistently rejected, as merging firms were found to be big or

---

12. In the US, an undue concentration is said to exist when four or less than four firms contribute at least 40 per cent of the total sales in the industry (Weston *et al.*, 1990).

bigger than the selected control sample or respective industry averages. The results regarding the 'risk spreading' motive (which is more often associated with vertical and conglomerate mergers) did not support risk reduction as a motive behind mergers. The 'economic disturbance' theory was corroborated in Sweden and Holland but rejected in the other five countries.[13] Although stock price movements were found to be related to some mergers, a consistent pattern was not discernible.

Evidence on agency cost, managerialism and free cash flow (FCF) hypotheses: As noted earlier, while payment of free cash to shareholder maximises shareholder's wealth, it reduces the resources controlled and power held by managers. Since managers' compensation is directly related to resources under their control and power held by them, they have a tendency to expand the firm's size through mergers and takeovers, even beyond the size that maximises shareholder's wealth.

Research studies in the US found that some mergers—especially horizontal mergers undertaken by declining industries that required exiting of resources—were solution of the agency problem of FCF, whereas few of the acquisitions, witnessed in the diversification programmes undertaken by oil industry that required shrinking on account of excess capacity, were symptoms of FCF (Jensen, 1988).

Jensen (1986b) also discussed the use of debt as one of the important factors reducing the agency cost and improving organisational efficiency. Increased use of debt (leading to increased leverage) automatically reduces the cash flows to be spent at the discretion of managers, as they are bound to pay compulsory interest and principal payments. The FCF theory along with greater use of debt, which results in lower agency cost, was also found to be consistent with the stock price movements resulting from financial restructuring of firms. Using stock price changes at the announcement of transactions that bring a change in the structure of capital, Jensen and Smith (1985) and Smith (1986) observed that most leverage-increasing transactions were associated with positive stock price movement whereas negative stock price movements were found to be due to leverage-

---

13. To analyse inter-country difference on causes and effects of merger, Mueller (1980c) initiated a research project. He covered seven countries; France, Belgium, Netherlands, West Germany, Sweden, the UK and the USA (also see Chapter 7, Table 7.17).

decreasing transactions. It was also reported that a higher value is created when the consideration for acquisition is made in cash or debt rather than in equity (Servaes, 1991).

The benefits obtained by LBOs and 'going private' transactions of the early 1980s in the US, further lend credence to the reduced agency cost function of debt. Most of the business division that turned into LBOs were the ones where agency cost of FCF was likely to be high, that is existence of firms with low growth opportunities along with high potential of generating cash.

Gibbs (1993) investigated corporate restructuring activity of very large corporations, which were insulated from takeovers by virtue of their large size. His results supported the hypothesis that financial and portfolio restructuring were motivated by the agency cost. However, factors other than agency cost were also driving restructuring. The findings further, confirmed the importance of corporate governance and well functioning market for corporate control (MCC) in preventing and controlling the agency problem. This implies excess financial resources or FCFs are a necessary but not sufficient condition for agency cost to arise.

What drove managers to diversify their businesses in the 1960s and conglomerate merger wave of 1960s in the US, is a well-researched area but with no consensus. Risk reduction is advanced as an important motive of the firm for engaging itself in conglomerate merger. But the fact that stockholders could achieve this through their own diversified portfolios raised the question as to why managers entered into conglomerate mergers? In the context of 'agency cost' and 'managerialism' propositions, Amihud and Lev (1981) hypothesised that managers diversified to achieve their personal objectives. They observed that managers engaged in such mergers tended to decrease their largely undiversifiable 'employment risk' of losing job and professional reputation. The study noted that: (i) manager-controlled firms engaged more in conglomerate acquisition than the owner-controlled firms, and (ii) regardless of the means through which a firm achieved diversification: operations of the manager-controlled firms were more diversified than those of the owner-controlled firms. These observations also tallied with the two early estimates by Boudreaux (1973) and Holl (1975) on the UK and the US firms, respectively.

However, using stock market response to acquisitions, Matsusaka (1993) did not support the hypothesis of Amihud and Lev (1981). He observed that market favoured acquisitions that intended to exploit the managerial synergies than the ones that were motivated to discipline the target management. On the basis of these observations, it was suggested that conglomerate merger wave was not driven by managerial objectives.

Consistent with FCF, several studies used free cash flows available with firms as one of the variables, to predict takeover of a firm as well as probability of a firm going for an acquisition. Palepu (1986) observed that firms with the resource-growth mismatch are more probable targets of takeover. Firms with high sales growth, high leverage and low liquidity (defined as 'high growth-low resource' firms) and with low sales growth, low leveraged and high liquidity (defined as 'low growth-high resource' firms) were more likely to be taken over. Hay and Liu (1998), focussing on the behaviour of acquiring firms, report that a firm with a forecast rise in its cash flow is more likely to make an acquisition.

3.5 Effects of Mergers

Turning to the empirical evidence on the effects of M&A activity, a large body of literature is available for the US and the UK dating back to the 1890s. For other industrial countries, a beginning was made only in the 1950s, when most of the leading industrial countries along with the UK and US, experienced merger waves. Most of the evidence provided here are from the UK and US.

The effects and desirability of takeovers essentially depend upon motives of merger. If the acquiring firm wishes to exploit economies of scale or replace inefficient management, mergers are expected to be wealth-enhancing. On the other hand, if managers pursue their self-interest or are affected by hubris, mergers are generally wealth-reducing.

Evidence on market power, concentration and competition: The creation of 'monopoly' or 'near monopolies' witnessed during the early merger movement in the US, led many to believe that mergers were driven by market power (Markham, 1955). Occurrence of economies of scale through large-scale production was doubted on the grounds that most of the firms involved in mergers were large-scale firms.[13] Several studies completed subsequently, reported the effect of mergers in the form of increased concentration for the West Germany (Muller, 1976) and UK (Hannah and Kay, 1977; Aaronovitch and Sawyer, 1975) during the 1950s to 1960s. But to what extent this concentration is due to mergers was questionable, since the change in concentration also depends on entry, exit and internal growth of firms. Further, it has also been reported that a rise in concentration was more due to increase in the number of plants operated by bigger corporations, rather than increase in the relative size of plants owned by such corporations. Hence economies of scale are a less plausible reason of increased concentration. Effects of mergers in terms of higher prices, increase in aggregate concentration and market power have been found, however, increase in market power as one of the motives behind the merger could not be established (Mueller, 1995).

Hay and Untiet (1981) and White (1982), on the other hand, concluded that mergers did not have an impact on aggregate concentration during the intense merger activity, as net entry of firms was also high during that period. A similar conclusion of a fall in aggregate concentration is also reported for the period 1970-1980 by Golbe and White (1988) for the largest 200 US corporations. This view was also endorsed by Ravenscraft and Scherer (1987), on the grounds that many of the mergers were failures in the long run that resulted in subsequent spin-offs. It was also suggested to examine, whether the composition of firms remained the same or changed, since the changing composition of firms reflects the vigour of competition in the economy (Weston *et al.*, 1990). Further, in order to see its impact on the competitive pattern among the incumbent firms, the effect on industrial concentration rather than aggregate concentration is a more appropriate index.[14] Along with aggregate concentration, several studies also reported a rise in industrial concentration during the 1960s in UK (Aaronovitch and Sawyer, 1975), West Germany (Jacquemin and de Jong, 1977) and the Netherlands (Peer, 1980). On the other hand, because of anti-trust laws, despite a rise in

13. Scale economies seem to be the motive when small rather than large firms are involved in combinations (Mueller, 1980c).

14. The present study has done this for the Indian drugs and pharmaceutical industry. For details, see Chapter 8.

aggregate concentration, the micro concentration was controlled in US- especially during the conglomerate merger movement (Mueller, 1980b).

As regards the effects on competition, increased concentration is not necessarily associated with lower competition. In fact, the rise in concentration witnessed in the 1960s in the US was in tandem with intense competition due to growth of international trade and a liberal policy regime followed in most of the industrial countries. Recent studies are more supportive of anti-competitive effects of increased industrial concentration. During the late 1970s, the governments of West Germany and UK became very concerned about the increased monopoly profits and other anticipated problems of inflation.

By examining the stock prices movement of rival firms, Stillman (1983) and Eckbo (1983) also rejected the market power hypothesis. If a merger results in higher prices due to increased market power, it must also benefit its competitors (through rise in prices) and thereby an increase in equity value of competing firms. On the other hand, the market power hypothesis predicts negative abnormal profits for the rival firms of those mergers for which a complaint is filed for anti-trust challenge (on the presumption that it will reduce the probability and expected price rise due to increased monopoly power). However, Stillman (1983) found no statistically significant abnormal returns for rival firms of 11 horizontal mergers, while Eckbo (1983) reported non-significant positive abnormal returns.

Effects on growth and efficiency: Effects of merger on the efficiency of a firm are manifested through price and output. In principle, a rise in efficiency should result in a fall in cost leading to a fall in prices and expansion in output, while a rise in market power must result in a rise in prices and a fall in output. In order to test this, three studies measured the market share of firms before and after the merger. Goldberg (1973), and Mueller (1985; 1986) found either a decline or no significant change in market share during the post-merger period. These pieces of evidence were suggestive of increased market power due to mergers. It is important to comment here that a fall (or an insignificant change) in market share could

15. Defined in detail in Chapter 7.

have occurred despite a rise in firm's output, if there are new entrants in the industry and higher output.

Mueller (1980c) also commented on the efficiency effects of merger through testing for growth in size of the merging firms and control group[15] firms in seven countries. In the Netherlands and US, slowdown in the growth rate of merging firms was observed in the post-merger period relative to the change in growth rate performance of the control group companies. No statistically significant difference in growth rates for two sets of firms was observed between the pre- and post-merger periods for the remaining countries. In addition to these, a study conducted on Australian firms (McDougall and Round, 1986) also observed a statistically non-significant change in the growth rates between merging and control group firms. This evidence, along with no change in market share, can be taken as an indicator of no improvement in efficiency of merging companies, following the merger.

Most of the attempts at measuring efficiency benefits of the MCC[16] have either focussed on behaviour of share price of acquiring and acquired firms (studies by finance specialists) or on the post-merger performance of merged firms, based on accounting data derived from companies' annual reports (industrial organisation studies). The conclusions of these studies, however, differ. The former squabble in favour of economic gains whereas the latter point to a fall in efficiency.

Effects on shareholder wealth: The impact of MCC on the shareholders' wealth has been carefully scrutinised in the late 1970s and early 1980s. Some have been sceptical about its gains to the society. It is argued that the value created does not arise from the increase in efficiency or productivity. Rather, it is due to the redistribution of gains from one group to the other, e.g., due to reneging in contracts with managers and employees, mistaken valuations, increased market power and lower tax

16. Originally, the term MCC was coined for only hostile acquisitions or open offers. However, research studies on it have included mergers, acquisitions and proxy contests as part of this market (Jensen and Ruback, 1983).

17. It is argued that managers are pressurised to maintain the short-term goals at the cost of long-term growth of the firm, for example, through a fall in expenditure on research and development.

payments. Further, it is also argued that the market has damaging effects on the morale, productivity and long-term growth[17] of the organisation.

Evidence regarding the 'effects of merger activity on shareholder wealth' is based on the 'event study' methodology. Event studies measure the effects of any uncertain event on stock prices that show how investors in stock market view the effect of an event on future benefits. Findings of any abnormal returns (returns left after correcting for the influence of general market activity on the prices), is taken as a reflection of the positive view of the event occurring in the market. This presupposes an efficient capital market.

In their comprehensive survey,[18] Jensen and Ruback (1983) advocated that the corporate takeovers generate positive gains where target firms' share holders gain and that of bidding or acquiring firms' do not lose. From the evidence on stock price changes (measured net of market-wide price movements) for both successful and unsuccessful takeovers, it is observed that in successful takeovers, target firms experience statistically significant abnormal stock price changes of 20 per cent in mergers and 30 per cent in tender offers, while bidding firms realise zero and 4 per cent in mergers and tender offers, respectively. In contrast to this, in unsuccessful cases, mergers were found to be associated with small negative abnormal stock price changes for both target and bidding firms. From this, they argued that gains from mergers and tender offers are realised only when assets are actually transferred to bidding firms. Further, they argued that these gains are realised on account of increased efficiency and synergies, however, they could not gather sufficient evidence to identify the sources of gains.

One of the major criticisms of MCC is that of 'short sightedness'. The fear of takeover makes market as well as managers to behave myopically i.e., they follow short-term growth strategies by sacrificing long-term growth of the corporation. In this context, Jensen (1988) has provided substantial evidence that does not tally with the short-term outlook of the market and managers. The evidence is based on the positive stock price reaction to increased investment and research and development (R&D)

18. It reviews evidence from about 40 research studies, covering the period from 1960s to the early 1980s in the US. The studies reviewed are based on 'event study' methodology.

expenditure of the firms. It is hypothesised that if the argument of short-term behaviour is accepted, the stock prices must respond negatively to increased R&D and other long-term investment expenditure, as these indicate a focus on the long-term growth. Two more studies by McConnell and Muscarella (1985) and by Securities and Exchange Commission (1985) also reported a positive stock price reaction to increased R&D and other investment expenditures. In a comparative study of acquired and industry-matched non-acquired firms, Hall (1988) found that the ratio of R&D to sales in both sets of firms is equal and there is no difference between pre- and post-merger R&D performance of merging and non-merging firms. This evidence was taken as a confirmation of the view that the firms with higher R&D expenditure were not vulnerable to takeovers.

Jarrell *et al.* (JB&N) (1988) extended the analysis to cover the heightened takeover activity of the 1980s and confirmed the earlier assertions reported by Jensen and Ruback (1983). They also reported that any criticism against MCC is ill-founded, as it performs a positive role. On the basis of evidence available from several other studies,[19] JB&N maintained the earlier results that target firm received bulk of the value created by mergers and there is a secular decline in the gains received by the bidders (acquirer) in the 1980s. Factors, such as greater regulations, multiple bidding, auctions/contests and pre-emptive bidding, use of defensive tactics against takeovers, and easy availability of sophisticated takeover advisors, (see Table 3.1) intensified competition during the 1980s and thus decreased (increased) the returns received by bidders (targets). Further, they also convincingly rejected the undervaluation theory (i.e., target firm is undervalued) and short-term myopia theory (i.e., market participants value short-term earnings rather than long-term earnings). The assertion that premium received by target firm is redistribution of gains from bondholder or from labourers of target firm (due to the exploitation of raiders to accept wage reductions) was also refuted. They strongly held the view that corporate transactions reflect economically beneficial restructuring of productive assets and share premiums from takeovers represented real wealth gains.

---

19. These included, Jarrell and Poulsen (1987); Lehn and Poulsen (1987); DeAngelo *et al.* (1984); Mikkelson and Ruback (1985).

Whether on average, takeover events are wealth-reducing or wealth-enhancing for acquiring firms, Gregory (1997) analysed the long-term returns to bidding/acquiring firms for UK. In order to avoid the issue of choice of benchmark that has a considerable effect on the measurement of abnormal returns from share price data, Gregory (1997) used six different models of normal returns. He unambiguously concluded that takeover events, on average, are wealth-reducing for acquiring firms and are not compatible with shareholders' wealth-maximising behaviour on the part of acquiring firms' management. He found this finding to be consistent with Roll's (1986) 'hubris' hypothesis and 'managerialist' theories.

Effects on operating performance: Regardless of the driving force behind a merger, if managers aim to maximise profits, acquiring firm must show higher profits after the acquisition, relative to the profits in pre-merger period. The results on profitability have varied depending on the measure of profitability used and also on the type of merger the firms are involved in. To find the effects of merger on profitability, it is important, (i) to compare the profit rates of newly formed firm after the merger with the weighted average of the profit rates of acquiring and acquired firms before the merger (instead of comparing with the profit rates of acquiring firm before the merger); and (ii) to discount for any change in the general economic condition, the comparison should be made with a control group of non-merging firms or industry averages of the merging firms (Hughes *et al.*, 1980).

Mueller (1995) reviews 19 studies (including six studies on US and five on UK) on the effects of merger on profitability. From this list, only three studies, *viz.*, Mueller, 1980b (for US); Cosh, *et al.*, 1980 (for UK); and Kumps and Witterwulghe, 1980 (for Belgium),[20] found an increase in post-merger profitability (profit after tax/total assets), relative to the control group. All others report either a fall or no change in profitability after merger. The two largest sample studies, *viz.*, Ravenscraft and Scherer (1987) for the US and by Meeks (1977) for UK, report a fall in the post-merger profitability. The conclusion that mergers do not increase profitability is thus hard to reject.

---

20. The study for Belgium is not considered to be reliable because of its small sample size.

Among the studies on mergers that took place during the 1980s and later, the results are mixed. Since equity value gain, as posited by capital market studies, could arise due to real economic gains or capital market inefficiencies, Healy *et al.* (1992) found a strong positive relation between the post-acquisition increases in operating cash flows and abnormal stock returns at the time of acquisition announcement. They also found a significant improvement in the operating cash flow returns caused by a rise in asset productivity,[21] which was especially strong for firms with high overlapping businesses. The R&D and other long-term investments were not found to be inversely affected after the acquisition.

To explore the sensitivity of accounting rate of profit to the main accounting treatments of takeovers described by regulators, Chatterjee and Meeks (1996) evaluated the UK takeovers during 1977 to 1990 by segregating their sample before and after 1984. The finding of a rise in profitability during 1987-1989 (as different from the fall in profitability reported for takeovers during 1977-1984) was not accepted as a reversal of the earlier trend. Rather, it was due in part to the distortions brought about by creative accounting practices.

Sharma and Ho (2002), in review of 10 studies using accounting measures (five based on earning measure and the rest on cash flow based method of performance) revealed an interesting finding. As opposed to studies using earning measures of performance, the studies using cash flow based method of performance showed improvement in post-acquisition profitability. They maintain that creative accounting practices do not affect operating cash flows to the same extent as they affect profitability. Hence, they recommended the use of both the earning and cash flow measures to investigate the effects of post-merger operating performance of companies. Results based on their study, consistently revealed a decline or no gain in operating performance following the merger. Also, the type of acquisition (i.e., conglomerate or non-conglomerate) and the form of acquisition financing (i.e. cash, shares or combination) were not linked to measures of post-merger operating performance.

21. For its meaning, refer to Chapter 6.

To sum up, comparing the results on the effect of mergers and takeover activity based on the use of accounting and stock price data, it is difficult to resolve the issue of efficiency gains of merger.

The studies by finance specialists based on stock price data, invariably maintain that merger represent an unambiguously positive reshuffling of assets into more productive uses. The views that gains are simply a redistribution of wealth from one section to another (redistribution theory) or that M&As make corporation shortsighted and thus endangers long-term growth, are refuted by finance specialists. They point to the impact on R&D activity, increase in wages and employment of merged firms and tax effects. However, it must be mentioned here that these conclusions are based on the premise that share prices are always efficient in the Tobin (1984) sense i.e., they reflect expected future benefit from the firm. Further, as the share prices are dominated by noise traders, the change in share prices cannot be accepted as a gain to the society (Singh, 1998).

The industrial organisation studies conclude that a decline in post-merger profitability is indicative of decrease in efficiency of merger. Keeping in view the sensitivity of results to the accounting measure used and the way figures in the annual reports of companies are manipulated, the conclusions remain open to question.

In view of the criticism put to the conclusion of both kinds of studies, it is suggested that, instead of concluding on the basis of share prices or accounting measures of profitability, the focus must shift to total factor efficiency or total factor productivity changes following merger. These measures analyse the changes in post-merger output of firm using input-output data, which better indicate the synergistic benefits of mergers. Several studies have researched the change in productivity levels occurring due to ownership changes. Lichtenberg and Siegel (1987) and McGuckin and Nguyen (1995) emphasise that changes in ownership are associated with higher productivity levels. The former study observed that the plants that experienced a change in ownership during 1972-1981 were preceded by declines in productivity and followed by increases in productivity. The latter study reported that the acquired plants experienced a rise in productivity. However, this rise was offset by a decline in productivity realised in plants already owned by the firms. Few other researchers also confirm these results.

In response to these results, Mueller (1995) makes two observations. First, these studies focus on the acquisition of plants during the period that corresponds to a large wave of spin-offs of the 1970s. Second, the studies do not indicate if the plants studied are acquired due to merger or due to spin-off. Further, in view of the observations reported by Ravenscraft and Scherer (1987) and Lichtenberg and Siegel (1987) units that were spun-off were performing badly, the above studies cannot be taken as indicative of the reversal of the earlier conclusion that mergers do not enhance efficiency. The findings of Bittlingmayer (1996) support the view that mergers in manufacturing industry serve to transfer intangible capital, and thus allow a low cost solution to the assets deployed post-merger. There are also studies by McGuckin and Nguyen (1995) and Schoar (2000) that confirm the productivity improvement of acquired plants.

3.6 Nature of Selection Mechanism and Characteristics of Firms

A very important aspect of M&As theory that still remains to be discussed is the nature of the selection process. Given the fact that two or more firms are involved in the merger process, few of the key issues are; on what basis does the market decide whether a firm is to be an acquiring or an acquired firm? Can these firms be differentiated on the basis of their size, profitability, leverage, growth and other features? Can the theory of merger predict the firms that are more likely to be acquiring or acquired? The following section throws light on these issues.

Nature of Selection Mechanism

The classical description of economic natural selection, on account of perfect competition in product market, argues in favour of profit maximisation as a goal of firms i.e., the firms that attempt to maximise profits would survive and others (non-maximisers) would be competed away from the market. This characterisation was found to be irrelevant in the world of modern corporations, which are essentially divorced through owner and control relationship. These corporations, on account of their diverse ownership, aim to satisfy their managerial motives such as, growth and sales maximisation. The managers of these corporations, regardless of profitability, work for the realisation of their own motives that may diverge from shareholder's wealth maxmisation motive. They attempt to increase the size or growth of the firm that determine their salary, job security, resources under their control, power and prestige, and managerial promotions.

With the advent of market for corporate control, neo-classical economists again argued that, despite the growth of large managerially controlled corporations, profit maximisation would still remain their main survival strategy. It is the efficiency in the capital market or the threat of takeover that forces firms to maximise their profits. It was further debated that the selection mechanism does not function entirely on the basis of profitability, as non-maximisers still survive on account of their size power.

Singh[22] (1971, 1975) pioneered research in this direction and systematically examined the nature of a firm's selection process. His findings supported the new managerial and behavioural theory of firm and provided little support to neo-classical theory of profit maximisation.

The acquiring firms in this study, on average were bigger, more profitable, faster growing, more liquidate and highly leveraged than their corresponding acquired firms. The most distinguishing feature was related to profitability improvement over the two years prior to merger. The acquiring firms on an average showed a small improvement in the profit records while acquired firms showed a marked decline. Though a considerable degree of stock market discipline for unprofitable firms was found, attempting to increase relative profitability as a survival strategy was found to be inferior than attempting to increase relative size—especially for large unprofitable firms. The most important finding is that the selection mechanism in the MCC encouraged a large unprofitable firm to immune itself to takeover by increasing its size rather than profitability. Kuehn (1975) found results consistent with Singh's finding that MCC does not provide much discipline over the managerial pursuit of growth.

---

22. His research was based on the mergers and takeovers that took place in the UK during the periods, 1954-1960 and 1967-1970, where the former was associated with a normal takeover activity and in the latter there was a takeover boom. The study covered five industries, *viz*., food, drink, clothing and footwear, and non-electrical engineering. This involved an in-depth comparative analysis by dividing the population in four sets of firms, *viz*., acquired, non-acquired, acquiring and non-acquiring.

In this context, the role played by 'innovations in financing technology' in the growth of takeover activity is worth mentioning. An important development, witnessed during the takeover activity of the late 1980s and the early 1990s in the US, was the emergence of innovative financing techniques, such as the high-yield non-investment-grade bonds (junk bonds). This enhanced the ability of firms to use debt financing and removed the obstacles to acquire bigger firms and removed size as an impediment to competition in the MCC. These techniques made possible for smaller firms to obtain resources to take over large corporation by issuing claims on the value of assets of the firm being targeted (Jensen, 1988). Does this mean that the large and unprofitable firms, which were earlier supposed to be insulated from takeovers, were not so due to their big size but on account of non-availability of finance to take over them? If yes, this implies that size, as a deterrent to take over activity, was not a valid argument against the market for corporate control during that period.

Characteristics of Acquiring, Acquired and Control Group Firms

Based on seven studies[23] for the UK firms during the 1970s, Cooke (1980) summarises findings on the financial characteristics of acquiring (AG) and acquired (AD) firms. All these studies reported that AD or taken over firms performed poorly than AG firms in terms of profitability, valuation ratio, P/E ratio and growth in net assets. However, in terms of gearing or leverage ratio, AD were less geared than AG firms and no difference in the liquidity ratios of two sets of firms was found.

Mueller (1980c) also covers comparison of pre-merger characteristics of different sets of firms on the basis of size, profitability, leverage and growth. In terms of almost all variables, a fairly consistent pattern emerged across the countries covered. Acquiring firms were found to be larger than three sets of firms, *viz.*, firms they acquired, average firm in the industry and a control group of firms selected randomly from their respective industries. AG firms grew faster than AD firms and as fast as or faster than their size-matched control group companies. AD firms did not differ in growth from their control group companies in all the countries except UK

23. These include Newbound (1970), Singh (1971), Buckley (1972), Tzoannos and Samuels (1972), Kuehn (1975), Firth (1976), Meeks (1977).

and West Germany, where they grew slowly. However, AD firms performed poorly or the same as compared to their AG, matched AD and the control group firms. It is only in UK where AD firms were significantly less profitable than AG and size-matched AD firms.

Results regarding AG and matched non-acquiring (MNAG) firms differed across countries. In four countries, *viz.*, the US, UK, Sweden and Germany profitability of both the groups was about equal and in Belgium and the Netherlands, AG firms were found to be performing poorly. France is the only exception where AG firms were better than the control group. In all countries, AG firms were either as highly leveraged or more leveraged than the companies they acquired as well as the control group firms. Between AD and matched non-acquired (MNAD), with the exception of Belgium, AD firms were either equally or more leveraged than their matched counterparts. AG firms had consistently lesser or same variability in profits than the firms they acquired and their matched group. No consistent pattern emerged from the profit-variability between AD and MNAD firms.

Reviewing the earlier and recent research work, Sorensen (2000) found that depending upon the motives of acquisition, characteristics of merging firms (AG and AD) changed from 1960s to 1970s to 1980s. During the 1996 calendar year, on the basis of 286, 232 and 217 targets, acquirers and non-merging firms respectively, he found that profitability is the single significant identifier of AG firms. Further, a single industry analysis was found to be better in analysing the financial ratios to correctly classify merging and non-merging companies.

Prediction of M&As

If the AD and non-acquired firms (NAD) can be distinguished, then an obvious question is regarding prediction—can the takeover targets be predicted?

In the context of MCC hypothesis, several studies attempted to predict the takeover target or analysed factors that affect the probability of a firm being acquired. Singh (1971) used discriminant analysis to find, if there existed any variable that discriminated between AD and NAD firms. He did not find any one variable that discriminated between the two sets of firms but at the same time he could not reject the null hypothesis that AD and NAD firms belong to the same population. Kuehn's (1975) study, using a probit model, found the valuation ratio to be a significant factor determining the probability of being acquired.

Consistent with Singh (1971) and Kuehn (1975) for UK; Schwarz (1982) finds evidence on the factors affecting the probability of acquisition of firms for the US Firms. Using a sample of 186 firms chosen randomly, for the period 1968 to 1977, he found that there is no critical value of the valuation ratio below which a firm is certain to be targeted for takeover. However, using probit analysis, he maintained that higher valuation ratio reduces the probability of a firm becoming a takeover target. Further, the study found that the probability of acquisition is negatively related to size, profitability,[24] retention ratio,[25] and maturity of the firm.

To predict takeover targets, Palepu (1986), based on nine independent variables[26] estimated a logit probability model. Though the model correctly identified a high percentage of actual targets, it also mistakenly predicted a large number of non-targets as targets. The author states that prediction of takeover target is difficult and the earlier studies overestimated prediction accuracy. Stevens (1973), using a sample of 40 AD and 40 size-matched NAD firms, demonstrated that low leverage and high liquidity are the two attributes of AD firms that distinguished them from their MNAD firms. Using Logistic regressions, Weir (1997) analysed the relationship between the probability of being acquired, the firm's performance and the governance structure. The study hypothesised that, if internal control mechanism described by key governance characteristics[27] fails to reduce or prevent the scope of managerial discretion (reflected in poor performance),

24. It is similar to Kuehn's (1975) result. The more profitable the firms are, the less likely they are to be targeted for acquisitions.

25. It is consistent with Mueller and Grabowski's (1972) argument that market prefers retention to dividends.

26. The choice of variables was based on six hypotheses, *viz.*, profitability (inefficient management hypothesis), growth-resource dummy (growth resource mismatch defined by growth of sales, liquidity and leverage), industry dummy (industry disturbance hypothesis), size (size hypothesis), market value/book value (market to book value hypothesis) and P/E ratio (P/E hypothesis).

27. The three governance characteristics used in the study were: (i) whether the role of CEO and chairman are combined, (ii) proportion of non-executive directors on the board, and (iii) the quality of non-executive directors.

the MCC acts as an effective monitoring mechanism of last resort. The findings of the study confirm that acquired firms are poor performers, suggesting their ineffective governance structure. Further, the results support the view that hostile acquisitions are disciplinary but throw doubt on the claim that non-hostile acquisitions are purely synergistic.

3.7 Conclusion

M&As have been one of the most important forms of restructuring strategy adopted to face the challenges posed by a change in business environment emanating from factors, such as liberalisation, deregulation, technological change, and foreign competition. M&A activity, being a cheaper and shorter route to growth, is also preferred as a growth strategy over the organic expansion of the firm.

A survey of voluminous literature reflects two important features of this activity; first, M&A activity occurs in waves i.e., there are periods of high and low activity; second, M&As cluster in industry i.e., the activity is not uniformly distributed across all industries. Rather, it is concentrated in a few industries, during different merger movements. These features provide a link between the macroeconomic factors and industry-specific factors that cause the M&As. Any change in the competitive forces brought about in the industry due to occurrence of any industrial shock, such as deregulation, foreign competition, excess capacity, low growth opportunities and a declining industry also stimulate M&A activity by the existing firms so as to adjust to the changing environment in the industry.

The driving force behind this activity from the firm's point of view is provided through firm-specific factors called 'motives' of M&As. Empirically, depending on the type of merger, several hypotheses have been put forward by researchers in explaining the reasons for M&A activity. These include, for example, achieving economies of scale, establishing market power, replacing inefficient management, use of free cash flows, achieving managerial motive of growth, risk reduction through diversification, gaining tax advantage and exploiting other synergistic gains through combining assets. Available evidence clearly suggests that the importance of these motives of merger has varied across different time periods as well as across industries in which they occurred. Motives of mergers along with government's regulatory framework have been effective in determining the kinds of merger. Encouraging attitudes of governments and relaxation in the anti-trust laws in the UK and US encouraged firms to involve in horizontal and vertical mergers during the first and second merger waves. However, tightening of restrictions on horizontal and vertical mergers due to their effects on undue concentration led to the conglomerate merger wave of the 1960s.

Concerning efficiency effects of M&As, there is no consensus among researchers. Whether the mergers reflect the desire of management to maximise the shareholder's wealth or the management's attempt to maximise their own wealth, is not easy to ascertain. Many managers do not add value but some managers do work to add to shareholders' wealth. Studies by finance specialists based on share prices and industrial organisation studies, using accounting data, have differing opinions. The former consistently view the reorganisation of resources brought through the M&As, bring gains to the society, while the latter associate this activity with a decline in efficiency. A thorough survey of empirical evidence on post-merger performance based on financial ratios reveals that mergers are wealth-reducing. However, the effects of M&As vary across factors, such as accounting measures of performance used, kind of merger the firm has undertaken, types of financing techniques used, motives of the merger, hostile or friendly merger and relative size of AG and AD firms involved in merger.

Taking note of issues highlighted, it is suggested that to get better insights into the motives, effects, and features of merging and non-merging firms, the research design should focus on a similar sample. Further, in view of the very well acknowledged industry-specific factors affecting the various features, such as average size, leverage and profitability in the industry, the general conclusion can be better drawn by focussing on industry-level studies.

4 Global Trends in Mergers and Acquisitions

M&As have been a natural way of restructuring business operations in the western world since the 19th century. A number of factors, such as opening of economies due to policy liberalisation and deregulation, increasing privatisation, financial liberalisation, global integration of production systems due to advancement of information and communication technologies,[1] and opening of foreign direct investments (FDIs) along with continuing liberal policies[2] have contributed to the rising global M&A activity since 1990s.

Cross-border M&As (foreign firm merging with a domestic firm, thus creating a new entity or foreign firm taking over the existing domestic firm and becoming a new foreign affiliate) and Greenfield investments (new investment made by setting up a new foreign affiliate) are two important forms of FDI flows. The former is the dominant form in the developed countries, while the latter dominates in developing countries. Firms from the developed world have constantly resorted to cross-border M&A transactions to consolidate their business processes and thereby attain market dominance. It has set the trend for large multinational companies (MNCs) to grow even larger and consequently, a smaller number of firms are controlling a large share of market.[3]

1. Bhoi (2000).
2. In 2003, there were 244 changes in laws and regulations affecting FDI, 220 of which were in the direction of more liberalisation of FDIs (UNCTAD, 2004). In 2004, out of 271 such changes, 235 were related to the opening of new areas to FDI (UNCTAD, 2005).
3. Concerns have been shown by both developed as well as developing countries regarding the increasing market power and possible anti-competitive effects of M&As. Suggestions have been made to pursue a global approach to competition policy that can respond effectively to cross-border M&As and anti-competitive practices of firms that affect the countries—especially the smaller ones (UNCTAD, 2000b).

The scheme of this chapter is as follows. It is organised in six sections. Section 4.1 links the movements in FDI with cross-border M&As. Section 4.2 provides a detailed analysis of cross-border M&A sales and purchases of the three groups of economies of the world. This section is divided in two sub-sections. The first sub-section analyses the number of cross-border deals and the second discusses the value of cross-border transactions. Section 4.3 gives the ranking pattern of individual countries, both as targets and acquirers. Section 4.4 describes industry-wise distribution of cross-border M&As. In Section 4.5, to deepen our understanding of global M&As, we identify the links of cross-border M&As with openness, institutional quality and gross national income of a country. Section 4.6 offers concluding observations.

4.1 Trends in FDI[4] Inflows and Cross-border M&As

It is observed that movements in M&As and FDI flows are aligned i.e., both have followed parallel paths (Figure 4.1). The similarity in the movement of world FDI inflows and cross-border M&As is indicative of the fact that the latter has become an important mode of global FDI since the early 1990s. The intense pressure created by globalisation drove the boom period created during the early years of 1990s up to 2000. The growth was particularly spectacular from the mid-1990s to 2000.[5] The proportion of M&As to FDI was high (above 0.7) during the late 1980s. From 1990 to 1995, the proportion fell and hovered around 0.5. The FDIs, M&As and ratio of M&As to FDI, reached their peak level in the year 2000, with their respective values recorded at US $1,400 billion, US $1,140 billion (7,894 measured in numbers) and 0.8 (See Table 4.1).

Both, FDI flows and cross-border M&As rose sharply till the year 2000 and declined thereafter for three years in a row. The fall occurred on account of a fall in FDI flows to developed countries and a lesser number of purchases made by the developed countries. The principal cause of decline during 2001-2003, particularly in M&As, was the slow down or end of

4. Foreign direct investment is defined as an investment involving management control of a resident entity in one economy by an enterprise resident in another economy. (UNCTAD, 2000a).

5. Increase in the number of M&As since the mid-1990s has been named as 'Fifth wave' by many researchers. For other waves, refer to Chapter 3.

privatisation in many countries (UNCTAD, 2004). After observing a decline in the activity from 2001 to 2003, the year 2004 witnessed a turn around in both the global FDI inflows and the value of cross-border M&As. The former increased by 3 per cent over the previous year, while the latter depicted a rise of roughly 30 per cent over 2003. A number of factors, such as higher economic growth in the home and host countries, improved corporate profitability and higher stock market valuation led to recovery of FDIs (UNCTAD, 2004). Apart from these factors, low interest rates and recovery in asset prices also caused an upturn in the M&A activity. The recovery in FDI is on account of increased flows to developing and transitional economies, while the rise in the value of cross-border M&A purchases is due to higher purchases by developed and developing economies that more than compensated for the decline in purchases by the transitional economies.

Analogous to the value of cross-border M&A, the number of deals also reflected a similar trend i.e., the latter reached its peak in 2000 and then observed a declining trend for the next two years. The number of M&A deals resumed an upward trend from 2003, *albeit* marginally (2 per cent over 2002).

Figure 4.1

Global FDI Inflows and Cross-border M&As, 1987-2004 (in billion dollars and numbers)

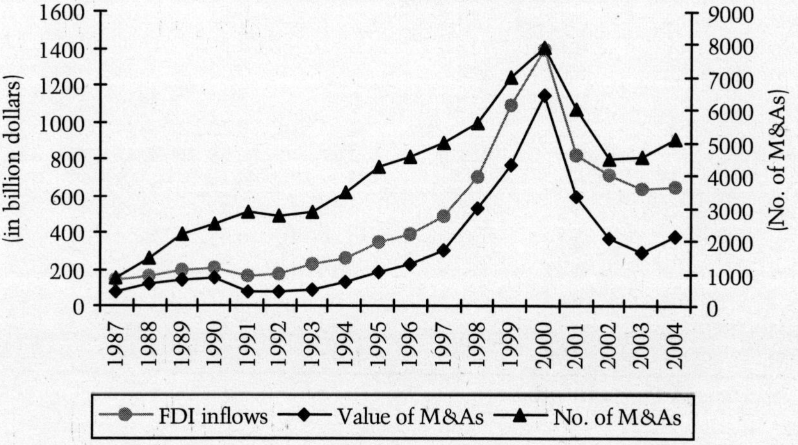

4.2 Detailed Analysis of Cross-border M&As

The analysis is carried out from the perspective of both the target (region or economy by seller) and the acquiring economies (region or economy by purchaser) by categorising the data in terms of number and value of deals. The data for the whole world is broadly sub-divided into three groups[6] of economies (UNCTAD, 2005), *viz.*

- *Developed countries and territories (DDE):* Europe, North America and Other Developed Countries (ODC).
- *Developing countries and territories (DGE):* Africa, Latin America and the Caribbean, Asia and Oceania.
- *Transition economies (TE):* Southeast Europe and Commonwealth of Independent States (CIS).

Number of Cross-border M&A Deals Purchased/Sold

As far as the number of total deals is concerned, in a span of 10 years beginning from 1990, the total deals more than trebled from 2,503 to 7,894 in 2000 (Table 4.1). After recording a decline for few years the number of

Table 4.1

Global FDI Inflows and Cross-border M&As, 1987-2004

Year	*FDI Inflows (in billion dollars)*	*Annual Growth Rate in FDI Inflows*	*M&As (billion dollars)*	*Annual Growth Rate in M&As (billion dollars)*	*Ratio of M&As /FDI*	*M&As (no. of deals)*	*Annual Growth Rate in M&As (no. of deals)*
1987	140.2		74.5		0.53	862	
1988	164.8	0.18	115.6	0.55	0.70	1480	0.72
1990	207.9	0.08	150.6	0.07	0.72	2503	0.14
1991	161.3	-0.22	80.7	-0.46	0.50	2854	0.14
1994	259.5	0.14	127.1	0.53	0.49	3494	0.23
1995	341.1	0.31	186.6	0.47	0.55	4247	0.22
1998	701.1	0.44	531.6	0.74	0.76	5597	0.12
1999	1092.1	0.56	766.0	0.44	0.70	6994	0.25
2000	1396.5	0.28	1143.8	0.49	0.82	7894	0.13
2001	825.9	-0.41	594.0	-0.48	0.72	6035	-0.24
2002	716.1	-0.13	369.8	-0.38	0.52	4493	-0.26
2003	632.6	-0.12	297.0	-0.20	0.47	4562	0.02
2004	648.1	0.02	380.6	0.28	0.59	5113	0.12

Source: Compiled from UNCTAD (2005).

6. For the further sub-division of three groups, refer to UNCTAD (2005).

deals attained a value of 5,113 in 2004. A pattern similar to the trends witnessed in the number of total deals and the value of cross-border M&As (i.e., a rising trend up to 2000 and a fall for two years and then again a turn towards a rise) is also evident across the three groups of economies, for both the purchase and sale of deals [Table 4.2; Figure 4.2(a) and (b)].

Figure 4.2 (a)

Total Number of Cross-border M&As by Three Groups of Economies (by purchaser)

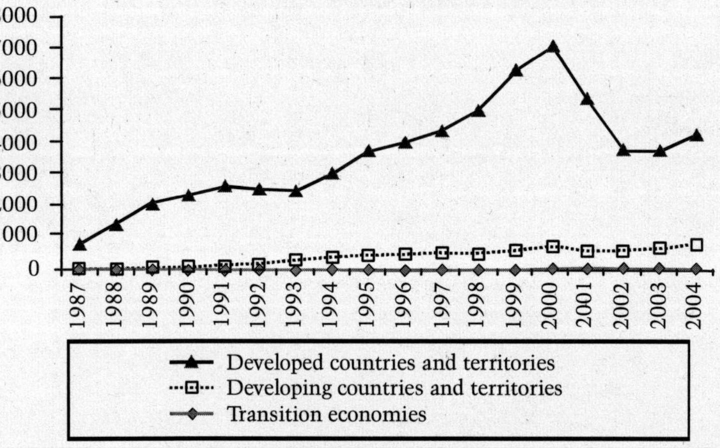

Figure 4.2 (b)

Total Number of Cross-border M&As by Three Groups of Economies (by seller)

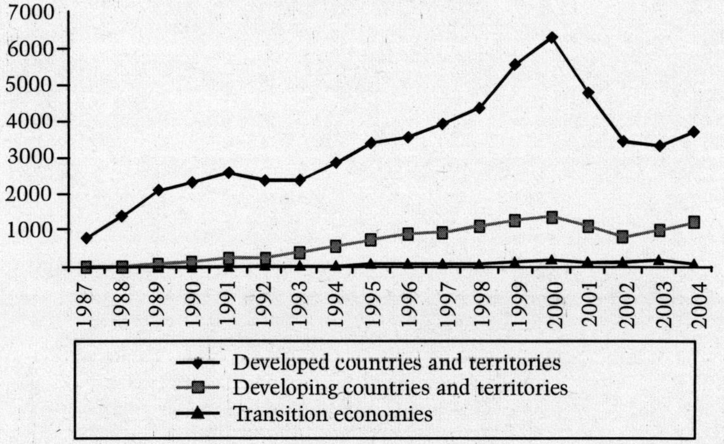

In terms of relative contribution in the total number of M&A deals by region, DDE's share as a purchaser is higher than as a target or seller, while for DGE economies, the share stands higher as target countries [Figure 4.3 (a) and (b)]. It is important to draw attention to the fact that both the groups of economies, DDE and DGE attained the highest deals in 2000; however, the former attained them as 'purchaser' and the latter as acquisition 'targets' or acquired countries as illustrated in Figure 4.3 (a) and

Figure 4.3 (a)

Total Number of Cross-border M&As Purchased and Sold by DDE

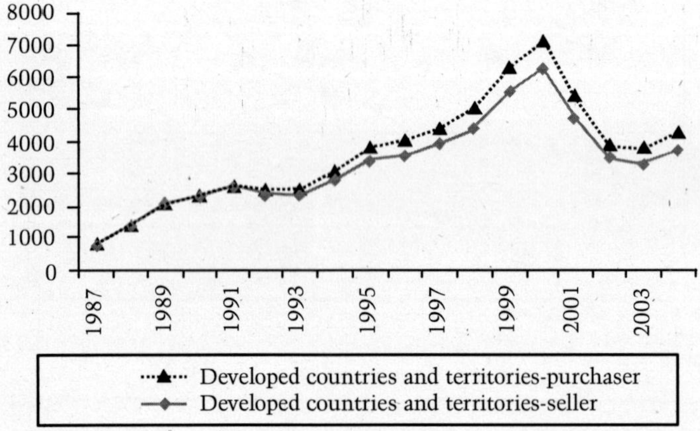

Figure 4.3 (b)

Total Number of Cross-border M&As Purchased and Sold by DGE

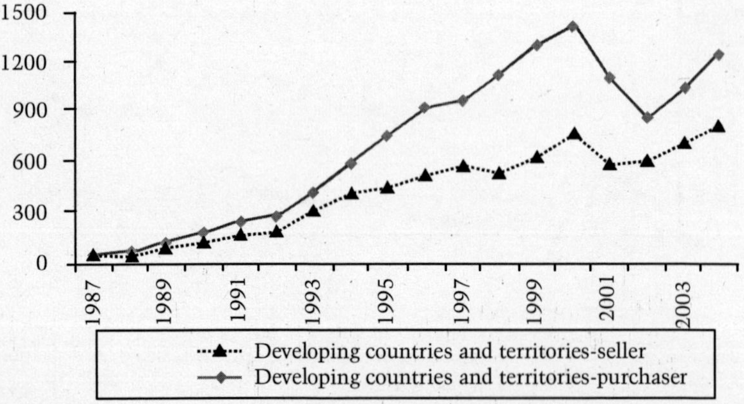

(b). Further, though both the groups of economies engaged in the highest total deals (both sold and purchased) in 2000, yet the difference in the deals sold and purchased was highest in 1999 for both the DDE and DGE. Comparing the deals purchased and sold for DGE, it is observed from the figure, that deals sold increased at a much higher rate than the deals purchased especially, from 1990 to 2000. In line with the above observation, DDE's numbers of deals as acquirer have grown at a higher rate than the rate at which they are targeted. On the other hand, DGE's numbers of deals as target (or seller) have grown at a much higher rate than as purchaser or acquirer during 1990-2000.

In order to validate the above observations and compute average annual trend growth, we fitted a semi-logarithmic trend equation (equation 1) to the series of number of total cross-border M&As[7] (from both the purchaser and seller's point of view, given in Table 4.2) for the period 1987 to 2004. Further, in order to observe variations in the average annual trend growth rates across different groups of economies and over different periods, we estimated the trend for both DDE and DGE and also for the periods 1980-2004 and 1990s, separately. The results obtained from the estimation are (numbers below the coefficient are t ratios and * denotes significance at 1 per cent level):

$$\ln(M\&A)_t = \alpha + \beta_1 t \qquad (1)$$

Results of regression for the group of economies as Purchasers:

Period: 1987 to 2004

$$\ln(\widehat{M\&A\text{-World}}) = \underset{(49.04)}{7.3} + \underset{(6.45)^*}{.089t}, \qquad t = 1 \ldots\ldots\ldots. 18 \qquad (2)$$

$$\ln(\widehat{M\&A\text{-DDE}}) = \underset{(47.43)}{7.3} + \underset{(5.74)^*}{.082t}, \qquad t = 1 \ldots\ldots\ldots. 18 \qquad (3)$$

$$\ln(\widehat{M\&A\text{-DGE}}) = \underset{(20.16)}{4.14} + \underset{(8.78)^*}{.167t}, \qquad t = 1 \ldots\ldots\ldots. 18 \qquad (4)$$

7. Due to large fluctuations in the value of cross-border M&A deals, caused by mega deals, the average annual growth has been calculated for the number of M&A deals only.

Period: 1990 to 2000

$$\ln(\widehat{M\&A\text{-}World}) = 7.7 + .12t, \quad t = 1 \ldots\ldots\ldots.10 \qquad (2)'$$
$$(150) \quad (14.9)^{*}$$

$$\ln(\widehat{M\&A\text{-}DDE}) = 7.6 + .12t, \quad t = 1 \ldots\ldots\ldots.10 \qquad (3)'$$
$$(123.4) \quad (12.1)^{*}$$

$$\ln(\widehat{M\&A\text{-}DGE}) = 5.2 + .156t, \quad t = 1 \ldots\ldots\ldots.10 \qquad (4)'$$
$$(40.2) \quad (7.55)^{*}$$

Results of regression for the group of economies as Sellers[8]

Period: 1987 to 2004

$$\ln(\widehat{M\&A\text{-}DDE}) = 7.3 + .074t, \quad t = 1 \ldots\ldots\ldots.18 \qquad (5)$$
$$(49.14) \quad (5.4)^{*}$$

$$\ln(\widehat{M\&A\text{-}DGE}) = 4.52 + .18t, \quad t = 1 \ldots\ldots\ldots.18 \qquad (6)$$
$$(20.15) \quad (8.5)^{*}$$

Period: 1990 to 2000

$$\ln(\widehat{M\&A\text{-}DDE}) = 7.6 + .11t, \quad t = 1 \ldots\ldots\ldots.10 \qquad (5)'$$
$$(116.1) \quad (10.4)^{*}$$

$$\ln(\widehat{M\&A\text{-}DGE}) = 5.46 + .20t, \quad t = 1 \ldots\ldots\ldots.10 \qquad (6)'$$
$$(52.8) \quad (11.86)^{*}$$

8 As seller, the regression is not repeated for the world because the figures for the world are the same, whether counted as seller or purchaser. When a cross-border M&A deal takes place, it is registered as both a sale in the country of the target firm and as a purchase in the home country of the acquiring firm.

Table 4.2

Cross-border M&A Sales/Purchases by Three Groups of Economies, 1987-2004
(number of deals)

Year	DDE				DGE				TE			
	Purchase	Proportion of Total	Sale	Proportion of Total	Purchase	Proportion of Total	Sale	Proportion of Total	Purchase	Proportion of Total	Sale	Proportion of Total
1987	819	0.95	810	0.94	40	0.05	52	0.06	1	0.00	0	0.00
1988	1437	0.97	1405	0.95	40	0.03	74	0.05	1	0.00	1	0.00
1990	2368	0.95	2309	0.92	127	0.05	188	0.08	1	0.00	6	0.00
1991	2674	0.94	2586	0.91	172	0.06	253	0.09	3	0.00	15	0.01
1994	3060	0.88	2834	0.81	423	0.12	598	0.17	7	0.00	62	0.02
1996	4004	0.88	3551	0.78	529	0.12	921	0.20	22	0.00	97	0.02
1999	6341	0.91	5527	0.79	627	0.09	1304	0.19	24	0.00	163	0.02
2000	7070	0.90	6277	0.80	769	0.10	1412	0.18	42	0.01	205	0.03
2003	3778	0.83	3328	0.73	710	0.16	1045	0.23	74	0.02	189	0.04
2004	4255	0.83	3741	0.73	817	0.16	1251	0.24	41	0.01	121	0.02
Average (1987-2004)	3633	.90	3284	.83	422	.09	709.7	.15	19.78	.00	86	.02
Average (1995-2004)	4789	.88	4236	.78	620.4	.12	1077	.20	33	.01	136.4	.03
Average (2000-2004)	4867	.86	4316	.76	698.4	.13	1138	.21	49.2	.01	165.4	.03

Source: Compiled from UNCTAD (2005).

From the above regression results regarding the average annual growth in cross-border M&As for the DDE and DGE during 1987-2004 and 1990-2000, it is noted that the growth is higher for DGE countries both as purchasers as well as sellers during both the periods. The higher growth during 1990-2000 as illustrated in the Figures 4.3(a) and (b) is also largely validated from the regression results. The average annual growth in the number of deals of DGE countries is double the growth of DDE both as an acquirer as well as target countries during 1987-2004 [compare equation (3) and (4), and (5) and (6)]. The DDE's deals purchased have grown at a higher rate than deals sold during both the periods [compare equation (3) and (3)' with (5) and (5)'. On the other hand, unlike DDE, DGE's deals sold or acquired grew at a higher rate than the deals purchased [compare equation (4) and (6) with (4)' and (6)'.

Comparing the relative shares in the number of deals from the acquiring and acquired point of view, it is observed that there has been a continuous decline in the proportion of developed countries and a rise in the share of developing as well as transitional economies. From the acquiring country's point of view [Figure 4.4(a)], the share of developed economies fell from 95 per cent to 83 per cent and that of developing economies' climbed from 5 per cent to 16 per cent. The contribution of transition economies changed from 0 per cent to 1 per cent. Though these economies account for only about one per cent of the world's deals, the rise in the number of deals from 1 to 74 during 1990-2003 is appreciable. Regarding the number of cross-border M&A deals from target countries' (seller's) point of view [Figure 4.4 (b)], though the share of developed countries in total deals sold has reduced by higher margin than as an acquirer, yet more than 70 per cent of the firms targeted for M&As in the world are from the developed countries and the rest are from developing (24 per cent) and transitional economies (2 per cent) in 2004.

The difference in the relative proportion of DDE and DGE in the total deals from acquisition point of view has fallen from 90 to 67 per cent during the period 1987-2004, while from the target countries' point of view, the gap has narrowed from roughly 90 per cent to less than 50 per cent during the same period [Figure 4.4 (a) and (b)]. This is on account of the fact that from 5 per cent share of the developing countries in the total number of M&A deals purchased and sold, the proportion for the former has increased to 16 per cent and that of the latter to 24 per cent. For developed countries, the corresponding shares decreased from 95 per cent (in both purchases and sales) in 1987 to 83 per cent and 73 per cent for purchases and sales, respectively [Figure 4.5 (a) and (b)]

Figure 4.4 (a)

Shares of Three Groups of Economies in Total Number of Cross-border M&As (by purchaser)

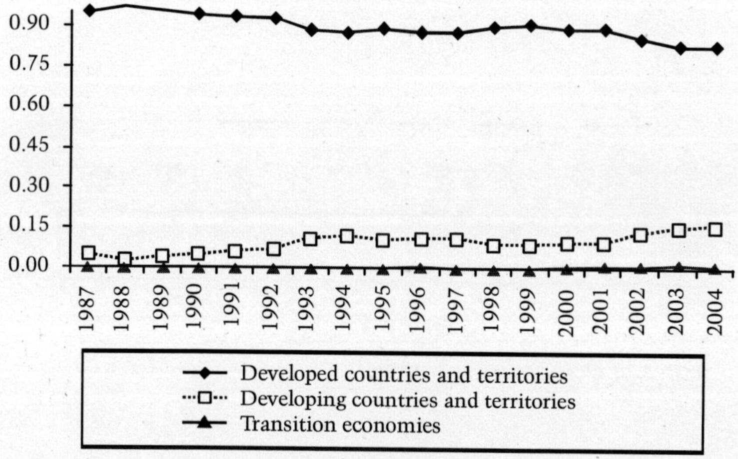

Figure 4.4 (b)

Shares of Three Groups of Economies in Total Number of Cross-border M&As (by seller)

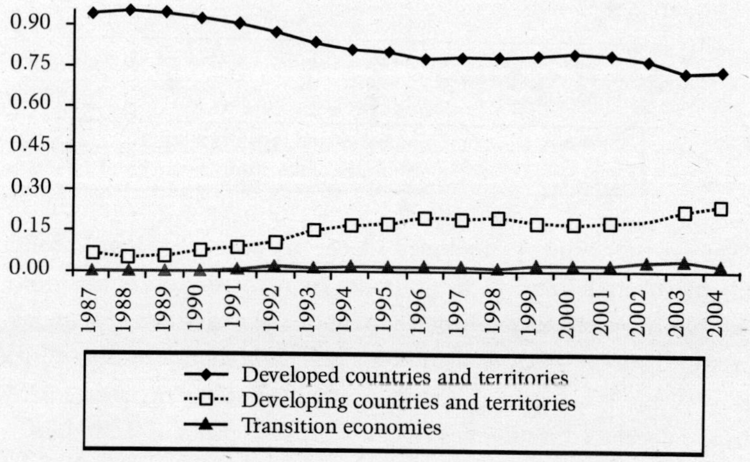

Figure 4.5 (a)

Shares of DDE in Total Number of Cross-border M&A Deals Purchased and Sold in the World

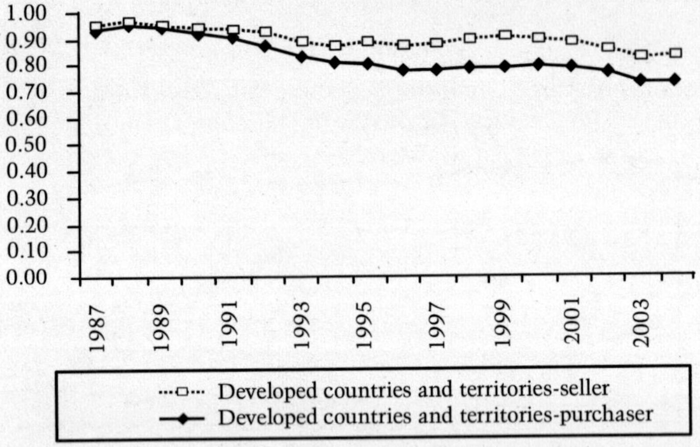

Figure 4.5 (b)

Shares of DGE in Total Number of Cross-border M&A Deals Purchased and Sold in the World

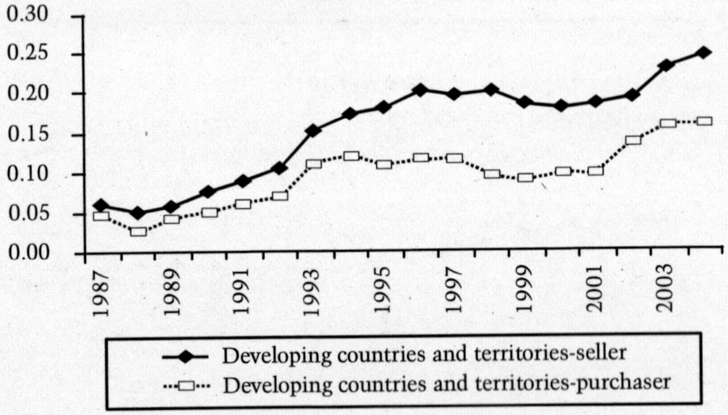

Among the countries included in the group of developed economies (DDE), the overall trend in the number of mergers and acquisitions, for Europe, North America and other developed countries is the same as that for the world's total M&A deals. But a significant change in their respective shares of these groups, in the total companies sold/purchased for M&As within the developed economies, is reflected in Figure 4.6 (a) and (b).

Figure 4.6 (a)

Shares of Europe, North America and Other Developed Economies in the Total Number of Cross-border M&As Purchased by the Group of DDE

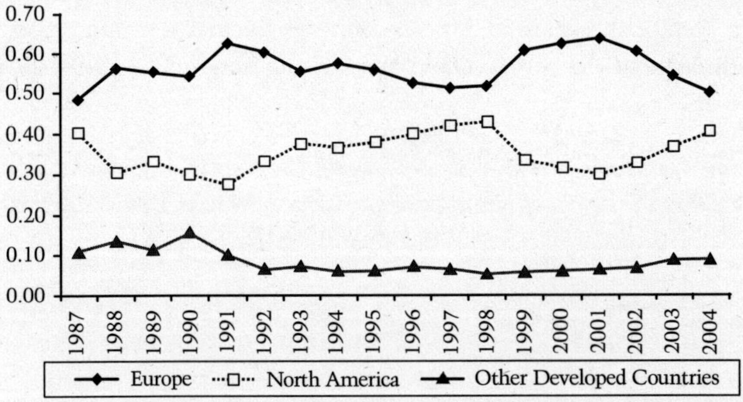

Figure 4.6 (b)

Shares of Europe, North America and Other Developed Economies in the Total Number of Cross-border M&As Sold by the Group of DDE

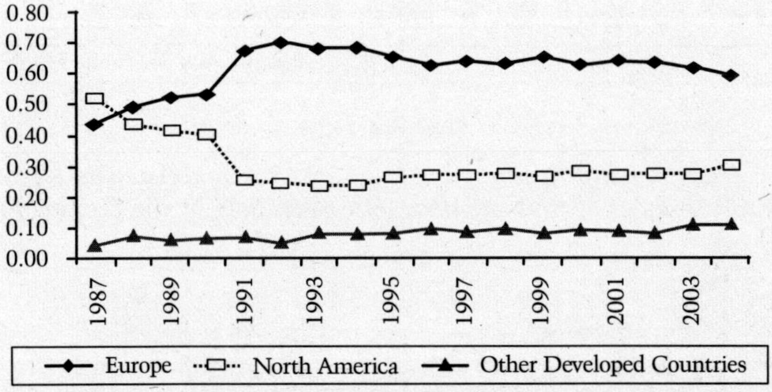

As sellers, the proportion of other developed countries reflects a continuous rising trend throughout the period under observation, with its share rising from 4 per cent in 1987 to 11 per cent in 2004. As purchasers, however, it witnessed a falling trend. From more than 50 per cent share during the late 1980s in total sales by DDE, North America's share witnessed a declining trend up to 1994 (24 per cent) and a rise thereafter, but at a very slow pace, reaching 30 per cent in 2004. A reverse pattern is observed for Europe showing a rising trend in its proportion up to 1992 (70 per cent), and a decline thereafter with 59 per cent in 2004. As acquirers also North America and Europe[9] reflect counter balancing movements with their average shares roughly at 35 and 57 per cent, respectively, in 2004.

Within the group of developing economies, as sellers, [Figure 4.7 (b)], on an average the share of African countries fluctuated around 8 to 9 per cent throughout the period. Observing a rising trend up to 1998, the share

Figure 4.7 (a)

Shares of Africa, Latin America and the Caribbean and Asia and Oceania in the Total Number of Cross-border M&A Deals Purchased by the Group of DGE

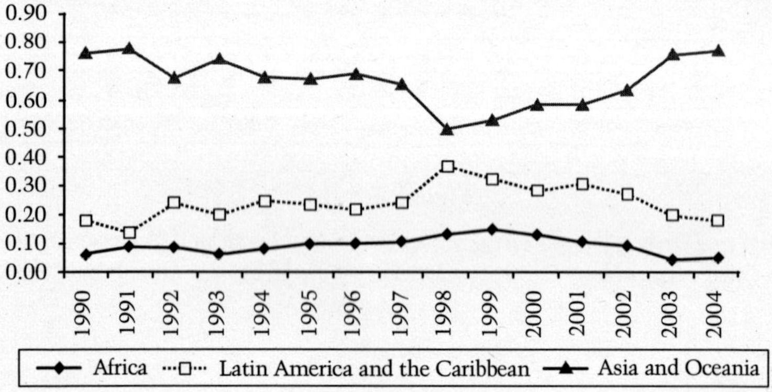

Figure 4.7 (b)

Shares of Africa, Latin America and the Caribbean and Asia and Oceania in the Total Number of Cross-border M&A Deals Sold by the Group of DGE

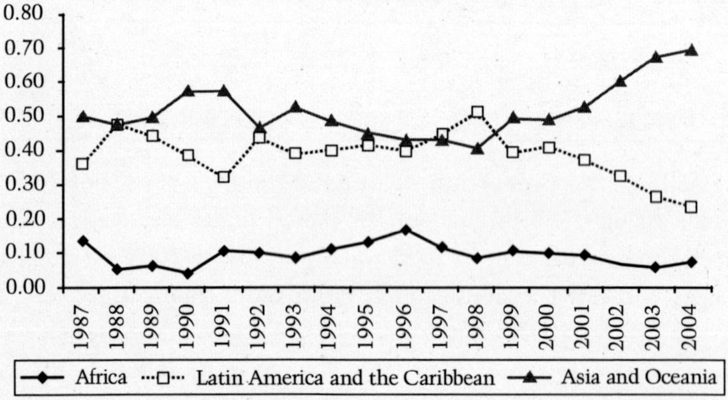

9. The main cause of Europe being the active participant in the M&A activity carried by the group of DDE is the introduction of a single currency of the European Monetary Union (EMU).

of Latin American economies targeted for M&As within DGE, grew up to 51 per cent and then registered a decline to date, with 24 per cent of share in 2004. The trend witnessed in the share of Asia and Oceania is just in the opposite direction. In 2004, 70 per cent of the targeted firms within the developing economies were from Asia and Oceania group of economies. As acquirers also [Figure 4.7 (a)], Asia and Oceania's share is far above that of the other two groups, controlling two-thirds of the total acquisitions made by DGE. Out of the remaining 33 per cent, Latin America on an average purchased 25 per cent of the acquisitions. The rising share of Asia and Oceania with Africa's share being more or less constant at around 9 per cent counterbalanced Latin America and Caribbean's decreasing proportions.

Value of Cross-border M&A Deals Purchased/Sold

On account of 90 per cent of the world's cross-border M&As' value being contributed by developed countries (Table 4.3), it is noted that the movements in the M&As value is largely controlled by the developed countries' purchases and sales [Figure 4.8 (a) and (b)].

The broad movements discernible from Figure 4.9(a) and (b), (reflecting relative shares of three groups of economies in the total value of cross-border M&A), are quite comparable to the movements in the number of deals purchased and sold [Figure 4.4 (a) and (b)]. However, the relative shares in the M&A activity when measured in value terms, exhibit greater year-to-year fluctuations than reflected in the shares measured in the total number of deals. This is essentially on account of the large-sized cross-border M&As (called mega deals—M&As worth more than US $1 billion), which despite being a small proportion of total number of deals, brought large changes in the value of transactions (Table 4.4). In the year 2000, only 2.2 per cent of mega deals worth US $866.2 billion accounted for 75.7 per cent of the total deals measured in value terms. The contribution of the remaining 97.8 per cent of deals valued at US $277.6 billion was merely 24.3 per cent in value terms. This distinctly highlights the importance of small number of mega deals having a substantial bearing on the value of deals and thus causing significant year-to-year fluctuation in the shares of the three groups of economies.

Table 4.3

Cross-border M&A Sales/Purchases by Three Groups of Economies, 1987-2004

(in billion dollars)

Year	DDE				DGE				TE			
	Purchase	Proportion of Total	Sale	Proportion of Total	Purchase	Proportion of Total	Sale	Proportion of Total	Purchase	Proportion of Total	Sale	Proportion of Total
1987	71.56	0.96	72.79	0.98	2.93	0.04	72.79	0.02	0.01	0.00	0	0.00
1988	113.39	0.98	112.75	0.98	2.20	0.02	112.75	0.02	0.00	0.00	0	0.00
1990	143.07	0.95	134.47	0.89	7.18	0.05	134.47	0.11	0.00	0.00	0.06	0.00
1991	77.45	0.96	74.39	0.92	3.26	0.04	74.39	0.07	0.00	0.00	0.54	0.01
1994	112.46	0.88	111.62	0.88	14.36	0.11	111.62	0.12	0.27	0.00	0.44	0.00
1997	271.27	0.89	234.17	0.77	33.33	0.11	234.17	0.21	0.16	0.00	6.02	0.02
2000	1088.96	0.95	1070.9	0.94	48.48	0.04	1070.9	0.06	0.39	0.00	2.40	0.00
2001	535.98	0.90	504.93	0.85	55.69	0.09	504.93	0.14	0.42	0.00	3.28	0.01
2003	256.94	0.87	244.43	0.82	31.06	0.10	244.43	0.14	8.99	0.03	12.39	0.04
2004	339.80	0.89	315.85	0.83	39.81	0.10	315.85	0.14	0.99	0.00	10.05	0.03
Average (1987-2004)	288.63	0.93	275.39	0.89	21.47	0.07	275.39	0.10	0.24	0.00	1.66	0.01
Average (1995-2004)	400.39	0.91	380.63	0.86	31.78	0.09	380.63	0.13	0.39	0.00	2.50	0.01
Average (2000-2004)	635.53	0.93	606.37	0.88	43.35	0.07	606.37	0.12	0.54	0.00	2.69	0.00

Source: Compiled from UNCTAD (2005).

Figure 4.8 (a)

Total Value of Cross-border M&As by Three Groups of Economies (by purchaser)

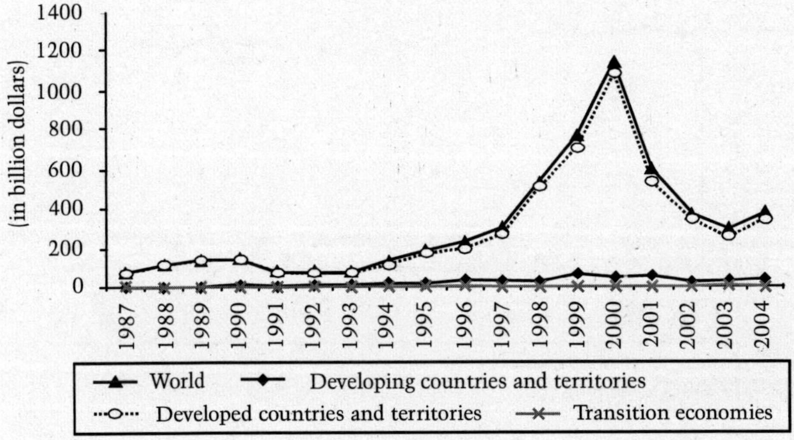

Figure 4.8 (b)

Total Value of Cross-border M&As by Three Groups of Economies (by seller)

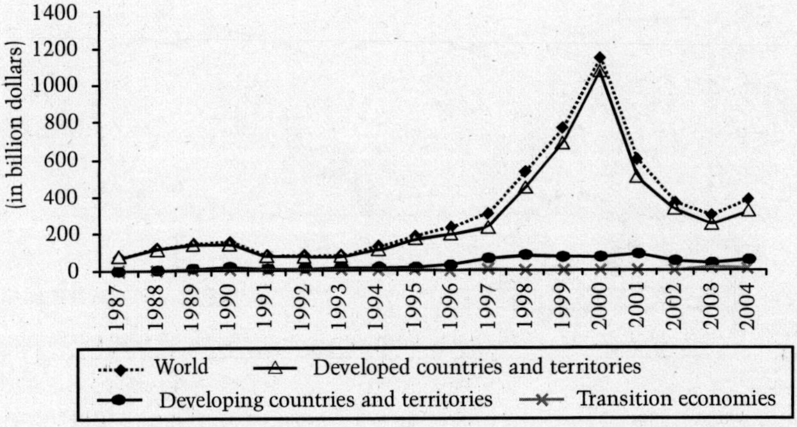

Figure 4.9 (a)

Shares of Three Groups of Economies in Total Value of Cross-border M&A (purchases)

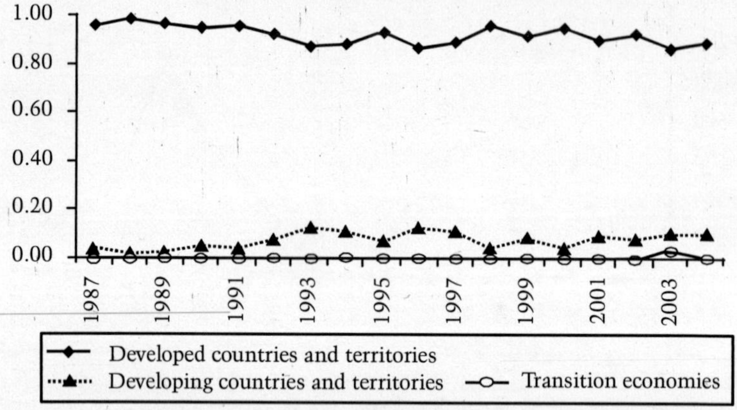

Figure 4.9 (b)

Shares of Three Groups of Economies in Total Value of Cross-border M&A (sales)

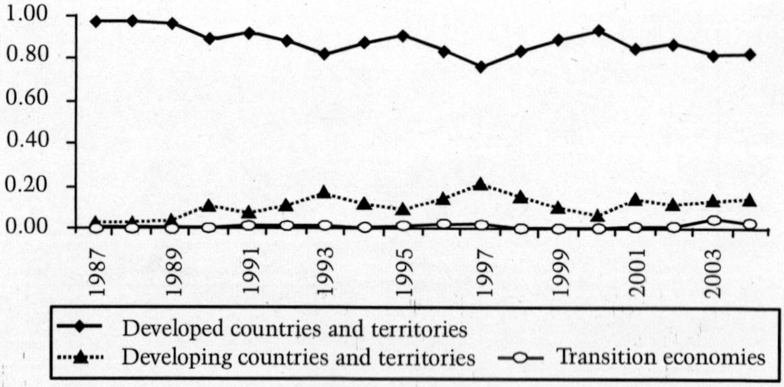

Till the late 1980s, the percentage share of developed (DDE) and developing (DGE) economies was 97 per cent and 3 per cent, respectively, in total value of cross-border M&A purchases as well as sales. As target and acquiring companies, the transition economies contributed a negligible amount in cross-border M&As. Since 1990s, the share of developed countries as target as well as acquirer reflects a declining trend; however, the decline as target country is 5 percentage points more than the decline as an acquirer country. The share of developing economies, on the other hand, witnessed a rising trend as targets as well as acquiring companies. From their share of 3 per cent as acquiring as well as target countries during 1987-1990, it climbed to 8 per cent as acquirer and 13 per cent as target during 1991 to 2004. This clearly indicates that the developing countries' firms are more often acquired than they themselves acquire firms from other countries.

Table 4.4

Cross-border M&As with Values of over $1 Billion, 1987-2003

Year	*Number of Deals*	*Percentage of Total*	*Value ($billion)*	*Percentage of Total*
1987	14	1.6	30.0	40.3
1988	22	1.5	49.6	42.9
1989	26	1.2	59.5	42.4
1990	33	1.3	60.9	40.4
1991	7	0.2	20.4	25.2
1992	10	0.4	21.3	26.8
1993	14	0.5	23.5	28.3
1994	24	0.7	50.9	40.1
1995	36	0.8	80.4	43.1
1996	43	0.9	94.0	41.4
1997	64	1.3	129.2	42.4
1998	86	1.5	329.7	62
1999	114	1.6	522.0	68.1
2000	175	2.2	866.2	75.7
2001	113	1.9	378.1	63.7
2002	81	1.8	213.9	57.8
2003	56	1.2	141.1	47.5

Source: UNCTAD (2004).

With virtually no participation in cross-border M&As till the late 1990s, the transition economies, on an average have accounted for 2 per cent of the total sales and 1 per cent of total purchases, for the past four to five years. In the year 2003, these economies contributed 3 per cent of total purchase value and 4 per cent of total sales value of cross-border M&As. The narrowing of the gap between the relative proportions of DDE and DGE in total sales value of M&As [Figure 4.9 (b)] is also noticeable from the number of deals sold [Figure 4.4 (b)].

Viewing the participation of DDE and DGE as sellers and purchasers in cross-border M&A activity measured in value terms [Figure 4.10 (a) and (b)], and comparing it to the number of deals [Figure 4.5 (a) and (b)], three basic differences can be highlighted. First, as compared to the number of deals, the average shares maintained by the group of DDE, both as seller and purchaser, in value terms are higher (Tables 4.2 and 4.3). The key reason being that the bulk of the mega deals (referred in Table 4.4) were undertaken by firms from

Figure 4.10 (a)

Shares of DDE in Total Value of Cross-border M&A Deals Purchased and Sold in the World

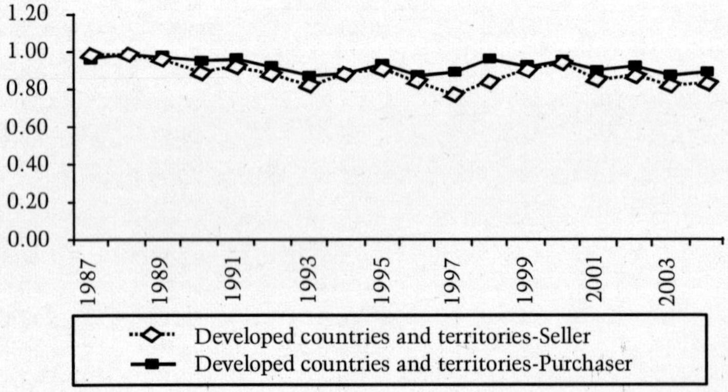

Figure 4.10 (b)

Shares of DGE in Total Value of Cross-border M&A Deals Purchased and Sold in the World

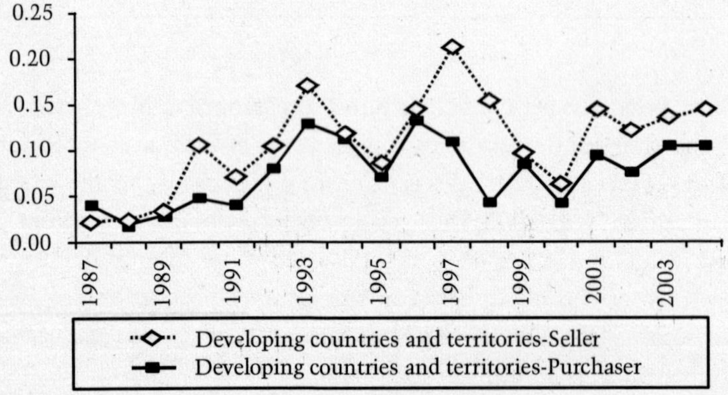

the developed world that influenced the value of deals more than the number of deals. Second, for both the groups of economies, the difference between the relative shares as targets and acquirer are greater, when measured in value terms. Third, the relative shares as sellers as well as purchasers, measured in value terms, exhibit greater fluctuations for DDE than DGE. This again implies that any change in the number of mega deals (despite being a very small percentage of total number of M&As) had a large impact on the value of deals and thereby affected the proportions held by respective countries in the total value of world's M&A deals.

From the subsequent sub-division of DDE, it is noticed that on an average, Europe roughly contributed 60 per cent of (55 per cent of the world's) cross-border M&A purchases and the rest was accounted for by North America and other developed countries in a 3:1 ratio during 1987-2004. In 2000, when the cross-border M&As reached their peak level, Europe's share was as high as 78 per cent within the group of DDE (75 per cent in the World's M&As). From an average of 15 per cent during 1987 to 1992, the share of other developed countries has declined at an average of 6 per cent during the previous decade. The year-wise data reflect wide fluctuations in the relative share of Europe, which is counterbalanced by North America [Figure 4.11 (a)]. Since 2000, on account of sharp fall in the value of M&A purchases by Europe, its share is continuously falling and that of North America is rising. During 2003-04 the share of Europe, North America and other developed countries is 51, 40, and 9 per cent, respectively.

As destinations of cross-border M&A, though, on an average Europe's share is lower as a target (50 per cent) region than as an acquirer (60 per cent), the gap in its relative contribution as a seller and as a purchaser, is declining over time [Figure 4.11(a) and (b)]. In contrast, the North American firms are more in demand as targets than as acquirers; however, their share as targets is slowly declining, as is evident from Figure 4.11 (b).

As acquirers, the relative contributions of Europe, North America and other developed countries are roughly the same in the number of deals and in value of M&As held by DDE [Compare Figures 4.6(a) and 4.11(a)]. A notable divergence is found, however, when the relative shares of the three groups especially, North America are compared in value and number of deals of M&A, as a target region. On an average, during 1991-2004, its share in value terms (38 per cent) was higher by 10 percentage points than its share in number of deals (28 per cent). The difference is balanced by the Europe and other developed countries that are involved in higher proportionate deals. This points to North America involving itself in smaller deals but of higher value, while an opposite trend is observed for Europe and Other Developed Countries.

Figure 4.11 (a)

Shares of Europe, North America and Other Developed Countries in the Total Value of Cross-border M&As Purchased by the DDE

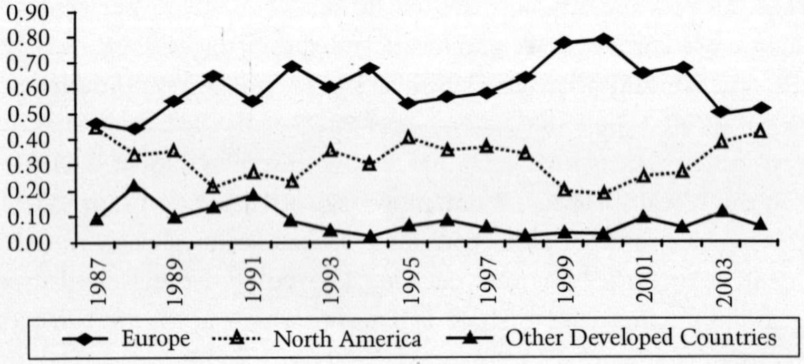

Figure 4.11 (b)

Shares of Europe, North America and Other Developed Countries in the Total Value of Cross-border M&As Sold by the DDE

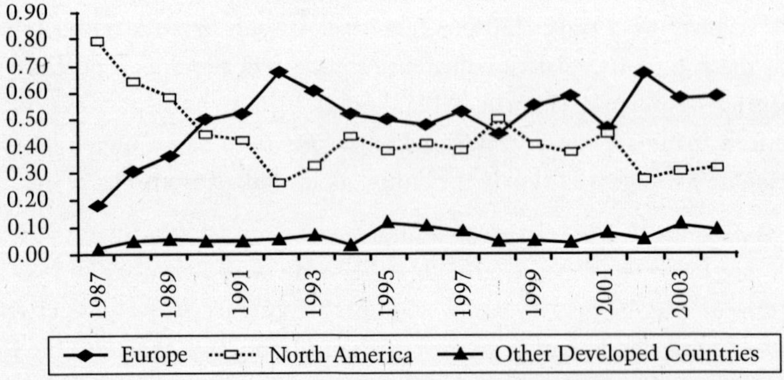

As regards the group of DGE [Figure 4.12 (a) and (b)], the respective shares of Asia, Africa and Latin American groups of economies have witnessed wide fluctuations in both purchases and sales of M&As. From a huge share of 80 per cent in the purchases of cross-border M&As by DGE, Asia and Oceania showed a declining trend till the end of 1990s. With an average of 55 per cent during 1990-1999, the share came down to as low as 20 per cent in 1999. Since 2000, a rising trend is again witnessed. After

Figure 4.12 (a)

Shares of Africa, Latin America and the Caribbean and Asia and Oceania in the Total Value of Cross-border M&As Purchased by the Group of DGE

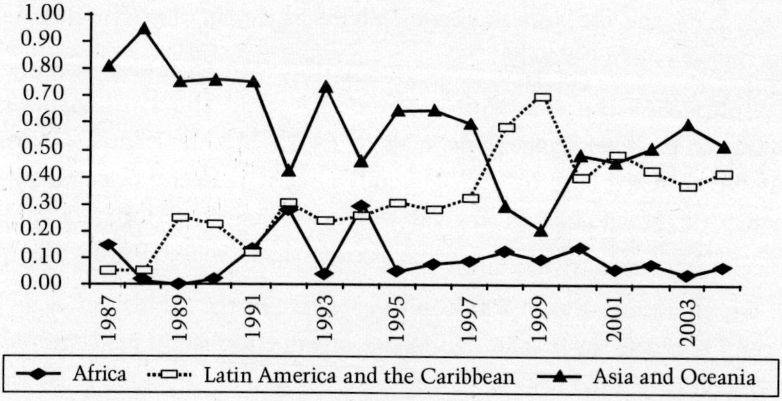

Figure 4.12 (b)

Shares of Africa, Latin America and the Caribbean and Asia and Oceania in the Total Value of Cross-border M&As Sold by the Group of DGE

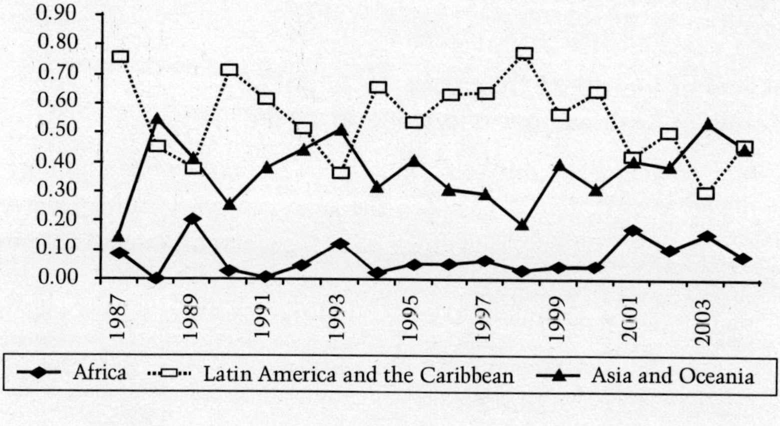

observing a rising trend up to 1994, with average of 11 per cent during 1987 to 1994, the average share of Africa reduced to 8 per cent during 1995-2004. In sharp contrast to Asia and Oceania, Latin America and the Caribbean depicted a rising trend in their shares up to 1999 and a decline thereafter. With a nominal share of 5 per cent in 1987 among the DGE, Latin America's share climbed to 71 per cent in 1999. Since then, these countries have witnessed a declining trend with average share of approximately 42 per cent. As targets of cross-border M&As, Latin America and the Caribbean maintain a higher share (55 per cent during 1995-2004). However, since the late 1990s their share as targets also witnessed a declining trend, reaching a level of 30 per cent in 2003. On an average, though Asia and Oceania countries' share as destinations for M&As is lower, but it is rising slowly.

Comparing the shares of Asia and Oceania and Latin American countries in the total acquisitions made by DGE's M&As, [Figures 4.7(a) and 4.12(a)] considered both in numbers and value, it is clearly perceptible that although the broad changes in their respective shares overtime are similar, there are significant differences in the average shares maintained by them.

On an average the African countries' share in the number of deals (65 per cent) is much larger than their share in value terms (50 per cent), while for Latin America the respective shares are 25 and 37 per cent. This makes palpable that amongst the group of DGE, in contrast to Latin American countries, the Asian economies are purchasing higher number of deals, however, of smaller values.

4.3 Ranking Patterns

Rankings of Individual Countries as Targets (in terms of both number and value of deals)

From individual country's point of view, in terms of the number of cross-border M&As, the US has been the largest targeted country followed by UK, throughout the period from 1987[10] to 2004, (Table 4.5). From

10. Up to 1980s, cross-border M&As were almost exclusively monopolised by US's MNCs. Since 1990s, European Union's MNCs have become principal participants of M&A activity. During 2001-2003, they accounted for 61 per cent of all M&A purchases worldwide (UNCTAD, 2004).

Table 4.5

Ranking of Countries in Cross-border M&As by Country of Seller during Selected Years

Country	1987	Country	1990	Country	1994	Country	1998	Country	2000	Country	2003	Country	2004
Ranking according to the Share (in proportion) of Countries in Total Number of Cross-border M&A Sales													
US	0.43	US	0.31	US	0.15	US	0.17	US	0.18	US	0.16	US	0.16
UK	0.16	UK	0.16	UK	0.11	UK	0.13	UK	0.11	UK	0.10	UK	0.09
France	0.08	Germany	0.07	Germany	0.09	Germany	0.07	Germany	0.06	Germany	0.06	Germany	0.07
Canada	0.06	Canada	0.06	France	0.08	France	0.06	France	0.05	China	0.05	Canada	0.06
Germany	0.05	France	0.06	Canada	0.05	Australia	0.05	Canada	0.05	France	0.05	France	0.05
Spain	0.03	Spain	0.04	Australia	0.04	Canada	0.05	Australia	0.04	Canada	0.04	China	0.04
										India (14)	0.02	India (17)	0.02
Ranking according to the Share (in proportion) of Countries in Total Value of Cross-border M&A Sales													
US	0.69	US	0.36	US	0.35	US	0.39	US	0.28	US	0.23	US	0.22
Canada	0.08	UK	0.19	France	0.13	UK	0.17	Germany	0.22	UK	0.11	UK	0.15
UK	0.07	France	0.05	UK	0.09	Brazil	0.06	UK	0.16	Germany	0.08	Germany	0.09
Australia	0.02	Argentina	0.04	Italy	0.05	Netherlands	0.04	Canada	0.07	France	0.06	France	0.05
France	0.02	Germany	0.04	Sweden	0.05	Germany	0.04	France	0.03	Italy	0.05	Canada	0.05
Bermuda	0.01	Canada	0.04	Germany	0.04	France	0.03	Netherlands	0.03	Japan	0.04	Australia	0.04
				Canada	0.03	Canada	0.03	Brazil	0.02	China (18)	0.01	China (12)	0.02
										India (37)	0.00	India (27)	0.01

Note: The countries' names are written in the order of ranking, wherever the order of ranking changes, figures in the bracket give the respective ranks. Rankings of individual countries as acquirers (in terms of both number and value of deals).

Source: Compiled from UNCTAD (2005).

greater than 30 per cent share till late 1980s, US's share has ranged between 16 to 18 per cent for more than a decade. UK, on the other hand, has maintained an average share of 10 to 11 per cent since 1994. For the 3rd, 4th and 5th positions Germany, Canada and France were the main competitors till 2002. A noticeable change since 2003 is that a few of the Asian countries are emerging as important destinations for cross-border M&A. In 2003, China emerged as a leading location and took the 4th position in the world (first among the developing economies) with 5 per cent of the total number of deals targeted. In 2004, China and Australia ranked 6th and 7th, respectively, each with roughly 4 per cent of the world's deals. Hong Kong (China) stood at the 8th position with 3 per cent of the total deals. Although India's position in the world's total number of deals as a target country is low, its rank has been improving over time. From the 19th place in 2001, it has moved up to the 17th in 2004, with its share doubling from 1 per cent to 2 per cent during the same period.

In terms of value of cross-border M&A deals (Table 4.5), the ranking pattern largely remains the same for developed countries. However, average shares maintained by the US and UK, are more than their shares in the number of deals, signifying that developed countries are involving into lesser number of bigger deals. So far as the Asian countries are concerned, they seem to have suffered a sharp deterioration in their positions, in terms of both ranking and percentage holding, when comparisons are made relative to the total value of world's cross-border M&As. China's ranking in the world fell from 4th in number of deals to 18th in value terms in 2003. Further, its holdings went down from 5 per cent in total deals to only 1 per cent in value terms in the same year. Similarly moving from number to value terms, India's position fell from 14th to 37th with its share falling from 0.2 to 0 per cent, over the same period. This clearly confirms our earlier finding that, although Asian economies (for that matter developing economies) are attracting a good number of world's deals, they are of smaller value.

In terms of contributions made by individual countries in the world's purchases (Table 4.6) of cross-border M&A deals (measured both in number and value terms), US and UK ranked at the 1st and 2nd positions, respectively, almost throughout the period from 1987 to 2004. On an average in value terms, US purchased 23 per cent and UK 19 per cent of the world's deals during 1991-2004.

In 1987, US topped the list by contributing 40 per cent of the world's acquisitions in value terms followed by UK (26 per cent), Canada (5 per cent), Italy (4 per cent) and France (4 per cent). In 1990 also, US topped the list; *albeit* its share reduced to 18 per cent followed by UK's 17 per cent, France's 14 per cent, Japan's 9 per cent and Sweden's 8 per cent. Similarly, in other years also wide fluctuations have been witnessed in the respective shares of many countries. In 1999, UK replaced US at the 1st position, contributing 28 per cent of the total value of M&A, followed by US with only 16 per cent. In 2000, when the activity was at its peak, US took 3rd position, with only 14 per cent of the total M&As, followed by Germany and the Netherlands, each with 5 per cent share. The scenario remained the same till 2001. In 2004, US again became the largest acquirer with roughly 30 per cent of its shares followed by UK (12 per cent), Canada (9 per cent) and Spain (9 per cent). As regards the average shares in the number of deals purchased, the respective shares of US and UK during 1991-2004 were 25 and 14 per cent. The fall in UK's average share suggests that it is acquiring lower proportion of total number of deals, which are bigger in value.

Among the Asian countries, Singapore has emerged to be the largest acquirer, holding 3 per cent of the total number of acquisitions since 2002. China and India, however, are placed at lower positions. In 2003, their respective positions were 16th and 20th in number of deals, while in value terms, they were at 24th and 25th ranks, respectively. As sellers also, Asian countries are holding lower positions in value terms. In 2003, for example, China, 4th in number of deals of M&A, stood 18th when measured in value term (Table 4.5). Similarly, in 2004 from 6th in number of deals, it stood at 12th position in value terms. The ranking going down in value terms again confirms the earlier conclusion that these countries are acquiring greater proportion of total number of deals that are smaller in value. The Asian countries holding high positions as sellers (targets) and low as purchasers (acquirers) also corroborates our earlier finding that these economies have more often been acquired than they themselves have gone for acquisitions.

Table 4.6

Ranking of Countries in Cross-border M&As by Country of Purchaser during Selected Years

Country	1987	Country	1990	Country	1994	Country	1998	Country	2000	Country	2003	Country	2004
Ranking according to the Share (in proportion) of Countries in the Total Number of Cross-border M&A Purchases													
US	0.32	US	0.23	US	0.26	US	0.32	US	0.23	US	0.23	US	0.25
UK	0.23	UK	0.20	UK	0.14	UK	0.13	UK	0.12	UK	0.12	UK	0.12
Canada	0.07	Japan	0.11	Germany	0.09	Canada	0.07	Germany	0.09	Canada	0.07	Canada	0.08
Australia	0.05	France	0.08	Canada	0.06	Germany	0.06	France	0.07	Germany	0.06	Germany	0.05
Japan	0.04	Germany	0.06	France	0.05	France	0.05	Canada	0.05	France	0.04	France	0.04
France	0.04	Canada	0.05	Netherlands	0.04	Netherlands	0.05	Netherlands	0.04	Singapore(9)	0.03	Singapore(7)	0.03
Netherlands	0.04	Netherlands	0.04	Australia	0.03	Spain	0.03	Sweden	0.03	Hong Kong, China (10)	0.02	Hong Kong, China (10)	0.03
										China (16)	0.02	India (19)	0.01
										India (20)	0.01	China (22)	0.01
Ranking according to the Share (in proportion) of Countries in the Total Value of Cross-border M&A Purchases													
US	0.38	US	0.18	US	0.22	US	0.26	UK	0.33	US	0.28	US	0.29
UK	0.26	UK	0.17	UK	0.21	UK	0.18	France	0.15	UK	0.19	UK	0.12
Canada	0.05	France	0.14	Switzerland	0.09	Germany	0.13	US	0.14	Germany	0.07	Canada	0.09
Italy	0.04	Japan	0.09	Netherlands	0.07	Switzerland	0.07	Germany	0.05	Canada	0.05	Spain	0.09
France	0.04	Sweden	0.08	Germany	0.06	Canada	0.07	Netherlands	0.05	Australia	0.05	Germany	0.05
Japan	0.04	Germany	0.05	France	0.05	France	0.06	Switzerland	0.04	France	0.03	France	0.04
										China (24)	0.006	China (30)	0.003
										India (25)	0.005	India (32)	0.002

Note: The countries names are written in the order of ranking, wherever the order of ranking changes, figures in the bracket give the respective ranks.

Source: Compiled from UNCTAD (2005).

4.4 Sector-wise Distribution of Cross-border M&A Deals

With regard to the distribution of M&A deals among three main economic sectors, viz., primary, manufacturing and tertiary, it is observed that in line with the total activity, M&A deals increased in each sector up to 2000 and observed a declining trend thereafter [Figure 4.13 (a) and (b)]. A major part of the rise in the activity is contributed by the tertiary sector. As compared to 1990, the total value of activity scaled up by four times in

Figure 4.13 (a)

Cross-border M&As by Sector of Purchaser (in billion dollars)

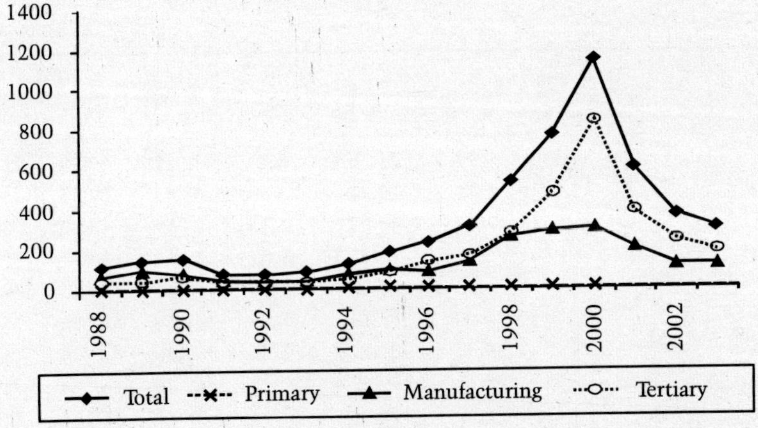

Figure 4.13 (b)

Cross-border M&As by Sector of Seller (in billion dollars)

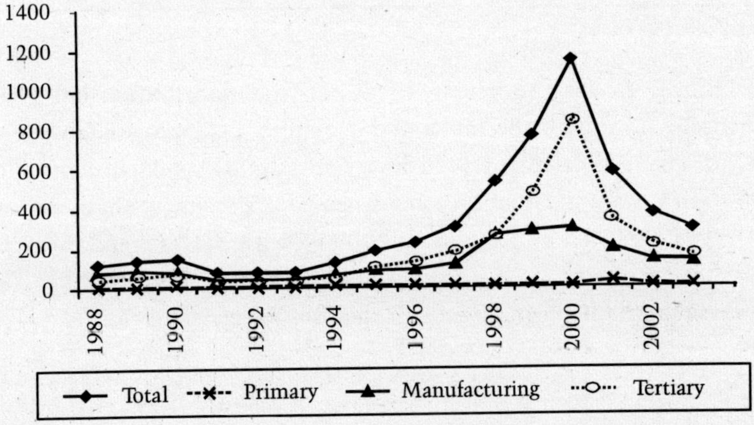

both the primary and manufacturing sector, while the tertiary sector witnessed an increase of 12 times in 2000. Out of the total M&A deals made (purchased/sold) in 2000, 73 per cent pertained to tertiary sector, 26 per cent to manufacturing and the remaining less than 1 per cent to the primary sector in 2000 [Tables 4.7 (a) and (b)]. On account of intangible nature of assets held by service industry, M&As rather than greenfield projects[11] have been extensively used as an important tool by MNCs to enter into industries, such as banking, telecommunication and water.

Table 4.7 (a)

Cross-border M&As by Sector of Purchaser/Seller, 1988-2003

(in billion dollars)

Year	*Primary*		*Manufacturing*		*Tertiary*		*Total*
	Purchase	*Sale*	*Purchase*	*Sale*	*Purchase*	*Sale*	
1988	4.40	3.91	71.75	73.73	39.22	37.99	115.63
1990	2.13	5.17	79.91	75.50	68.43	69.91	150.58
1991	1.56	1.17	44.99	36.18	33.99	43.30	80.65
1994	5.03	5.52	72.55	69.32	49.52	52.27	127.11
1997	7.15	8.73	133.20	121.38	164.46	174.74	304.85
1999	7.40	10.00	287.13	288.09	471.50	467.85	766.04
2000	8.97	9.82	302.51	291.65	832.30	842.34	1143.82
2001	6.54	28.28	199.89	197.18	387.43	347.46	572.92
2002	9.31	12.75	115.46	137.41	243.77	219.62	369.79
2003	4.23	7.71	112.76	129.71	180.00	159.56	296.99
Average (1988-2003)	5.37	8.12	126.70	127.02	192.60	188.35	324.84
Average (1994-2003)	6.77	10.98	166.33	167.09	281.47	274.56	454.78
Average (2000-2003)	7.26	14.64	182.65	188.99	410.88	392.25	601.14

Source: UNCTAD (2005).

During the last 15 years, the sector-wise distribution has changed immensely, from both the target and acquirer's perspective [Table 4.7 (b)]. The primary sector maintained its average share at 2 per cent till late 1990s, with a few fluctuations. It witnessed a rise in its share during the mid-1990s, followed by a decline till 2000 [Figure 4.14 (a) and (b)]. Of late, the sector again witnessed a rise during 2000-2002. The other two sectors reflected just the opposing trends in their respective shares.

11. The greenfield projects are more common in 'goods industries' in which technological skills and production technology are key than in 'service industry'.

Table 4.7 (b)

Percentage Share of Each Sector in Cross-border M&As, Purchases/Sales

	% of the Total Purchases			% of the Total Sales		
Year	Primary	Manufacturing	Tertiary	Primary	Manufacturing	Tertiary
1988	3.80	62.05	33.92	3.38	63.76	32.85
1990	1.42	53.07	45.44	3.43	50.14	46.43
1991	1.93	55.73	42.11	1.44	44.82	53.64
1994	3.96	57.08	38.96	4.34	54.54	41.12
1995	4.26	50.26	45.46	4.55	45.27	50.18
1998	1.03	48.38	50.50	1.99	49.51	48.50
1999	0.97	37.48	61.55	1.31	37.61	61.07
2000	0.78	26.45	72.77	0.86	25.50	73.64
2001	1.10	33.65	65.23	4.94	34.42	60.65
2002	2.52	31.22	65.92	3.45	37.16	59.39
2003	1.42	37.97	60.61	2.60	43.68	53.73
Average (1988-2003)	2.43	45.80	51.69	3.10	45.97	50.90
Average (1994-2003)	2.09	40.53	57.33	3.04	40.65	56.30
Average (2000-2003)	1.46	32.32	66.13	2.96	35.19	61.85

Source: Compiled from UNCTAD (2005).

Further, the composition of M&A has drastically shifted in favour of tertiary (services) sector. From one-third of the total M&A activity during the late 1980s, tertiary sector involved 55 per cent during the mid-1990s and by 2000 its share climbed to roughly 65 per cent. The change in the share of tertiary sector is wholly counterbalanced by manufacturing sector that witnessed a declining trend as clearly illustrated in Figure 4.14 (a) and (b). The shift towards services is a worldwide phenomenon. The trends in the Indian M&As (reviewed in the next chapter) also indicate a clear move towards this sector. The most important reason behind this change is the worldwide liberalisation of services.

To sum, an insignificant difference is found in the M&A purchases and sales made in the primary sector. On the other hand, share of tertiary sector is reflecting a rising trend, counterbalanced by a falling share of manufacturing sector in both the M&A sales and purchases. However, since the beginning of 2000, opposing movements are witnessed in the respective shares of both the tertiary and manufacturing sectors in M&A purchases and sales.

Figure 4.14 (a)

Shares of Three Sectors in the Total Cross-border M&A Purchases

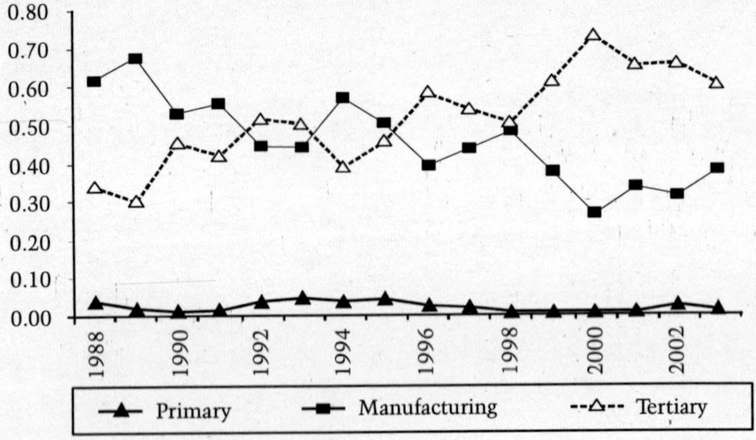

Figure 4.14 (b)

Shares of Three Sectors in the Total Cross-border M&A Sales

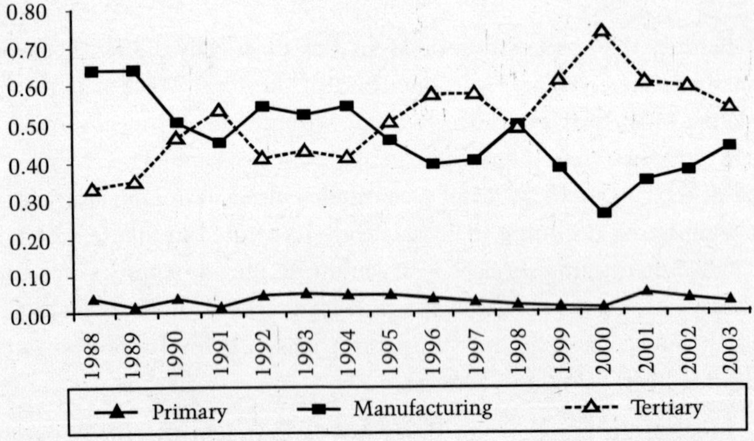

With reference to the industry-wise distribution of M&As, again trends are broadly the same from destination as well as acquirer's point of view. Regarding primary sector, more than four-fifths of deals are from 'mining, quarrying and petroleum', while agriculture, hunting, forestry, and fishing have a share of less than 20 per cent. In the year 2002, 99.6 per cent of M&A purchased from primary sector pertained to the former industry. Within the manufacturing sector, the four industries namely, food, beverages and tobacco; coke, petroleum and nuclear fuel; chemicals and chemical products; and electrical and electronic equipment are the key pullers of M&As. On an average, more than two-thirds of the M&A deals from this sector are concentrated in these four industries. Industries such as textiles, clothing and leather; wood and wood products; rubber and plastic products and non-metallic mineral products have taken a back seat, attracting less than 8 per cent of deals carried out by the manufacturing sector.

In the tertiary sector, finance has been the leading industry since 1990s, attracting roughly one-third of the total deals of tertiary sector. Transport, storage and communication; business services; electricity, gas, and water; and public administration and defence are the other key industries that all account for more than 40 per cent of the tertiary sector deals.

4.5 Determinants of Cross-border Mergers and Acquisitions

Recognising the importance of cross-border M&As for the firms' competitiveness and for the economy as a whole, it is imperative to throw some light on the driving force behind this phenomenon. Several factors, such as geographic proximity, market size and growth of market, level of development, openness, bilateral trade, exchange rate or institutional variables are considered important in determining the cross-border M&As. However, in this section, we examine the roles of openness and quality of institutions in any country in determining the magnitude of cross-border M&As during 2000-2004.

Cross-border M&As and Openness Index

With regard to FDIs, a major part takes place in the form of international M&As.[12] Consequently, the effect of trade restrictions is

12 Cross-border M&As constituted more than 80 per cent of the world total—some $1 trillion FDI in 2000 alone (UNCTAD, 2004).

ambiguous. In identifying the factors that affect FDI, Aminian *et al.* (2005) suggest that distinction must be made between two types of FDI: market-seeking (horizontal in nature) and non-market seeking (vertical in nature). In the case of the former, production and sales take place in the host country, while in the latter, goods are produced in the host country and exported outside.[13] Accordingly, the effect on trade volumes differs. Further, in the theoretical literature also, it is established that for vertical FDIs, trade and investment complement each other i.e., move in the same direction, while they are substitutes of each other and move in the opposite direction for horizontal FDIs (e.g. Carr *et al.*, 2001).

The kind of FDIs received by a country therefore, depends on the restrictions imposed by it. It has been witnessed that restricted economies[14] receive more of horizontal FDIs whereas open economies get engaged in more of vertical investments. This makes the effect of openness on total FDI uncertain, as it is determined by the relative strength of the two effects (Aminian *et al.*, 2005). On account of this, it is essential that conclusions should be drawn by distinguishing two types of investments.

Theoretically, the relationship between resources obtained through cross-border M&As (or FDIs) and openness i.e., percentage of goods traded, can be explained in terms of the Rybczynski Theorem.

The theorem state: if a country experiences an increase in its endowment of any one factor, holding all other things constant (including factor and product prices), the output of the good that uses the factor intensively will rise, and the output of the other good will fall. Further, if the good using the increased factor more intensively is import-competing and the other being the exportable good, the theorem directly implies a fall in trade volumes, on account of fall in both imports and exports of the country.[15] This signifies that trade and resources are substitutes of each other, in this case. Using production possibility curve and indifference curves, this can also be explained through Figure 4.15.

---

13. The vertical investments are called export-substituting investments and horizontal investments are called factor-seeking investments.
14. The argument stems from the tariff-jumping hypothesis i.e., source countries shun tariffs by producing and selling in the host country.
15. It is based on the assumption that both importable and exportable goods are normal goods.

Assuming an economy, with good X to be an import-replacing and Y to be an exportable good, whose production or supply (given by tangency of production possibility curve (PPC) and world price ratio) and consumption or demand (given by tangency of indifference curve and world price ratio) patterns are shown by points A and B, respectively. Here, country imports ab (ob – oa) of good X and exports cd (oc – od) of good Y. Considering a rise in the resource used more intensively in good X, PPC shifts rightward i.e., biased in favour of its production. The new supply and demand positions change to A' and B', respectively. In this new situation, on account of higher production of import-replacing good X (by aa') and lower production of other good (by cc'), the amount of imports and exports fall to a'b' (ob'– oa') and c'd' (oc'– od') respectively.[16] In other words, trade volumes of a country fall (from (ab + cd) to (a'b' + c'd') as it experiences a rise in its resources, used more intensively in its importable good.

Figure 4.15

Graphical Representation of Rybczynski Theorem

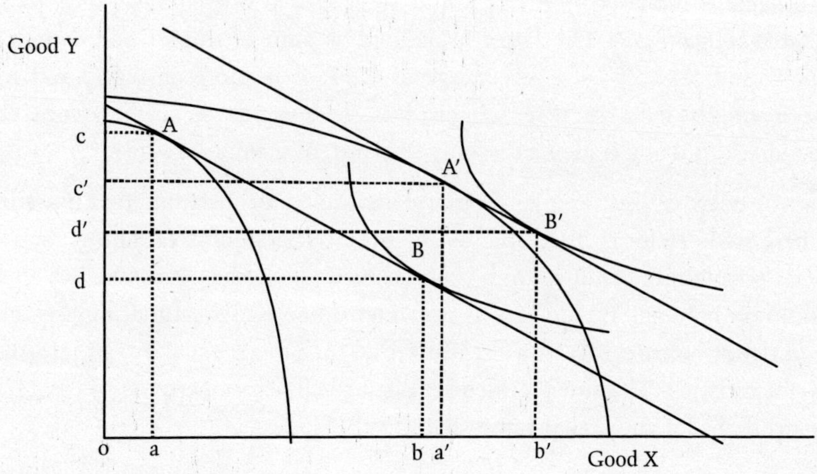

Source: Based on Kindleberger (1996).

---

16. On the other hand, if the growth in factors used intensively in the production of exportable goods takes place, it will promote world trade through both exports and imports; consequently, trade and investment will be positively related to each other.

Methodology and Variables

To carry out this analysis, in accordance with the availability of data, regressions were run on cross-country data. The relationship posited is specified below:

CBMA = f (openness index,[17] Institutional index and income dummy variable);

where CBMA is average of the sum of total sales and purchases undertaken by any country during 2000-2004. It has been measured both in number as well as value of deals sold and purchased.

Openness index: The role of openness of an economy is well researched with respect to economic growth, (Rodriguez and Rodrik, 2000; Rodrick *et al.*, 2004), Poverty reduction and inequality (Gaiha and Imai, 2005 and Gaiha *et al.*, 2005) and FDIs (Aminian *et al.*, 2005). There are two alternative measures of openness available, *viz.*, Sachs-Warner index and the other is based on the ratio of trade-to-GDP. The former defines all countries in only two categories and is available in zero-one dummy, taking the value 0 if the economy is found to be closed on the basis of 5 trade-related indicators.[18] The latter is defined as sum of import and export of goods and services as a percentage of GDP. It is more objective and has been widely used in research studies.[19] However, it suffers from the drawback of using trade as the only measure of openness.

In view of this, Frankel-Romer constructed an instrumented measure, where trade share is instrumented by other geographical variables, such as area, population, distance from each other, and whether the countries share common borders. Trade share is first instrumented by estimating a gravity equation, where bilateral trade flows are regressed on geographic characteristics. The fitted values are aggregated across partners to create an instrument for the actual trade share.[20]

---

17. For a detailed review of existing openness measures, see Yanikkaya (2003).
18. These include: (i) tariff rates exceeding 40 per cent, (ii) non-tariff barriers covering more than 40 per cent of imports, (iii) socialist economic system, (iv) state monopoly of major exports, and (v) black market premium exceeding 20 per cent during 1970s or 1980s. For details, see Vu (2004).
19. For details, see Vu (2004).
20. For details, see Frankel and Romer (1999).

For the purpose of our study, we have used Frankel-Romer openness index, which is based on geographically constructed trade shares, and another estimated measure, instrumented on the basis of institutional quality index of a country and regional dummies.

Institutional quality index: To highlight the quality of institutional and legal infrastructure, we have used seven governance indicators[21] (see Box 4.1 for their detailed description), *viz*., regulatory quality (RQ), rule of law (RoL), control of corruption (CoC), voice and accountability (VA), political stability (PS), government effectiveness (GE), and an aggregate index (Agg.I) calculated as the average of the six measures. The scores of each of the six indicators during 2000-2004, are calculated as averages of the scores in 2002 and 2004. All these estimates are normally distributed with zero mean and standard deviation of one, implying all scores range from -2.5 to +2.5, with higher scores corresponding to better outcomes.

Following World Bank's classification, the data are classified on the basis of both region and income of the country. Accordingly, dummies (given in brackets) were used for both income and regional classification using 'low income countries' for the former and 'other developed countries' for the latter, as the reference or benchmark countries.

The four income classifications are:

1. Low income countries,
2. Lower middle income countries (D_1),
3. Upper middle income countries (D_2), and
4. High income countries (D_3).

As far as regional classification is concerned, all the countries included in the sample are divided into five regions, namely:

1. Africa (R_1),
2. Asia and Oceania (R_2),
3. Europe (R_3),
4. Latin America and the Caribbean (R_4), and
5. Other developed countries.

21. These governance indicators, available for 209 countries from 1996-2004, are based on 350 variables obtained from several institutions worldwide. The six dimensions are measured through two of each of the political, economic and institutional dimensions of governance.

Box 4.1

Definitions of the Six Measures of Institutional Quality Index

1. *Regulatory quality:* It includes measures of incidence of market-unfriendly policies, such as price controls or inadequate bank supervision, as well as perceptions of the burdens imposed by excessive regulation in areas, such as foreign trade and business development.
2. *Rule of law:* It includes several indicators, which measure the extent to which agents have confidence in and abide by the rules of society. These include perceptions of the incidence of crime, the effectiveness and predictability of the judiciary, and the enforceability of contracts. Together, these indicators measure the success of a society in developing an environment in which fair and predictable rules form the basis for economic and social interactions, and importantly, the extent to which property rights are protected.
3. *Control of corruption:* It measures perceptions of corruption, defined as the exercise of public power for private gain. This aspect of corruption measured differently by the various sources, ranging from the frequency of 'additional payments to get things done,' to the effects of corruption on the business environment, to measuring 'grand corruption' in the political arena or in the tendency of elite forms to engage in 'state capture'. The presence of corruption is often a manifestation of a lack of respect (public official or politician) for the rules, which govern their interactions, and hence represents a failure of governance.
4. *Voice and accountability:* It includes a number of indicators measuring various aspects of the political process, civil liberties and political rights. These indicators measure the extent to which citizens of a country are able to participate in the selection of governments. Indicators measuring the independence of the media, which serves an important role in monitoring those in authority and holding them accountable for their actions, are also included in this category.
5. *Political stability:* This index combines several indicators, which measure perceptions of the likelihood that the government in power will be destabilised or overthrown by possibly unconstitutional and/or violent means, including domestic violence and terrorism. This index captures the idea that the quality of governance in a country is compromised by the likelihood of wrenching changes in government, which not only has a direct effect on the continuity of policies, but also at a deeper level undermines the ability of all citizens to peacefully select and replace those in power.
6. *Government effectiveness:* The main focus of this index is on 'inputs' required for the government to be able to produce and implement good policies and deliver public goods. It combine into a single grouping responses on the quality of public service provision, the quality of the bureaucracy, the competence of civil servants, the independence of the civil service from political pressures, and the credibility of the government's commitment to policies.

Source: Kaufmann *et al.* (2003)

Regression Results of the Instrumental Variable (IV) Estimates of Openness Index

In view of the endogeneity of openness and institutional quality index, as hypothesised in several studies,[22] we also constructed an instrumental variable (IV) estimate of openness. To obtain this, the openness index i.e., ratio of trade-to-GDP was constructed by averaging the ratios during 2000-2004 and then it was regressed[23] separately on each of the seven measures of institutional index (including the aggregate index) along with four regional dummies (equation 7). The latter are included to capture the effects of omitted variables that are specific to region, such as competitiveness among firms, motives of merger, and corporate culture. The fitted values of openness index are the required IV estimates of openness index. Accordingly, based on above regressions, we obtained seven variants of instrumented openness index (O_{RQ}, O_{RoL}, O_{CoC}, O_{VA}, O_{PS}, O_{GE}, and $O_{Agg.I}$) that are used for the analysis of CBMA.

$$O_t = \alpha + \beta_o I_t + \beta_1 R + \varepsilon \quad (7)$$

Here, O is the ratio of trade-to-GDP (per cent), averaged during 2000-2004, I is institutional index, and R is regional dummy variable. α and ε are constant and error terms, respectively. In all, seven regressions were run, using one of the seven institutional measures at a time. Each regression was tested for Breusch-Pagan heteroscedasticity (B-P Hetero) and robust regression was run wherever it was found to be significant. The regressions clearly indicated that all institutional indicators play a highly significant and positive role in determining the trade shares of countries (Table 4.8). The better the quality of institutions in a country, the greater is the trade share. If a country needs to improve upon its trading volumes, it must progress in the field of its institutions.

In trying to determine the role of openness and institutional quality in CBMA and taking into consideration the endogeneity of the two indices, we estimated the relationship in two different specifications given below.

---

22. For details, see Gaiha and Imai (2005); Rodrik *et al.* (2004); and Gaiha *et al.* (2005).
23. The Frankel-Romer openness index did not account for differences in institutional quality of countries.

$$CBMA_t = \alpha' + \beta'_0 O_t + \beta'_1 D_t + \varepsilon' \qquad (8)$$

and

$$CBMA_t = \alpha'' + \beta'' I_t + \varepsilon'' \qquad (9)$$

where O is instrumental variable estimate of openness and D is dummy variable for income and α' and ε' are constant and error terms, respectively. In equation (9), I is the institutional quality index. In accordance with seven instrumental variable estimates of openness based on seven institutional quality indices, and Frankel-Romer openness index (O_{FR}), we estimated eight regressions from the equation (8) and seven from equation (9). Though data on CBMA are available on 188 countries, matching data on all variables restricted our sample size to 100 countries. However, our sample accounted for approximately 95 per cent of the average CBMA activity undertaken during 2000-2004 in both the number and value of deals. Further, for the present analysis, no distinction is made between various types of M&As. The regression results with respect to number of deals in cross-border M&As sales and purchases are shown in Tables 4.9 and 4.10.

Results of Regression Estimates

Regardless of the variant of openness index used, it can be observed from the Table 4.9, that the CBMA (measured in number of deals) are negatively related to openness. This implies that trade and resource endowments or investments received in the form of cross-border M&As are on an average, inversely related. The estimated coefficients are highly significant with respect to six instrumented openness index (including Frankel-Romer index) and non-significant to two instrumented indices based on rule of law and aggregate institutional index.[24] The inverse relationship between openness and CBMA deals is justified in terms of the Rybczynski Theorem.

---

24. Results with respect to CBMA, when measured in value terms, (not shown here) are negatively and non-significantly related to all instrumented openness indices based on institutional quality. However, the relation is negative and significant when regressed on Frankel-Romer openness index.

Table 4.8

Results of Robust[a] Regressions to obtain Instrumental Variable Estimates of Openness
(Dependent variable: average of ratio of trade-to-GDP during 2000-2004)

Specification	*1*	*2*	*3*	*4*	*5*	*6*	*7*
Independent Variables	*Estimated Coefficient*	*Estimated Coefficient*	*Estimated Coefficient*	*Estimated Coefficient*	*Estimated Coefficient*	*Estimated Coefficient*	*Estimated Coefficient*
Constant	21.28 (1.63)	24.3 (2.2)	24.4 (1.67)	28.2 (1.9)	20.5 (1.5)	20.7 (1.5)	18.14 (1.35)
VA	17.4*** (3.5)						
PS		16.9*** (4.6)					
GE			11.6** (2.4)				
CoC				9.12* (1.93)			
RoL					14.7*** (3.05)		
RQ						16.74*** (3.3)	
Agg. I							17.4*** (3.5)
Regional Dummies							
R_1	53.9*** (3.5)	50.6*** (3.95)	47.8*** (2.8)	43.2*** (2.5)	53.8*** (3.3)	54.2*** (3.3)	57.1*** (3.6)
R_2	59.8*** (3.9)	56.1*** (4.3)	49.4*** (3.03)	47.41*** (2.8)	55.5*** (3.5)	58.3*** (3.6)	60.4*** (3.9)
R_3	33.7*** (2.6)	36.3*** (2.9)	38.1*** (2.8)	37.5*** (2.7)	37.8*** (2.8)	38.3*** (2.8)	36.9*** (2.8)
R_4	41*** (3)	44.8*** (3.5)	45.3*** (2.8)	41*** (2.5)	50.5*** (3.2)	45*** (3)	50.3*** (3.4)
B-P Hetero. $chi^2(1)$	25.36***	20.03***	37.5***	37.3***	33.3***	32.2***	32.31***

Notes: Figures in brackets are t-values. *** significant at 1 per cent; ** significant at 5 per cent; * significant at 10 per cent.

[a]: In each of these regressions, the Breusch-Pagan test for heteroscedasticity was found to be significant; hence, robust regressions were run for estimation.

It is well established in the operations of MNEs that trade and investment are likely to be complements when the investment is of vertical type, while investment may substitute for trade in the case of horizontal mergers. In case of vertical mergers, MNCs segregate their manufacturing operations and shift their production facilities to the locations of cheaper factors of productions and export the final goods to the home countries. In these mergers, trade volumes and resources move in the same direction because growth in resources takes place in factors used more intensively in the production of exportable goods. In terms of Rybczynski Theorem, the countries attracting vertical deals experience an increase in the resources used more intensively in the export-promoting goods, and hence exhibit a rise in their trade volumes. In contrast to this, horizontal mergers are generally market-seeking. Here, MNEs take the resources to the host countries and produce the goods to sell in their markets and hence substitute for trade especially, imports. In other words, countries involved in horizontal mergers receive investments in import-competing goods, and thereby bring in a fall in the trade shares.

Focussing on cross-border M&As alone, it cannot be discerned whether a more liberalised trade policy (i.e., openness) and investment received through global M&As are positively or negatively related to each other. It largely depends on the nature of cross-border M&A deals received by a country. When cross-border M&As are horizontal in nature, the effect of openness is reflected in terms of negative relation between trade shares and resources received, and in vertical mergers, the effect is positive.

The estimated negative coefficient of openness in our analysis suggests that on an average openness has negative impact on investments received through cross-border M&As. The negative link between CBMA and openness is established from the fact that a large part of cross-border M&As is in the form of horizontal mergers.[25] These mergers aim at consolidation within the industry and are in search of new markets. The more restricted economies attract these merger deals and thereby receive resources in import-replacing goods. This in turn is exhibited in negative relation between trade and investment (Rybczynski Theorem). Therefore, it implies that the market-seeking effect outweighs the non-market seeking outcome of cross-border M&As. In other words, the export-promoting

25. In 1999, 70 per cent of cross-border M&As value corresponded to horizontal FDI, less than 10 per cent of deals were vertical in nature and the remaining were from unrelated industries (UNCTADb, 2000).

Table 4.9

Results of Robust Regressions using Various IV Estimates of Openness
(Dependent variable: average number of deals of CBMA sales and purchases during 2000-2004)

Specification	1	2	3	4	5	6	7	8
Independent Variables	*Estimated Coefficient*	*Estimated Coefficient*	*Estimated Coefficient*	*Estimated Coefficient*	*Estimated Coefficient*	*Estimated Coefficient*	*Estimated Coefficient*	*Estimated Coefficient*
Constant	2.76	6.5	4.35	21.5	27.6	1.68	6.5	4.21
	(1.64)	(2.7)	(3.0)	(4.64)	(6.2)	(.9)	(2.8)	(3.85)
$O_{Agg.I}$	-.02							
	(.74)							
O_{VA}		-.07**						
		(2.2)						
O_{PS}			-.04**					
			(2.1)					
O_{GE}				-.31***				
				(4.5)				
O_{CoC}					-.40***			
					(6.1)			
O_{RoL}						-.001		
						(.05)		
O_{RQ}							-.08**	
							(2.3)	
O_{FR}								-.05***
								(3.94)
Income Dummies								
D_1	1.18	1.66	1.4*	3.7**	3.4**	1.15	1.72	2.7**
	(1.51)	(1.5)	(1.7)	(2.1)	(2.13)	(1.5)	(1.6)	(2.14)
D_2	3.17***	3.78***	3.54***	6.6***	5.6***	2.96***	3.57***	5.6***
	(3.4)	(2.9)	(3.7)	(3.1)	(3.01)	(3.1)	(2.8)	(3.8)
D_3	150.9***	178.8***	151.3***	167.4***	168.1***	150.5***	178.9***	183.3***
	(177)	(156)	(178)	(85)	(97)	(174)	(152)	(141)
B-P Hetero. chi^2 (1)	201.4***	181.5***	222***	206***	221.6***	201.1***	199.2***	170.2***

Notes: Same as in Table 4.8.

investments are weaker than the import-replacing resources that give rise to a negative relation between trade volumes and CBMA sales and purchases.

The regression results obtained (not shown here) by using value of CBMA deals and openness though directionally negative, are not that clearly established, especially, in terms of significance of coefficients. This could be on account of the presence of mega deals, which despite being small in numbers affect the total value by very large amount (see Table 4.4).

So far as coefficients of income dummy variables are concerned, we find all are positive. However, coefficients with respect to 'high income countries' (both OECD and non-OECD) and 'upper middle income' countries are statistically significant at less than 1 per cent level and those with respect to 'lower middle income' are either not significant or are significant at more than 5 per cent (less than 10 per cent). The magnitude of the coefficient is highest for 'high income countries' followed by the 'upper middle income' countries. The estimated coefficient of income dummies with respect to sign, magnitude and significance level are similar when regressions are obtained by using value of CBMA sales and purchases.

Finally, turning to the regression results of CBMA on institutional index (Table 4.10), CBMA are positively and highly significantly related to all individual institutional indices (except political stability) and to aggregate institutional index. This clearly implies that to encourage inflow of skill, technology, physical capital through cross-border M&As, countries must improve upon the quality of their institutions.

4.6 Conclusion

From the analysis of cross-border M&As, it is noted that the trends with regard to the roles of DDE and DGE, as acquirer and destination countries, are in opposite directions. The former group witnessed a fall, offset by the rise observed for the latter group of economies. Bulk of the rise in the share of developing economies in total number of M&A target is captured by Asia and Oceania economies.

Table 4.10

Results of Robust Regressions using Various Institutional Quality Indices

Specification	1	2	3	4	5	6	7
	Voice and Accountability	*Political Stability*	*Government Effectiveness*	*Regulatory Quality*	*Rule of Law*	*Control of Corruption*	*Aggregate Index*
Independent Variables	*Estimated Coefficient*	*Estimated Coefficient*	*Estimated Coefficient*	*Estimated Coefficient*	*Estimated Coefficient*	*Estimated Coefficient*	*Estimated Coefficient*
Constant	12.3 (5.9)	3.5 (6.6)	23.9 (7.9)	18.74 (6.3)	10.3 (7.3)	23.1 (7.6)	24.6 (7.2)
Institutional Index	11.1*** (5.0)	.45 (.77)	32.9*** (11.3)	23.62*** (7.6)	8.75*** (6.5)	27.8*** (9.8)	30.9*** (8.6)
B-P Hetero. $chi^2(1)$	56.1***	13.98***	105.1***	70.83***	94.4***	107.2***	77.93***

Notes: Same as in Table 4.8.

Within the group of developed economies, the participation of Europe has gone up greatly as purchaser as well as seller of cross-border M&As since the late 1980s. On an average, the share of Europe is greater as acquirer (62 per cent) than as target (55 per cent) and that of North America is more as target (38 per cent) than as acquirer (31 per cent) since 1990s. The contribution of other developed countries is roughly 8 per cent as purchaser as well as seller among the group of developed economies.

There have been wide fluctuations in the relative shares of Africa, Latin America and Asia within the group of developing economies. The participation of African countries has marginally moved up as purchaser as well as seller since the late 1980s. The participation of Latin American countries has increased greatly as acquiring countries. However, as target economies they have witnessed a declining trend. Although the share of Asian economies has witnessed large changes during the last 15 years as acquiring as well as acquired countries, it maintains more than 50 per cent of share in both the purchases and sales of cross-border M&As made by the developing economies.

From an individual country point of view, since the year 1987, US has been the largest seller (target country) as well as a purchaser (acquirer) of cross-border M&As. However, its share is slowly declining. On an average UK maintains its position at the 2nd rank, while its share declines as purchaser and fluctuates as target country. Germany, France and Canada are the three chief competitors for the 3rd, 4th and 5th ranks within the developed economies. Among developing countries of the world, few of the Asian countries such as China, Hong Kong (China), Japan and Singapore are recently showing their existence in the number of world's cross-border M&A deals. This indicates that Asian countries are attracting a good number of deals, but of smaller value.

With respect to the role of openness in determining the cross-border M&As, using cross-country data, it is noted from our analysis that trade or openness and resources attained through M&As are inversely related to each other. In fact, the relationship between trade and investment depends upon the type of investment that comes through cross-border M&As. The negative sign obtained in our results implies trade and resources are substitutes for each other. This is, plausibly, on account of the fact that horizontal M&As outweigh the vertical M&As i.e., the market-seeking effect of the former overshadows the non-market seeking outcome of the latter. This implies that countries involved in cross-border M&As are more in search of new markets to sell their products in the host country, rather than in search of factors of production due to differences in relative factor endowments. The latter is the case of vertical cross-border M&As, where trade and investment are complements for each other. If openness is interpreted as a measure of trade restrictions, it can be concluded that a country with greater restrictions (or lower openness) attract more of horizontal investments, which seek to produce and sell in the host country. This, as a result, brings lower trading volumes, and hence, resources and trade move in the opposite direction. So far as the income-classification of countries is concerned, leaving aside the 'lower middle income' group countries, coefficients with respect to dummies used for 'upper middle income countries' and 'high income countries' are positive and significant.

With respect to the role of institutional quality, the regression estimates indicate that institutional quality index in any country has a positive and a significant role to play in obtaining investments through cross-border M&As. It can also be concluded from our analysis that trade restrictions just determine the type of investment a country would be receiving, and not the amount. However, if a country desires to attract greater resources through cross-border M&As (or FDIs), it must improve upon its institutional quality index as it directly impacts the cross-border M&As.

5 Trends in Mergers and Acquisitions in India

The chapter focusses on the response of the Indian corporate sector in the post-liberalised period. As mentioned in the earlier chapters, the prevalence of policy-induced rigidities before reforms constrained firms to take independent decisions regarding allocation of resources. Also, the protection from internal and external competition made firms complacent and did not force them to improve their business strategies. In the phase of intensified competitive pressure from the domestic as well as the world market during the post-reform period, a high degree of response in any case was expected. This is not only because liberalised policies gave freedom to firms to take decisions regarding their investment, plant size, location and entry in any industry, but also in the wake of external competition firms had to think of survival strategies.

The main objective of this chapter is to delineate trends in merger and acquisition activities in India. The chapter is divided into seven sections. Section 5.1 outlines the response of the Indian firms in general. Section 5.2 comprehensively reviews the Indian studies on M&As, giving details of the nature of activities undertaken since 1990s. The recent trends from 2000 onwards are presented in Section 5.3. Section 5.4 provides rationale for an industry-specific analysis to be conducted in the next four chapters. Section 5.5 is devoted to an overview of the drugs and pharmaceutical (D&P) industry in India. The consolidation wave in this industry in the post-reform period is discussed in Section 5.6. The chapter ends with concluding observations in Section 5.7.

5.1 Corporate Sector Response

In the last 40 years of control, diversification was a preferred mode of growth. Indian corporate sector was full of large conglomerate firms. The regulatory framework forced firms to diversify in various unrelated sectors.

Hazari (1966) in his pioneering work, reports the effects of the policies adopted post-independence that led to the emergence of conglomerate firms that were specific in character. Unlike western firms,[1] the Indian firms consisted of legally independent firms that diversified into various unrelated areas, but were controlled by a single central decision-making authority. It is the lacunae in the policy structure that made the expansion through separate units easier.[2] Subsequent work pointed out that Indian business groups were not only specific but also stable in character. Various factors, such as financial strength of business groups, power to influence policy decisions in their favour and the resultant negligible threat of entry from outside, brought in the element of stability in the intensity of competition they faced (Chandrasekhar, 1999). Further, industrial licensing and small-scale reservation inhibited firms from reaping economies of scale and minimising costs. Misuse of licensing practices led to a reduced amount of connection between targeted, licensed and actual capacities.

Over a period of time, experience demonstrated that diversified companies did not perform well. It was difficult to develop managerial capabilities required to run different kinds of businesses. As a result, even the most competent managements did not run companies efficiently. Until the MRTP Act was abolished in 1991-92, large firms remained in the businesses they had entered into, as there were no exit provisions. Consequently, companies with underutilised capacities on one hand and companies that were expanding capacities on the other, were co-existing.

A shift from the early regulated regime to a new liberal regime in the early 1990s exposed the Indian industry to intense domestic as well as global competition. This forced the corporates to adopt strategies to meet the emerging competitive challenges. With the purpose of consolidating their capacity and focussing on their core business the Indian private corporate sector adopted restructuring strategies at an unparalleled rate. The most common and obvious way, the Indian corporate sector restructured itself, was in the form of mergers and acquisitions (M&As). Mergers and acquisitions were not uncommon to the Indian situation.

1. Western firms were single business units that diversified into linked areas (Roy, 1999).
2. Chandra (1977) provides detailed description of loopholes that led to growth of such business units.

However, on account of several restrictions, it was a low-key affair. Known Indian businessmen like the Birlas, the Tatas, the Goenkas, the Piramals and the Modis acquired profit-making companies in the 1980s. To avail tax and other fiscal benefits, a good number of M&As were related to sick units.[3] After the introduction of FERA Act in 1973, some of the MNCs changed hands, as they were not ready to comply with the regulations (Shinde, 1995).

However, M&As emerged as an important, regular and market-driven phenomenon of the Indian corporate world only in the post-liberalised era.[4] Increasing market share, brand power, gaining synergies, and quick expansion were among the major motives behind the M&As wave that swept the Indian corporate world since 1991-92. The number of M&As, which was as low as 15 in 1988, rose to 114 in 1993 (Shinde, 1995). During the year 2005, the number of deals crossed the 2000 mark (CMIE[4], November 2005).

Restructuring in this form allowed firms to focus on their core competencies i.e., the area in which the firm had competent managerial skill. After the change in the policy regime, the conglomerates[5] also rationalised their portfolio by focussing on areas of their main businesses, by giving away unrelated businesses and acquiring the related ones. For instance, in 1994, in order to focus on core competencies, the Tatas expanded their steel and vehicle manufacturing capacity at Tata Iron and Steel (TISCO) and Tata Engineering and Locomotive Company (TELCO) and disposed of Tata Oil Mills (TOMCO) to Hindustan Lever Ltd. (HLL). Later, HLL too involved in merger with Brooke Bond Lipton India Ltd.[6] (BBLIL) and Ponds India Ltd., to attain core competency and quick expansion.

3. To encourage the merger of sick units with the healthy units, Section 72 A of Income Tax Act was also introduced in 1977.

4. The M&As that took place in the pre-reform period were not market-driven, rather, were policy-induced, i.e., financial institutions and Government agencies arranged them, Bhoi (2000).

5. Tyabji (1999) discusses in detail, the restructuring operations undertaken by five conglomerate firms in response to changed economic environment.

6. This company was formed by the amalgamation of Brooke Bond India Ltd. and Lipton India Ltd. in 1992.

Based on work done on India, the next section delineates the pattern of M&As that took place in the pre- and post-reform period.

5.2 Review of Indian Studies on Mergers and Acquisitions

It is almost one and half a decade since the Indian corporate sector undertook restructuring operations in response to liberalisation measures. Several studies have analysed issues, such as nature of M&As, industrial clustering in M&As, pre-merger characteristic of acquiring (AG) and acquired (AD) firms, post-merger performance of amalgamated firms, role of multinationals (MNCs), response of MRTP companies, mergers of sick units and prediction. Few studies have also covered the M&A activity during the pre-liberalised period. Based on the findings of these studies (listed in Table 5.1), this section discusses the important features of trends in M&As in India.

Pattern of Mergers and Acquisitions in Pre- and Post-liberalised Period

From the descriptive analysis of trends in M&As in Indian private corporate sector the following findings are reported.

- M&As as a means of restructuring existed in India even during pre-reform years but the merger movement accelerated in the early 1990s due to a change in the policy environment. The number of mergers more than doubled from 1985-1989 to 1990-1994 (Beena, 1998; also see Figure 5.1).
- Both the mergers and acquisitions rose during the post-liberalised period. However, the former exceeded the latter in terms of number of deals. Basant (2000) reports that out of 402 merger and acquisition deals undertaken in India during the period 1991-1997, two-thirds were in the form of mergers and the remaining one-third were in the form of acquisitions.
- M&A process was spread across various industry groups, such as manufacturing, financial, banking, services and service related areas. Further, on account of deregulation of production and capacity restrictions, a major part of this activity took place in the private

manufacturing sector. Approximately three-fourths of M&As were undertaken by the manufacturing sector and the remaining one-fourth in financial services and other related areas (Basant, 2000; Das, 2000). Predominance of mergers in manufacturing sector *vis-à-vis* non-manufacturing sector is also illustrated in Figures 5.1 and 5.2. Before liberalisation, more than 70 per cent of the mergers and 93 per cent of acquisitions took place in the manufacturing sector. Although, the trend continued in the post-reform period (1990-1994), there has been a rise in M&A activity in the non-manufacturing sector. This is on account of financial liberalisation in 1990s that helped firms to gain competitive edge through mergers and also facilitated early listing in the stock market. The latter is also evidenced from the fact that a greater number of private companies indulged in merger strategies (Beena, 1998).

- Horizontal mergers dominated in both mergers and acquisitions. The respective proportions of horizontal, vertical and conglomerate deals were 53, 16, 31 per cent in 252 mergers and 74, 5, 21 per cent in 145 acquisition deals (see Table 5.2). Predominance of horizontal[7] nature of mergers is identified in several studies undertaken during the post-liberalised years. Beena (1998) observed that 70 per cent of mergers in a sample of 45 mergers undertaken during 1990-91 to 1993-94 were of horizontal nature and the rest 30 per cent were equally distributed between vertical and conglomerate types. Roy (1999) also reports a high percentage of horizontal mergers during 1995-1997 (Table 5.2).
- This pattern clearly highlights the fact that during the liberalised era Indian companies corrected for their early over-diversified strategies and focussed on their core areas of production. Consequently, firms reaped the advantages of large-scale production (economies of scale), reduced cost (through avoidance of duplicate facilities) and attained higher market shares. A low, but significant proportion of mergers in the form of conglomerate mergers (Table 5.2) suggests that the erstwhile tendency of over-diversification had slowed down but not eliminated, during the post-reform period (Basant, 2000).

7. The first merger wave experienced in the US and other developed countries also dominated in horizontal mergers.

Table 5.1

A Summary of Studies on Mergers and Acquisitions in India

S.No.	Authors	Title of the Study	Period of Study	Sample Size	Nature of Work Done
1.	Kaveri (1986)	*Financial Analysis of Company Mergers in India.*	1975-1984	9 case studies	Comparative analysis of actual post-merger performance of sick units *vis-à-vis* the expectations laid down
2.	Rao and Rao (1987)	*Regulation of Mergers under the MRTP Act 1969: A Critical Study.*	1970-1986	94 mergers	Nature and motives of mergers of MRTP companies, highlights rationale for approving or rejecting a merger proposal
3.	Singh and Kumar (1994)	*Corporate Rehabilitation and BIFR.*		3 case studies	Analyse the role of BIFR in the revival of sick units
4.	Yadav *et al.* (1994)	*Profitability of Mergers: Some Case Studies.*		4 case studies	Compares the post-merger performance of firms merged with Indian and foreign companies
5.	Beena (1998)	*Mergers & Amalgamations: An Analysis in the Changing Structure of Indian Oligopoly.*	1973-74 to 1994-95		Trends in M&A in private corporate sector in India from 1973-74 to 1994-95; Nature, motives and consequences of mergers during 1990-91 to 1994-95
6.	Sankar and Rao (1999)	*Takeover and Turnaround.*	1987-1998	8 case studies	Examines the post-takeover performance of sick units
7.	Roy (1999)	*Mergers and Takeovers: The Indian Scene during the 1990s.*	1995-1997	116 mergers, 170 takeovers 5 business groups	Pattern of mergers and takeovers, An in-depth analysis of five big business houses

contd...

...contd...

S.No.	Authors	Title of the Study	Period of Study	Sample Size	Nature of Work Done
8.	Basant (2000)	*Corporate Response to Economic Reforms.*	1990-1997	252 mergers and 145 acquisitions	Examines corporate strategies in response to economic reforms
9.	Das (2000)	*A Study of Corporate Restructuring of Indian Industries in the Post-New Industrial Policy Regime: The Issue of Amalgamation/Mergers.*	1994-1998		Nature, structure and composition of mergers
10.	Saple (2000)	*Diversification, Merger and their Effects on Firm Performance: A Study of the Indian Corporate Sector.*	1992-1995	36 AG 36 AD 30 NAG	Pre-merger characteristics of AG&AD and post-merger analysis
11.	Agarwal (2002)	*An Analysis of Mergers in India.*	1973-74 to 1997-98	1810 mergers 94 MRTP firms 58 sick units	Nature of mergers, Industrial clustering in India, factors affecting M&As
12.	Sood and Kaur (2004)	*Predicting Corporate Takeovers in India: An Empirical Analysis.*	1993-94 to 1997-98	37 AG 37 control firms	Examines the M&A activity in India, predict takeovers in India, evaluate post-takeover performance
13.	Kaur (2005)	*Corporate Mergers in India.*	1990-2000	254 mergers 51 mergers	Lays down the financial and strategic motives of M&A activity and analyses pre- and post-merger performance

Figure 5.1

Distribution of Mergers and Takeovers, 1974-75 to 1993-94
(according to manufacturing and non-manufacturing sectors)

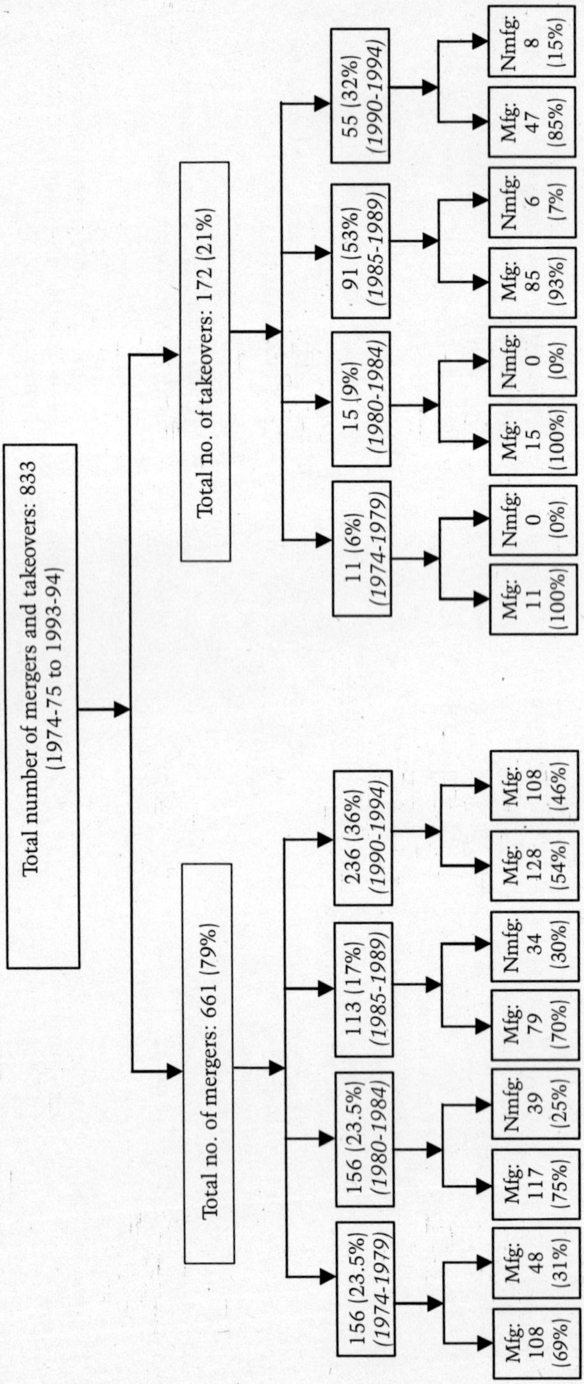

Note: Mfg.-manufacturing, Nmfg.-non-manufacturing.
Source: Based on Beena (1998, 2000).

Figure 5.2

Distribution of Mergers and Takeovers, 1974-75 to 1993-94 (according to MRTP and non-MRTP firms)

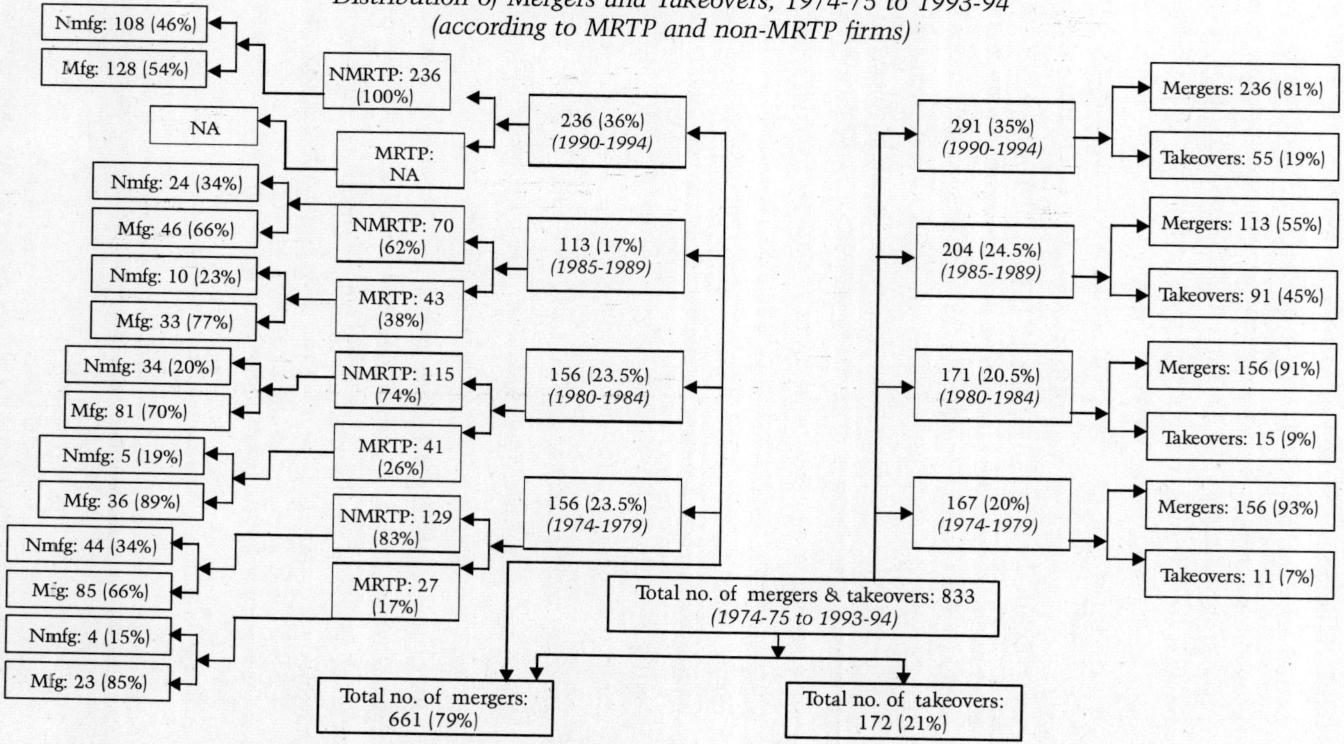

Note: Mfg.-manufacturing, Nmfg.-non-manufacturing, NMRTP- non-MRTP, N.A.- not applicable.

Source: Adapted from Beena (1998).

- Another dominant feature of M&A activity during the post-reform period was the high proportion of mergers from within group companies[8] (Table 5.2). It was meant to avoid competition between intra-group companies. Basant (2000) observed 74 per cent of mergers from within the same group, whereas only 16 per cent from unrelated groups. Beena (2000) witnessed 71 per cent from the same management and the rest from unrelated managements. Similar pattern is also reported by Roy (1999), as 82 per cent of mergers were within the same group and 10 per cent outside the same group. The in-depth study of 51 cases of mergers during 1990-2000, in a study by Kaur (2005) included 44 per cent of horizontal mergers and 50 per cent from within group mergers. This further strengthens the observed trends of consolidation in similar line of businesses as well as within same groups. The likely reason for consolidation within same group companies arose from the market for takeovers that emerged from the evolution of takeover code in 1994. Through M&A activity, companies strengthened their controlling stake to protect themselves against the takeover bids (Beena, 1998).

In an attempt to identify merger waves, Agarwal[9] (2002) divided the entire period covered into three sub-periods,[10] *viz*:

(a) Stagnant merger activity (1973-74 to 1988-89),

(b) Moderate merger activity (1989-90 to 1994-95), and

(c) Heightened merger activity (1995-96 to 2000-01).

Out of the reported 1,810 cases of merger, 49 per cent took place in the first 22 years (i.e., the period covered by the first two sub-periods) whereas 51 per cent of the cases occurred in the third sub-period that covers only six years. Out of the 512 cases of within group mergers

8. When two merging firms belong to the same group, it is named as 'within' group merger

9. Agarwal's (2002) work is one of the rarest attempts to build an exhaustive database on mergers in India, across 28 years, from 1973-74 to 2000-01. The study covers many aspects of mergers that have been completely neglected so far in studies for India. Apart from analysing the nature of mergers in India, his work also tests the hypothesis of industrial clustering and impact of amendments to the MRTP Act in 1991 on the incidence of mergers by MRTP firms.

10. In order to demarcate one period from the other, Agarwal (2002) applies the rule that the highest number of mergers in a year for a period should be lower than the lowest number of mergers achieved in the immediate succeeding period.

identified from the total M&A activity, 340 were reported to have occurred during the third sub-period (see Figure 5.3). Further, group mergers account for 15, 24 and 37 per cent of the total merger activity during the respective three sub-periods. This indicates the preponderance of consolidation activity during 1995-96 to 2000-01.

- To highlight the companies' strategy to use mergers as means to consolidate their activities in their core business, Agarwal (2002) also provides insights into intra- and inter-industry mergers. Of the 1,573 cases of mergers, 55 per cent belonged to intra-industry mergers (see Figure 5.4). Further, a decomposition of intra- and inter-industry mergers into the three sub-periods reveals that the number of inter-industry mergers exceeded the intra-industry merger in the first sub-period whereas dominance of the latter group is reported during the next two periods of moderate and high merger activity.
- To investigate further, he calculated the intensity index[11] (defined as intra-industry mergers minus inter-industry mergers/total mergers in the industry) to capture the pattern of mergers among various industries. Industries, such as banking and insurance, electricity, cosmetic, petroleum, rubber, and paints dominated in intra-industry mergers and crude petroleum, natural gas, other food products, printing and publishing, road transport, jewellery, aircraft, space craft and parts, ship building, cement, fertilisers and pesticides dominated in inter-industry mergers. These findings are in line with the earlier findings (Beena, 1998; Roy, 1999; Basant, 2000) that in the post-reform period mergers were used as a corrective measure for the earlier business strategies such as over-diversification and competing with the group companies that largely resulted from the erstwhile licensing regime.
- In the context of the size distribution of firms involved in mergers, Beena (1998) makes a significant observation regarding the

11. An industry with an intensity index equal to or greater than 0.25 (i.e., intra-industry greater than inter-industry mergers by at least 25 per cent of the total mergers in that industry) was taken as dominating in intra-industry mergers while a value, -0.25 implied its domination in inter-industry merger.

12. A firm with the size of Rs 100 crore of assets was a cut-off figure in the diluted MRTP Act of 1985.

Table 5.2

Distribution of Mergers and Acquisitions by Various Categories during Post-reform Period*

Study	Size of Sample	Nature of Mergers			No. of Loss-Making/Sick Units	Within Same Management	Outside Same Management
		Horizontal	Vertical	Conglomerate			
Beena (2000)	45 mergers (1991-1994)	31 (70%)	7 (15%)	7 (15%)	N.A.	32 (71%)	13 (29%)
Roy** (1999)	116 mergers (1995-1997)	47	14	37[a]	18	92 (82%)	12 (10%)
Roy** (1999)	170 takeovers (1995-1997)	97	12	24[a]	31	N.A.	N.A.
Basant** (2000)	252 mergers (1991-1997)	134 (53%)	39 (15%)	79[a] (31%)	N.A.	186 (73.8%)	40 (16%)
Basant[b] (2000)	145 acquisitions (1991-1997)	107 (74%)	5 (3.5%)	33[a] (22.5%)	N.A.	N.A.	N.A.

Notes: * Roy (1999) used the term 'takeover' for 'acquisition'.

** Information could not be ascertained regarding the types of all the cases of mergers and takeovers as well as their managements.

a Mergers and takeovers under the category of conglomerate related and conglomerate unrelated are added.

b Information regarding management could not be ascertained for all cases.

Source: Based on Beena (2000); Roy (1999); Basant (2000).

Figure 5.3

Distribution of Mergers, 1973-74 to 2000-01
(according to within and outside group mergers)

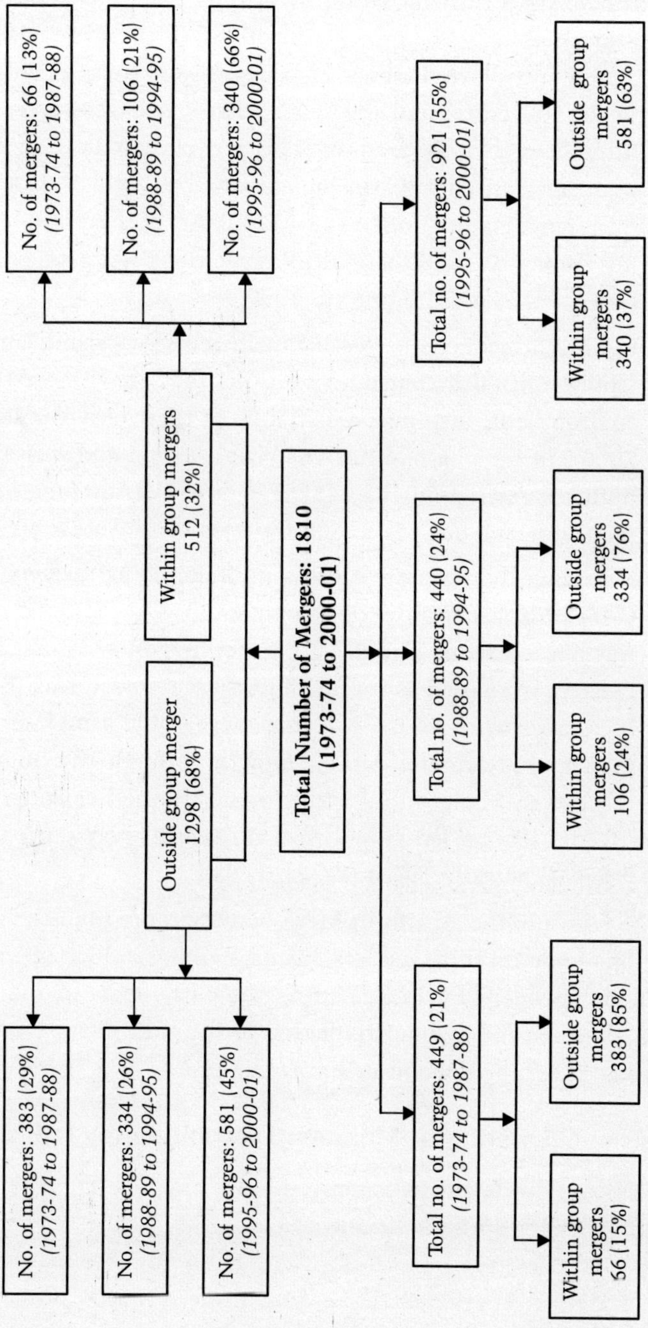

Source: Based on Agarwal (2002).

composition of firms in terms of total assets. Out of the 94 firms examined, 39 (41 per cent) belonged to the asset size of Rs 100 crore[12] and above. Further, 20 per cent were from medium size (Rs 5 to Rs 100 crore) and the remaining 40 per cent were small-sized firms (less than Rs 5 crore). This is a clear indication that mergers were not concentrated in big corporations, which were required to take permission under the MRTP Act. Therefore, it would be misleading to state that MRTP regulations were responsible for the slower M&A activity prior to 1990.

- In order to reduce the existing inefficiencies, a significant part of the family-controlled conglomerate firms that grew under the protected environment, also adopted M&As as their survival strategy (Das, 2000). In the phase of increased competition and with the arrival of multinational companies (MNCs), these firms preferred shedding their non-core businesses and focussed on key areas.
- Regarding the motives of firms in undertaking mergers during early years of post-reform period i.e., 1991-1994, the basic aim of firms was not to expand further in terms of market or assets share. Rather, mergers were used as means of internal restructuring (Beena, 1998). It is indicated from the fact that most of the sample firms included in her study financed their growth through the buoyant capital market and borrowings rather than retained earnings or through M&As. Merger-led growth had no role to play during the merger wave of the early 1990s (Beena, 1998).

To sum up, the growth in M&A activity came from the restructuring operations undertaken by various business groups, which operated through several independent entities. During the early years of the post-reform period, these business groups preferred to integrate themselves into single entities and with production in similar activities.

Industrial Clustering of Mergers: Distribution by Industry

The worldwide phenomenon of M&A being distributed non-uniformly across industries during different merger waves (witnessed in the UK and US) is also observed in India. The phenomenon of mergers being concentrated in few industries is supported by many studies (Bhaumik, 2002; Basant, 2000; Kaur, 2005). Basant (2000) observed that the industry

Figure 5.4

Distribution of Mergers, 1973-74 to 2000-01
(according to intra- and inter-industry mergers)

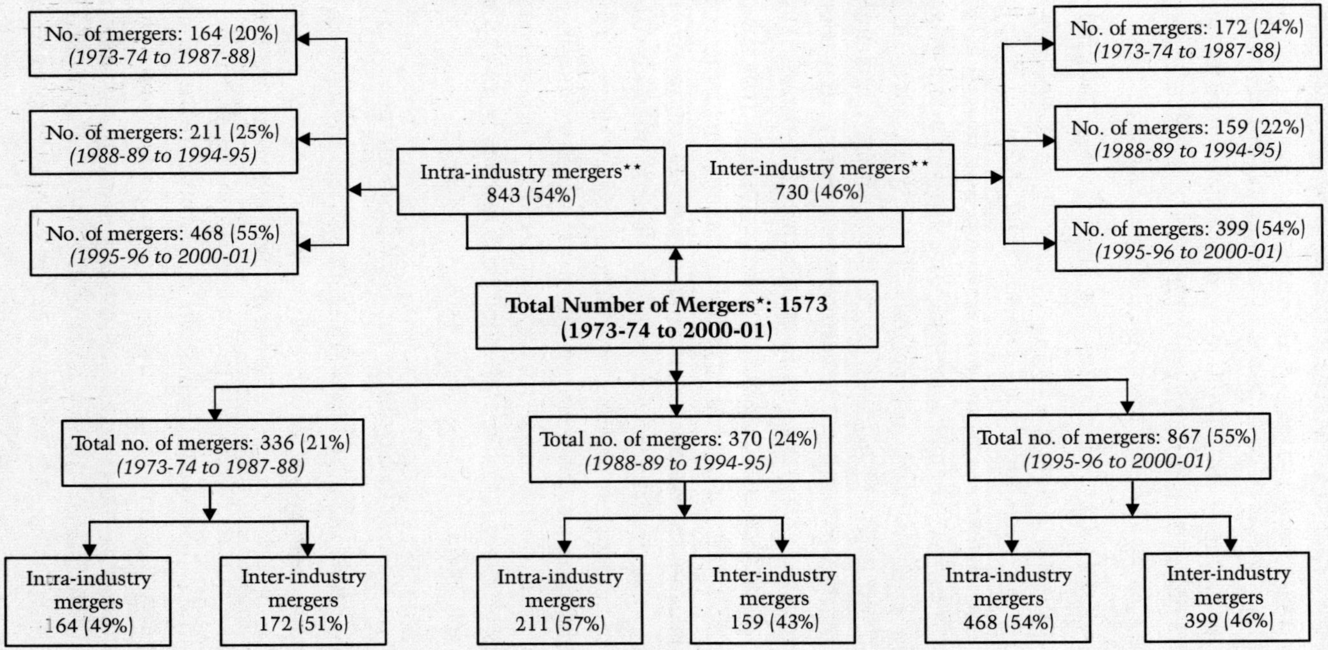

Notes: * Total number of mergers for which information on the product category of both acquiring and acquired companies was available.
** Both intra- and inter-industry mergers are classified from the perspective of acquiring firm.

Source: Based on Agarwal (2002)

groups beverages, spirit and vinegar (16 per cent), chemical including drugs and pharmaceutical (15 per cent), financial services (12 per cent) and electrical machinery (7 per cent) together accounted for 50 per cent of total M&A activity during 1991-1997. Mergers in industry groups, such as wood and wood products, paper and paper products, construction and electricity and power played an insignificant role during the same period.

Agarwal (2002) investigates the presence of clustering of merger activity in India from 1973-74 to 2000-01 in a few industries and also econometrically tests for certain industry level shocks in determining this activity. He identified 76 industries, which experienced 1,795 mergers during this period. The phenomenon of industrial clustering was found to be present in all three sub-periods. Industries, such as drugs and pharmaceutical (D&P), textiles, electrical machinery, machinery (other than electrical and transport), investment and trading, were found to have higher concentration of mergers in all the three sub-periods. However, the relative importance of each industry varied across different sub-periods. In order to test the hypothesis that industrial restructuring is caused by industrial shocks, such as delicensing, foreign competition, growth prospects in an industry, growth in sales, capacity utilisation and number of mergers undertaken by other rival firms in the industry, Agarwal (2002) considered a sample of 72 mergers from 52 industries during 1982-83 to 1998-99. The results suggest that merger activity varied with deregulation measures of 1990s, capacity utilisation, and mergers by rival firms (the so called ripple effect).

Merger as a Revival Strategy for Sick Companies

Even before the introduction of economic reforms, mergers were used as an important and effective corrective measure to restructure the operations of sick units in India. Reviving these units, by merging them with healthy units, has always been preferred to the alternative of closure of sick units. The special provision mentioned in the section 72A of Income Tax Act, 1961, and the Sick Industrial Companies (Special Provisions) Act (SICA), 1985, delineate the role of government in promoting the mergers of sick units with healthy companies. The former deals with tax benefits to the acquiring company, by setting off the accumulated losses and unabsorbed depreciation of sick companies, against its (healthy or acquiring company) profits. The latter came into force w.e.f. May 1987, along with an appointed body called, Board for Industrial and Financial Reconstruction (BIFR), which was empowered to work out and sanction the rehabilitation scheme with regard to sick industrial companies. In view of the importance of mergers, being used for rehabilitation of sick units, several studies have identified such mergers.

Agarwal (2002) identified 98 cases of mergers that involved sick units, out of which approximately 50 per cent (45 cases) were within group mergers. Decomposing these mergers between intra- and inter-industry mergers 45 belonged to the former and the rest to the latter. Further, looking at the industry-wise distribution, 51 per cent of these mergers were from metal products (9 per cent), textiles (9 per cent), electricity machinery (8 per cent), machinery other than electrical and transport (8 per cent), iron and steel (5 per cent), miscellaneous chemical products (6 per cent) and organic and inorganic (5.6 per cent). Kaur (2005) observed 15 cases (from a sample of 51) of mergers that involved sick units and out of which 60 per cent were from the category of within group mergers.

In order to analyse the effectiveness of mergers as a means to rehabilitate the sick units, Kaveri (1986) and Singh and Kumar (1994) carried out an in-depth analysis of few specific case studies. Both the studies concluded that mergers have proved to be an effective means to revive sick units. The former study covered nine cases of such mergers undertaken during 1975-1984 and concluded that on an average, mergers were mutually advantageous to both sick and healthy units. The latter study based on three cases referred by BIFR, found tax savings was the main motivating factor for healthy units in undertaking mergers with sick firms.

Using various financial ratios, such as profitability, earning price share (EPS) and cost ratios, Yadav *et al.* (1994) tested the ownership issues i.e., whether mergers with MNCs were more successful than the ones involving Indian companies. Comparing the pre-merger (based on three years before merger) and post-merger (three years after merger) values, the study reported that mergers with MNCs performed better with respect to most of the ratios used. In this regard Sankar and Rao (1999) also analysed eight cases of takeovers[13] (instead of mergers) in turning around sick firms. The results, based on financial ratios indicated that sick companies, undertaken by better-known industrial group performed better and faster post-takeover, than the ones taken over by relatively lesser-known management groups.

Reverse Mergers

Since the amendments of 1994, SICA also included the provision for reverse mergers, where a profitable company merges into a sick company.[14] Here the sick company does not lose its identity. Rather, it continues business, generally, with a changed name. Basant (2000) mentions four cases of reverse mergers in a sample comprising 252 mergers. Kaur (2005) considers three such cases in a sample of 51 mergers and finds acquiring firms to be performing better post-merger in all the three cases.

Mergers by MRTP Companies

The study of mergers undertaken by MRTP companies during the pre- and post-reform period has become of great relevance especially after the abolition of MRTP Act in 1991. Several studies (Rao and Rao, 1987; Beena, 1998; Agrawal, 2002) have contributed to the analysis of the extent to which MRTP Act acted as a hindrance to M&A activity, undertaken by MRTP companies[15] (Figure 5.2). Removal of institutional barriers encouraged mergers among large-sized firms (Beena, 1998). During 1990-1991 to 1994-95, one-third of a sample of acquiring firm that adopted the merger route belonged to the large-sized group (assets greater than or equal to Rs 100 crore), which could not have adopted this route without the dilution of the MRTP Act in 1991-92. An important feature observed, however, is that the absolute as well as the relative proportion of MRTP companies undertaking mergers increased during 1974-1979 to 1985-1989. As regards the decomposition of total mergers between MRTP and non–

---

13. The sick units maintained their identity and experienced a change in their management and policies followed thereby.
14. Eicher Tractors Ltd. merging into Royal Enfield Motors Ltd. in 1995-96 and Godrej Soaps Ltd. merging into Gujarat Godrej Innovative Chemical Ltd. in 1994-95, are two examples of reverse mergers, Kaur (2005).
15. Merger of Hindustan Lever Ltd. with Tata Oil Mills (TOMCO) in 1993-94 and later, with Lakme in 1995-96 is a classic example because all three companies involved, were MRTP companies. Without the dilution of MRTP Act, it would not have been easy for these mergers to take place.

MRTP companies, it is observed that the latter were more involved in larger numbers (Figure 5.2). This indicates that the non-MRTP firms might have used merger strategy to exploit the advantage of size to improve their competitive strength.

Assuming amendment to the MRTP Act in 1991-92, as an event or shock affecting the merger behaviour of MRTP companies (unlike deregulation that affected the industry as a whole), Agarwal (2002) carried out an analysis of mergers undertaken by the MRTP companies five years before (1986-87 to 1990-91) and after (1992-93 to 1996-97) the 1991 amendments to MRTP Act. To find the statistical significance of 1991 amendments and also to account for the factors (at firm level) that led MRTP companies to undertake mergers, he used a fixed-effects logit regression on a sample of 85 acquiring MRTP companies during 1986-87 to 1996-97. His analysis, as that of Beena's, supported the view that amendments to the MRTP Act encouraged MRTP firms to opt for merger in greater number in the post-amendment period. Notably, in post-amendment period, a significantly high percentage of these mergers belonged to intra-industry (63 per cent as compared to 13 per cent in pre-amendment period) and within group mergers (53 as compared to 38 per cent in pre-amendment period). In judging the variables that increased the likelihood of mergers opted by MRTP companies, the study found that higher sales growth, higher cash flow and capacity utilisation encouraged firms to expand through mergers after the amendment to the Act.

Mergers and MNCs[16]

In the wake of liberalised policies, both the Indian and multinational enterprises (MNEs) undertook mergers and acquisitions with different purposes. Domestic firms consolidated their position to reap the economies of scale and gain other synergies while the MNCs took this opportunity to increase their control on the Indian corporate sector. The MNCs played an important role in M&A activity in India in the early 1990s. The dilution of controls on the operations of foreign firms in India in the post-liberalised

16. MNCs comprise parent enterprises and their foreign affiliates: a parent enterprise is defined as one that controls assets of another entity or entities in a country or countries other than its home country, usually by owning a capital stake. An equity capital stake of at least 10 per cent is normally considered as a threshold for the control of assets in this context (UNCTAD, 2000a).

period encouraged them to establish themselves in the Indian market. Instead of entering through green field projects[17] and thereby helping the Indian economy,[18] the MNCs preferred the M&A route. The latter helped them to have an easy and quick access to the Indian market. Through their deep pockets, MNCs paved their way in Indian markets and established themselves in no time (Kumar, 2000). Basant (2000) reported that 8 per cent of the total mergers and 32 per cent of the total acquisitions during 1991–1997, were by MNCs. That MNCs adopted the acquisition route to strengthen their presence in the Indian market, is also supported by the fact that 70 per cent of the total M&A deals undertaken by MNCs were in the form of acquisitions.

In an exploratory attempt, Kumar (2000) examines the trends, motives and industrial composition of M&A activity undertaken by MNCs during the post-reform period. He reported that 93 per cent of the total 256 M&A deals undertaken by MNCs during 1993-94 to 1999-2000 were in the form of acquisitions, most of which concluded during the last four years of the period studied (i.e., 1996-2000). Regarding industrial composition, a large proportion (74 per cent) of deals took place in the manufacturing sector. Non-electrical machinery (31deals), food and beverages (25 deals), industrial chemicals and allied (20 deals), drugs and pharmaceuticals (17 deals) and auto components (13 deals) together accounted for 56 per cent of the total M&A activity in manufacturing. Share of services recorded an increasing trend. From 9 per cent (3 out of 32 deals) during 1993-1995 and 19 per cent (27 out of 144 deals) of total deals during 1996-1999, share of services increased to 30 per cent in 1999-2000. Within services (54 deals), banking and financial services (19 deals), advertising and marketing research (11 deals) and software (9 deals) dominated the total deals. MNCs largely invested in products, such as consumer goods and personal care products, which are sensitive to brand loyalties and marketing and distribution network. Due to this reason, MNCs preferred to enter the Indian market through acquisition of

17. Approximately, 40 per cent of the FDI inflows in India during 1997-1999 came in the form of M&As, whereas until 1990, almost all FDI took the form of green field projects, Kumar (2000).

18. Green field investments add to the stock of capital, bring in new knowledge, technology, organisational and entrepreneurial skill, management know-how and lead to knowledge spillovers (Kumar, 2000).

domestic joint venture partners (either through outright purchase or through increased equity stake) that had established market and distribution facilities. This way the MNCs could save time required to establish production facilities and marketing network and thereby, could also show their effective presence in the Indian market.

Another important feature, similar to Indian firms, is that even the MNCs related mergers belonged to the same management. However, unlike Indian firms, they engaged in all horizontal mergers (Beena, 1998; Kumar, 2000). Of the 256 deals in Kumar's (2000) dataset, only 3 could be classified as vertical and the rest were horizontal in nature. The phenomenon of acquisition of foreign firms by Indian firms also began in the late 1990s *albeit*, at a smaller pace.

Pre-merger Characteristics

Comparing the pre-merger characteristics with respect to size, debt and profitability,[19] Das (2000) noticed, that as compared to AD firms, 90 per cent of the AG firms had higher net worth, 68 per cent had lower debt burden and 70 per cent had higher pre-merger profitability. The AD firms were found to be smaller in size, lower in profitability and higher in debt burden than their corresponding AG firms.

Beena (2000) found the AG firms to be less profitable and less leveraged. The greater dependence of AG firms on debt and on retained earnings implied that acquiring firms used more of both internal and external resources for their growth. Acquiring firms were found to be better performing than the overall manufacturing private corporate sector.

Comparing the mean characteristics of AG and AD firms prior to merger, Saple (2000) surprisingly, did not find any statistical difference with respect to the average size, profitability, capital structure and tax provisions between the two sets of firms, after adjusting for industry averages. The AG firms were better than their corresponding AD firms, only in terms of growth and equity ratios. This could be attributed to the fact that the sample of 36 AG firms examined in the study, included only 14 horizontal

19. In her study, the size of sample undertaken for each variable differed because of unavailability of data. Data on size, debt and profitability was available for 52, 38 and 25 merger cases respectively.

mergers (less than 40 per cent) and approximately two-third cases of merger between subsidiary and group companies. In the latter, it was often witnessed that a larger company merged into a smaller company to take advantage of tax provisions. The samples considered by other studies reported here, had much larger share of horizontal mergers than the other. Further, both AG and AD firms were found to be high in terms of size, profitability and liquidity ratio and lower in terms of leveraged ratio and tax provisions than their industry averages.

Post-merger Performance

Saple (2000) reported on the effects of merger by comparing the post-merger performance of the acquiring firms to the weighted average of the pre-merger performance of acquiring (AG) and acquired (AD) firms. The results indicate a once-and-for-all increase in assets, sales and operating profit margins, with no increase in growth rate of acquiring firms in the subsequent years. Further, post-merger profitability and liquidity were found to be lower than the corresponding industry average. However, leverage increased significantly, post-merger. With these results, Saple points to the possibility that mergers were driven by managerial pursuit of growth maximisation that give firms increased capital to pursue other investment plans.

Saple (2000) further, attempted to identify the contribution of merger in the post-merger performance i.e., whether the effects are due to merger induced monopoly events or due to persistence of profit, indicating the possibility of profit even in the absence of merger. The results support the view that mergers do not generate high monopoly rents and they do not impede the competitive process. The merger outcome was found to be affected by the type of merger i.e., whether it was horizontal or BIFR or between the group companies.

For most of the acquiring firms included in the dataset[20] for post-merger performance, Das (2000) recorded a rise in average sales and net worth but only 15 per cent of the firms showed a decline in post-merger profitability. However, results on post-merger profitability vary across the

20. Depending on the measure used, the sample included only 14 to 18 acquiring firms for post-merger performance in Das (2000).

measure of profitability used. Fifty-four per cent of the firms recorded a rise in profitability measured as a ratio of gross profit to net sales whereas only 36 per cent showed a rise, if the measure changed to ratio of gross profit to total capital employed. Approximately, 70 per cent of the firms recorded a rise in returns over net worth and the same per cent of firms found to have declined their gearing ratio. The results imply that firms sought to improve their financial position through a viable capital structure (Beena, 1998).

Further, shareholders of acquired firms grabbed major part of the gains (Beena, 1998). Empirically, Jensen and Ruback (1993) and Jarrell *et al.* (1988) also found the acquired firms to be the main beneficiary of M&A activity. Through the process of merger, more than 80 per cent of the acquiring firms registered a rise in equity share of the major controlling block. This plausibly throws light on two basic motives of M&A activity. First, M&As were used as a means of guarding against takeover attempt that resulted from the increased internal and external competition; and second, they were used to avoid a dilution of control of the shareholding level that could have resulted from the greater financial liberalisation or a desire of the firm to exploit the buoyant capital market (Beena, 1998).

Based on size, leveraged ratio and ownership structure, Bhaumik (2002) explores the agency problem by examining the post-merger performance of 81 firms. Contrary to expectation, the results suggest that the probability of post-merger performance of acquiring firms, relative to the pre-merger period, is negatively related to leverage and inside control (i.e., management owning a controlling stake in the firm) and positively related to the foreign control or ownership of a firm.

Prediction of M&As

Sood and Kaur (2004) attempted to identify takeover targets using financial ratios, such as profitability, leverage, liquidity, activity and valuation ratios of the firms. A sample comprising a set of 37 target companies[21] and a matched sample of 37 control[22] companies, during

21. The takeover target was defined to cover even an attempt to takeover, whether met with success or not.

22. Control group was matched by the business and size of the sample company, size ranging within ± 50 per cent of the market capitalisation of the targeted company.

1997-98 to 2000-01, was considered for the purpose. Before takeover attempt, targeted firms were found to be less profitable, less leveraged and with lower liquidity but with higher valuation ratio than the control group firms. Discriminant analysis performed on the financial ratios to predict takeover targets, showed moderate success in discriminating between target and non-target firms.

5.3 Trends in Mergers and Acquisitions during 2000-2005[23]

Total M&A Deals

Broadly speaking, trends in M&A deals observed during 2000-2005[24] are in conformity with the trends witnessed during 1990s, as reviewed earlier. Out of the total M&A deals, roughly 75 to 80 per cent are in the form of acquisitions (Table 5.3). After recording the highest number of deals in the year 2000, the activity showed a declining trend till 2004. In the 10 months of year 2005, the activity touched new heights, with total deals announced at 2,044 level, which was more than double the deals announced in the year 2004. Further, the number of both the mergers and acquisitions rose (Figure 5.5).

Table 5.3

Year-wise Distribution of M&A Deals, 2000-2005

Year	*2000*	*2001*	*2002*	*2003*	*2004*	*2005**	*Total Deals*
Total no. of acquisitions	1234	1046	974	805	785	1517	6361
Total no. of mergers	278	276	366	307	221	527	1975
Total no. of M&A deals	1512	1322	1340	1112	1006	2044	8336

Note: * January to November 2005.

Source: Compiled from CMIE[4], various issues.

23. The analysis is based on CMIE's publication of *Mergers and Acquisition* document, which started in November 2001. The document gives comprehensive coverage of M&A deals announced in India since 2000.

24. Each year is considered as calendar year i.e., January to December.

Figure 5.5

Number of M&A Deals, 2000-2005

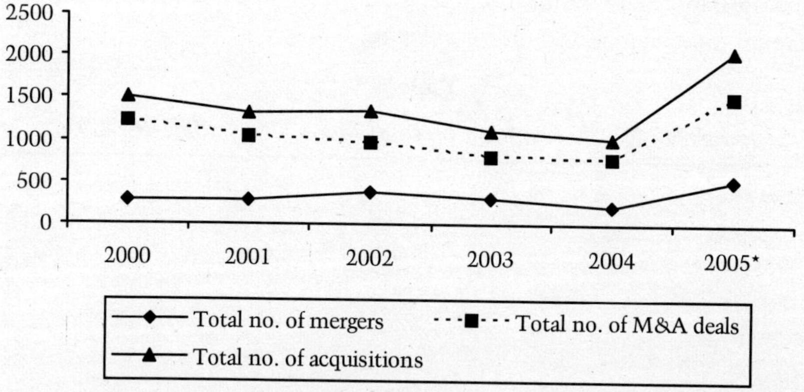

Regarding the industry-wise distribution (Table 5.4) of deals during 2001-2005, 40 per cent of the deals were registered in the services sector and the rest 60 per cent were struck in the manufacturing sector. Within the latter, the chemical industry witnessed the highest deals, followed by electronics and food & beverages. Services other than financial, accounted for one-fourth of the total deals. Industries such as non-ferrous metals,

Figure 5.6

Industry-wise Distribution of Total Number of M&A Deals, 2001-2005

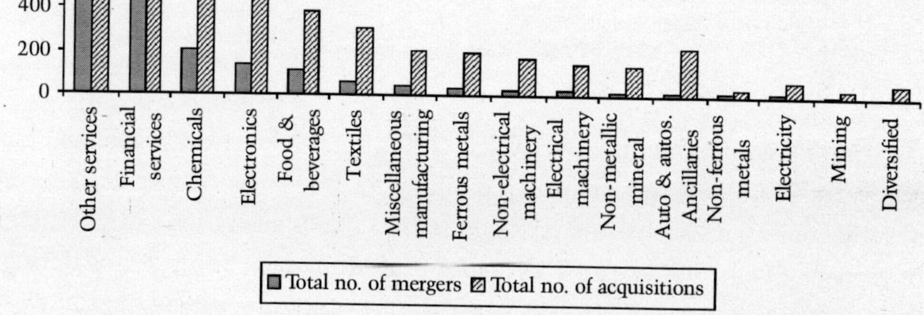

electricity, mining and diversified recorded 1 per cent each of the total M&A deals. Automobiles and automobile ancillaries and diversified industries are the two industry groups in which acquisition deals are much more prominent than the mergers (Figure 5.6).

Table 5.4

*Industry-wise Distribution of Total M&A Deals, 2001 to 2005**

Industry	*Total No. of Mergers(M)*	*Total No. of Acquisitions(A)*	*Total No. of M&A Deals*	*Percentage of the Total Deals*	*Ratio of A/M*
Other services	530	1178	1708	25	2
Financial services	449	494	943	14	1
Chemicals	201	769	970	14	4
Electronics	137	662	799	12	5
Food & beverages	112	380	492	7	3
Textiles	57	306	363	5	5
Miscellaneous manufacturing	41	209	250	4	5
Automobiles & automobile ancillaries	21	222	243	4	11
Ferrous metals	34	196	230	3	6
Non-electrical machinery	28	169	197	3	6
Electrical machinery	26	147	173	3	6
Non-metallic mineral products	21	137	158	2	7
Non-ferrous metals	13	37	50	1	3
Electricity	13	66	79	1	5
Mining	12	38	50	1	3
Diversified	2	61	63	1	31
Real estate transactions	N.A.	56	56	1	–
Total	1697	5127	6824	100	3

Note: * January to November.
Source: Compiled from CMIE[4], various issues.

Total Merger Deals

After recording its highest level in 2002, total merger deals declined for two years. With still two months remaining for 2005, the merger deals have already gone much above the previous levels. The industry-wise distribution of mergers (Table 5.5) changed in favour of non-manufacturing sector during 2000-2005. Though the trend towards non-manufacturing sector was established in the early post-reform period, the manufacturing sector dominated the aggregate merger activity during the pre-liberalised period and the early post-reform years (Beena, 1998; Basant, 2000). The distinguishing feature of aggregate merger activity during 2001-2005 is a clear domination of the non-manufacturing sector. During this period, roughly 60 per cent of the total merger activity took place in services related sector within which financial sector took the major share (Figure 5.7).

Table 5.5

Industry-wise Distribution of Total Merger Deals

Industry	*2001*	*2002*	*2003*	*2004*	*2005**	*Total Mergers (industry-wise)*
Food & beverages	18	24	14	16	40	112
Textiles	10	6	6	9	26	57
Chemicals	33	34	25	39	70	201
Non-metallic mineral products	3	2	3	4	9	21
Ferrous metals	7	5	12	1	9	34
Non-ferrous metals	0	6	1	2	4	13
Non-electrical machinery	5	7	6	1	9	28
Electrical machinery	4	5	4	5	8	26
Electronics	29	24	17	20	47	137
Automobiles & automobile ancillaries	3	5	6	2	5	21
Miscellaneous manufacturing	4	13	0	3	21	41
Diversified	1	0	1	0	0	2
Mining	1	2	1	3	5	12
Electricity	0	2	4	2	5	13
Financial services	96	114	98	37	104	449
Other services	62	117	109	77	165	530
Total mergers (year-wise)	276	366	307	221	527	1697

Source: Same as Table 5.4.

The earlier trend of industrial clustering exhibited during 1990s is also established during 2001-2005. Within the manufacturing sector, chemical industry witnessed the highest number of mergers, hovering between 10-15 per cent every year, followed by clcctronics, food & beverages and textiles (Figure 5.8).

Figure 5.7

Industry-wise Trend in Total Number of Merger Deals, 2001-2005

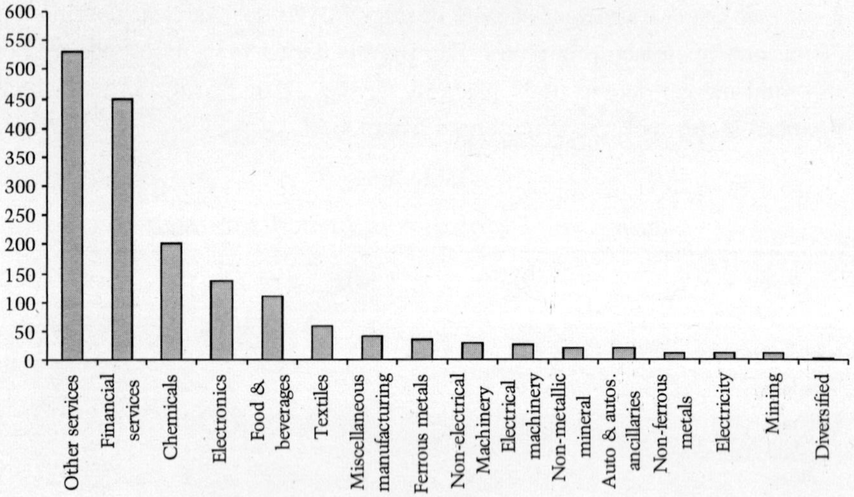

Figure 5.8

Percentage Share of Each Industry in Total Merger Deals, 2001-2005

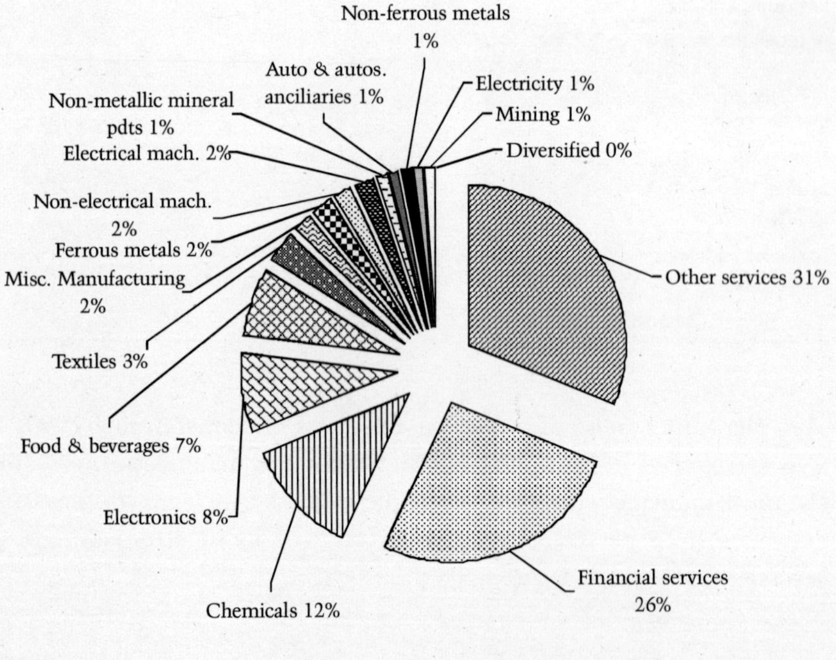

Total Acquisition Deals

Unlike the total merger deals, on acquisition front the manufacturing sector still dominates. Two-thirds of the total 5,127 acquisition deals (Table 5.6) took place in manufacturing and the rest one-third in services. In contrast to 26 per cent of mergers in the financial sector, the acquisition deals witnessed less than 10 per cent of total deals. Within the manufacturing sector, the pattern of industrial clustering is the same as exhibited by the merger deals. The chemical industry tops the list with 15 per cent of total deals followed by electronics, food & beverages and textiles (Figure 5.9).

Table 5.6

Industry-wise Distribution of Total Acquisition Deals, 2001-2005

Industry	*2001*	*2002*	*2003*	*2004*	*2005**	*Total Acquisitions (industry-wise)*
Food & beverages	99	69	67	54	91	380
Textiles	48	54	53	52	99	306
Chemicals	171	146	128	120	204	769
Non-metallic mineral products	26	25	23	20	43	137
Ferrous metals	32	34	37	36	57	196
Non-ferrous metals	7	11	6	5	8	37
Non-electrical machinery	30	48	28	20	43	169
Electrical machinery	35	41	27	15	29	147
Electronics	169	125	86	96	186	662
Automobiles & automobile ancillaries	44	31	40	34	73	222
Miscellaneous manufacturing	31	28	26	30	94	209
Diversified	18	11	10	8	14	61
Mining	5	4	6	7	16	38
Electricity	12	11	12	10	21	66
Financial services	95	115	77	72	135	494
Other services	186	213	169	206	404	1178
Real estate transactions	38	8	10	0	0	56
Total acquisitions (year-wise)	1046	974	805	785	1517	5127

Source: Same as Table 5.4.

Figure 5.9

Industry-wise Trend in Total Number of Acquisition Deals, 2001-2005

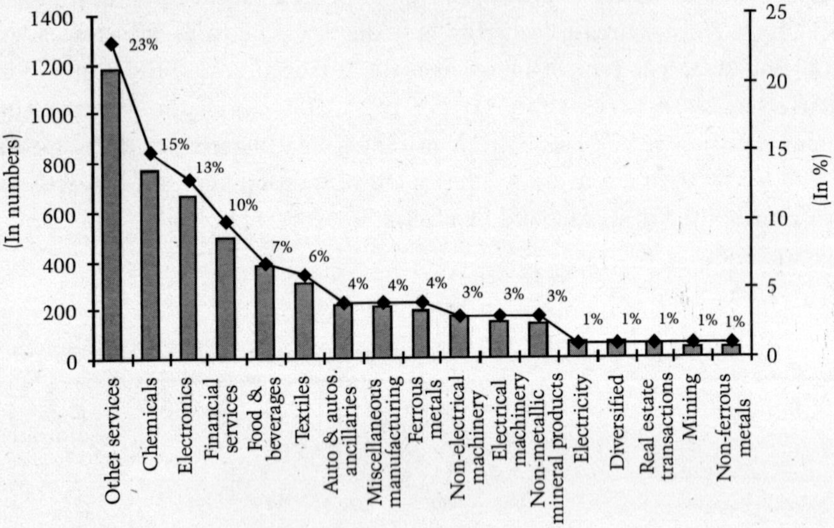

In order to rule out any possibility of aggregation bias and on account of inter-industry differences in the features of firms, the analysis in the next four chapters is carried out on an individual industry, namely, drugs and pharmaceutical.

5.4 Rationale for an Industry-specific Analysis

Studies on mergers and acquisition reveal that both the incidence and the motivation for M&As differ greatly across industries and large inter-industry differences exist in the characteristics of firms. Further, it has been suggested in the empirical literature that pooling across industry can lead to statistically biased results. However, pooling across time is less risky if there are no drastic changes in economic conditions, such as a change in the policy regime. Trahan and Shawky (1992) suggested that the identification of merging and non-merging firms with a particular financial ratio differed across industries. Singh (1971), Trahan (1994) and Sorensen (2000) also documented that results differ across industries.

Referring to inter-industry differences in India, we find that not only do the averages with respect to different variables differ, the trends over time differ as well. For example, with respect to the average profitability (PAT/ sales) during 1997-98 to 2003-04, aluminium industry maintained 13 to 14 per cent of profits, mining was roughly at 10 per cent, while non-ferrous metals ranged between 8 to 9 per cent. Industries, such as electrical machinery, metal and metal products, cement and plastic products, on the other hand, earned negative profits throughout this period (CMIE[2], 2003, 2004). Further, focussing on changes over time, the tea industry witnessed a sharp decline in average profitability from 12 per cent in 1997-98 to negative margins in 2003-04, mining industry increased from 10 to 18 per cent during the same time periods, and automobile sector experienced a decline from 5 per cent in 1997-98 to negative margin in 2000-01 and again regained initial level in 2003-04. So far as leverage ratios are concerned, similar inter-industry variations can be witnessed. Referring to the same period, on an average, industries such as sugar, cement, steel and ferrous metals have their debt-equity ratio between 2.5 to 3 times. Mining, non-ferrous metal and tea and coffee averaged nearly 0.5 times during 1997-98 to 2003-04. Taking note of these variations among industries, it is suggested that examining the selection process in M&A activity through a sample from different industries would certainly lead to an aggregation bias.

Further, variations in industry-level factors, such as motives, structure and industry-specific regulations also induce differences in the kind of corporate structuring that takes place in each industry. Also, effects of mergers on concentration and competition are better understood if the focus is on the industrial concentration and composition of firms that are in competition with each other in an industry.

Listing factors more specifically,

- The characteristics of average firm in terms of size, profitability may differ among industries.
- The main motivation behind M&A activity may differ.
- Structure of industry differs i.e., whether the industry consists of a large number of small firms or is it dominated by small number of big firms, this in turn determines the opportunities available for further growth.
- Extent of competition faced from domestic or foreign firms differs.

- The extent to which an industry is subject to industrial shock differs.
- Number of mergers experienced by each industry also differs. In India, it is observed that the M&A activity is not uniformly distributed across industries.[25]

The industry chosen for our analysis is Indian Drugs and Pharmaceutical (D&P). Partly on account of its importance and partly due to its analytical value, the D&P industry is preferred to understand the distinguishing features of acquired, acquiring, and non-merging firms, and other aspects of mergers. Also the D&P being one of the most merger-intensive industries in post-liberalised regime in India, along with the availability of data on both the acquiring and the acquired firms, enables us to work on the mergers that took place in this industry. The analysis focusses on all mergers that took place during the period 1992-93 to 2005-2006 and considers only those merging firms for which data are available on both the acquiring and acquired firms.[26]

5.5 An Overview of the Indian Pharmaceutical Industry

The pharmaceutical industry showed its presence in India only in the post-independence period when the government took the initiative to establish Hindustan Antibiotics Ltd. in 1954 followed by the Indian Drugs and Pharmaceutical Ltd. in 1961. The domestic producers just processed the imported bulk drugs into formulations. Initially, to have access to advanced technology and international manufacturing practices, the government also encouraged multinational companies (MNCs) to set up their units in India. Till 1970s, the MNCs dominated the Indian market, holding 80 per cent of the market share. Over the last five decades, the government gave considerable boost to the domestic industry through its regulatory framework. As a result, the domestic companies made phenomenal progress. On account of factors, such as availability of cheap manpower giving competitive edge to the domestic producers, large population base giving larger demand, developed chemical industry

25. For details, see Agarwal (2002) and Basant (2000).

26. This restricted the analysis to only those firms that are listed on various stock exchanges of the country.

supporting the growth of bulk drugs, and above all, government's policy initiative giving boost to the domestic firms, the pharmaceutical industry in India has established an international presence.

There has been an unparalleled growth in the number of firms engaged in the manufacture of pharmaceutical products. The number of units increased from 2,257 in 1969-70 to 5,156 in 1979-80. According to estimates of the Organisation of Pharmaceutical Producers of India (OPPI, 2004), the number stood at 10,702 in 2003-04, employing a total of 2.9 million workers. The total assets of the pharmaceutical firms in the organised sector[27] were valued at roughly Rs 200 crore in 2003-04, of which gross fixed assets account for 90 crore. Currently, the Indian pharmaceutical industry is the fourth largest in terms of volume, holding 8 per cent of the global pharmaceutical sales and 13th largest in value, holding, however, a small share of 1 per cent, on account of low prices of pharmaceutical products. The share of domestic companies increased from 20 per cent of industry sales in 1970 to 70 per cent in recent years (ICRA, 2005b). Also in 2003-04, 40 per cent of the sales value was from exports with imports accounting for only 8 per cent of the total sales (CMIE[3], 2004). Following the global trend, the Indian industry has also been undergoing a process of consolidation since the mid-1990s.

The pharmaceutical industry in India, like the global pharmaceutical industry is also fragmented with high concentration at the top level.[28] Out of the total 10,000 units manufacturing pharmaceutical products, approximately 300 are in the organised sector and the rest are highly unorganised very small units. Even within the former, there are large variations in market share. From Table 5.7 we observe that during all the three selected years, more than 85 per cent of total firms maintained less than 1 per cent of market share and merely 5 per cent of firms had a market share of more than 2 per cent. The top 10 players accounted for 43 per cent of the market whereas the top 5 players supplied 30 per cent of the total sales during 2003-04. On account of a series of M&As in the

27. The data on firms within organised sector is collected by Prowess Corporate database (CMIE). Currently, it covers financial data of 425 pharmaceutical companies, many of which are closed or extinguished on account of losses or mergers.

28. The top 10 companies of the world accounted for 44 per cent of the global market in 2003, with no individual player catering more than 9 per cent of the market (ICRA, 2004).

pharmaceutical industry, the shares of top players have increased since the mid-1990s. Ranbaxy Laboratories Ltd. remained the largest firm, supplying 7, 8 and 11 per cent of the total sales, respectively, during 1994-95, 1999-2000 and 2003-04. The intensity of competition among the next 10 to 15 firms is indicated by the change in their relative positions in the industry every year. Apart from M&As, the players also focussed on production of formulations, brand building and establishing wide distribution and marketing networks to ensure a deeper penetration of the domestic market and to increase the market share.

Table 5.7

Distribution of Firms according to Market Share during Selected Years

Market Share (in %)	*2004-05*	*1999-2000*	*1994-95*
0.05	67 (31)	74 (32)	56 (29)
1	122 (57)	129 (56)	108 (56)
1.5	9 (4)	12 (5)	13 (7)
2	7 (3)	5 (2)	7 (4)
3	2 (1)	6 (3)	6 (3)
4	5 (2)	5 (2)	1 (.5)
>4	3 (1)	1 (0)	3 (1.5)
Total firms	215	232	194

Note: Figures in parentheses are percentages of the respective totals.

Source: Calculations are based on data collected from Prowess database (CMIE).

An important distinguishing feature of this industry is low bargaining strength of end-consumers. This is largely because the choice of drugs lies with the doctors. This makes a widespread marketing and distribution network of vital importance for the success of the company. Further, on account of a large number of brands for the same product, companies employ aggressive marketing techniques to grab a larger market share.

Research is an important driver of growth of the pharmaceutical industry. It is basically concentrated in developed countries—the US alone, for example, accounts for 44 per cent of total global research expenditure. Having obtained protection through process patent,[29] Indian pharmaceutical industry concentrated research in process engineering of bulk drugs and development of novel drug delivery systems (NDDS) for formulations, focussing on anti-infective. With the enactment of patent bill,[30] Indian companies cannot simply rely on finding alternative manufacturing processes for making new drugs (patented) launched overseas, which they would no longer be able to sell. Therefore, focussing on R&D, innovative research discovery of new chemical entities (NCE) and NDDS for existing drugs, expenditure on R&D is becoming extremely important along with technically qualified manpower and access to technology.

Performance Measures in the Indian Pharmaceutical Industry

The overall production of pharmaceutical industry is divided in two parts: (a) bulk drugs and (b) formulations. Bulk drugs refer to the active pharmaceutical ingredients (APIs) that provide raw material for the manufacture of formulations. Adding other substances named, excipients to APIs produce the end-product called formulations. Unlike bulk drugs, the formulations can be administered directly to the patient and are sold by brand names in various forms, such as tablets, capsules, syrups and injections. By 1980s, the industry had attained a considerable degree of self-sufficiency in the requirement of bulk drugs and had also acquired technical capability to produce them. Bulk drugs production is controlled by the organised sector. Its production also forms a large part in the total exports of our pharmaceutical products. With regard to formulations, India is self-sufficient in domestic demand. The manufacture of formulations is also dominated by the organised sector. However, a large number of small-scale producers are also engaged in its production. During 1980-2004, the

29. To develop the domestic pharmaceutical industry, initially, the Indian government issued the Indian Patent Act (IPA) in 1970. Its main objective was to provide protection through process patent rather than product patent, as is prevalent in other countries. The Indian firms could expand their share and consequently, share of MNCs declined.

30. On account of India's commitment to World Trade Organization (WTO) signed in 1994, there has been a shift from the process patent to product patent, beginning from 2005.

share of bulk drugs in the total production of pharmaceutical products increased from 15 per cent to 22 per cent whereas that of formulations fell from 85 per cent to 75 per cent (Figure 5.10).

Figure 5.10

Share of Bulk Drugs and Formulations in Total Production, 1980-2004

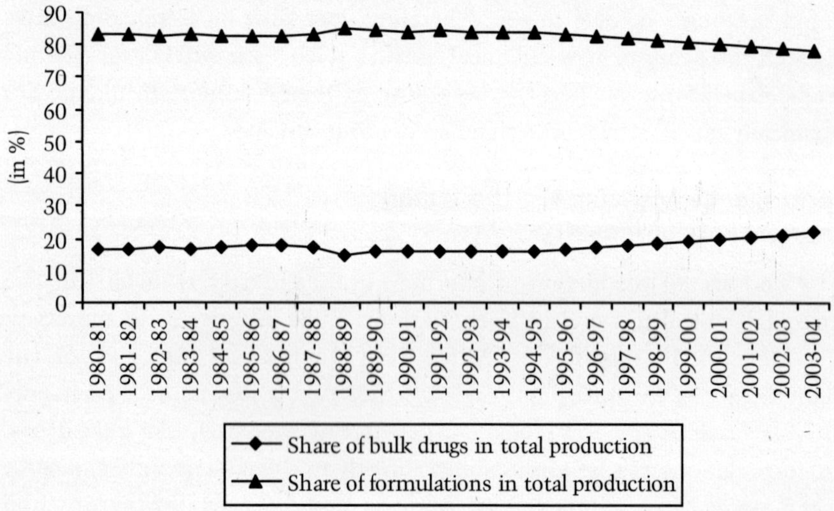

Bulk drugs' production forms a large part in the total exports of our pharmaceutical products. Figure 5.11 reflects wide fluctuation in the shares of bulk drugs production and formulations, observed in the exports of the Indian pharmaceutical industry over a period of 20 years from 1980-81 to 1999-2000. From less than one-fourth of exports in the form of bulk drugs during 1980-1986, the share rose to more than 60 per cent during the late 1980s. In recent years, both the segments have roughly shared equal proportions in total exports. The rise in the export market is largely accounted for by high quality products, which are supplied at competitive prices. Government incentives, R&D competitiveness and vision to grow and exports have played an important role in encouraging Indian firms to enter into export markets. Over time, there has also been a shift in the export-destination countries from Asia and East European countries to US and China. Today the Indian pharmaceutical industry exports to 65 countries with its total exports valued at Rs 167 billion in 2004 (CMIE[3], 2005). To enhance exports and establish themselves in developed markets, in recent years, few big Indian pharmaceutical companies have also entered into alliances, setting up their subsidiaries, joint ventures, and acquisition of overseas companies especially in the USA and Europe.

Figure 5.11

Share of Bulk Drugs and Formulations in Total Exports

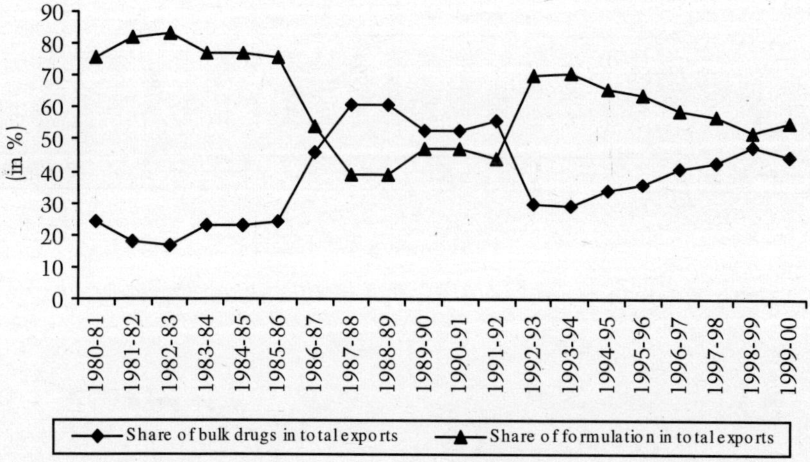

With regard to imports, the predominance of bulk drugs imports indicates the dependence of India's pharmaceutical industry on it. Although the relative importance of bulk drugs in total imports declined over time, it still accounted for 75 per cent of imports in 2003-04. The average proportion of 93 per cent and 7 per cent for bulk drugs and formulations, respectively, in total imports during 1980s, changed to 81 per cent and 19 per cent during 1990s (Figure 5.12). During the 1980s, share of imports in total production exceeded that of exports. However, by the late 1980s, share of imports and exports almost coincided roughly at 10 per cent. Since the early 1990s, the share of imports has exhibited a downward trend, as against an upward trend in the share of exports in total production (Figure 5.13).

Figure 5.12

Share of Bulk Drugs and Formulations in Total Imports

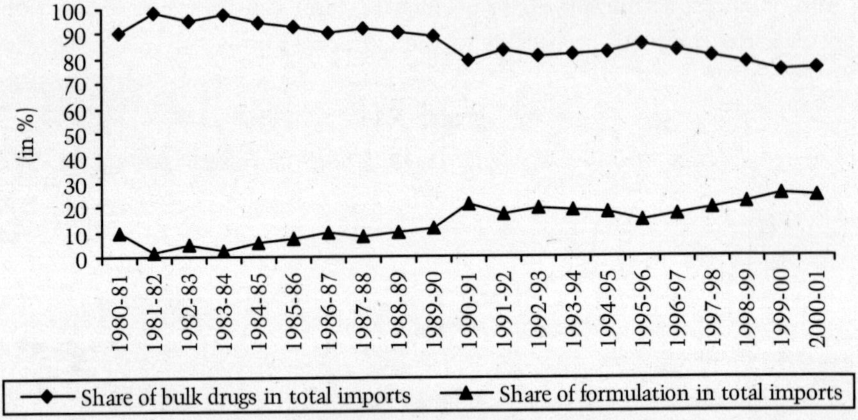

Figure 5.13

Share of Exports and Imports in Total Production of Pharmaceuticals

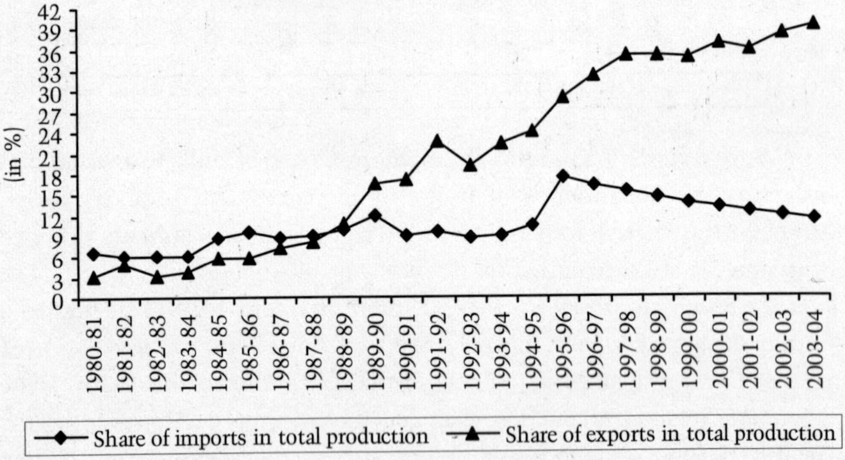

Higher annual growth of exports and its increasing share in total production has made the balance of trade (BoT) in pharmaceutical industry very favourable for the Indian economy. Till late 1980s, the balance of trade was negative. However, since early 1990s, the balance of trade is not only positive, it is rising consistently. In fact, in recent years, exports of pharmaceutical industries is 3.5 times more than imports (Figure 5.14).

Figure 5.14

Balance of Trade in Pharmaceutical Industry, 1980-81 to 2003-04

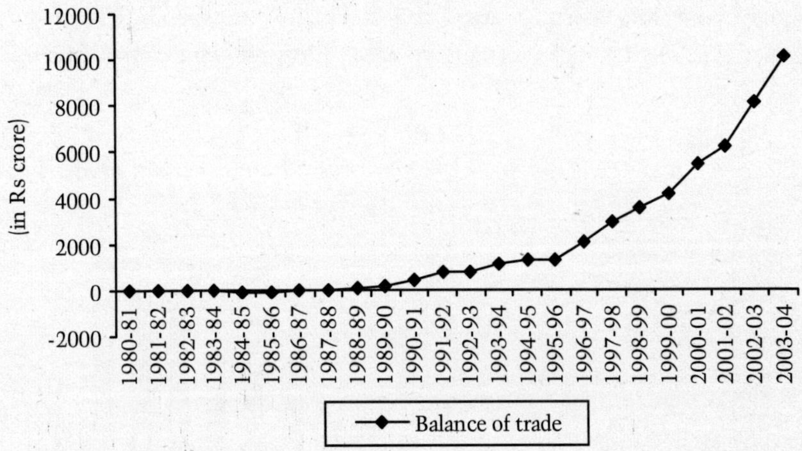

As pharmaceutical industry is one of the most knowledge-driven industries of the world, R&D expenditure has considerable impact on its growth, export intensity and competitiveness. Evidence suggests that pharmaceutical industry is one of the most research-intensive industries in India. Although the expenditure on R&D has consistently increased in value terms (Figure 5.15), its ratio to total production in the industry has either remained constant or has fallen. The expenditure incurred on R&D by Indian firms, stands nowhere in comparison to the expenditure made by pharmaceutical firms in the US.[31] The Indian government has also been encouraging R&D activities in this industry through various measures, such as tax incentives, relaxation in import licensing to R&D units and relaxation in industrial licensing for using results of R&D units.

On account of the new intellectual property rights (IPR) regime, which is putting pressure on the domestic industry to launch new products, top Indian pharmaceuticals are steadily increasing R&D expenditure. On an average R&D expenditure rose from 4 per cent of net sales in 2002-03 to 5.8 in 2003-04 and 7.74 per cent in 2004-05. After the launch of IPR, reverse capital engineering is not allowed. The only option, therefore, for

31. US companies' R&D to sales ratio is 17 per cent (Aggarwal, 2004).

domestic companies to have their own intellectual property (IP) portfolios, is through R&D. According to recent estimates, Ranbaxy and Dr. Reddy's are investing around 10 per cent, which is close to the international standard, and Sun Pharmaceutical and Wockhardt are spending between 8 to 9 per cent of their sales revenue on R&D (Prowess database—CMIE).

Figure 5.15

Research and Development Expenditure in Pharmaceutical Industry

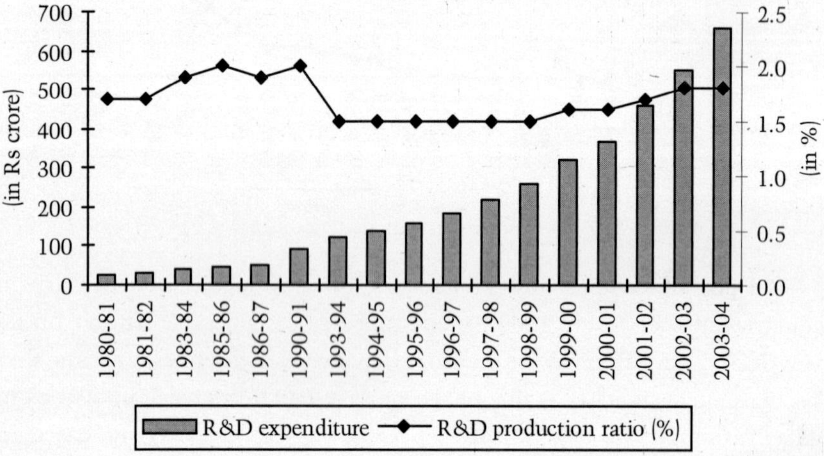

The following sub-section presents distribution of firms according to sales, total assets, profitability, debt-equity ratio, and R&D indicators during the two selected periods.

Distribution of D&P Firms according to Various Indicators

In order to further explore the other characteristics of the pharmaceutical industry and to gain insights into inter-firm variations, we have also presented the more disaggregated data compiled from Prowess database (CMIE).

Size Distribution of Firms according to Sales and Total Assets

Size, measured in terms of total assets and sales, was distributed in three classes: small size (< Rs 200 crore), medium size (Rs 200–Rs 500 crore) and large size (>Rs 500 crore). The distribution of firms during

1994-95, among various size classes (Tables 5.8) was found to be the same irrespective of the variable used to measure. Ninety-five per cent of firms were small-sized, 5 per cent belonged to medium size and only 1 per cent of the 215 firms had their total assets and sales greater than Rs 500 crore. During 2004-05, the distribution of firms changed in favour of medium and large-sized firms. From 6 per cent of firms in these two classes in 1994-95, 22 per cent of 218 had their total assets greater than Rs 200 crore. The average size of industry, measured in terms of both total assets and sales, increased by 3.5 times during the period 1994-95 to 2004-05.

Table 5.8

Size Distribution of Indian Pharmaceutical Firms, 1994-95 and 2004-05

→ Sales (Rs crore) / *↓ Total Assets (Rs crore)*	*< 200*		*200-500*		*> 500*		*Total*	
	1994-95	*2004-05*	*1994-95*	*2004-05*	*1994-95*	*2004-05*	*1994-95*	*2004-05*
< 200	199[a]	166[aa]	3	4	0	0	202 (95)	170 (78)
200 – 500	2	9	7	16	1	5	10 (4)	30 (14)
> 500	1	1	1	1	1	16	3 (1)	18 (8)
Total	202 (95)	176 (81)	11 (4)	21 (9.5)	2 (1)	21 (9.5)	215 (100)	218 (100)

Notes: a. It includes 21 companies that had positive assets but 0 sales.
aa. It includes 4 companies that had positive total assets but 0 sales.
Figures in parentheses are percentages of the grand total.

Distribution of Firms according to Sales and Profitability

In order to have a clear depiction of the levels of profitability (measured as profit after tax, PAT/sales) among various sized firms, we further sub-divided small-sized firms in four parts: less than Rs 25 crore, Rs 25–50 crore, Rs 50–100 crore and Rs 100–200 crore (Tables 5.9 and 5.10). A noticeable pattern that emerged in 1994-95 was that all firms with negative profit margin as well as very high profit margins (>15 per cent) concentrated in the small-sized class (<Rs 200 crore). Within the small-

sized firms, approximately 79 per cent of the firms had sales less than Rs 50 crore. This indicates that very small firms were either running losses or enjoying very high profits. The medium and large-sized firms were clustered in medium or high ranges of profitability.

In 2004-05, the distribution of firms changed according to their profitability levels. The absolute as well as relative proportion of firms with negative profitability increased considerably. Eighty-six per cent of the 56 firms had assets less than Rs 100 crore as against 100 per cent firms in this size in 1994-95. Among the firms with very high profitability, no firm out of the 24 belonged to the medium and large size classes in 1994-95; whereas 67 per cent of the 22 firms in 2004-05 were in medium and large size classes. Among very small-sized firms (<Rs 25 crore), those with negative profitability increased from 7 per cent to roughly 40 per cent. There is a tangible shift in very small firms towards negative and low profitability in 2004-05 whereas medium and large-sized firms shifted towards higher profitability levels.

Table 5.9

Distribution of Pharmaceutical Firms according to Sales and Profitability, 1994-95

→ *Sales (Rs crore)* / ↓ *Profit Margin (in %)*	*< 25*	*25 – 50*	*50 – 100*	*100 –200*	*200 –500*	*>500*	*Total*
< 0	8	1	2	0	0	0	11 (6)
0 – 5	38	10	8	6	5	1	68 (35)
5 – 10	32	6	9	12	4	0	63 (33)
10 – 15	15	5	3	1	2	1	27 (14)
> 15	16	3	1	4	0	0	24 (12)
Total	109 (56)	25 (13)	23 (12)	23 (12)	11 (7)	2 (1)	193 (100)

Note: Figures in parentheses are percentages of the grand total.

Table 5.10

Distribution of Pharmaceutical Firms according to Sales and Profitability, 2004-05

Profit Margin (in %) ↓ / Sales (Rs crore) →	< 25	25 – 50	50 – 100	100 –200	200 –500	>500	Total
< 0	39	4	5	7	0	1	56 (26)
0 – 5	22	15	19	8	3	2	69 (32)
5 – 10	10	10	5	8	9	2	44 (21)
10 – 15	4	3	2	3	3	8	23 (11)
> 15	5	1	1	1	6	8	22 (10)
Total	80 (37)	33 (15)	32 (15)	27 (13)	21 (10)	21 (10)	214 (100)

Note: Figures in parentheses are percentages of the grand total.

Distribution of Firms according to Sales and Leveraged Structure

Gearing levels are comfortable in the Indian pharmaceutical industry with certain prominent companies having an almost debt-free structure. Sixty-five per cent of the firms have maintained D-E ratio less than 1 per cent and only 22 per cent of 196 firms have their leveraged levels greater than 1.5 per cent (Tables 5.11). Ninety-three per cent of the latter firms are small-sized firms and a significant number of medium and large-sized firms have low D-E ratios. Distribution of firms among various levels of D-E ratio remained the same over a period of 10 years i.e., 1994-95 to 2004-05. The MNCs were found to be less leveraged than the Indian firms (CMIE[1], 2004).

Distribution of Firms according to Sales and R&D Expenditure

To trace the changes in the number of firms undertaking R&D expenditure[32] as well as the amount incurred on R&D, an analysis is

32. In Prowess database (CMIE), R&D expenses are available both on capital and current account; therefore R&D expenditure incurred is calculated by adding the expenses available on both the accounts.

carried out for the periods 1994-95, 2004-05. The number of firms undertaking R&D expenditure rose from 80 in 1994-95 to 102 in 2004-05 (Tables 5.12). During 1994-95 only 80 out of 215 firms were found to be incurring expenditure on R&D, 33 per cent of which maintained R&D/ sales ratio greater than 2 per cent and majority of which belonged to small size i.e., with sales less than Rs 200 crore.

Table 5.11

Distribution of Pharmaceutical Firms according to Sales and Leverage, 1994-95 and 2004-05

→ *Sales (Rs crore)* ↓ *D-E Ratio*	*< 200*		*200-500*		*> 500*		*Total*	
	1994-95	*2004-05*	*1994-95*	*2004-05*	*1994-95*	*2004-05*	*1994-95*	*2004-05*
<0.5	80	57	2	10	1	10	83 (42)	77 (42)
0.5 – 1	42	33	2	4	1	7	45 (23)	44 (24)
1 – 1.5	21	23	4	3	0	1	25 (13)	27 (15)
1.5 – 2	21	15	1	0	0	1	22 (11)	16 (9)
>2	19	17	2	1	0	1	21 (11)	19 (10)
Total	183 (93)	145 (79)	11 (6)	18 (10)	2 (1)	20 (11)	196 (100)	183 (100)

Note: Figures in parentheses are percentages of the grand total.

In 2004-05 firms with greater than 2 per cent of R&D/sales ratio, increased to 41 per cent. Another important change is that a considerable number of large-sized firms are undertaking R&D expenditure. Most of the firms undertaking R&D/sales ratio greater than 2 per cent are medium and large-sized firms. This number increased from 12 per cent in 1994-95 to 62 per cent in 2004-05. Out of the large-sized firms, 20 per cent undertook R&D/sales greater than 6 per cent whereas among medium-sized firms, 50 per cent maintained R&D/sales ratio greater than 2 per cent. This has resulted in a rise in the average R&D/sales ratio of the industry from 2 to 2.5 per cent, respectively, during the two years selected for the analysis.

Table 5.12

Distribution of Pharmaceutical Firms according to Sales and R&D, 1994-95 and 2004-05

→ Sales (Rs crore) / ↓ R&D/Sales (in %)	< 200		200-500		> 500		Total	
	1994-95	2004-05	1994-95	2004-05	1994-95	2004-05	1994-95	2004-05
<1	33	31	6	6	1	3	40 (49)	40 (39)
1 – 2	14	16	1	4	15	0	15 (17)	20 (20)
2 – 4	12	10	3	6	0	8	15 (18)	24 (23)
4 – 6	6	3	0	1	1	3	7 (9)	7 (7)
>6	4	3	0	2	0	6	4 (6)	11 (11)
Total	69 (85)	63 (61.5)	10 (1)	19 (19)	2 (3)	20 (19.5)	80 (100)	102 (100)

Note: Figures in parentheses are percentages of the grand total.

After an overview of the broad trends in the Indian pharmaceutical industry, in the next section we present the trends in M&As in the Indian D&P industry.

5.6 Consolidation in Indian Pharmaceutical Industry through M&As

Akin to the global pharmaceutical industry, the Indian D&P industry is also one of the most merger-intensive industries. Soon after the initiation of the economic reform process in 1991-92, the pharma companies started consolidating their capacities through mergers and acquisitions of brands, plants and assets, divisions and units of firms. The driving force behind M&A was to consolidate the highly fragmented pharma sector to achieve faster growth, to avoid delays associated with building a new plant and increasing their shares.

The growth of few companies, such as Sun Pharmaceutical and Matrix Laboratories Ltd., in the current scenario is spectacular and worth mentioning. With both organic and external growth through aggressive and strong M&A strategy, Matrix Laboratories Ltd. has grown by more than 17 times i.e., from a turnover of Rs 45 crore in 1999-2000, to approximately Rs 800 crore in 2005-06, and its market capitalisation has grown by 300 times i.e., from Rs 10 crore to Rs 3,000 crore, during the same period. From a negative profit margin of Rs 9 crore in 2000, its net profit grew to over Rs 182 crore during 2005-06. After successfully merging with Medicorp Technologies India Ltd. and Vorin Laboratories Ltd.[33] in 2002-03, it continued its appetite for M&As. In 2004-05, it struck a number of deals, such as merger with Strides Arcolab, acquisition of controlling state in Belgian Dockpharma,[34] joint ventures with South African Aspen Pharmacare Holdings Ltd., and alliance with Chinese Xiamen Mchem Pharma Group and purchase of a dosage facility in Nasik. Further, it merged with Fine Drugs and Chemical Ltd. (FDCL) and Vera Laboratories Ltd. in 2003-04 and 2004-05 respectively. With the ability to integrate various entities and successfully consolidate them, Matrix is on a high-rise growth path. Similarly, Sun Pharmaceutical, through mergers and acquisitions has grown by 8 times in total assets, 6 times in net profits, and 3 times in sales, during 1999-2000 to 2005-06.

Concerning trends in mergers in D&P industry, it is observed that approximately 109 mergers[35] took place during 1990-91 to 2004-05. With a few exceptions, most of these mergers were horizontal in nature. In the initial phase of economic liberalisation, merger activity was quite slow and acquisition of brands was more common among the firms. In the mid-1990s, the M&A activity picked up moderately and in the early years of this century, the merger activity accelerated rapidly (Table 5.13 and Figure 5.16). More than 65 per cent of the total mergers in D&P industry during 1990-2005 were undertaken in the last five years. This has also led to a rise in concentration levels[36] in the industry since 2000-01. An important feature of this activity is that about 30 to 35 firms are involved in

33. Both Vorin and Medicorp were underperforming, however, they had the necessary potential to grow.

34. Matrix acquired 22 per cent of this company. This was one of the largest foreign acquisitions by any Indian pharma company during that period.

35. The number includes both private and public limited companies.

36. Effect of mergers on the level of concentration in Indian D&P industry is covered in Chapter 8.

undertaking more than 100 mergers. Few firms are very aggressive in nature and have undertaken mergers in large numbers. For example, during the period in question, Sun Pharmaceutical undertook 7 mergers, NPIL[37] (8), Cadila Healthcare Ltd. (4), Matrix Laboratories (4) and Dr. Reddy's Laboratories Ltd. involved in (4) mergers.

Table 5.13

Total Number of Mergers[a] in Pharmaceutical Industry

Year	*No. of Mergers*	*Year*	*No. of Mergers*	*Year*	*No. of Mergers*
1990-91	2	1995-96	5	2000-01	10
1991-92	1	1996-97	4	2001-02	14
1992-93	4	1997-98	3	2002-03	12
1993-94	4	1998-99	5	2003-04	15
1994-95	4	1999-2000	5	2004-05	21
Total	15	Total	22	Total	72
% of Grand total	13.76		20.18		66.06

Note: [a] The numbers are written from the perspective of acquiring firm belonging to D&P.

Source: Based on various issues of CMIE[4]; Company News and Notes; website of Bombay Stock. Exchange <*www.bseindia.com*> and the data compiled by National Informatics Centre.

Figure 5.16

Number of Mergers in Pharmaceutical Industry, 1990-2005

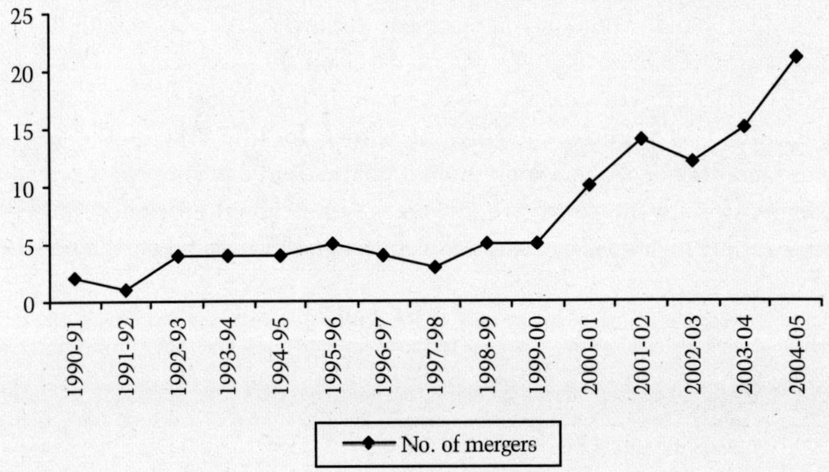

37. Nicholas Piramal India Ltd. (NPIL) was later renamed as, Piramal Healthcare Ltd.

Comparing the M&As in Chemical and D&P[38] industries since 2001,[39] we find, on an average, close to 30 per cent of mergers and acquisitions taking place in the chemical industry are from D&P industry (Table 5.14 and Figure 5.17). Further, both mergers and acquisitions are rising in D&P industry. However, the extent of rise in the number of mergers is more than in the acquisitions.

Table 5.14

M&As in Chemical and D&P Industry, 2001-2005

Year	*Total No. of Mergers in Chemical Industry*	*Total No. of Mergers in D&P Industry*	*Total No. of Acquisitions in Chemical Industry*	*Total No. Acquisitions in D&P Industry*
2001	33	10 (30)	171	51(30)
2002	34	14 (41)	146	55 (38)
2003	25	12 (48)	128	32 (25)
2004	39	15 (39)	120	37 (31)
2005*	70	21 (30)	204	65 (32)
Total	201	72 (36)	769	240 (31)

Note: * The year 2005 is covered from January to November. Figures in parenthesis are M&As in D&P as a percentage of M&As in chemical industry in the corresponding year.

Source: Compilation is based on CMIE[4], various issues.

Acquisitions in Global Markets

Indian pharmaceutical industry is truly becoming global in nature (Table 5.15) and making its presence felt worldwide. India's strength lies in its cost competencies and formulation development. According to Frost and Sullivan (a growth consulting company), Indian pharmaceutical is positioned as a perfect partner of choice for the rest of the world pharmaceutical collaborations. Indian pharmaceutical companies provide competitive advantage in five key areas, *viz*., capital efficiency, process engineering, high quality, qualified chemists and low capital cost. Since the

38. D&P is one of the 16 sub-groups of the chemical industry. The remaining 15 sub-groups are: inorganic, alkalies, fertilisers, pesticides, paints & varnish, dyes & pigments, soap & detergents, cosmetics, organics chemical, other chemical, polymers, plastic products, petroleum products, tyres & tubes, and rubber & rubber products. The D&P accounts for approximately one-third of the total firms in the chemical industry.
39. The systematic compilation of industry-wise distribution of M&As is available from 2001 onwards.

Figure 5.17

M&As in D&P Industry, 2001-2005

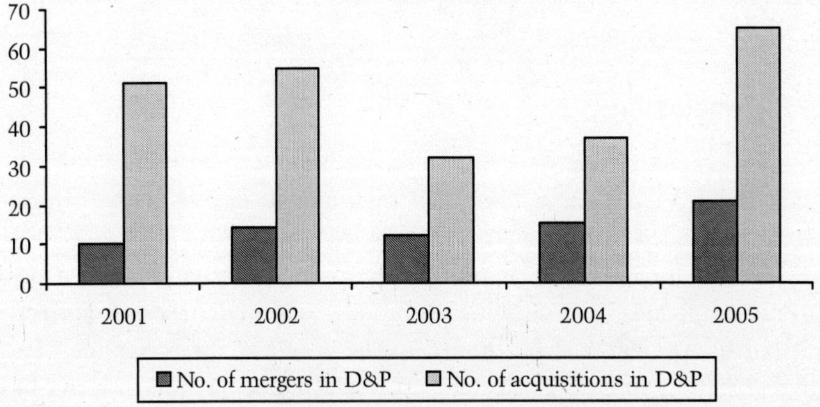

Table 5.15

The Indian Acquisitions of Foreign Companies, 2005-06

	Acquirer	*Target*	*Country*	*Deal Size ($ million)*
February 2006	Aurobindo	Milphar Ltd.	UK	Undisclosed
December 2005	Glenmark	Bouwer Barlett	South Africa	Undisclosed
November 2005	Sun Pharma	Able Labs	US	23.15
November 2005	Dr. Reddy's Labs	Roche's API Unit	Mexico	59
October 2005	Nicholas Piramal	Avecia Pharma	UK	16.25
August 2005	Sun Pharma	Valeant Pharma Unit	Hungary	10
July 2005	Jublant Organosys	Trinity Labs	US	12.3
June 2005	Torrent	Heumann Pharma	Germany	30
June 2005	Matrix Labs	Docpharma	Belgium	263
June 2005	Ranbaxy	Efarmes Sa	Spain	18
April 2005	Dishman Pharma	Synprotec	UK	3.48
February 2005	Strides Arcolab	Strides Latina	Brazil	16

Source: *Business Standard*, 13 February 2006.

last few years, Indian pharmaceutical firms have been active participants in foreign acquisitions and are even having their presence felt in US. In less than seven years, they have established themselves in the US markets and are also posing a challenge to the US firms. Today 8 to 10 companies are active in the US, either on their own or through partnerships, and entering into M&As with US firms.[40] Ranbaxy and Wockhardt are planning to acquire large US companies worth billions of dollars. Cadila, Torrent and Dishman Pharma are also growing via acquisitions and green field facilities in the US and Europe.

5.7 Conclusion

For a country like ours, where the economy moved from a controlled and regulated regime to a liberalised environment in 1990s, the corporate sector responded extensively by adopting M&As. M&As embraced almost all sectors, *albeit* at a different pace. In the early years of the post-liberalised periods, restructuring operations were undertaken as corrective measures to the earlier business strategies, for instance, from diversification to core competency. Over a period of time, M&As have become an essential part of the restructuring operations of the Indian corporate sector.

Owing to intense competition from both the domestic and global fronts in the post-reform period, firms preferred merger-led growth. Firms of all sizes participated in restructuring operations. Predominance of mergers in manufacturing sector, horizontal mergers within manufacturing sector, and within group mergers have been essential features of M&As in India. All this points to the fact that firms through these strategies aimed at bigger size, higher market share, exploiting economies of scale, and adopting cost-minimising techniques. With the purpose to have easy and quick access in Indian markets, MNCs also preferred to grow through mergers and acquisitions with established companies. Increase in mergers and acquisitions in services—especially financial services—is a development of the late 1990s. From less than one-fourth of share of services in 1990s, roughly 40 per cent of the total M&As deals took place in this sector during 2000-2005.

Soon after the initiation of liberalised policies, the D&P industry started its restructuring operations through mergers, brand acquisition, buying and selling of plants and units, alliances and acquisitions of other firms. It is one of the most merger-intensive industries. Since the inception of economic reforms in 1990-91, close to 100 mergers have taken place in

40. Yet, India's share is just $1 billion in $25 billion US generic market.

the industry. An important feature of this activity is that a few firms have been instrumental in undertaking a majority of these mergers which are horizontal in nature. Over the past few years, Indian pharma firms have also become active in foreign acquisitions.

Despite commencing its production in the mid-1950s, the Indian D&P industry has grown phenomenally. It is characterised by intense competition, high level of fragmentation with concentration at top level, and low prices. Less than 3 per cent of the total firms are in organised sector, of which top 10 players hold more than 40 per cent of the total sales. The growth of the industry has been particularly robust in the post-reform period.

Several studies on M&As have been undertaken, covering issues, such as trends, industrial clustering, reverse mergers, mergers by sick companies, MRTP and MNCs, and pre- and post-merger performance. However, most of the studies lack in application of econometric tools. Given the voluminous size of M&A activity, its wide-ranging effects on the economy are not in doubt. The existing literature shows that the phenomenon could have wide implications that differ across countries, depending on their stage of development and availability of financial resources. Hence, it is crucial to deepen our understanding of the subject and assess its impact on issues, such as competitive environment, industrial structure, motives of acquisition and thus, on the overall growth of the Indian economy.

In order to understand the distinguishing features of acquired, acquiring, and non-merging firms and other aspects of mergers, a detailed analysis is carried out in the next four chapters.

6 Pre-merger Characteristics of Merging Firms

It is often argued that the basic aim of every firm, small or big, is to grow bigger. Growth can take place through internal or external expansion. The internal, also called, generic expansion, is embodied in creation of new physical assets and in external growth, firms adopt mergers and acquisition as part of their investment strategy. As discussed earlier, the growth strategy chosen by the firm is influenced by exogeneous as well as endogeneous factors. The former include the policy environment in which the firm operates, for instance, industrial framework, foreign competition, technical know-how, pattern of industrial growth, and demand and supply balance in industry. The latter, however, are firm-specific factors that include motives of the firm (such as attainment of synergy, increase in market power, desire to build an empire), resources available to the firm, and risk-taking capacity of the firm. Hence, the growth strategy adopted by the firm is determined by complexities of both endogeneous and exogeneous factors.

M&As became an integral part of Indian corporate structuring after the change in regulatory regime—especially since the mid-1990s. Firms resorted to these means, as a part of their growth as well as survival strategy. Liberalised policies and intensified competition from domestic as well as external producers, pushed firms to embark upon these measures. As noted in the previous chapter, it is almost a decade since the M&A activity has been on the rise, though the rate differs among industries. To examine the various issues related to the M&A activity, different analyses are carried out in the following four chapters. It is important to emphasise that the analysis is based on mergers[1] that took place in the Indian drugs and pharmaceutical industry during 1992-93 to 2005-06. The present and

1. The terms merger, acquisition and takeover are used interchangeably, to mean merger as defined in Chapter 3.

the next chapter analyse the distinguishing features of participant and non-participant firms in the M&As activity, while the following two focus on the determinants of acquiring and acquired firms.

This chapter is arranged in six sections. Section 6.1 gives the motivation for the analysis. Section 6.2 briefly discusses the sample chosen. Section 6.3 describes the variables used for comparisons followed by the methodology used in Section 6.4. In Sections 6.5, an analysis of pre-merger characteristics of acquiring (AG) and acquired (AD) firms is carried out. The chapter ends with some remarks to put the analysis in perspective.

6.1 Nature of Selection Process

The present chapter focusses on the pre-merger characteristics of firms that participate in the merger activity. A question that crops up is: how does the market distinguish between the acquiring and acquired firms? i.e., what is the nature of selection process that gets generated in the market? The argument put forward by neoclassical theorists is that competition in the product market always forces firms to maximise their profits and remain efficient. The process of 'natural selection' would force firms to do so because of the survival of the efficient i.e., profit-maximisers and elimination of the non-maximisers. However, managerial capitalism theorists argue, in today's world where modern corporations are characterised by the divorce of ownership and control, the salaried managers are more interested in maximising the rate of growth rather than maximising profits. Managers' goals, such as higher salaries, power, perks, and prestige, are all positively related to the firm's size than its profits. Recognising this, neoclassical economists, nonetheless, argued that despite the divorce between ownership and control in big corporations, it is the competition in the capital market, i.e., the takeover threat that would force a firm to pursue profit maximisation. It was emphasised that even if managers prefer other goals, profit maximisation is thrust upon them by sheer necessity of survival, for without it, non-maximisers will disappear through acquisitions or mergers. Singh (1971) pioneered research in this direction and systematically examined the nature of the selection process. The central finding of his work was contrary to the neoclassical theory. It was argued that the selection process in the takeover market does not take place entirely on the basis of profitability, as size also matters. Market is more likely to favour the firms that pursue fast growth than those that aim at profit maximisation. Large firms, regardless of their profitability, are immune to takeover on account of their size power.

To examine the nature of the selection process in the market and how takeover market provides a disciplinary device, it is necessary to systematically examine the pre-merger characteristics of different kinds of firms i.e., the participants and non-participants in the market. The former, also called, merging firms, are of two types, *viz.*, acquiring (AG) and acquired (AD) firms. While the non-participants, are those firms that are not involved in any kind of merger activity, therefore also named non-merging firms. These can also be grouped into two; non-acquiring (NAG) and non-acquired (NAD). The present chapter focusses only on the first two sets of firms i.e., the AG and AD firms.

6.2 The Sample

By pooling all the mergers over time, the present study focusses on those mergers that took place during the period 1992-93 to 2005-06 in the D&P industry. The sample comprises only those merging firms for which data are available on both the acquiring and acquired firms. The availability of data on both acquired (AD) and acquiring (AG) firms restricted the study to those firms that are listed in various stock exchanges of the country. The analysis in the present chapter considers a sample of 32 mergers[2] (i.e., 32 AG firms with their corresponding 32 AD firms) having the following features:

- All these mergers are horizontal in nature i.e., in which both merging firms, the AG and AD, engaged in the same lines of business.[3]
- The mergers included are those for which data are available on both the merging firms i.e., the acquiring and the acquired. The sample

2. The list of AG and AD firms included in the sample is given in Annexure II. The AD firm 'Alpha Drug India Ltd.' and its corresponding AG firm 'Punjab Chemicals and Crop Protection Ltd.', are excluded from the list for the analysis purpose in this chapter, as the latter does not pertain to the D&P industry.
3. Out of the 32 AD firms, 2 firms, *viz.*, 'TTK Biomed Ltd.' and 'TTK Medical Devices Ltd.' pertain to the chemical industry (of which D&P is a further sub-division). The similarity in the production lines of the corresponding AG firms, allows us to consider them as horizontal mergers.

contains 32 acquiring firms, all from the D&P industry and their corresponding 32 acquired firms.

- An AG firm that undertook more than one merger in a given year or in different years is considered as many times as the number of mergers it undertook, provided the data on the corresponding AD firm is available. Out of the 32 acquiring firms under consideration, six firms are considered twice, two firms thrice and one firm four times, as each of these firms in the sample was involved in more than one merger.

In making comparisons of pre-merger characteristics of the two sets of firms, the data are collected for five years preceding a merger. Since, the comparisons have been made on both the short- and long-term basis, the averages have been calculated one and two years before the merger for the short-term, while five years before the merger for the long-term comparisons.

As referred to earlier, the records of firms are pooled over the whole period i.e., 1992-93 to 2005-06, under consideration. If the comparisons of the characteristics of both sets of firms were done each year separately, we would have got a much smaller sample, with unreliable results. From the economic point of view, it is not unjustifiable to do so, since the major changes in the policy environment took place in 1991-92 and the whole period considered for our analysis here, pertains to the post-reform years. Further, from statistical point of view we are better off because, grouping together all the merging firms, across all the years, allows us to work on a larger sample.

6.3 Variables Used

To obtain the distinguishing features of AG and AD firms, comparisons are made on the basis of five main variables:

- size,[4]
- profitability,
- investment turnover ratio,
- leverage, and
- growth.

---

4. All indicators of size are measured in Rs crore.

Each variable is measured by several different indicators, based on the financial data of firms. The definition of each indicator is given in Annexure I.

1) Size: The size of a firm is measured by five indicators, *viz.*, total assets (TAs), gross fixed assets (GFA), net assets (NAs), net worth (NW) and sales.[5]

Total assets are inclusive of both gross fixed assets and current assets. The former, are long-term resources that include assets such as land, building, plant, machinery and investments. The latter, also called liquid assets, are short-term assets and include cash, marketable securities, account receivable, bills payable and inventories. GFA play a key role in the future earning of the firm. Net assets, a measure of capital employed by the firm, are computed by subtracting short-term liabilities (STLs) from TAs or adding net current assets to GFAs. The capital employed includes both long-term funds and equity capital. It measures TAs owned by the firm, exclusive of STLs i.e., NAs measure long-term funds owned by the firm. NW measures the claims of owners of the firms against the assets of the firms.

2) Profitability: The operating efficiency of the firm is measured by different profitability ratios, expressed as returns to different measures of size of the firm, such as NAs, NW and sales. The post-tax profit on equity (PAT/NW) is calculated to find return on equity and post-tax profit on net assets (PAT/net assets) shows return on capital employed. The latter, reflect the efficiency with which long-term funds of a firm are being used. The most common ratio used is 'net profit margin' which is computed over sales (PAT/sales). The four other measures of earning records are:

- PBDIT/sales—profit before depreciation, interest and taxes as a ratio of sales,
- PBIT/sales—profit before interest and taxes (after depreciation) as a ratio of sales,
- PBDT/sales—profit before depreciation and taxes (after interest) as a ratio of sales, and

5. The four measures of size, *viz.*, TAs, GFAs, NW and NAs are calculated from the 'balance sheet account' and sales are calculated from the 'profit and loss account'. The former account is given at a point of time and the latter, over a period of time, usually, a year.

- PBT/sales—profit before taxes (after depreciation and interest) as a ratio of sales.

These ratios are computed to compare the effects of operating expenses on the firm's profits.

3) Asset/investment turnover ratio: It measures the efficiency with which assets are utilised to generate sales i.e., it shows what part of the long-term funds is converted or turned into sales. It is measured by sales/ net assets. It is also called activity or asset management or productivity of assets ratio.[6] This ratio measures sales per rupee of net assets and is an indicator of efficiency in utilisation of assets employed. The higher the ratio, greater the efficiency with which assets are turned into sales.

The relevance of investment turnover ratio can be found from the following equation:

$$\frac{\text{PAT}}{\text{Net assets}} = \frac{\text{PAT}}{\text{Sales}} \times \frac{\text{Sales}}{\text{Net assets}}$$

The rate of return on net assets (PAT/NA)—also termed as profitability on assets, can be decomposed in terms of profitability on sales (profit margin-PAT/Sales) and profitability of investments (investment turnover ratio-Sales/NA). The overall operating efficiency of a firm is judged on the basis of both the ratios. A firm can have a higher return on assets either because of its higher profit margins or because of higher investment turnover ratio or both.

4) Leverage or capital structure ratio: In order to compare the financial position, also called 'financial leverage' or 'financial gearing' of firms, five measures of leverage are calculated. They mainly determine the proportion of debt in total finances of the firm. The measures, though related, are different in their significance for the firm. These are expressed in five ways:

a) Debt-equity ratio (D/E): It measures total borrowings (short and long-term) as a proportion of the net worth. It measures lenders' contribution (borrowed funds) in relation to the owners' contribution (equity funds).

6. It has also been termed as 'productivity of investment', see Singh (1998).

b) *Total Debt as a ratio of total assets (TD/TA):* Here, both the numerator and denominator are more inclusive in their coverage than the D/E ratio. Besides total borrowing, the former also includes 'current liability and provisions'. The latter, includes both total debt and net worth. It signifies the average proportion of total assets financed through lenders. The remaining, by definition is financed through owners.

c) *Long-term liability as a ratio of total assets (LTL/TA):* It measures the portion of TAs financed through only LTLs, as total debt can be raised through short as well as long-term means. For two firms with the same debt burden, the one more dependent on LTL, is subject to greater risk.

d) *Long-term liability as a ratio of short-term liabilities (LTL/STL)* and

e) *Short-term liabilities as a proportion of total assets (STL/TA).*

The latter three ratios are calculated to find if the difference in total debt of two groups of firms is due to a greater proportion of STL or LTL or both.

5) *Growth:* Growth of a firm is measured in terms of two size indicators, namely, sales and NAs.

6.4 Methodology

The characteristics of two sets of firms are compared on a cross-section basis. The statistical analysis followed here compares the group means (using arithmetic, geometric and weighted means) for each of the indicators and the observed difference is also tested for statistical significance by using the standard t-test.

$$t = \frac{\overline{X}_1 - \overline{X}_2}{\text{pooled variance}}$$

where the formula for 'pooled' sample variance depends upon the variance of the two samples i.e., whether the two samples have equal variance or not. The test statistic for the equality between two sample variances[7] is given as,

7. For details, see Levin and Rubin (1995).

$$F_{(n_1-1)(n_2-1)} = \frac{S_1^2}{S_2^2}$$

where n_1 = sample size of group 1; n_2 = sample size of group 2

$n_1 - 1$ = degrees of freedom in group 1; $n_2 - 1$ = degrees of freedom in group 2

S_1^2 = sample variance in group 1; S_2^2 = sample variance in group 2

Depending upon the significance of the F-test, i.e., whether the two samples have equal or unequal variance, our analysis calculates appropriate t-values (using two-tailed distribution).

In order to incorporate outlier[8] firms, wherever found necessary, weighted averages of certain ratios are also calculated. Depending upon the variable in the denominator, the period for which averages are calculated, and the set of firms, weights for each ratio were calculated. For example, to calculate weighted average of the ratio, PAT/sales for one year before the merger for AD firms, the weights used are [assuming t to be the year of merger, (t-1) are values one year before the merger].

$$W_i = \frac{\text{sales of } i^{th} \text{AD firm in year } (t-1)}{\Sigma_i \text{ sales in year } (t-1) \text{ for all AD firms}}$$

And weights for computing weighted averages of PAT/sales for five years before merger:

$$W_i = \frac{\text{average sales of } i^{th} \text{ firm in } (t-5) \text{ years}}{\Sigma_i [\text{average sales in } (t-5) \text{ years of all AD firms}]}$$

Since the growth variable is calculated over five-year period, the weights are calculated from the averages of (t-5) years before the merger. Depending upon the variable for which growth is calculated, the weights are:

$$W_i = \frac{\text{average sales (or net assets) of } i^{th} \text{ firm in } (t-5) \text{ years}}{\Sigma_i [\text{average sales (or net assets) in } (t-5) \text{ years}]}$$

8. Removing outlier firms is the most commonly used technique because of pure convenience. However, if the sample is small, removing outlier is not advisable.

6.5 Pre-merger Characteristics of AG and AD Firms

Focussing on five variables, *viz*., size, profitability, productivity of assets, leverage and growth, each approximated by several indicators, an in-depth analysis of the characteristics of merging firms is carried out below. To highlight short and long-term changes, value of each indicator is averaged for one, two and five years preceding the merger. For the growth variable, each indicator is averaged over five accounting years[9] before the acquisition.

Size Comparisons

Using all the indicators of size (Table 6.1) calculated over one year, two years and five years preceding the mergers, it is found that acquiring firms are larger than acquired firms and the t-ratio is statistically significant at the 1 per cent level. The AG firms are three to four times larger than the set of AD firms for averages calculated over one and two years and are 2.5 to 3 times larger for averages calculated over the five-year period before the merger. This holds true for all indicators and across both the methods of measurement (arithmetic and geometric mean). The relative differences between the averages for all indicators decrease marginally, when the method of measurement is changed from arithmetic mean to geometric mean. The relative difference in the average size, calculated over two years, is larger than that calculated over five years before the merger. It is attributed to the fact that increase in the average size of acquiring firm just before the merger is much more than that of acquired firms. The standard deviation for acquiring firms is much larger than that of acquired firms for all indicators and the relative difference is larger when calculated over two years than over five years preceding the merger. The F-test for equality of variances is significant for all indicators.

Turning to Tables 6.2(a) to 6.2(d) showing the joint distribution of AG and AD firms in various size-classes of total assets (TAs), calculated for the year just before the merger, it is observed:

1. AD firms are mainly concentrated in lower size-classes and AG firms are in the middle and higher size-classes.

---

9. For three firms data are not available for all the five years before merger. In such cases, averages over long period are based on the figures of three or four years, as per the data availability.

2. From Table 6.2(a), it is observed that 69 per cent of the AD firms have total assets less than Rs 100 crore, 25 per cent have between Rs 100 to 400 crore and just 6 per cent have TA greater than Rs 400 crore. The figures for AG firms in these classes are 15, 41 and 44 per cent, respectively.

Table 6.1

Size Comparisons (Rs crore) of AD and AG Firms

Size	*Mean Value AD* (X_1)	*Mean Value AG* (X_2)	*Ratio* X_1/X_2	$\sigma (X_1)$	$\sigma (X_2)$	*F-Statistic*	*t-Statistic*
Total assets							
A.M. (-1)	106.4	408.2	3.8	171.6	313.8	3.4***	4.13***
A.M. (-2)	102.0	374.5	3.7	161.8	292.7	3.3***	4.09***
A.M. (-5)	87.8	275.6	3.1	141.1	207.1	2.1**	3.98***
G.M. (-2)	101.6	371.3	3.7	161.5	292.8	3.3***	4.07***
G.M. (-5)	85.6	256.8	3.0	139.8	190.7	1.8*	3.8***
Total sales							
A.M. (-1)	106.0	396.4	3.9	122.5	301.4	6.3***	4.6***
A.M. (-2)	105.9	367.7	3.6	131.5	282.0	4.8***	4.3***
A.M. (-5)	98.6	297.9	3.1	120.6	237.6	4.0**	3.9***
G.M. (-2)	113.5	366.0	3.2	130.7	281.7	4.5***	4.3***
G.M. (-5)	96.7	286.9	3.0	119.4	234.1	3.8***	3.8***
Net assets							
A.M. (-1)	72.6	299.4	4.1	121.6	23769	3.8***	4.14***
A.M. (-2)	69.3	275.4	4.0	117.0	225.4	3.7***	3.99***
A.M. (-5)	59.9	197.1	3.3	105.5	151.3	2.1**	3.86***
Net worth							
A.M. (-1)	42.8	229.9	5.4	64.5	209.9	11.1***	4.85***
A.M. (-2)	42.0	220.5	5.3	61.2	195.2	11.1***	4.88***
A.M. (-5)	35.0	159.5	4.6	52.2	134.7	8.3**	4.55***
GFA							
A.M. (-1)	46.8	164.1	3.5	76.7	116.2	2.1**	4.25***
A.M. (-2)	45.0	146.1	3.3	74.5	104.0	2.0***	4.12***
A.M. (-5)	41.2	115.5	2.8	68.1	87.8	1.7*	3.57***
G.M. (-2)	45.4	145.7	3.2	74.2	103.4	1.9**	3.06***
G.M. (-5)	39.9	109.0	2.7	67.3	82.3	1.5	3.31***

Notes: *** significant at 1 per cent level; ** significant at 5 per cent level; * significant at 10 per cent level.

3. Within higher classes, it can be seen that 35 per cent of AG firms have total assets greater than Rs 500 crore whereas only 3 per cent (one out of 32) acquired firms lie in this range.
4. In Table 6.2(b), 81 per cent of the AD firms have net assets <Rs 100 crore whereas only 28 per cent of AG firms lie in this size class. There is only one AD firm with greater than Rs 400 crore of NAs where as 14 (44 per cent) of AG firms lie in this range.
5. The distribution of firms in various size-classes of sales [Table 6.2(c)], shows a similar picture. In three size-classes, *viz.*, less than Rs 100 crore, Rs 100-400 crore and greater than Rs 400 crore of sales, the distribution of AD firms is 69 per cent, 28 per cent and 3 per cent, respectively, and that of AG firms is 12, 31, and 56 per cent, respectively. So far as the distribution of AD firms across various classes of net worth is concerned, only one firm had its net worth between Rs 200-300 crore and over 75 per cent of firms had less than Rs 100 crore of their net worth (not shown here). Approximately 45 per cent of AG firms had net worth over Rs 300 crore. The difference in concentration of AD and AG firms in various size classes of total assets (one year and five years before the merger) is also reflected in Figures 6.1 and 6.2.

Table 6.2(a)

Joint Distribution of AD and AG Firms

(classification based on total assets (in Rs crore), one year pre-merger)

→ *AD* ↓ *AG*	*0-50*	*50-100*	*100-200*	*200-300*	*300-400*	*400-500*	*>500*	*Total*
0-50	0	0	0	0	0	0	0	0
50-100	3	0	2	0	0	0	0	5
100-200	3	1	0	0	0	0	1	5
200-300	2	0	1	0	0	0	0	3
300-400	2	2	1	0	0	0	0	5
400-500	2	1	0	0	0	0	0	3
>500	4	2	3	1	0	1	0	11
Total	16	6	7	1	0	1	1	32

Table 6.2(b)

Joint Distribution of AD and AG Firms
(classification based on net assets (in Rs crore), one year pre-merger)

→AD / ↓AG	0-50	50-100	100-150	150-200	200-250	250-300	>300	Total
0-50	3	1	0	0	0	0	0	4
50-100	5	0	0	0	0	0	0	5
100-200	3	1	0	0	0	0	1	5
200-300	3	1	0	0	0	0	0	4
300-400	2	0	1	0	0	0	0	4
400-500	2	1	0	1	0	1	0	4
>500	3	1	1	1	0	0	0	6
Total	21	5	2	2	0	1	1	32

Table 6.2(c)

Joint Distribution of AD and AG Firms
(classification based on sales (in Rs crore), one year pre-merger)

→AD / ↓AG	0-50	50-100	100-200	200-300	300-400	400-500	500-600	Total
0-50	1	1	0	0	0	0	0	2
50-100	0	1	0	0	0	0	1	2
100-200	5	3	1	0	0	0	0	9
200-300	0	0	0	0	0	0	0	0
300-400	0	0	1	0	0	0	0	1
400-500	2	1	2	1	1	0	0	7
>500	6	2	0	2	1	0	0	11
Total	14	8	4	3	2	0	1	32

Table 6.2(d)

Joint Distribution of AD and AG Firms (classification based on average total assets (in Rs crore), five years pre-merger)

↓AG \ →AD	0-50	50-100	100-200	200-300	300-400	400-500	>500	Total
0-50	1	2	0	0	0	0	0	3
50-100	6	0	0	0	0	0	0	6
100-200	3	1	0	0	0	0	1	5
200-300	2	3	2	0	0	0	0	7
300-400	1	0	0	0	0	0	0	1
400-500	3	0	1	0	1	0	0	5
>500	2	0	3	0	0	0	0	5
Total	18	6	6	0	1	0	1	32

6. Tables 6.2(a) and 6.2(d) show the difference in concentration level of firms in various size-classes of TAs over time, before the merger. As far as the distribution of AD firms is concerned, there is no clear movement towards higher size-classes, while AG firms are clearly moving to higher size-classes when observed from five years before the merger to one year before the merger. The number of acquiring firms in size-classes of TA, less than Rs 100, Rs 100-400, and greater than Rs 400 crore, changes from 9, 13, 10 to 5, 13, 14, respectively (see Figures 6.1 and 6.2). Within the highest class, it is found that five years before the merger, there were two firms with TA greater than Rs 600 crore and the number increases to 8, when observed one or two years before the merger. A similar pattern was observed for other indicators over time (not shown here).

Figure 6.1

Distribution of AD and AG Firms in Various Size-Classes of TAs (one year before merger)

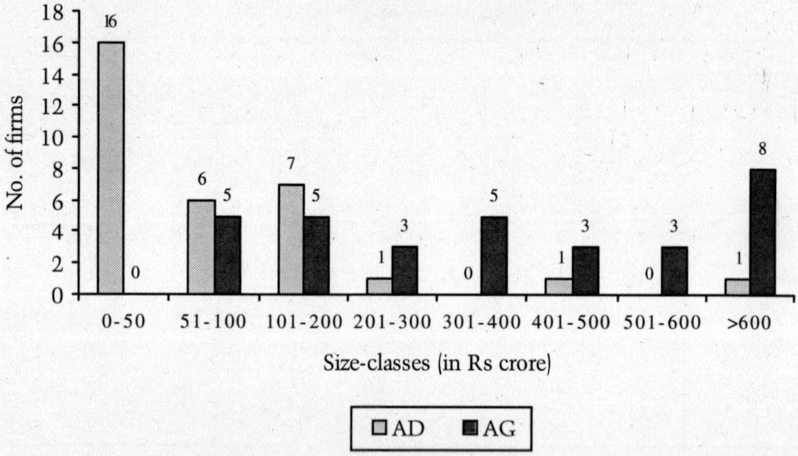

Figure 6.2

Distribution of AD and AG Firms in Various Size-Classes of TAs (five years before merger)

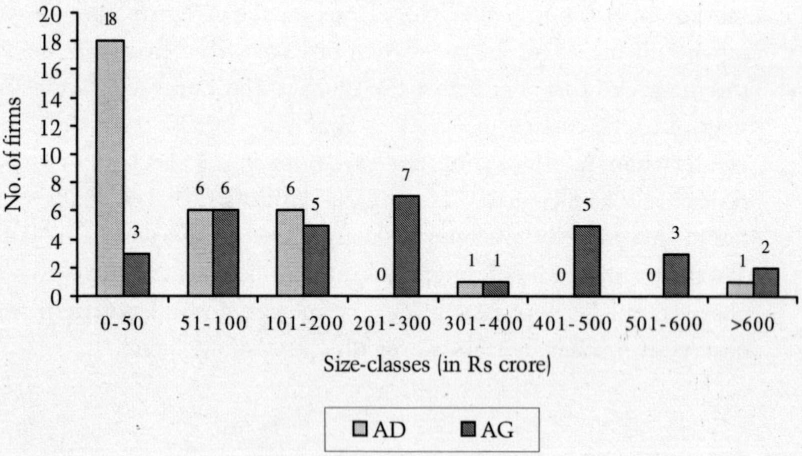

Profitability Comparisons

Analysing the results on performance, based on profit records of merging firms (see Table 6.3), it is confirmed that AG firms, in terms of all the indicators of profitability (with few exceptions), are significantly more profitable than the acquired firms. Also, it can be seen that AG firms are earning relatively higher average profits in the years just before the merger than over five years before the merger. This result also holds true for AD firms, however, only for those measures of profitability that are expressed as a ratio of sales. The relative difference in the average profit levels between AD and AG firms is higher when observed over one or two years before the merger than the ones observed over five years preceding merger.

Table 6.3

Profitability Comparisons of AD and AG Firms

Profitability Ratio	*Mean Value AD (X_1)*	*Mean Value AG (X_2)*	*Ratio X_1/X_2*	$\sigma (X_1)$	$\sigma (X_2)$	*F-Statistic*	*t-Statistic*
PAT/sales							
A.M. (-1)	.01	.11	7.53	.125	.06	3.8***	3.39***
A.M. (-2)	.01	.10	7.22	.10	.07	1.8*	3.55***
A.M. (-5)	-.04	.08	N.R.	.25	.08	8.3***	2.45**
PBDIT/sales							
A.M. (-1)	.10	.21	2.01	.15	.09	2.2**	2.88***
A.M. (-2)	.11	.20	1.78	.13	.08	1.9*	2.84***
A.M. (-5)	.13	.18	1.39	.13	.08	2.2**	1.820*
PBDT/sales							
A.M. (-1)	.06	.15	2.88	.13	.09	1.6	3.18***
A.M. (-2)	.05	.14	3.36	.11	.09	1.1	3.23***
A.M. (-5)	.02	.13	6.34	.20	.09	4.3***	2.59***
PBIT/sales							
A.M. (-1)	.08	.16	2.12	.14	.08	2.6***	2.88***
A.M. (-2)	.08	.16	1.95	.10	.07	1.6*	3.19***
A.M. (-5)	.06	.15	3.35	.17	.08	4.5***	2.78***
PBT/sales							
A.M. (-1)	.02	.13	5.33	.15	.07	4.5***	3.44***
A.M. (-2)	.02	.12	5.06	.11	.10	1.4	2.98***
A.M. (-5)	-.04	.10	N.R.	.28	.10	6.7***	2.25**
PAT/NA							
A.M. (-1)	.06	.14	2.41	.12	.10	1.4	1.89*
A.M. (-2)	.08	.14	1.92	.13	.09	1.9*	1.74*
A.M. (-5)	.06	.12	1.52	.13	.08	2.6***	1.54
PAT/NW							
A.M. (-1)	.02	.20	8.22	.41	.21	8.3***	2.34***
A.M. (-2)	-.05	.23	N.R.	.77	.18	14.3***	1.91*
A.M. (-5)	.06	.16	2.66	.35	.15	8.3***	1.56

Note: N.R.: not reported, whenever average profitability is negative, ratio of X_2/X_1 is not computed.

*** significant at 1 per cent level; ** significant at 5 per cent level; * significant at 10 per cent level.

Broadly speaking, the conclusions are the same for all measures of profitability. The main findings from Table 6.3 are summarised below:

1. The AG and AD firms earned relatively higher average profits in the years just before the merger than averaging out over a longer period, preceding the merger. The relative difference between average profitability of AD and AG firms is highest when observed one year ahead of the merger and lowest for averages based on five years before the merger.
2. The difference in profit ratios is significant for all indicators of average profitability, calculated over one year and two years before the merger. However, the difference based on measures over five years prior to the merger, is not statistically significant for PAT/NW and PAT/NA.
3. An important observation regarding the profitability, expressed as a ratio of sales, (measured over one or two years before the merger) is that the extent of difference in average profit ratios, continues to rise when measure of profitability change from PBDIT/sales to PBIT/sales to PBDT/sales to PBT/sales to PAT/sales i.e., the relative difference in average profits is least for PBDIT/sales and highest for PAT/sales. This suggests that the relative difference in average profitability levels increases when adjustment for deprecation and payments for interest and taxes are made out of the total profits. The rise in the ratio of relative profitability of AG and AD companies is much lower when moving from PBDIT/sales to PBIT/sales than moving from PBDIT/sales to PBDT/sales. This implies that interest payments have affected AD companies much more adversely than AG companies and depreciation adjustments made in profits affect both AG and AD in almost the same manner. This is also revealed in comparisons of PBIT/sales and PBT/sales, since the rise in the ratio of average profitability for AG and AD firms is more than double, implying that the interest payments are much more burdensome for AD firms. Concerning the burden of tax payments, it seems to be higher on AG firms, since the relative fall in averages from PBT/sales to PAT/sales is lesser for AD firms (also see Table 6.4).

4. The average rate of return on equity (PAT/NW) is higher for AG companies for all averages, though it is statistically significant only for averages calculated one and two years before the merger at the 1 and 10 per cent, respectively. The mean difference in average profitability between AG and AD companies is highest for PAT/NW when calculated over one or two years preceding the merger
5. The average rate of return on assets (PAT/NA)[10] is higher for AG companies. However, surprisingly, the relative difference between averages of AD and AG firms is much lesser and is also statistically non-significant at the 5 per cent significance level, for records based on five years preceding the merger.

The distribution of AD and AG firms in three classes, *viz.*, less than 0.5 (lower), between 0.5 and 0.15 (middle) and greater than 0.15 (higher), for all profitability ratios is given in Table 6.4 and the following results are noted.

1. Using PBDIT/sales, it is observed that the concentration of AD firms in the three classes <0.5, between 0.5 and 0.15, >0.15 is 28, 34, and 38 per cent, respectively. In contrast to this, 3, 28 and 69 per cent of the AG firms have profitability levels in the three respective classes. There is a slight movement of both AD and AG firms towards lower ranges of profitability, as the indicator of profitability is changed from PBDIT/sales to PBIT/sales. This implies that the distribution of both the sets of firms across the two indicators of profitability remains more or less the same, since deprecation adjustments have affected them in the same manner. The concentration of firms based on averages over one, two and five years preceding merger also nearly remains the same, suggesting that adjustments made for depreciation just before the merger or on average, made five years before the merger do not alter the concentration levels of both the sets of firms.
2. On the other hand, the concentration of AD firms differs greatly in favour of lower profitability class, across PBDIT/sales and PBDT/sales;

10. The rate of return on assets, as referred earlier, is the combined effect of a firm's profit margins (PAT/sales) and the efficiency with which net assets are utilised (sales/net assets) in production.

Table 6.4

Frequency Distribution of AD and AG Firms (classification based on average profitability)

Profitability	*<0.5 (Lower)*		*0.5-0.15 (Middle)*		*>0.15 (Higher)*	
	AD (%)	*AG (%)*	*AD (%)*	*AG (%)*	*AD (%)*	*AG (%)*
PAT/sales						
A.M. (-1)	56	22	38	56	6	22
A.M. (-2)	69	19	28	63	3	19
A.M. (-5)	66	28	34	53	0	19
PBDIT/sales						
A.M. (-1)	28	3	34	28	38	69
A.M. (-2)	28	0	34	31	38	69
A.M. (-5)	28	3	34	38	38	59
PBDT/sales						
A.M. (-1)	50	6	28	38	22	56
A.M. (-2)	47	9	34	34	19	56
A.M. (-5)	47	15	38	47	16	38
PBIT/sales						
A.M. (-1)	28	7	44	28	28	65
A.M. (-2)	32	3	41	38	27	59
A.M. (-5)	30	10	50	45	20	45
PBT/sales						
A.M. (-1)	56	6	25	56	19	38
A.M. (-2)	56	9	31	56	13	34
A.M. (-5)	56	19	34	59	9	22
PAT/NW						
A.M. (-1)	39	6	14	25	46	69
A.M. (-2)	36	6	18	22	46	72
A.M. (-5)	31	13	17	19	52	69
PAT/NA						
A.M. (-1)	46	10	25	52	29	38
A.M. (-2)	38	7	32	52	30	41
A.M. (-5)	32	17	32	48	36	34

however, it varies slightly for AG companies. Notably, the difference in concentration for AG is the same as it appeared while shifting from PBDIT/sales to PBIT/sales. This once again reflects that interest payments are more of a burden for AD than for AG firms. The concentration of AD firms changes from 28, 34 and 38 per cent using PBDIT/sales to 50, 28 and 22 per cent, using PBDT/sales in the lower, middle, and higher classes of profitability, respectively.

3. These results are more clearly reflected in Tables 6.5 (a) and 6.5 (b), in which firms are distributed according to two profit classes, 'lower' and 'middle and higher' (formed by clubbing middle and higher). The upper panel of the Table 6.5 (a) clearly shows that the concentration of AD firms between the two classes, changes very drastically when profitability ratio change from PBDIT/sales to PBDT/sales and remains the same when changed from PBDIT/sales to PBIT/sales. While change in the concentration of AG firms (Table 6.5(b)) remains the same across PBDIT/sales to PBIT/sales or PBDIT/sales to PBDT/sales, indicating that the impact of depreciation and interest payments is equally burdening for AG firms. Comparing the lower and the upper panels, it is also found that the relative difference in the concentration levels of AD and AG firms, across different profit classes are less morbid when measured over five years before merger. This implies that the differences become more prominent when measured over short period, prior to the merger.

4. The impact of tax payments on AD and AG firms can also be seen in change in the concentration of firms, across PBT/sales and PAT/sales ratios of profitability. Table 6.4 clearly indicates that the change in concentration levels for AG firms is more pronounced than that of AD firms in different profit classes. This further emphasises that tax payments have a more burdening effect on AG firms. This is primarily on account of two reasons; firstly, a large number of AG firms are high profit-earning companies. Secondly, AD firms being more leveraged than AG firms, (see leverage ratio comparisons in Table 6.9) also get an advantage of their higher interest costs,[11] which is deducted from their profits for the purpose of their tax calculations.

---

11. Interest on debt is treated as cost and is deducted from earnings before calculating taxes.

Table 6.5 (a)

Frequency Distribution of Acquired Firms in Various Ranges of Profitability Ratios based on Sales (in %)

Profitability Ratio	*PBDIT*	*PBDT*	*PBIT*	*PBT*	*PAT*
A.M. (-1) & A.M. (-2)					
Lower	28	49	30	56	63
Middle & higher	72	51	70	44	47
A.M. (-5)					
Lower	30	47	30	56	66
Middle & higher	70	53	70	44	34

Table 6.5 (b)

Frequency Distribution of Acquiring Firms in Various Ranges of Profitability Ratios based on Sales (in %)

Profitability Ratio	*PBDIT*	*PBDT*	*PBIT*	*PBT*	*PAT*
A.M. (-1) & A.M. (-2)					
Lower	3	8	7	7	20
Middle & higher	97	92	93	93	80
A.M. (-5)					
Lower	3	15	10	19	19
Middle & higher	97	85	90	81	81

5. So far as the concentration of firms based on PAT/NA is concerned, it is observed that on an average, distribution of AD firms remains unchanged, when analysed from averages calculated over two years and five years preceding the merger, and AD firms are equally distributed over the three classes of profitability ratio. However, there is an increase in the number of firms in the lower class counterbalanced by the reduction in the middle class, in the year just preceding the merger. The AG firms are unevenly distributed across three classes, with highest concentration in the middle class (50 per cent) followed by the higher (42 per cent) and lower (18 per cent) classes. The concentration of firms remains unchanged over one and two years before the merger, while, over five years, it

changes in favour of the lower class at the cost of the higher size-class of profitability.

6 Analysing PAT/NW, it is noted that on an average, over one and two years before the merger, the distribution of AD firms is 37, 16, 46 per cent and that of AG firms is 6, 23, and 71 per cent in the three classes of profitability, respectively. Observing the changes in concentration, it is noted that moving from five-year period to one year before the merger, the distribution changes in favour of the higher class for AG firms and that of lower class for AD firms.

To sum up, it is concluded that AG firms are significantly more profitable than their corresponding AD firms over both the short and long-term periods before the merger. The AG firms cluster more in the middle and high classes whereas AD firms concentrate in the lower and middle ranges of profitability. The difference in concentration levels of AD and AG firms across the various size-classes is lower when found from the averages measured over five years before the merger. This holds true for almost all the measures of profitability.

To see correspondence between size and profitability, we have also found distribution of both the sets of firms according to TAs and PAT/sales [see Tables 6.6 (a) and 6.6 (b)]. Although, AD firms are significantly smaller and less profitable, an important observation regarding these firms remains concealed. More than 90 per cent of the AD firms being small-sized firms, roughly, less than 50 per cent of them have negative or low profitability. About one-fifth of the small-sized AD firms were earning very high profits before becoming a merger target [Table 6.6 (a)]. AG firms, on the other hand, are definitely superior, as only one out of 10 small-sized AG firms has negative profitability. However, there are cases where small and profitable companies are merging into relatively bigger and lesser profitable companies. It is important to mention here, that most of these cases[12] are of a subsidiary merging into its parent company. From these observations, it is difficult to say that the takeover mechanism did not provide a disciplinary device or that size matters more than efficiency. But the

12 For example, Wyeth Laboratories Ltd. getting merged into Wyeth Ltd.; Croslands Research Laboratories Ltd. to Ranbaxy Laboratories Ltd.; Croydon Chemical Works Ltd. to Glaxosmithkline Pharmaceuticals Ltd. and Max India Ltd. to Maxxon India Ltd. (later, its name was changed to Max India Ltd.)

relevant issue is whether acquiring firms at all aimed at disciplining their targets or was attaining synergistic gains remain their basic motive? In fact, corporate restructuring in India especially, in the form of M&As points more to the latter case. Exploiting opportunities provided by the market due to liberalised policies and thereby, achieving benefits through increase in scale and increasing market share are the plausible goals of AG firms behind mergers. This also suggests that firms are restructuring their businesses to become bigger as a survival strategy in the phase of increased competition especially, from foreign firms.

Table 6.6 (a)

Distribution of Acquired Firms according to TAs and PAT/Sales (both measured one year before merger)

PAT/Sales (in %) ↓ / TA (Rs crore) →	0-200	200-400	400-600	>600	Total
<2	14	0	0	0	14 (44)
2-6	7	0	0	1	8 (25)
6-10	2	1	0	0	3 (9)
>10	6	0	1	0	7 (22)
Total	29 (91)	1 (3)	1 (3)	1 (3)	32 (100)

Note: Figures in parenthesis are per cent of the grand total.

Table 6.6 (b)

Distribution of Acquiring Firms according to TAs and PAT/Sales (both measured one year before merger)

PAT/Sales (in %) ↓ / TA (Rs crore) →	0-200	200-400	400-600	>600	Total
<2	1	0	0	0	1 (3)
2-6	5	2	1	1	9 (28)
6-10	3	1	1	1	6 (19)
>10	1	5	4	6	16 (50)
Total	10 (32)	8 (25)	6(18)	8 (25)	32 (100)

Note: Figures in parenthesis are per cent of the grand total.

Investment Turnover Ratio Comparisons

As referred earlier, the return on capital employed can be decomposed between profit margins and investment turnover ratio or productivity of investment. Table 6.7 shows that AD firms have greater investment turnover ratio than the AG firms. However, it is significant at only the 10 per cent level when compared for the averages calculated over two, three or five years preceding the merger. The ratio of average productivity of AD firms is nearly 1.5 times that of the AG firms, when records over five years before merger are used and it falls marginally, when compared over two years just preceding the merger. Table 6.7 shows that there has been deterioration in the average level of productivity of assets of both the AD and AG firms just before the merger, however it is lesser for the latter. Yet, on an average, AD firms perform better than AG firms in terms of generating sales out of their net assets. This conclusion helps in the analysis of the results obtained earlier with respect to PAT/NA comparisons. It was found from Table 6.3 that on an average, profit margins (PAT/sales) of AG firms are 7.5 times higher but the return on assets ratio (PAT/NA) is only 2.4 times higher, than those of AD firms. This is because, a part of the higher profit margins of AG firms is offset by their lower turnover ratio. It seems, one of the reasons of selecting a particular company for merger may well be its higher assets turnover ratio.

Table 6.7

Investment Turnover Ratio Comparisons of AD and AG Firms

Sales/ NA	*Mean Value AD (X_1)*	*Mean Value AG (X_2)*	*Ratio@ X_1/X_2*	*σ (X_1)*	*σ (X_2)*	*F-Statistic*	*t-Statistic*
A.M. (-1)	2.11	1.66	1.27	1.82	.82	7.1***	1.47
A.M. (-2)	2.26	1.68	1.34	1.85	.84	12.5***	1.81*
A.M. (-3)	2.30	1.72	1.31	1.72	.88	5.6***	1.76*
A.M. (-5)	2.36	1.75	1.44	1.66	.80	5.0***	1.71*

Notes: *** significant at 1 per cent level * significant at 10 per cent level.

@: In this table the ratio X_1/X_2 has been calculated (instead of X_2/X_1 in previous tables) as the value of average investment turnover ratio is relatively higher for AD firms.

Two observations are pertinent here. Firstly, the variation (comparing standard deviations) in the productivity of AD firms is more than double than that of AG firms. This testifies that AD firms are unevenly distributed over various size-classes of sales/NA. This conclusion also emerges from Table 6.8, illustrating the concentration levels of AD and AG firms in different classes of investment turnover ratio. It can be seen that almost all AG firms have productivity of less than 3 whereas only 80 per cent of AD firms lie in this range. The difference in the concentration levels becomes more evident when averages are compared over longer period before the merger. It is observed that five years prior to the merger, approximately 50 per cent of AD firms had productivity greater than 3 while, no AG firm lies in this range. Secondly, the high sales/NA ratio of AD firms could also be on account of their low amount of net assets.

Table 6.8

Frequency Distribution of AD and AG Firms (classification based on average investment turnover ratio)

Sales/NA	<3		>3	
	AD	*AG*	*AD*	*AG*
A.M.(-1) & A.M.(-2)	81	97	19	3
A.M. (-5)	52	100	48	0

It can be concluded that, as compared to AD firms, AG firms have significantly higher profit margins (PAT/sales) but non-significantly (at 5 per cent significance level) higher returns on assets (PAT/assets), on account of their low productivity. These differences are more pronounced when compared over a longer period before the merger.

Leverage Ratio Comparisons

Table 6.9 shows five indicators that are used to make leverage comparisons between the AD and AG firms and Table 6.10 indicates the differences in distribution of both sets of firms across various classes[13] of leverage ratios. The averages for all indicators are calculated over two and five years preceding the merger.

13. Depending on the range of average of leverage ratio, the lower and upper limits of various classes differ across different indicators of leverage ratios.

Using TD/TA indicator of leverage ratio, it is observed that AD firms are significantly more leveraged than AG firms at the 10 per cent level of significance, over both short and long periods before merger. The concentration of AG firms is in the lower and middle ranges over both short and long period ahead of the merger. The AD firms are uniformly distributed across the three classes in the short period, while concentration increases in the middle range over the long period preceding the merger.

Table 6.9

Leverage Ratio Comparisons of AD and AG Firms

Leverage Ratio	*Mean Value AD (X_1)*	*Mean Value AG (X_2)*	*σ (X_1)*	*σ (X_2)*	*F-Statistic*	*t-Statistic*
TD/TA						
A.M. (-2)	.61	.47	.32	.15	2.0 **	2.3**
A.M. (-5)	.61	.49	.27	.14	1.9 **	1.88*
G.M. (-1)	.59	.42	.33	.15	2.3 ***	2.1**
G.M. (-2)	.59	.45	.28	.14	2.0 **	1.93
D/E[@]						
A.M. (-2)	1.93	.80	3.51	1.47	4.3 ***	1.69*
A.M. (-5)	1.51	.84	1.77	1.28	2.0 **	1.65*
LTL/STL						
A.M. (-2)	.96	.56	1.41	.56	7.7 ***	1.59
A.M. (-5)	.97	.62	1.55	.59	2.9 ***	1.56
G.M. (-2)	.89	.53	1.32	.54	6.7 ***	1.55
G.M. (-5)	.89	.57	1.51	.56	2.7 ***	1.17
STL/TA						
A.M. (-2)	.38	.31	.22	.12	3.1 ***	1.64*
A.M. (-5)	.38	.32	.20	.11	3.1 ***	1.75*
G.M. (-2)	.37	.30	.22	.12	3.8 ***	1.52
G.M. (-5)	.37	.31	.19	.11	3.1 ***	1.56
LTL/TA						
A.M. (-2)	.23	.17	.26	.14	4.0 ***	1.4
A.M. (-5)	.23	.17	.21	.13	2.1 **	1.5
G.M. (-2)	.21	.16	.23	.14	4.2 ***	1.38
G.M. (-5)	.20	.15	.21	.13	2.0 ***	1.25

Notes: @ Firms with negative D/E are excluded in calculating average D/E;
*** significant at 1 per cent level;
** significant at 5 per cent level; * significant at 10 per cent level.

Although average D/E ratio is very high for AD firms (2.5 times that of AG firms), it is statistically significant only at the 10 per cent level. This is mainly due to skewed distribution of average level of D/E ratio among AD firms. While 50 per cent of AD firms lie in the lower range, one-third of the AD firms have their average ratios in the higher range as well. The AG firms, on the other hand, are heavily concentrated in the lower range (approximately 70 per cent) with a small cluster in the higher range (Table 6.10).

Table 6.10

Frequency Distribution of AD and AG Firms (classification based on average leverage ratio)

TD/TA	*<0.5*		*0.5 – 0.75*		*>0.75*	
	AD (%)	*AG (%)*	*AD (%)*	*AG (%)*	*AD (%)*	*AG (%)*
A.M. (-2)	38	66	34	25	28	9
A.M. (-5)	28	60	47	31	25	9
D/E	*< 1*		*1 – 2*		*>2*	
	AD (%)	*AG (%)*	*AD (%)*	*AG (%)*	*AD (%)*	*AG (%)*
A.M. (-2)	50	71	18	23	32	6
A.M. (-5)	55	69	7	25	38	6
LTL/TA	*<0.25*		*0.25 – 0.4*		*>0.4*	
	AD (%)	*AG (%)*	*AD (%)*	*AG (%)*	*AD (%)*	*AG (%)*
A.M. (-2)	60	87	15	3	25	10
A.M. (-5)	58	82	23	9	19	9
STL/TA	*<0.25*		*0.25 – 0.5*		*>0.5*	
	AD (%)	*AG (%)*	*AD (%)*	*AG (%)*	*AD (%)*	*AG (%)*
A.M. (-2)	20	41	50	56	30	6
A.M. (-5)	25	28	47	63	28	9

LTL/STL	*<0.2*		*0.2–0.8*		*0.8-1.4*		*1.4-2.0*		*2.0 -3.0*		*>3.0*	
	AD (%)	*AG (%)*	*AD (%)*	*AG (%)*	*AD (%)*	*AG (%)*	*AD (%)*	*AG (%)*	*AD (%)*	*AG (%)*	*AD (%)*	*AG (%)*
A.M. (-2)	46	24	27	51	6	9	6	16	6	0	10	0
A.M. (-5)	56	41	16	34	6	9	6	16	6	0	10	0

In order to find out 'what makes AD firms more leveraged', we have further decomposed TD between STL and LTL, and have calculated average STL/TA and LTL/TA ratios. The average LTL/TA is marginally and non-significantly higher, while STL/TA is significantly higher at the 10 per cent level for AD firms. This result holds over both the short and long periods before the merger. It is further supported by the distribution of firms across different classes of both the leverage ratios (Table 6.10). Approximately, 90 per cent of AG firms have their average LTL/TA in the lower range and only 10 per cent lie in the higher range. For AD firms, 60 per cent are in the lower range while out of the remaining 40 per cent, 25 per cent lie in the higher class. This distribution largely remains unchanged in the short and long periods. As far as STL/TA is concerned, roughly, 50 per cent of both AD and AG firms are concentrated in the middle range, but it is the difference in concentration levels in the lower and higher classes that explains the differences in the averages of AD and AG firms. More than 40 per cent of the AG firms have their average STL/TA lying in the lower range (i.e., less than 0.25) while only 20 per cent of AD firms have their average in this range. So, the AD firms are more leveraged on account of higher amount of both ratios, i.e., LTL/TA and STL/TA, however none of them is significant at 5 per cent level.

The fifth indicator of leverage ratio that explains the average amount of LTL in proportion to STL is given by LTL/STL. Though average LTL/STL is higher for AD firms, the difference is statistically not significant. In order to reason out this difference in averages, we have shown the distribution of AD and AG firms in more than three classes of average LTL/STL. Despite the fact that the number of AD firms in the lowest class (i.e., < 0.2) is approximately 50 per cent and is almost double than that of AG firms in this class, AD firms have high relative averages. This is mainly on account of the difference in the concentration level in the highest two classes (i.e., 2.0–3.0 and >3.0). The number of AD firms in these two classes is 16 per cent while no AG firm lies in these two classes. Further, comparing changes in distribution of firms from long-term to short-term averages; it is observed that AG firms are moving towards lower ranges while AD firms are moving towards higher classes before the merger.

Here, in light of these results, it is vital to discuss Modigliani and Miller's irrelevance theorem[14] regarding the capital or financing mix (or degree of leverage) of the firm. Under the assumptions of perfect capital market, costless information, no transaction costs, and rationality of investors, Modigliani and Miller theorem states that the cost of the capital and therefore, the total value of the firm is invariant to the financing mix of the firm between debt, equity, and other claims.[15] A firm cannot have higher value simply because it has a different capital-mix than the other firm. The value of the firm essentially depends on the variables, such as productivity, technical progress and market demand of output, and any change in the proportion of debt to equity in the capital-mix will have no effect i.e., financing has a passive role to play in firm's investment decisions.

However, the irrelevance of capital structure is essentially based on the perfect capital market assumption. The introduction of real world imperfections in the form of taxes, bankruptcy costs, institutional restrictions on lending and restriction on investment behaviour can bring certain advantages to the use of debt and hence, there is a need to find an optimal capital-mix that maximises the firm's value. This invalidates Modigliani-Miller's irrelevance theorem. Further, introduction of more complex situations of asymmetric information, moral hazards, and agency costs also point to the significance of a firm's financial structure for the firm's investment decisions. Several empirical studies have established that factors, such as product characteristics, capital intensity, size, proportion of tangible to intangible assets, profitability and tax consideration are significant in explaining inter-firm and inter-industry differences in the corporate debt structure (Singh and Hamid, 1992).

With reference to the present work, it is found that the AD companies are more leveraged or indebted than AG companies and this higher leverage is on account of the greater proportion of both LTL and STL in the total debt. However, there is no significant difference in average D/E ratios over

---

14. Modigliani and Miller first put forward this proposition in their paper published in (1958).

15. The justification of the theorem is provided in terms of arbitrage process. See, for example, Van Horne and Wachowicz (2001).

two or five years preceding the merger. The AG firms are heavily grouped in the lower class whereas AD firms are distributed over both the lower and higher classes. This also elucidates the fact that AD companies have higher standard deviation for all ratios used.

Growth Comparisons

As far as the growth variable (Table 6.11) is concerned, it is measured for sales and net assets over five years prior to the merger. On account of large differences in the average growth of individual firms (i.e., presence of outlier firms), the growth comparisons have been made using both the simple average growth (excluding outlier firms) as well as weighted average growth. The weights used are the relative share of each company's sales (or net assets) in the total sales (or net assets) of the corresponding set of AD or AG companies. Results of growth vary across variables as well as across the measures used to calculate the average growth. The weighted growth of sales is not significantly higher for AD companies whereas the weighted growth of net assets is significantly higher for AG companies. This finding is consistent with the higher productivity of (sale/assets) of AD firms, shown in Table 6.8.

Table 6.11

Growth Comparisons of AD and AG Firms

Growth	*Mean Value AD (X_1)*	*Mean Value AG (X_2)*	*σ (X_1)*	*σ (X_2)*	*t-Statistic*
Sales					
A.M. (-5)	1.21	1.74	4.25	7.92	1.34
A.M. (-5)@	.45	.27			
W.A.M. (-5)	.32	.25	—	—	1.01
Net assets					
A.M. (-5)	.83	.36	3.3	.3	.88
A.M. (-5)@	.21	.34			1.34
W.A.M. (-5)	.21	.36	—	—	4.42**

Notes: @ Excluding outlier firms' average growth from the calculation of overall average for AD firms.

** significant at 5 per cent level.

6.6 Conclusion

This chapter examined the pre-merger characteristics of AG and AD firms on a cross-section basis in the D&P industry during 1992-93 to 2005-06. The following main points emerge from the analysis.[16] The AG firms are undoubtedly significantly bigger and more profitable than their corresponding AD firms. On an average, the former are 3.5 times larger than the latter. All profitability measures, though affected by difference in gearing levels, are significantly higher for AG firms. The main cause of low profit margins of AD firms lies in their heavy debt burden that gives rise to high interest payment to be deducted from their profits. An important observation that requires special mention is that despite, large difference in profit margins, the return on assets (PAT/NA) is not significantly different (at the 5 per cent level) for the two sets of firms. Lower profits margins of AD firms are largely counterbalanced by their higher assets turnover ratio, thus resulting in higher returns on assets. AD firms show an edge over AG firms in converting a greater proportion of their net assets in production activity, however, it could be on account of AD firms' lower net assets. So far as growth is concerned, AG firms are growing faster in terms of net assets, while AD firms are faster in growth of sales.

As regards the results from other empirical studies (see Table 7.17 in the next chapter), despite the difference in the coverage of sample examined,[17] largely speaking, results are in conformity with those for other countries. Pertaining to size, profitability, and growth of assets, our results are in complete agreement with those for all other countries. However, there is lack of correspondence in results concerning leverage levels. In complete contrast to our result of AG firms being less leveraged, AG firms in all other countries are either equally or more leveraged than AD firms. The rationale for this could be provided in two ways. Firstly, from the difference in the sample examined. Most of the studies considered a sample comprising very large firms (from various industries) that in any case have larger requirement of debt. The sample in our study examines all mergers

16. The results are also summarised in Table 7.18, in the next chapter.

17. Table 7.17 summarises the results based on seven countries.The samples considered for analysis, in all the seven countries were not single industry based. Rather, they were drawn from many industries. See for details, Mueller (1980c).

in D&P industry and includes firms that are uniformly distributed across various size-classes. Secondly, this could also be due to difference in the financing patterns of developed and developing economies.[18] It has been observed that firms in the developed world prefer internal to external finance and within external finance, equity is the least preferred means of finance while for developing countries like India, equity funds dominate over debt finance.

Though this study does not test motives for merger, some comments are in order. AG firms, relatively, are several times larger than AD firms; this does not mean that all AG firms are large-sized firms. It can be observed [see Tables 6.2(a) to 6.2(d)] that AG firms are distributed almost uniformly across different size-classes. Since, approximately 60 per cent of AG firms belong to small and medium-sized firms, achieving scale economies through merger cannot be ruled out as one of the important motives of firms adopting merger.[19] A large proportion of mergers being horizontal in nature, also support economies of scale, as an important plausible factor determining the M&A activity in D&P industry. Further, the fact that a large number of mergers is 'within group' mergers, also suggests that firms are restructuring their businesses to attain synergistic benefits. Becoming bigger and grabbing a larger market share to compete in the phase of increased competition—especially from foreign firms—seems to be the driving force for firms.

Altogether, we find AG firms are superior to their corresponding AD firms, in terms of size, profitability and leverage. This is not to imply, however, that AD firms are inferior in all respects. These firms have significantly high productivity of assets and high growth of sales. Generally speaking, larger and more profitable companies acquire relatively smaller and less profitable yet, more productive companies. Further, to comment on whether AG firms are more efficient than all other firms in the industry or AD firms are the most inefficient in the industry, we also need to investigate 'merging firms' *vis-à-vis* 'non-merging firms'. For this, we turn to the next chapter.

---

18. It is also discussed in Chapter 8. For details of inter-country differences in corporate debt structure, see Singh and Hamid (1992).

19. For details, see Mueller (1980c).

7 Pre-merger Characteristics of Merging and Non-merging Firms

The basic motivation behind the work in this chapter is to investigate, whether firms that participated in merger activity (acquiring and acquired firms) differ from the firms that did not. The analysis essentially makes an exploratory attempt to trace the factors that prevented non-merging firms from becoming a part of M&As process. This involves a comparative assessment of merging (participant) and non-merging (non-participant) firms. A non-participant to a merger or a non-merging firm is defined as the one, which neither acquires nor is itself acquired by any firm during the period under study. A comparison of this kind will further facilitate our analysis carried out in the next two chapters.

The order of discussion in this chapter is as follows. Section 7.1 is concerned with control sample selected for AG and AD firms. A detailed analysis of pre-merger characteristics of AG and matched non-AG is presented in Section 7.2. The same exercise with respect to AD firms is carried out in Section 7.3. Section 7.4 briefly covers a summary of findings for other countries. The concluding remarks are presented in Section 7.5.

7.1 Selection of Control Sample

As stated in the previous chapter, firms that acquire and firms that get acquired are called acquiring (AG) and acquired (AD) firms, respectively. Correspondingly, the firms that do not acquire or get merged are called non-acquiring and non-acquired firms, respectively. Now, the issue addressed here is: how to decompose non-merging firms into non-AG and non-AD firms?

To compare the pre-merger characteristics of merging and non-merging firms, our study defines a control sample. Since the analysis considers the data over a five-year period before a merger, the control sample comprises the firms that were not involved in a merger[1] during 1988-89 to 2005-06.

Depending on the data availability, the choice of control group has varied across empirical studies. Most of the studies[2] considered the same control sample for both AG and AD firms that consisted of entire non-merging firms from the respective industry. Singh (1971) analysed AD and non-AD firms by classifying the latter, as a set of firms that include all surviving[3] firms from the respective industry. And to examine AG firms, a set of non-AG firms was chosen at random from the same industry-year. With reference to our study, based on the evidence that size can have an important influence on some of the indicators,[4] the construction of a control sample of non-merging firms is done by reference to size. The size, measured by total assets,[5] as reported in the balance sheet for the accounting year just before the merger, is considered to construct a control sample. For each merging (acquired or acquiring) firm, a firm (from the group of non-merging firms) is chosen in the control sample such that, its TAs lie within ± 20 per cent of the total assets of the merging firm. This may seem arbitrary but some degree of arbitrariness is unavoidable.

Accordingly, two separate control samples are constructed for both the groups of merging firms. Corresponding to the set of AG firms, we created another set of firms that matched each AG firm by its TAs (within ± 20 per cent) as reported in the balance sheet for the year just prior to the merger. It was named matched non-acquiring (MNAG) firms. Analogous to this, we constructed a set for AD firms,[6] called, matched non-acquired

1. Many a time mergers go unreported especially, when small or unlisted companies are involved. Therefore, despite careful selection of control sample, it might have included some firms that were involved in merger during the period under study.

2. For details, see Mueller (1980c).

3. Surviving firms included all acquiring firms and non-merging firms i.e., comprised all firms in the industry, other than the acquired ones.

4. The criterion is used to avoid systematic differences in the performance of matched firms due to size. See, for example, Jenny and Weber (1980); Singh (1971); Singh and Whittington (1975); Mueller (1980c).

5. Total assets is the most commonly used indicator of size, as it includes both the current and fixed assets.

6. For AD firms, TAs' one year before the merger happens to be the last year for which its figures for assets and sales are reported in the balance sheet.

(MNAD) firms. An AG firm that undertook more than one merger in a given year or in different years, was considered as many times as the number of mergers it undertook i.e., all mergers were considered separately. Further, an AG firm that undertook more than one merger in a given year is paired with the same firm whereas, a firm undergoing more than one merger in different years may or may not have been matched by the same controlled firm, depending on its size in the year just before the merger. To create a completely matched sample in terms of size for all merging firms, a few control firms were required to be used more than once. The earlier studies showed that a control group with repeats[7] may actually better represent the control group than the one with lesser number of matched firms. Further, in view of the fact that it was possible to create a good matched sample (see Table 7.1 and Table 7.9) for both the sets of AG and AD firms, the comparison is not likely to be vitiated by size.

Finally, to carry out a detailed analysis of the characteristics of the merging and non-merging firms in the Indian D&P industry, the firms are divided in two groups, *viz*.:

(i) Acquiring and Matched Non-acquiring Firms,

(ii) Acquired and Matched Non-acquired Firms.

Here the sample consists of four sets of firms: acquiring (AG), acquired (AD), matched non-acquiring (MNAG) and matched non-acquired (MNAD). For comparisons, each AG (AD) firm is paired with a matched non-AG (non-AD). Depending on the availability of data, size of sample differed for each group.

Size of Sample

For the first group, the study considers a sample of 82 firms consisting of 41 acquiring[8] firms and a control sample of 41 matched non-acquiring firms, from the D&P industry. The control sample has 9 non-acquiring firms that have been matched more than once to different acquiring firms,

7. See, Mueller (1980c: 119).

8. Out of this group of 41 acquiring firms, ten firms did not have data on their corresponding merged firms. So they were excluded from the pre-merger analysis of AD and AG firms, carried in the previous chapter.

though for different years. The second group includes a sample of 62 firms[9] consisting of equal number of acquired and matched non-acquired firms, from the D&P industry. To compare the characteristics of AD and MNAD firms, data for each matched non-AD firm are collected for the same years as for the corresponding AD.

We refrain from repeating the details of the variables used, as it is the same set used in the earlier chapter. Regarding the methodology, after testing for the variability of samples through the F-test, we applied the appropriate t-test for the groups i.e., AG and their MNAG and AD and MNAD firms.

7.2 Characteristics of Acquiring and Matched Non-acquiring Firms

As referred above, the sample used here has 82 firms, comprising 41 acquiring[10] and 41 non-acquiring firms. This set has a larger number of AG firms[11] than included in the pre-merger analysis of AG and AD firms. The present analysis includes all the firms from the D&P industry that have gone for acquisition during the period under study, irrespective of the data availability on their corresponding acquired firms. The control sample includes a set of non-merging[12] (i.e., neither acquiring nor acquired) firms matched (by total assets) to each acquiring firm in the year just preceding the merger. The averages for all indicators of various variables for this set of firms are shown in Tables 7.1 to 7.8.

9. Out of the 32 AD firms considered for the analysis of AD and AG firms in the previous chapter, two firms, *viz.*, TTK Biomed Ltd. and TTK medical Devices Ltd., do not belong to the D&P industry. Hence they were excluded from the sample for the present analysis. Another AD firm from D&P industry, Alpha Drug India Ltd. (acquired by Punjab Chemicals and Crop Protection Ltd., in 2005-06) which was excluded earlier, is also considered here for the analysis of AD and MNAD firms.

10. A few acquiring firms have been included more than once because, as referred earlier, a firm engaging in two mergers (either in the same year or in different years) is considered separately.

11. In this set of 41 AG firms, Ranbaxy Laboratories Ltd. (considered in the previous chapter), despite being an acquiring firm in 1996-97, has been excluded from the analysis, because it being the largest firm in the industry, no non-merging firm could be matched to it within the range of ± 20 per cent of its total assets in the pre-merger year i.e., 1995-96.

12. In view of shortage of matched non-acquiring firms—especially, corresponding to large-sized acquiring firms—a few non-acquiring firms had to be used more than once either for the same year or for different years.

Size Comparisons

The size-comparisons[13] are shown in Table 7.1. It is observed that AG firms have lower average net assets than MNAG firms. However, in terms of average net worth and sales, AG firms are larger than MNAG firms. But these differences are statistically not significant. The mean sales of AG firms measured over one, two and five years before the merger is 1.3 times of the mean sales of MNAG firms measured over the same years. The relative difference between AG and MNAG companies remains the same for average sales and net worth, over short as well as long periods.

Table 7.1

Size Comparisons (in Rs crore) of AG and MNAG Firms

Size	*Mean Value AG (X_1)*	*Mean Value MNAG (X_2)*	*Ratio X_1/X_2*	*$\sigma(X_1)$*	*$\sigma(X_2)$*	*F-Statistic*	*t-Statistic*
Sales							
A.M. (-1)	314	243.7	1.3	285	198	2.7**	1.2
A.M. (-2)	298	228.1	1.3	267	194	2.1**	1.2
A.M. (-5)	242	179.0	1.4	223	146	1.9***	1.4
Net assets							
A.M. (-1)	238	219	1.1	193	253	1.1	.45
A.M. (-2)	223	202	1.1	185	5	1.2	.41
A.M. (-5)	167	155	1.1	1	279	1.0	.31
Net worth							
A.M. (-1)	188	145	1.3	176	163	1.1	.99
A.M. (-2)	170	144	1.2	165	155	1.2	.76
A.M. (-5)	129	114	1.1	122	120	1.0	.85

Note: *** significant at 1 per cent level; ** significant at 5 per cent level.

Profitability Comparisons

Concerning profitability, using the five ratios over sales, it can be seen from Table 7.2 that AG firms are certainly more profitable than MNAG firms across all the measures. PBDIT/sales and PBIT/sales are higher but not significantly whereas PBDT/sales and PBT/sales are significantly higher for AG firms. Since the latter two ratios are calculated after deducting

13. Since the control sample is matched according to total assets, size comparisons of merging and non-merging firm do not include it.

interest payments, it can be inferred that the interest payments are more burdening for MNAG firms. This result is also confirmed from the comparisons of leverage ratios where MNAG firms are found to be more leveraged than the AG firms.

Table 7.2

Profitability Ratio Comparisons of AG and MNAG Firms

Profitability	*Mean Value AG (X_1)*	*Mean Value MNAG (X_2)*	*Ratio X_1/X_2*	σ *(X_1)*	σ *(X_2)*	*F-Statistic*	*t-Statistic*
PBDIT/sales							
A.M. (-1)	.19	.16	1.2	.08	.09	1.31	1.44
A.M. (-2)	.18	.16	1.1	.08	.08	1.14	1.12
A.M. (-5)	.20	.16	1.3	.18	.08	5.6***	1.51
PBDT/sales							
A.M. (-1)	.15	.10	1.5	.09	.09	1.1	2.13**
A.M. (-2)	.13	.10	1.4	.09	.09	1.0	1.95**
A.M. (-5)	.15	.09	1.6	.19	.11	3.4***	1.89*
PBIT/sales							
A.M. (-1)	.16	.13	1.2	.08	.08	1.1	1.55
A.M. (-2)	.15	.13	1.2	.08	.08	1.0	1.44
A.M. (-5)	.17	.12	1.4	.16	.08	3.7***	1.73*
PBT/sales							
A.M. (-1)	.12	.06	1.79	.10	.09	1.1	2.22**
A.M. (-2)	.12	.06	1.78	.10	.09	1.1	2.16**
A.M. (-5)	.13	.05	2.26	.18	.12	2.3**	2.13**
PAT/sales							
A.M. (-1)	.10	.05	1.88	.09	.09	1.3	1.67*
A.M. (-2)	.08	.05	1.65	.09	.09	1.5	1.55
A.M. (-5)	.09	.05	2.07	.14	.11	1.2	1.8*
PAT/NA							
A.M. (-1)	.16	.08	1.91	.11	.13	1.3	2.39**
A.M. (-2)	.15	.08	1.86	.10	.12	1.5	2.6***
A.M. (-5)	.14	.08	1.81	.10	.11	1.2	2.6***
PAT/NW							
A.M. (-1)	.22	.12	1.83	.13	.17	1.8**	2.45**
A.M. (-2)	.22	.14	1.64	.13	.19	16.7***	2.25**
A.M. (-5)	.20	.14	1.42	.15	.18	4.2***	1.64*

Note: *** significant at 1 per cent level; ** significant at 5 per cent level; * significant at 10 per cent level.

The relative difference between the average profitability of AG and MNAG firms is least for PBDIT/sales (1.2 times) and is highest for PBT/ Sales (1.8 times). Further, comparing these ratios over short and long periods prior to the merger, it clearly emerges that across all the ratios, the difference is higher over the latter. This is mainly due to a fall in the average profitability of AG firms before the merger whereas MNAG firms show a rise, though marginal, in average profitability over the short period.

Table 7.3

Frequency Distribution of AG and MNAG Firms (classification based on average profitability)

Profitability	*<0.5(lower)*		*0.5- 0.15(middle)*		*>0.15(higher)*	
	AG (%)	*MNAG (%)*	*AG (%)*	*MNAG (%)*	*AG (%)*	*MNAG (%)*
PAT/sales						
A.M. (-1)	20	32	64	58	16	11
A.M. (-2)	20	24	66	71	14	5
A.M. (-5)	25	39	55	53	20	8
PBDIT/sales						
A.M. (-1)	0	8	37	37	63	55
A.M. (-2)	3	5	32	39	66	55
A.M. (-5)	3	11	37	37	61	53
PBDT/sales						
A.M. (-1)	16	11	50	71	34	18
A.M. (-2)	3	13	32	63	66	24
A.M. (-5)	11	16	63	61	26	24
PBIT/sales						
A.M. (-1)	11	13	37	63	53	24
A.M. (-2)	8	8	42	55	50	37
A.M. (-5)	11	8	42	61	47	32
PBT/sales						
A.M. (-1)	11	13	63	76	26	11
A.M. (-2)	8	13	66	82	26	5
A.M. (-5)	11	13	71	79	18	8
PAT/NW						
A.M. (-1)	26	24	32	47	42	29
A.M. (-2)	34	37	26	29	40	34
A.M. (-5)	37	37	21	29	42	34
PAT/NA						
A.M. (-1)	13	32	47	37	40	32
A.M. (-2)	11	32	42	34	47	34
A.M. (-5)	16	26	47	58	37	16

Finally, using the rate of return on equity (PAT/NW) and net assets (PAT/NA), it is found that AG firms are significantly more profitable over short as well as long periods before the merger. MNAG companies show a fall in return on equity over short periods and the average return on assets and equity is marginally higher over short period before merger for AG companies.

Examining the distribution of AG and MNAG (Table 7.3) firms across the three size-classes of profitability ratios, it is found that the concentration of AG firms is lower in the lower class and greater in the higher class than those of MNAG firms.

The concentration in the middle range is almost the same for both AG and MNAG firms. The distribution does not differ much across the two periods for all ratios of profitability measured over sales. Using PAT/NW, it is observed that relatively high per cent of AG firms lie in the higher range and the concentration of both the AG and MNAG firms remain the same over short and long periods. While AG firms throughout concentrate more in the middle and higher classes, MNAG firms are equally distributed (33 per cent) across the three classes of PAT/NA during the short periods and move towards the middle profit classes during the long period.

Investment Turnover Ratio Comparisons (productivity of investment)

The average asset turnover ratio (Table 7.4) over one and two years ahead of merger, both using simple and weighted mean, is higher for AG firms. However, the difference is statistically significant when weighted averages are used. The proportionate gap in the averages is also higher when weighted mean is used. Though the average productivity is higher over the long period for both AG and MNAG set of firms, the relative difference in the productivity levels of the two sets of firms remains unchanged over the short and the long periods.

The distribution of AG and MNAG (Table 7.5) in the three ranges of productivity is 50, 45 and 5 per cent, respectively, for the former and 65, 30, 5 per cent for the latter.

Table 7.4

Investment Turnover Ratio Comparisons of AG and MNAG Firms

Sales/NA	Mean Value AG (X_1)	Mean Value MAG (X_2)	Ratio X_1/X_2	σ (X_1)	σ (X_2)	F-Statistic	t-Statistic
A.M. (-1)	1.78	1.71	1.04	.99	.92	1.1	.26
A.M. (-2)	1.88	1.73	1.09	1.09	.94	1.5	.58
A.M. (-5)	1.92	1.96	.98	1.03	1.2	1.4	.14
W.A.M. (-1)	1.45	1.04	1.4	—	—	—	5.71**
W.A.M. (-2)	1.48	1.06	1.4	—	—	—	4.14**
W.A.M. (-5)	1.67	1.2	1.4	—	—	—	7.51***

Note: *** significant at 1 per cent level; ** significant at 5 per cent level.

Table 7.5

Frequency Distribution of AG and MNAG Firms (classification based on average productivity of investment)

Sales/NA	0–2		2–4		4–6	
	AG (%)	MNAG (%)	AG (%)	MNAG (%)	AG (%)	MNAG (%)
A.M. (-1) & A.M. (-2)	50	67	45	33	5	0
A.M. (-5)	53	65	42	30	5	5

Leverage Ratio Comparisons

With respect to leverage ratios (Table 7.6), MNAG firms are significantly more leveraged than AG firms. The average TD/TA and D/E are significantly higher for MNAG firms. The reason for higher leverage lies with greater proportion of LTL in TA, reflected in significantly higher ratio of LTL/TA and LTL/STL for MNAG firms.

The ratio of STL/TA is the same for both AG and MNAG firms. Among the four ratios used to measure leverage (excluding STL/TA), the relative difference in the average ratios between AG and MNAG firms is highest for LTL/STL and least for TD/TA. The proportionate difference across all ratios remains unchanged for all records calculated over one, two and five years before the merger. It is important to recall here, that AD firms were also found to be more leveraged than their corresponding AG firms. However, this was due to higher proportion of both LTL and STL in total assets.

Table 7.6

Leverage Ratio Comparisons of AG and MNAG Firms

Leverage Ratio	*Mean Value AG (X_1)*	*Mean Value MNAG (X_2)*	*Ratio@ X_2/X_1*	σ (X_1)	σ (X_2)	*F-Statistic*	*t-Statistic*
D/E							
A.M. (-1)	.74	1.16	1.6	.92	.89	1.3	1.89*
A.M. (-2)	.85	1.57	1.8	1.12	2.3	5.0***	1.82*
A.M. (-5)	1.04	1.44	1.4	1.16	1.37	1.4	1.37
LTL/STL							
A.M. (-1)	.47	1.11	2.4	.7	1.04	3***	2.95***
A.M. (-2)	.52	1.06	2.0	.53	1.04	3.8***	2.85***
A.M. (-5)	.56	1.2	2.1	.53	1.2	10***	2.31**
TD/TA							
A.M. (-1)	.47	.58	1.2	.16	.21	1.8**	2.3**
A.M. (-2)	.49	.58	1.2	.16	.21	1.7*	2.2**
A.M. (-5)	.51	.59	1.2	.14	.19	1.8**	2.0**
STL/TA							
A.M. (-1)	.32	.33	1	.13	.15	1.2	.44
A.M. (-2)	.33	.33	1	.14	.14	1.1	.13
A.M. (-5)	.35	.34	1	.13	.15	1.1	.34
LTL/TA							
A.M. (-1)	.14	.25	1.8	.15	.15	1.1	2.95***
A.M. (-2)	.15	.25	1.6	.13	.14	1.1	3.05***
A.M. (-5)	.16	.24	1.5	.13	.13	1.1	2.76***

Notes: *** significant at 1 per cent level; ** significant at 5 per cent level; * significant at 10 per cent level.

@: In this table the ratio X_2/X_1 has been calculated (instead of X_1/X_2 in previous tables) as the value of average leverage ratio is relatively higher for MNAG firms.

The concentration level differs across AG and MNAG firms. On an average, the spread of AG firms is approximately 50, 30 and 20 per cent in the lower, middle and higher classes, respectively. For MNAG firms, it is 20, 60 and 20 per cent, respectively (Table 7.7).

Table 7.7

Frequency Distribution of AG and MNAG Firms
(classification based on average leverage ratio)

TD/TA	*<0.4*		*0.4 – 0.75*		*>0.75*	
	AG (%)	*MNAG (%)*	*AG (%)*	*MNAG (%)*	*AG (%)*	*MNAG (%)*
A.M. (-2)	45	11	47	82	8	8
A.M. (-5)	32	11	58	74	11	16

LTL/TA	*<0.15*		*0.15 – 0.4*		*>0.4*	
	AG (%)	*MNAG (%)*	*AG (%)*	*MNAG (%)*	*AG (%)*	*MNAG (%)*
A.M. (-2)	58	29	32	55	11	16
A.M. (-5)	47	29	45	61	8	11

STL/TA	*<0.25*		*0.25 – 0.5*		*>0.5*	
	AG (%)	*MNAG (%)*	*AG (%)*	*MNAG (%)*	*AG (%)*	*MNAG (%)*
A.M. (-2)	37	29	53	58	11	13
A.M. (-5)	18	32	66	55	16	13

LTL/STL	*<0.25*		*0.25 – 0.5*		*>0.5*	
	AG (%)	*MNAG (%)*	*AG (%)*	*MNAG (%)*	*AG (%)*	*MNAG (%)*
A.M. (-2)	50	29	26	26	24	25
A.M. (-5)	45	26	32	29	24	45

D/E	*<0.5*		*0.5 – 1*		*1 - 1.5*		*>1.5*	
	AG (%)	*MNAG(%)*	*AG (%)*	*MNAG(%)*	*AG(%)*	*MNAG(%)*	*AG (%)*	*MNAG(%)*
A.M. (-2)	53	18	16	32	21	18	10	32
A.M. (-5)	39	11	24	34	21	24	16	32

Growth Comparisons

Large differences in the growth rates of firms—especially, within the set of AG firms—necessitated the calculation of weighted averages for comparisons of growth. The higher standard deviation in the growth rates for the AG firms in comparison to the MNAG firms reflects greater number of outliers present within the former set. The growth results between AG and MNAG firms vary across both the indicator and the method of measurement used (Table 7.8).

Using weighted average, it is found that during the five years preceding merger AG firms have grown at marginally higher rates as far as net assets are concerned and have grown at higher rates if sales are taken as a variable for growth comparison. The average growth of sales of AG companies varies by high margin across the method of measurement. It changes from 1.48 to .29 when the method of measurement is changed from simple to weighted average. This is attributed to higher standard deviation in the growth rates within the set of AG companies. Irrespective of method of measurement, average growth of sales is almost the same for MNAG firms. However, the difference in the growth measured in terms of both the simple and the weighted arithmetic mean is non-significantly higher for AG firms.

Table 7.8

Growth Comparisons of AG and MNAG Firms

Growth	*Mean Value AG (X_1)*	*Mean Value MNAG (X_2)*	*σ (X_1)*	*σ (X_2)*	*F-Statistic*	*t-Statistic*
Sales						
A.M. (-5)	1.48	.26	6.9	.2	1188.4***	1.08
W.A.M. (-5)	.29	.25	—	—	—	.00
Net assets						
A.M. (-5)	.51	.43	.94	.43	4.8***	.48
W.A.M. (-5)	.39	.37	—	—	—	.24

Note: *** significant at 1 per cent level.

7.3 Characteristics of Acquired and Matched Non-acquired Firms

This analysis is carried out to find the distinguishing features that set apart the AD firms from their size-matched NAD firms. A sample of 62 firms from the D&P industry, comprising 31 acquired and 31 matched non-acquired firms[14] is used for this purpose. The choice is on the basis of a set of AD firms that are acquired from the D&P industry.[15] Based on

14. In this set of 31 matched non–acquired firms, only one firm, Unichem Laboratory Ltd. was required to be used twice for the control sample.

15. Out of these 31 acquired firms from the D&P industry, only 3 firms were acquired by firms outside the D&P industry and the remaining 28 firms were acquired within the D&P industry.

various indicators of the five variables, Tables 7.9 to 7.16 give the differences between AD and MNAD firms. As mentioned earlier, the control group is chosen by matching the total assets of AD firms i.e., corresponding to each AD firm we have a similar-sized non-acquired firm. Matching is done with respect to the total assets of AD firms, as reported in the year just prior to the merger.[16]

Size Comparisons

The size comparisons are based on the sales, NAs and NW. However, Table 7.9 also gives the average figures for total sssets, to confirm that a good matched sample is created.

Table 7.9

Size Comparisons (in Rs crore) of AD and MNAD Firms

Size	*Mean Value AD* (X_1)	*Mean Value MNAD* (X_2)	*Ratio* X_1/X_2	σ (X_1)	σ (X_2)	*F-Statistic*	*t-Statistic*
Sales							
A.M. (-1)	102.9	82.1	1.25	68.6	96.5	2.0**	.91
A.M. (-2)	99.8	79.1	1.26	68.4	96.2	2.0**	.91
A.M. (-5)	85.8	67.5	1.26	59.3	87.4	2.2**	.93
Net assets							
A.M. (-1)	57	50	1.14	66.8	49.1	1.9*	.42
A.M. (-2)	53.3	46.7	1.14	64.2	45.5	2.0**	.43
A.M. (-5)	43.3	40	1.06	52.9	42	1.6	.43
Net worth							
A.M. (-1)	36.7	30.7	1.2	50.6	38	1.8*	.4
A.M. (-2)	34.4	27.7	1.2	48.1	34.6	1.9**	.6
A.M. (-5)	7.7	22.5	1.2	38.2	26.4	2.1**	.6
Total assets							
A.M. (-1)	86	79	1.1	88	71	—	—

Note: ** significant at 5 per cent level; * significant at 10 per cent level.

Acquired firms are slightly bigger than MAD firm in terms of sales, NA and NW. However, the difference is statistically not significant. As

16. In fact for AD firm, the year just prior to the merger is the last year for which its balance sheet is published.

compared to MNAD firms, average net assets, net worth and sales of AD firms are 1.1, 1.2 and 1.3 times, respectively.

Profitability Comparisons

The comparison of average profitability ratios by computing simple averages does not seem to be the right method due to the presence of large variations in profitability levels—especially, within the set of MNAD firms. This is also confirmed by the comparisons of standard deviation, which is more than double for MNAD firms.[17]

To make meaningful comparisons and adjustments for such variations, weighted arithmetic mean of each ratio is also computed. The results indicate that average profitability based on weighted means is higher for AD firms than that of MNAD firms. The difference, however, is statistically not significant for all ratios calculated over one, two and five years prior to the merger. The relative difference in average profitability between the two groups is highest for the return on equity (PAT/NW) and lowest for PBDIT/sales (Table 7.10).

The distribution of AD and MNAD firms (Table 7.11) across three size-classes, *viz.*, lower (<0.5), middle (0.5 to 0.15) and upper (>0.15) is largely the same for all ratios, except PBDT/sales. In this case the concentration of AD firms in lower range (54 per cent) is much more than that of MNAD (30 per cent) firms.

Asset/Investment Turnover Ratio Comparisons

Irrespective of the method of measurement, in turning assets into sales, the AD firms appear to be slightly better in their performance over short as well as long periods than MNAD firms (Table 7.12). Approximately three-fourth of both AD and MNAD firms have productivity levels below 3, while the remaining one-fourth lie in the range of above 3, over both the short and the long periods (Table 7.13).

---

17. Within the MNAD set, firms such as, Shrishma Fine Chemicals & Pharma. (Kar.) Ltd., Pharmacia Ltd., and Southern Herbals Ltd. had PAT/sales, -52 per cent, 68 per cent and –55 per cent, respectively. However, among AD firms, PAT/sales varied within ± 15 per cent.

Table 7.10

Profitability Ratio Comparisons of AD and MNAD Firms

Profitability Ratio	*Mean Value AD (X_1)*	*Mean Value MNAD (X_2)*	*Ratio X_1/X_2*	*σ (X_1)*	*σ (X_2)*	*F-Statistic*	*t-Statistic*
PBDIT/sales							
A.M. (-1)	.13	.12	.9	.08	.19	5.0***	—
A.M. (-2)	.13	.07	.9	.08	.19	21.7***	—
A.M. (-5)	.13	.05	1	.09	.19	29.3***	—
W.A.M. (-2)	.15	.13	1.1	—	—	—	.18
W.A.M. (-5)	.15	.14	1.1	—	—	—	.24
PBIT/sales							
A.M. (-1)	.10	.07	1.4	.07	21	8.3***	—
A.M. (-2)	.10	.07	1.5	.07	25	12.5***	—
A.M. (-5)	. 07	.09	.76	.16	22	1.8*	—
W.A.M. (-2)	.11	.11	1.1	—	—	—	.04
W.A.M. (-5)	.11	.11	1.1	—	—	—	.00
PBDT/sales							
A.M. (-1)	.08	.09	.8	.09	.19	5.0***	—
A.M. (-2)	.07	.10	.7	.08	.18	5.0***	—
A.M. (-5)	.03	.08	.4	.20	.18	1.3	—
W.A.M. (-2)	.10	.09	1.1	—	—	—	.06
W.A.M. (-5)	.10	.08	1.2	—	—	—	.11
PBT/sales							
A.M. (-1)	.05	.03	1.5	.09	.22	5.6***	—
A.M. (-2)	.05	.03	1.6	.09	.25	8.3***	—
A.M. (-5)	-.01	.03	N.R.	.27	.22	1.5	—
W.A.M. (-2)	.08	.07	1.2	—	—		.12
W.A.M. (-5)	.07	.05	1.4	—	—		.10
PAT/sales							
A.M. (-1)	.03	.02	1.9	.07	.21	8.3***	—
A.M. (-2)	.03	.02	1.3	.07	.24	12.5***	—
A.M. (-5)	-.03	.02	N.R.	.25	.20	1.6	—
W.A.M. (-2)	.05	.05	1	—	—		.01
W.A.M. (-5)	.05	.04	1.2	—	—		.00

Note: N.R.: Not reported, whenever average profitability is negative, ratio of X_2/X_1 is not computed.

*** significant at 1 per cent level; ** significant at 5 per cent level; * significant at 10 per cent level.

Table 7.11

Frequency Distribution of AD and MNAD Firms (classification based on average profitability)

Profitability Ratio	<0.5(lower)		0.5–0.15(middle)		>0.15(higher)	
	MNAD (%)	AD (%)	MNAD (%)	AD (%)	MNAD (%)	AD (%)
PAT/sales						
A.M. (-1)	65	59	23	37	12	4
A.M. (-2)	66	67	22	30	12	4
A.M. (-5)	63	67	30	33	7	0
PBDIT/sales						
A.M. (-1)	15	22	56	44	30	33
A.M. (-2)	22	22	47	37	37	41
A.M. (-5)	15	22	59	37	26	41
PBDT/sales						
A.M. (-1)	**30**	**54**	**52**	**26**	**18**	**20**
A.M. (-2)	41	44	41	33	19	22
A.M. (-5)	41	41	41	41	19	19
PBIT/sales						
A.M. (-1)	26	26	56	48	19	26
A.M. (-2)	30	26	52	48	19	26
A.M. (-5)	22	26	56	48	22	26
PBT/sales						
A.M. (-1)	56	56	33	30	11	15
A.M. (-2)	63	56	26	30	11	15
A.M. (-5)	59	56	22	33	19	11
PAT/NW						
A.M. (-1)	35	39	19	18	46	43
A.M. (-2)	23	36	38	21	38	43
A.M. (-5)	19	32	35	18	46	32
PAT/NA						
A.M. (-1)	44	41	26	26	30	33
A.M. (-2)	41	37	33	30	26	33
A.M. (-5)	37	37	37	26	26	37

Table 7.12

Investment Turnover Ratio Comparisons of AD and MNAD Firms

Sales/ NA	*Mean Value AD (X_1)*	*Mean Value MNAD (X_2)*	*Ratio X_1/X_2*	*σ (X_1)*	*σ (X_2)*	*F-Statistic*	*t-Statistic*
A.M. (-1)	2.6	2.2	1.2	1.8	1.4	2.0**	.88
A.M. (-2)	2.7	2.2	1.2	1.9	1.5	1.7*	1.2
A.M. (-5)	2.6	2.3	1.2	1.8	1.4	1.5	.96
W.A.M. (-1)	1.9	1.7	1.2	—	—	—	.17
W.A.M. (-2)	1.9	1.7	1.1	—	—	—	.15
W.A.M. (-5)	2	1.7	1.2	—	—	—	.51

Note: ** significant at 5 per cent level; * significant at 10 per cent level.

Table 7.13

Frequency Distribution of AD and MNAD Firms (classification based on average investment turnover ratio)

Sales/NA	*0-3*		*>3*	
	AD	*MNAD*	*AD*	*MNAD*
A.M. (-1) and A.M. (-2)	75	79	25	21
A.M. (-5)	72	74	28	26

Leverage Ratio Comparisons

The leverage ratio of both the sets of firms differs across ratios as well as time, but by a very small margin. The weighted average of STL/TA and LTL/TA ratios are marginally higher for MNAD firms over both the short as well as the long periods whereas average LTL/STL is higher for AD firms when calculated over two years preceding the merger and slightly higher for MNAD firms calculated over five years before the merger (Table 7.14). On an average, the MNAD and AD firms have more or less the same leverage ratios. However, MNAD firms are burdened by higher amount of LTLs.

Correspondingly, the concentration levels differ across ratios. With regard to LTL/STL and LTL/TA, it is observed that AD firms are heavily clustered in the lower range, while MNAD are concentrated in the middle range. There is no difference in concentration levels, when STL/TA is used. For both sets of firms, the cluster is in the middle range (Table 7.15).

Table 7.14

Leverage Ratio Comparisons of AD and MNAD Firms

Leverage Ratio	*Mean Value AD (X_1)*	*Mean Value MNAD (X_2)*	*σ (X_1)*	*σ (X_2)*	*F-Statistic*	*t-Statistic*
LTL/TA						
A.M. (-2)	.19	.22	.24	.15	2.5**	.32
A.M. (-5)	.20	.23	.18	.14	1.8*	.44
W.A.M. (-2)	.20	.23	—	—		.56
W.A.M. (-5)	.19	.27	—	—		1.52
LTL/STL						
A.M. (-2)	.74	.70	1.26	.7	3.2***	.15
A.M. (-5)	.65	.72	.88	.6	1.8*	.33
STL/TA						
A.M. (-2)	.41	.39	.22	.15	2.0**	.5
A.M. (-5)	.42	.40	.18	.14	1.7*	.5
W.A.M. (-2)	.35	.37	—	—		.22
W.A.M. (-5)	.36	.36	—	—		.10
TD/TA						
A.M. (-2)	.59	.60	.21	.30	2.1**	.16
A.M. (-5)	.61	.62	.17	.24	2.1**	.13

Growth Comparisons

The growth rates of sales as well as NA measured on the basis of simple as well as weighted average growth are higher for that of AD firms. The relative difference in average growth rates for AD and MNAD firms is higher for sales than for net assets. The weighted average growth of sales of AD firms is more than twice the average growth of MNAD firms. This substantiates our earlier finding of AD firms having greater asset turnover ratio than AG firms. The drastically different simple and weighted average growth rates obtained for AD set of firms is because of the presence of a number of outlier firms in the set of AD firms (Table 7.16).

Table 7.15

Frequency Distribution of AD and MNAD Firms (classification based on average leverage ratio)

LTL/TA	<.15		0.15–0.4		>0.4	
	AD (%)	MNAD (%)	AD (%)	MNAD (%)	AD (%)	MNAD (%)
A.M. (-2)	60	33	21	56	19	11
A.M. (-5)	48	33	40	59	12	7
STL/TA	<.25		0.25–0.5		>0.5	
	AD (%)	MNAD (%)	AD (%)	MNAD (%)	AD (%)	MNAD (%)
A.M. (-2)	15	19	52	56	33	26
A.M. (-5)	14	15	52	67	37	19

LTL/STL	<0.2		0.2 –0.4		0.4 - 0.6		0.6 -0.8		0.8 - 1.0		>1	
	AD (%)	MNAD (%)	AD (%)	MNAD (%)	AD (%)	MNAD (%)	AD (%)	MNAD (%)	AD (%)	MNAD (%)	AD (%)	MNAD (%)
A.M. (-2)	60	22	0	19	15	19	4	4	0	15	22	22
A.M.(-5)	41	15	19	26	15	19	4	4	0	11	22	26

Table 7.16

Growth Comparisons of AD and MNAD Firms

Growth	Mean Value AD (X_1)	Mean Value MAD (X_2)	Ratio X_1/X_2	t-Statistic
Sales				
A.M. (-5)	1.32	.19	—	—
A.M. (-5)[@]	.23	.19	—	—
W.A.M. (-5)	.34	.15	2.3	.29
Net assets				
A.M. (-5)	.94	.24	—	—
A.M. (-5)[@]	.27	.20	—	—
W.A.M. (-5)	.28	.19	1.5	.59

Note: @ Excluding outlier firms' average growth from the calculation of overall average for AD firms.

7.4 Summary of Research Findings for Other Countries

A summary of the findings of the studies undertaken in seven countries (Belgium, the Netherlands, UK, USA, France, Germany and Sweden) is given in Table 7.17.

Table 7.17

Summary of Characteristics of AG, AD and Control Group Firms for Seven Countries

Size	*AG and AD*	*AG, MAG or Control*		*AD, MAD or Control*
For all countries	AG >AD	Belgium, Netherlands and UK	AG > C AG > MAG	AD ≥ C(UK) AD ≅ C (Belgium, Netherlands)
		Germany, France, Sweden and USA	AG > MIND	AD ≥ MAD (Germany) AD > MIND (Sweden)
Overall	*AG >AD*		*AG > MAG*	*AD ≥ MAD*
Profitability	*AG & AD*		*AG, MAG or Control*	*AD, MAD or Control*
Belgium	AG ≅ AD		AG < C	AD ≤ C
Germany	AG ≥ AD		AG ≅ MAG	AD < MAD
France	AG ≥ AD		AG ≥ MAG	AD ≤ MAD
Netherlands	AG ≅ AD		AG ≤ MAG	AD ≅ MAD
Sweden	AG ≥ AD		AG ≅ MAG	AD ≅ MAD
UK	AG > AD		AG ≅ MAG	AD < MAD
USA	AG ≅ AD		AG ≅ MAG	AD ≅ MAD
Overall	*AG ≥ AD*		*AG ≤ MAG*	*AD ≤ MAD*
Profit Variability	*AG & AD*		*AG, MAG or Control*	*AD, MAD or Control*
Belgium	AG ≅ AD		AG ≤ C	AD ≅ C
Germany	AG < AD		AG < MAG	AD < MAD
France	AG ≤ AD		AG ≅ MAG	AD ≅ MAD
Netherlands	AG ≅ AD		AG ≤ MAG	AD ≥ MAD
Sweden	AG ≤ AD		AG ≅ MIND	AD ≅ MAD
UK	AG ≤ AD		AG ≅ MAG	AD ≥ MAD
USA	AG ≅ AD		AG ≅ MAG	AD ≤ MAD
Overall	*AG ≤ AD*		*AG ≤ MAG*	*AD ≥ MAD*
Leverage	*AG & AD*		*AG, MAG or Control*	*AD, MAD or Control*
Belgium	AG ≥ AD		AG ≅ C	AD < C
Germany	AG ≅ AD		AG > MAG	AD ≅ MAD
France	AG ≅ AD		AG ≅ MAG	AD > MAD
Netherlands	AG ≅ AD		AG ≅ MAG	AD ≅ MAD
Sweden	AG ≅ AD		AG ≅ MIND	AD ≅ MIND
UK	AG > AD		AG > MAG	AD > MAD
USA	AG > AD		AG > MAG	AD ≅ MAD
Overall	*AG ≥ AD*		*AG ≥ MAG*	*AD ≥ MAD*
Growth	*AG & AD*		*AG, MAG or Control*	*AD, MAD or Control*
Belgium	AG > AD		AG > C	AD ≅ C
Germany	AG ≥ AD		AG ≅ MAG	AD < MAD
France	AG ≅ AD		AG ≅ MAG	AD ≅ MAD
Netherlands	AG > AD		AG ≅ MAG	AD ≅ MAD
Sweden	AG > AD		AG ≅ MIND	AD ≅ MIND
UK	AG > AD		AG > MAG	AD ≤ MAD
USA	AG > AD		AG > MAG	AD ≅ MAD
Overall	*AG ≥ AD*		*AG ≥ MAG*	*AD ≤ AD*

Notes: MIND = matched industry; C = control group (all non-AG and non-AD); MAD = matched non-acquired; MAG = matched non-acquiring; ≤ less than or equal to; ≥ greater than or equal to; ≅ about equal; < significantly lesser; > significantly greater.

Source: Mueller (1980a).

The first set of comparisons is of the size of the acquiring and acquired firms. These results are quite consistent across all countries. Acquiring firms are larger than randomly selected firms in their industries, larger than the average firms in the industry and larger than the firms they acquire. Regarding profitability, the evidence is inconclusive. In Belgium and the Netherlands, for example, the acquiring firms were found to be somewhat less profitable than the control group companies; in France, slightly more so. In the other four countries, the two groups appear to be roughly equal in profitability. Drastic differences in variability in profits were not observed across the 7 countries. In Belgium, West Germany and the Netherlands the acquiring firms were found to have less volatile profits than for the companies they acquired.

In all countries the acquiring firms were either as highly leveraged or more leveraged than the control group firms. In France and UK, the acquired firms also tended to be somewhat more leveraged than non-acquired firms and in Belgium the opposite was found. A fairly consistent pattern of growth rate differences was found across all countries. The acquiring firms grew as fast as or faster than the size matched or control group non-acquiring firms. The acquired firms also grew as fast as the control group companies, except in the United Kingdom and West Germany where they grew slowly. With the exception of France, where the acquiring and acquired firms grew at roughly equal rates, acquiring firms in all other countries were generally faster growing than the companies they acquired.

7.5 Conclusion

In the earlier chapter, comparing AG and AD firms, we observed that AG firms are significantly more profitable and larger in size. Further, they are significantly less leveraged and are growing faster in terms of net assets. However, using sales as an indicator, AD firms showed faster growth and to corroborate this, we also found AD firms to have significantly high productivity of investment. These results are in conformity with several earlier studies. Now, the more pertinent and lesser-explored issue is with regard to the characteristics of merging and non-merging firms. In the present chapter, we constructed a specific sample to control the effect of size and compared the AG and AD firms with their size-matched non-merging firms.

The most noticeable difference between AG and MNAG firms is with regard to gearing levels and, as a result, profitability ratios. The former are significantly less leveraged—especially on account of lesser proportion of LTL in their total assets. This in turn resulted in significant difference in profitability margins, calculated after the deduction of interest payments i.e., PBDT or PBT or PAT. In terms of productivity and growth of sales, AG firms are marginally better than MNAG firms. It is important to draw attention to the fact that both AD and MNAG firms are more leveraged than AG firms. However, MNAG firms are particularly long-term debt laden and AD firms are more burdened on account of both the short and long-term funds.

Among the four sets of firms examined in the present study, namely, AG, AD, MNAG and MNAD; AG firms are the least debt loaded. Two points require a special mention here. First, our results invalidate Modigliani-Miller's irrelevance theorem that total value or cost of capital is invariant to the capital-mix. Our findings are that AG firms are not only largest in size, faster growing in assets, and most profitable, but they also have lowest debt-equity ratio. This confirms the traditional approach that factors, such as size, profitability, tax considerations and growth of firm are vital in determining its optimal capital structure. Second, apart from inter-firm differences, efficiency and growth of the financial system in any country also has an important role in determining the optimal capital-mix. On account of stock market reforms (see details in Chapter 2) the average corporate debt-equity ratio has fallen in India. Large firms have particularly exploited the situation by raising finance through equity issues. This accounts for inter-country differences in the optimal capital-mix.

Compared to other empirical studies (summarised in Table 7.17), our results regarding profitability are comparable to only France and in all the other countries MNAG and AG firms were found to have nearly same profitability. In terms of growth, our observations are consistent with other countries. So far as leverage ratios are concerned, in contrast to our results, all other countries found AG firms to be more debt-burdened. As stated, this is a result of inter-country differences in financing patterns (Singh and

Hamid, 1992). As compared to India, the developed world countries have a preference for long-term debt over the equity issue (discussed in Chapter 8). Also, since the initiation of economic reforms, particularly stock market developments, the relative use of equity financing has augmented in our country. This has caused a general fall in the corporate debt-equity ratio (discussed in Chapter 2). In effect, difference in leverage ratios between developed and developing countries also account for difference in profitability ratios of firms.

Concerning AD and their size-matched non-acquired firms, the former performed better in terms of profitability, asset turnover and growth and are also less leveraged than the latter. However, the difference is marginal and statistically not significant for all variables. Leaving growth, with respect to all other variables our results are quite similar to those obtained for other countries.

Altogether, it is concluded that acquiring companies are larger, more profitable and better managed companies and thus are more successful than other sets of companies. When compared with their MNAG firms, it clearly appears that they differed only in their leverage ratios. MNAG firms are significantly more dependent on long-term borrowing for financing their production activity. This also caused them to differ in terms of profitability ratios—especially, after deducting interest payments. From these first stage investigations, it can be inferred that long-term borrowings seem to be a constraint for MNAG firms to acquire other firms and be a participant in the merger activity. Contrary to Modigliani-Miller's irrelevance theorem, the capital structure of a firm has an important bearing on its future growth strategy.

The firms that are made merger targets, though less efficient than their corresponding AG firms, are very similar to other size-matched non-AD firms. Therefore, only on the basis of pre-merger comparisons, it is difficult to answer the question, as to why a particular firm is taken as a merger target or why a firm goes for an acquisition. To find out the factors that determine the probability of an acquisition or of becoming a merger target, we shall turn to the next chapter.

Table 7.18

Summary of Pre-merger Characteristics of AG, AD, MNAG and MNAD Firms

Size	
Sales:	AG > MAG > AD > MAD
Net assets:	MAG = AG > AD = MAD
GFA:	AG > AD
Net worth:	AG > MAG > AD > MAD
Total assets:	AG > AD
Profitability	
PAT/sales:	AG > MAG > AD > MAD
PBDIT/sales:	AG = MAG > AD > MAD
PAT/NW:	AG > MAG > AD > MAD
PAT/assets:	AG > MAG = MAD > AD, AG > AD
PBIT/sales:	AG > MAG = AD < MAD
PBT/sales:	AG > MAG > MAD > AD, AG > AD
Investment Turnover Ratio	
Sale/assets:	AD > MAD > AG > MAG
Leverage Ratio	
TD/TA:	AD > AG < MAG, AD = MAG
D/E:	AD > MAG > AG
LTL/STL:	MAG > AD = MAD > AG
STL/TA:	AD = MAD > AG = MAG
LTL/TA:	MAG > AG > AD < MAD
Growth	
Sales:	AD > AG = MAG > MAD
Net assets:	AG = MAG > AD > MAD

Notes: > and < signify statistically significant, ≥ quantitatively higher but non-significant; = neither quantitatively higher nor statistically significant.

8 Determinants of Acquisition

Why does a Firm Acquire?

From a detailed study of pre-merger characteristics of acquiring (AG) and matched non-acquiring (MNAG) firms, attempted in the previous chapter, it was observed that the former were significantly more profitable and less leveraged than their size-matched MNAG firms. In terms of growth and asset turnover ratio also, AG firms were better than their corresponding MNAG firms. However, the difference was not significant.

Now, in order to find a set of determinants that predicts the probability of a firm acquiring another, a question arises, why does a firm acquire? Hence, this chapter is organised in six sections. Section 8.1 outlines the motivation for the analysis. Section 8.2 briefly describes the size of the sample used for the analysis. The methodology used is outlined in Section 8.3. Section 8.4 gives a detailed description of all the variables, their construction and rationale for inclusion in the analysis. This section also discusses the trends in market share and concentration levels in the drugs & pharmaceutical industry. . The findings of the study are reported in Section 8.5. Finally, Section 8.6 concludes with some observations.

8.1 Motivation for Answering the Query

A key question that comes to our mind is that despite being in a similar macroeconomic environment and with same industrial level factors, why do some firms acquire while others do not? We analyse whether various firm-specific factors, such as size, profitability, capital structure, investments, financing pattern, and age of the firm at the time of merger matter in determining its growth strategy. So the focus is on the determinants of M&As from the firm's point of view in the D&P industry. Our analysis particularly attempts to answer this query:

'Why amongst a similarly-sized set of firms, some acquire and others do not?'

More specifically, the objective is to understand the relationship between a set of attributes describing a firm and the probability that it will go for a merger.

Such a study in Indian conditions is being attempted for the first time. Even the existing literature on other countries has focussed more on other areas, such as effect on post-merger performance of a firm, distribution of gains from merger between AD and AG firms, and probability of a firm being acquired by other firms. The behaviour of AG firms has received little attention and is a less explored research area. Jensen (1988) and Bhagat *et al.* (1990) have emphasised the role of acquisition strategy by firms in response to low returns from the existing business—especially when the industry to which they belong is declining or stagnant. Jensen (1988), in particular, has advocated 'free cash flow'[1] in which he emphasised that a firm goes for an acquisition because it has surplus cash, which it is not interested in distributing among its shareholders. Hay and Liu (1998), focussed on the determinants of mergers and behaviour of acquiring firms by considering a sample of only AG firms over a period of eight years.

Our study differs from the earlier work by having a few special features. First, the study analyses mergers within an industry. Second, it seeks to evaluate the behaviour of both AG and MNAG firms where the latter are matched by the size of AG firms, measured one year prior to the merger. Our focus, therefore, is on the variables that contribute to the explanation of the acquisition strategy of firms. There are two ways of approaching this issue. What variables or factors increase the probability of firm in undertaking mergers (hence, allowing firm to become an acquiring firm) is one. What variables restricted and constrained the other firms, despite being of similar size, in adopting the strategy of undertaking mergers and acquisitions is the second approach. Third, the study incorporates many new variables that have never been considered in the existing empirical literature. The study may also throw light on a few important aspects, which have been neglected in the literature available on mergers and acquisitions.

---

1. Free cash flow theory of acquisition highlights the fact that firms make acquisitions to mop up excess cash, which they are unwilling to payout to shareholders. For details, see Chapter 3.

8.2 Size of Sample

A sample comprising acquiring (AG) and matched non-acquiring (MNAG) is chosen. All the firms that undertook mergers during 1992-93 to 2005-06 are taken within a set of AG firms and for each AG firm a control firm was chosen that matched the AG firm in terms of size. The size is measured in total assets in the year that preceded the year of the merger. The size of the matched sample is allowed to vary within ± 20 per cent of the total assets of AG firms in the similar period. For a few AG firms no matched firms could be found within these limits. For example, Ranbaxy Laboratories Ltd., being the largest firm in the D&P industry, did not have any matched firm within ± 20 per cent of its size just prior to the merger. Therefore, the number of AG firms included in the sample is more than that of the matched firms.

It is important to mention here that each AG firm is considered only once irrespective of the number of mergers it has undertaken in a year or in different years. During the period under consideration, e.g., Dr. Reddy's Laboratories Ltd. undertook the merger with American Remedies Ltd. and Cheminor Drugs Ltd.[2] in the year 2000-01, Sun Pharmaceutical Industries Ltd., one of the most aggressive firms, undertook more than 10 mergers, *albeit* in different years, during 1993-2006. Similarly, TTK Healthcare Ltd., Matrix Laboratories Ltd., and Novartis India Ltd. are the firms that undertook more than one merger. All such firms are considered only once in the sample. The AG firms included in the sample accounted for approximately 45 per cent of the total industry's sales[3] in 1999-2000. On account of high merger activity during 2001-2005,[4] this share rose to 56 per cent[5] in 2004-05.

---

2. Cheminor Drugs Ltd. is considered as an AG firm as well. It undertook merger in 1994-95 and later itself got merged into Dr. Reddy 's Laboratories Ltd. in 2000-01.
3. The industry's sales are calculated on the basis of the data of approximately 300 firms available from Prowess database source. This set largely accounts for sales of organised sector in D&P industry and includes listed as well as unlisted firms.
4. See Table 5.13 of Chapter 5.
5. Fifty-six per cent is accounted for by 29 firms because data on three firms, *viz*., Core Healthcare Ltd., SOL Pharmaceutical Ltd., and Cheminor Drugs Ltd. were not available for 2004-05.

8.3 Methodology

As mentioned earlier, with the objective to find out factors that affect the acquisition behaviour of a firm, a sample of AG and MNAG firms is considered. Here, the firms are faced with a choice between two alternatives i.e., whether to go for a merger or not, and the choice in turn depends upon a few identifiable characteristics of firms. The dependent variable considered in such cases is of a qualitative nature, which can take the value 1 (if the firm is an acquiring firm) or 0 (if the firm is a non-acquiring firm). The method of ordinary least square regression analysis, for reasons explained below, is not applicable here.

Such cases of 'yes or no' dependent variable are handled by binary choice models,[6] also called 'dichotomous' or 'dummy dependent variable' regression models. There are three commonly used approaches to deal with cases of 'dummy dependent variable' i.e., when dependent variable takes 0 or 1 value.

1. The Linear Probability model (LPM),
2. The Logit model,
3. The Probit model.

Consider the following simple model with one independent variable in equation (1):

$$Y_i = \beta_1 + \beta_2 X_i + u_i, \tag{1}$$

Y_i = 1, if a firm acquires,

= 0, if a firm does not acquire.

where, let X_i be the size of the firm, and i is the number of firms.

Here Y_i is a linear function of the explanatory variable X_i and the function is called linear probability model. E (Y_i/X_i) is the conditional expectation of Y_i given X_i. It gives the probability of the firm going for an acquisition, whose size is given by amount X_i.

In order to estimate LPM the standard OLS technique cannot be applied for two reasons: (i) the assumption of normality of disturbances u_i

6. Such kinds of models are commonly used in survey data where qualitative behavioural responses are involved, e.g., an individual will vote or not, a firm will be acquired or not etc.

is not satisfied. Rather, it follows the binomial distribution i.e., variance of u_i is heteroscedastic[7], (ii) LPM does not guarantee that the estimated conditional probabilities of Y_i will lie between 0 and 1. Also, LPM is not logically a very attractive model because it assumes that $P_i = (Y_i=1/X_i)$ increases linearly with X i.e., marginal or incremental effect of X remains constant throughout. In our case, it means, as the size of the company increase by a unit, probability of a firm going for an acquisition increases by the same constant β_2, irrespective of the initial size. This is unrealistic. Keeping in view these limitations of LPM, an alternative approach is required which essentially has two properties: (a) its probability lies between 0 and 1, and (b) it varies non-linearly with X.

These requirements can be taken care of by the use of cumulative distribution probability function (CDF). Depending upon the type of CDF, we have various models. The most commonly used are Logit and Probit models. A detailed analysis of both the models is provided in Annexure III.

The present study analyses the problem using Logit specification. The justification of choice of Logit over Probit is as follows:

1. Logit and Probit formulation are quite similar,[8] however, Logit is convenient to use computationally.
2 It directly yields an estimate of the probability of the occurrence of an event. Logit models transform the problem of predicting probability within (0, 1) interval to the problem of predicting the odds of an event occurring within the range of the real line.

With respect to the present work, the estimating equation is written as

$$L_i = \ln\left(\frac{P_i}{1 - P_i}\right) = Z_i = \beta_0 + \beta_1 X_{1i} + \ldots + \beta_k X_{ki} + u_i \qquad (2)$$

where i = N = 59 (number of firms in the sample), n_1 = Prob(Y_i = 1, firm is an acquiring) = 32, n_2 = Prob(Y_i = 0, firm is a non-acquiring) = 27; n_1 +

7. For details see Pindyck and Rubinfeld (1998).

8. The slope of cumulative logistic distribution is maximum at P=½. It implies that any change in independent variable will have its greatest impact on the probability of choosing a given option at the mid point and will be lower near the end points. This is why, when plotted on a graph, logistic has slightly flatter tails (Pindyck and Rubinfeld, 1998).

n_2 = N, and no. of explanatory variables, i.e., k, vary from specification to specification with a maximum limit of 7. Since the observations considered in the data are individual observations, the logit model is estimated by using maximum likelihood estimation (MLE) procedure. Also, it yields consistent estimates. A brief outline of this method is given below.

The maximum likelihood function has the following form:

$$Q = \text{Prob}\,(Y_1 \ldots Y_N) = \text{Prob}\,(Y_1) \ldots \text{Prob}\,(Y_N)$$

Assuming Prob (Y_i= 1) has n_1 (=32) observations and Prob (Y_i = 0) has n_2 (=27) observations such that $n_1 + n_2$ = N (=59), and ordering the observations such that first 32 observations represent AG firms, the ML function can be rewritten as:

$$Q=\prod_{i=1}^{n_1} P_i \prod_{i=n_1+1}^{N} (1-P_i)=\prod_{i=1}^{N} P_i^{Y_i}(1-P_i)^{1-Y_i}$$

[since Prob (Y_i =1) = P_i, therefore Prob (Y_i=0) =1 - P_i]

Taking log on both the sides of the above equation we obtain,

$$\log Q = \sum_{i=1}^{n_1} \log P_i + \sum_{i=n_1+1}^{N} \log (1-P_i)$$

The significance of the estimated coefficients is tested by using Z-test, as the ratio of the estimated coefficient to its standard error follows a normal distribution. In order to test the overall significance[9] of logit regression estimates, likelihood ratio (LR) test[10] is used. This statistic follows a chi-square (χ^2) distribution with degrees of freedom equal to the number of parameters in the model.

8.4 Variables: Construction and Rationale for their Inclusion

The choice of variables is made partly on the basis of the similar kind of studies available for other countries and partly on the basis of analysis of

9. In binary dependent variable R^2 is not preferred as a measure of goodness of fit. For details, see Pindyck and Rubinfeld (1998) and Gujarati (2003).
10. It tests the hypothesis that all the parameters in the model are simultaneously equal to zero.

pre-merger characteristics of AG and MNAG firms carried out in the Chapters 6 and 7. This section presents some of the major hypotheses postulated empirically regarding the likelihood of a firm going for merger and accordingly, discusses the selection of variables and their measurement. For convenience, the variables included in the analysis are divided into the following seven broad groups:

- Profitability as a measure of a firm's performance,
- Gearing or leverage ratio,
- Market share,
- Age of the firm in the year it goes for merger,
- Valuation ratio,
- Investment made in physical assets, and
- Financing pattern of the firm: Internal and external financing.

All these variables, either individually or in combination with other variables, may influence a firm's probability of going for a merger. Various alternative indicators[11] are used to measure the above variables. Depending on the significance of the variable, each indicator[12] (except age) is measured for the year that just precedes the merger and also as an average of two years prior to the merger.

1. *Profitability:* Profitability, as an indicator of performance of a firm is considered as one of the important factors determining its likelihood of going for a merger. This variable is hypothesised to have positive influence on the acquisition strategy i.e., the greater the profitability of a firm the greater is the likelihood that it will adopt merger strategy for its expansion. Four indicators of profitability, *viz*., PBDIT/sales, PAT/sales, PAT/NA and PAT/NW are used in the analysis.

a) *PBDIT/sales*: This measure is taken as a proxy for cash flows. It has been argued that the greater the free cash flow left with the firm, the greater is the probability that the firm will go for an acquisition (Jensen, 1988).

---

11. In total 50 indicators are calculated to measure the variables over one year and as average of two and three years prior to merger. However, because of data unavailability, the variable 'valuation ratio' could not be calculated for the all 59 firms

12. For definition of indicators used for various variables, see Annexure I.

b) *PAT/sales:* It measures the profits of firms left after making payments for depreciation, interest and taxes, as a ratio of sales, also called profit margins.

c) *PAT/NA (Return on net assets):* It measures the profits of firms left after paying taxes as a ratio of net assets.

d) *PAT/NW (Return on equity):* It measures the profits of firms after paying taxes as a ratio of net worth.

2. *Leverage ratios (LR):* Empirically, leverage ratio of the acquiring company is one of the most important and significant determinants of merger activity and is found to be negatively affecting the decision to undertake a merger. This is reasoned as greater the leverage ratio greater the interest to be paid and lesser the free cash flow left with the firm for acquisition or investment purposes. Our results in the previous chapters have also suggested that the leverage ratio between AG and AD companies differs significantly, the former being less leveraged. In addition to this, it was also observed that a high gearing ratio of the latter firms was on account of a higher proportion of both long-term and short-term liabilities in the total assets. For the present study, we considered three indicators of gearing ratio that differ in terms of definition of 'debt' in the numerator as well as the denominator, to which it is expressed as a ratio of.

a) *Debt/equity (D/E):* Here 'debt' includes total borrowings consisting of long-term liabilities and short-term borrowings from banks and commercial paper. It is expressed as a ratio of the net worth of a company.

b) *Total debt/total assets (TD/TA):* The term total debt is more inclusive than the term 'debt' defined in the above measure. Apart from 'debt', it also includes 'current liabilities and provisions' and 'deferred tax liability' i.e., it consists of whole of the debt (both short and long-term) taken by a firm. It is expressed as a ratio of total assets of a company.

c) *Long-term liabilities/short-term liabilities (LTL/STL):* This ratio is used to focus on the composition of total debt in terms of long-term liabilities and short-term liabilities. The latter includes short-term borrowings from banks, commercial papers, current liabilities and provisions and deferred tax liability.

3. Market share (MS): Given the highly fragmented nature of the drugs and pharmaceutical industry, market share becomes an important variable in this industry. Out of the total, approximately, 10,000 firms in the industry (including the organised and unorganised sectors) roughly 300[13] (less than 2 per cent) firms are in the organised sector. The sample of 30 acquiring firms considered for this study accounted for 56 per cent of the total sales of the industry in 2004-05. This indicates a very high concentration of sales among very few firms in the industry. In the last six to eight years, the drugs and pharmaceutical industry has witnessed intense competition among firms in undertaking M&As. The inter-firm rivalry to increase market share is discernible not only through competitive bids made by different firms, but also through acquisition of brands and plants and other assets of firms. In a situation where a firm's rivals are making acquisitions, it may also be compelled to make acquisitions to prevent rivals from building dominant market positions.[14] Ranbaxy Laboratories[15] Ltd. made many acquisitions in 1996-97 with the objective to counter the threat from relatively smaller pharma companies merging to create larger entities. It acquired 30 per cent stake in Vorin Laboratories in December 1996, Gufic Laboratories in January 1997, Rima Pharmaceuticals in Ireland, Ohm Laboratories in USA in 1996 and Crossland Research Labs in February 1997. However, finally, it undertook merger with the latter in 1996-97. Similarly, NPIL acquired three companies (namely, Roche Products, Sumitra Pharmaceuticals and Boehringer Mannhiem India) in 1996-97 and later, all were merged with it. In a span of 10 years, Sun Pharmaceutical (incorporating its business in D&P industry in 1993) has grown its sales from Rs 54 crore in 1994 to Rs 1,400 crore in 2005-06, with its net profit increasing from Rs 7 crore to Rs 460 crore over the same period. It has grown big, merely, by adopting external growth strategy i.e., through M&As. Within 1996-97, it acquired three firms and got merged with them. In a span of eight years, it made more than 10 acquisitions and as a result, Sun Pharmaceutical grew its portfolio in the areas of cardiology, psychiatry, neurology and

13. This figure is based on Prowess database (CMIE) and ICRA (1999; 2002) reports.

14. For details, see Hay and Liu (1998).

15. Ranbaxy Laboratories Ltd. was the largest firm in 1996-97, accounting for 7.4 per cent of industry's sales.

gastroenterology. As a result, today it is among the 10 largest firms in the industry.

In light of the above discussion and in view of the fact that D&P industry is one of the most merger-intensive industry witnessing competitive bids and high rivalry among firms in the post-liberalised period, this phenomenon requires special attention from the point of view of its effect on the market shares of firms and level of concentration in the industry.

Empirically, we find that several research studies have focussed on the effects of horizontal merger activity on industrial concentration. It was observed that during the first and second merger wave[16] in the US, M&As raised industry and aggregate concentration levels substantially. Markham (1955) in his study estimated that the first great merger wave in the US created near monopolies in 71 industries and thus the first and second merger movements were labelled as for 'monopoly' and 'oligopoly', respectively.

In actual practice, changes in concentration level are affected by three processes, namely, (1) entry and exit of firms, (2) internal and generic growth of firms, and (3) external growth through merger of existing firms. Hay and Untiet (1981) and White (1982) have emphasised that intense merger activity in the 1970s and 1980s could not bring any rise in the concentration level because it took place in times of prosperity when the entry of firm outstripped the exit.

Concentration Ratio: Herfindahl (HF) Index

The concentration ratio is a summary statistics used to measure the degree to which an industry is dominated by a few large firms. It can be measured by the percentage of total industry sales[17] supplied by the largest 4, 8 and 12 firms in the industry. If the four-firm concentration ratio is

16. Researchers in US earlier classified merger activities into various waves, such as First merger wave (1898-1903), Second merger wave (1926-1929), Third merger wave (1940-1947), Fourth (1980s), and Fifth (1990s) merger wave. The latter two waves are caused by three macro trends as globalisation of industry, deregulation of industrial sector and increasing threat of takeover bids. For detail, see Ramu (1996).

17. The industry's sales are based on all the firms covered in Prowess database (CMIE, 2007).

close to 100 or even greater than 60 per cent, the concentration is high and it is known as an oligopolistic firm. If it is low or less than 60 per cent, then the concentration is low. However, the limitation of this method is that it does not consider the sales of each firm in the industry.

Another method of estimating the degree of concentration in an industry is the Herfindahl index (denoted by HF). The advantage of this method is that it measures the information on all the firms and is not limited to the shares of the few largest firms in the industry.

Assuming there are N firms in an industry, let s_i be the market share of the ith firm (defined as the ratio of sales of ith firm to total sales of the industry), the Herfindahl index is the sum of the squared values of the market shares (measured in percentage) of all the firms in the industry. Thus,

$$HF = s_1^2 + s_2^2 + s_3^2 + s_4^2 + ... + s_n^2$$

The index takes a value between 0 and 10,000 ($0 \leq HF \leq 10{,}000$), where the value 0 indicates no concentration and 10,000 indicates the case of monopoly. If there is only one firm in the industry, then HF = $(100)^2$ = 10,000. If there are two firms in the industry sharing the market equally, then HF = $(50)^2 + (50)^2$ = 5,000. With the 100 equal-sized firms in the industry (perfectly competitive) HF = $(1)^2 + (1)^2 + ... + (1)^2$ = 100. The lower the value of HF, the more dispersed is the industry in the concentration of market share and the higher the HF, the greater is the concentration. Another advantage of this method is that, by taking the squares of share of each firm, the index gives higher weight to larger firms (Salvatore, 1996).

From Table 8.1, it is noted that despite the high level of M&A activity in D&P, the results clearly show a drastic fall in HF index, indicating a fall in concentration level in the D&P industry. During the time span of 10 years i.e., 1988-89 to 1998-99, the HF index has fallen to less than half of its value in 1988-89. During 1999-2000 to 2002-03, there is a rise in concentration level, and HF index value rose from 154 to 240. However, the index again is showing a downward trend since the year 2003-04. To find concentration level in assets, the HF index with respect to total assets was also computed (Table 8.1). The broad trends are similar, fall in the index till 2000 and a rise for three years and again a fall thereafter. In

Table 8.1

Concentration Levels in D&P Industry, 1989-2006

Year	*Herfindahl Index*	*Sum of Squares of Shares in Total Assets*
March 1989	372.6	450.5
March 1990	304.9	349.8
March 1991	286.8	296.6
March 1992	251.6	241.7
March 1993	236.3	225.3
March 1994	194.8	326.4
March 1995	192.2	234.9
March 1996	186.4	222.2
March 1997	193.1	281.8
March 1998	199.2	265.3
March 1999	154.0	217.1
March 2000	176.7	212.9
March 2001	188.1	214.6
March 2002	210.6	227.7
March 2003	240.3	240.0
March 2004	228.1	221.4
March 2005	224.7	243.4
March 2006	203.4	239.0

Note: Calculations based on data obtained from Prowess database (CMIE) until 2007.

Figure 8.1

Trends in Concentration Levels in D&P Industry, 1989-2006

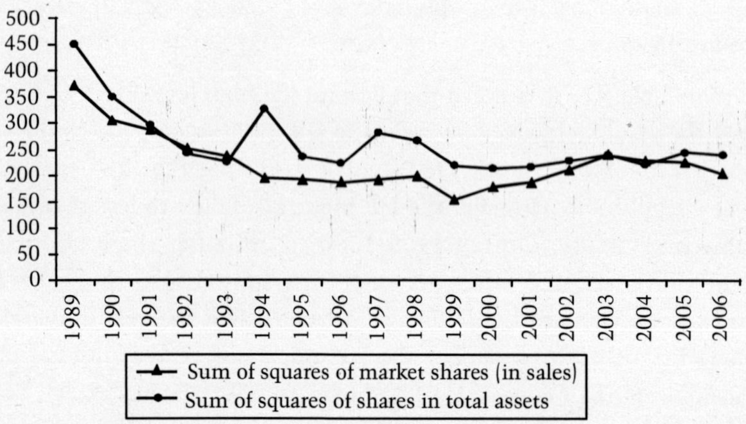

trying to further explore this issue and provide an explanation for the change in the concentration level, we further analysed the entry and exit phenomenon in Table 8.2 as well as the changes in concentration levels of 4, 8, and 12 largest firms in Table 8.3 for the period 1988-89 to 2005-06.

Table 8.2

Year-wise Distributions of Firms Registered and Merged in D&P Industry

Year	*No. of Firms Registered in D&P*	*No. of Firms with Sales Greater than Zero*	*No. of (listed) Firms Merged from D&P*
1989	224	62	N.C.
1990	241	78	N.C.
1991	256	100	N.C.
1992	277	120	N.C.
1993	297	145	1
1994	311	190	2
1995	323	202	0
1996	326	260	1
1997	327	237	4
1998	329	250	3
1999	334	280	0
2000	338	280	1
2001	342	279	7
2002	350	280	7
2003	370	283	6
2004	400	300	2
2005	405	340	2
2006	410	340	3

Note: Based on the Prowess database (CMIE), 2007; N.C.- not considered.

From Table 8.2, we observe that although, the number of new firms getting registered to the industry has not increased much during 1990-2000, there has been roughly a fourfold net rise in the number of firms contributing to industry's sales in this period. One of the plausible reasons of continuous reduction in the concentration ratio is entry of new firms with positive sales outstripping the exit of firms. During 2000-2003, on the other hand, a complete stagnation in the number of firms contributing to the industry's sales along with a rise in merger activity, is a clear indication of the exit of firms dominating in this period. In a span of three years i.e.,

2000-2003, 21 listed firms got merged to other firms within the D&P industry. The share of these merged firms in 1999-2000 was 10 per cent of the total sales of industry in that year.

To further highlight and corroborate our earlier findings, it is observed from Table 8.3 that the concentration levels of the first 4, 8 and 12 firms fell from 1989 to 1999, the most affected being the largest four firms in the industry [also see Figure 8.2 (b)].

Table 8.3

Percentage Shares of 12 Largest Firms in D&P, 1989-2006

Year	*Share of 4 Largest Firms*	*Share of 8 Largest Firms*	*Share of 12 Largest Firms*	*Share of 5 to 8 Largest Firms*	*Share of 9 to 12 Largest Firms*
March 1989	29.0	45.1	56.3	16.1	11.2
March 1990	25.5	40.4	49.8	14.9	9.4
March 1991	25.8	38.4	47.1	12.6	8.7
March 1992	23.7	34.6	42.8	10.9	8.2
March 1993	22.1	34.0	42.1	12.0	8.1
March 1994	18.8	29.2	37.2	10.4	8.0
March 1995	19.9	29.0	36.4	9.2	7.4
March 1996	19.6	28.7	35.8	9.2	7.1
March 1997	18.6	29.4	37.0	10.8	7.7
March 1998	18.8	30.2	37.6	11.4	7.4
March 1999	15.7	25.5	32.7	10.0	7.2
March 2000	17.5	28.0	35.8	10.5	7.8
March 2001	18.6	29.7	37.3	11.1	7.6
March 2002	20.6	32.6	40.8	12.1	8.2
March 2003	22.0	34.7	43.2	12.7	8.5
March 2004	21.8	33.4	40.7	11.6	7.3
March 2005	21.5	32.6	40.6	11.1	7.9
March 2006	20.2	31.8	39.9	11.7	8.1
Average (1989-1999)	21.6	33.1	41.3	11.6	8.2
Average (2000-2006)	20.3	31.8	39.7	11.5	7.9
Average (1989-2006)	21.1	32.6	40.7	11.5	8.1

Note: Calculations based on the Prowess database (CMIE), 2007.

The share of the largest 4 firms fell from 30 per cent to15 per cent and that of the next four largest firms (i.e., 5th to 8th ranked firms) decreased from 16 to 10 per cent and further for the next set of four firms (9th to 12th), it reduced from 11 to 7 per cent during 1989-1999. It is only after the year 1999, when this trend reversed and that the concentration level of the 12 largest firms rose from 32 in 1998-99 to 43 per cent in 2002-03 [Figure 8.2 (a)]. The rise in concentration level for the four largest firms from 15 to 22 per cent is noteworthy. From this, it is concluded that the changes in HF index shown in Table 8.2 are mainly accounted for by changes in the shares of few largest firms in the industry. A detailed analysis further shows that

Figure 8.2(a)

Percentage Shares of 4, 8, and 12 Largest Firms in D&P Industry, 1989-2006

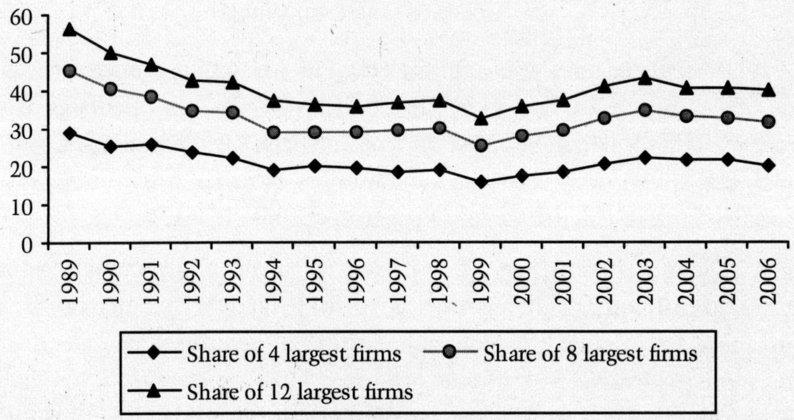

Figure 8.2(b)

Percentage Shares of 4, 5-8, 9-12 Largest Firms in D&P Industry, 1989-2006

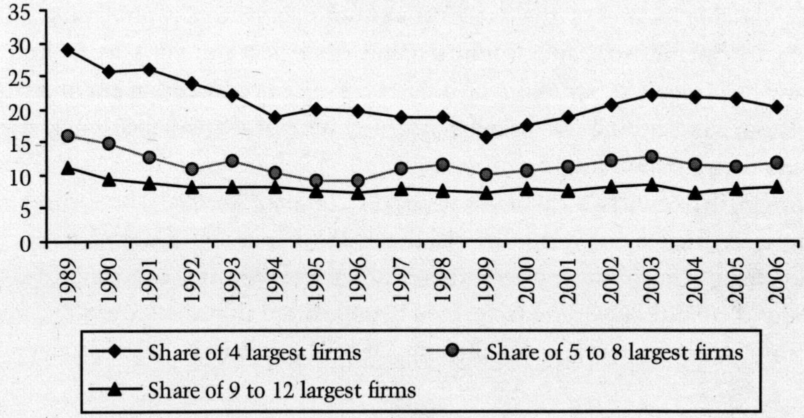

approximately the same 15 to 20 firms that are in competition with each other for the first 12 positions in the industry. The change in the ranking pattern of firms and their respective market shares is a clear reflection of power of competitive forces prevalent in the industry. In the group of largest 20 firms, all but four adopted the strategy of M&As, at least once during the period of study.

For these reasons, it is appropriate to include market share as one of the factors affecting the probability of a firm going for a merger. The variable market share (MS) of a firm is defined as:

$$\text{Market share in year t} = \frac{\text{firm's sale in year t}}{\text{industry's sales in year t}}$$

It is calculated in a year just preceding as well as an average over two years preceding the merger. Here the industry's sales are calculated from Prowess database, which is based on sales of firms in the organised sector. In fact, it is found that, despite a large number of firms in the unorganised sector, its share in the industry is almost negligible (ICRA, 2002).

4. *Age of the firm (Age):* The reason to consider this variable as one of the determinants of acquisition is to find out whether mature firms being more experienced, go for acquisitions or relatively younger firms being more aggressive and vibrant are more likely to acquire. Empirically, this variable has been considered with respect to the study of AD firms, as a proxy for the firm's maturity. It is hypothesised that older firms are more mature and, therefore, are less desirable acquisition targets (Schwartz, 1982). With respect to the study of AG firms, it is believed that the sign of this variable as one of the determinants of acquisition, would vary from industry to industry and would depend upon factors, such as technical know-how required, structure of industry, kind of competition the industry is facing, importance of brand names, extent of dependence on foreign technology, requirement of research and development expenditure, and share in the country's exports and export competitiveness. The Drugs and Pharmaceutical being one of most knowledge-driven and dynamic industry, and presuming that younger firms are more vibrant and adaptive to changed conditions, *prima facie*, it is hypothesised that the lower the age of a firm, the greater the probability that it will adopt the merger strategy to

gain its standing in the industry. Age of the acquiring firm is calculated in the year it goes for a merger and is defined as:

Age of the AG firm at merger =year of merger[18]–year of incorporation of the firm under consideration.

Age of the MNAG firm is calculated with respect to the merger year of the acquiring firm for which it is taken as a control firm.

5. *Valuation ratio (VR):* This variable becomes very important when the merger takes place through exchange of shares of two firms involved. The greater the market valuation of the acquiring firms, the cheaper would be the exchange for it and thus, greater the incentive to undertake merger activity. Theoretically, the valuation ratio of acquired firms is more relevant in explaining the merger activity but here, since our study focusses on the behaviour of AG and similar-sized MNAG firms, we have used valuation ratio of AG and MNAG firms to explain the determinants of acquisition strategy. It is defined as,

$$\text{Valuation ratio} = \frac{\text{market value of the share}}{\text{book value of the share}}$$

The calculation of this variable requires the market value as well as the book value prices of shares.

$$\text{Market value of the share in a year} = \frac{\text{365 days average market capitalisation}}{\text{no. of shares outstanding}}$$

The numerator '365-days average market capitalisation' is measured as an average of monthly averages from 1 April of a year to March end of the next year. Monthly average is further calculated by using the closing price of share in each day. Number of shares outstanding is considered on March of that year.

$$\text{Book value of the share} = \frac{\text{net worth of the firm in a year}}{\text{no. of shares outstanding}}$$

This variable is calculated for one year and average of two years before the merger. The requirement of data on share prices confined our sample to

18. If the year of merger is 1993-94, then age is calculated with respect to 1993.

only quoted firms in the industry. Given the paucity of data on share prices, this variable could be constructed for only 51 firms.

6. *Investment in physical assets (Invt):* Generally speaking, a firm will use its funds either for acquiring other firms (external growth) or alternatively, in the form of investment in physical assets (organic or internal growth). As mentioned earlier, a firm can strategically choose to grow internally or externally. If a firm adopts the external route and also undertakes investment simultaneously, this would mean that the firm is growth-oriented and is very aggressive in its policies. Accordingly, internal and external expansion routes are complementary to each other. On the other hand, external and internal expansion growths are substitutes if the firm adopts one of the routes for the expansion. This would imply that funds used by firms compete between investment and acquisition strategy. The sign of the coefficient of this variable would determine, whether the AG firms are using these two strategies as complementary or substitutes to each other. The construction of this variable is done from 'Sources and Uses of Funds' statement of firms, shown in Table 8.4.

Table 8.4

Sources & Uses of Funds: Manufacturing Companies

	Sources of Funds		*Uses of Funds*
X1	Internal sources	X3	Gross fixed assets
A	Retained profits		Capital WIP
B	Depreciation	X4	Investments
X2	External sources		In group/associate companies
A	Fresh capital (excluding bonus issue)	X5	Current assets
	Share premium reserves	A	Inventories
B	Borrowings	B	Debtors
	Bank borrowings	C	Cash & bank balance
B1	Short-term bank borrowings		Advances/loans to corporate bodies
	Financial institutional borrowings	D	Group/associate companies
	Debentures/bonds	E	Other receivables
	Fixed deposits	X6	Deferred tax assets
	Borrowings from corporate bodies	X7	Total sources/uses of funds
	Group/associate companies		
	Other borrowings		
C	Current liabilities & provisions		
	Sundry creditors		
D	Deferred tax liabilities		

Note: Capital WIP-Capital work-in-progress.

Broadly, the funds used by firms are shown under four heads, *viz.*, 'gross fixed assets', 'investment in group and associate companies', 'current assets (including inventories, debtors, advances and loan to corporate bodies etc.)' and 'deferred tax assets'. To construct the variable investment in physical assets, we have included funds used in creating GFA and inventories (included in current assets). Investment in group companies and deferred tax assets, both being non-physical items, are not included in this variable. This variable is calculated for the year that just precedes the merger and also as an average of two years before the merger.

Investment in physical asset (Invt) = X3 + X5 (A)

7. *Financing pattern:* This variable is considered to find out if the financial structure of AG firms affects their probability to undertake a merger. This variable focusses on sources of funds obtained to finance the growth of a firm. Every firm, growing internally or externally, requires resources to finance its growth of assets. Mainly, there are two sources of funds available to a firm: (a) internal and (b) external. The latter could further be decomposed in terms of funds raised through long-term borrowing (also called long-term debt) and through equity. It is the financing pattern of the firm that determines its structure of capital,[19] also called a firm's capitalisation. Although the financial structure includes both long-term and short-term sources, here, since the focus is on the financing of net assets (total assets minus short-term liabilities), sources of only long-term funds, such as equity shares, preference shares, long-term loans and retained earnings are considered.

The basic difference between debt and equity is one of its cost to the firm. Debt is a liability on which interest is to be paid irrespective of a firm's profitability position i.e., it is a committed payment. The payment to equity holder, also called dividend, is a discretionary payment and depends on the company's policies and profit position. Our corporate tax system considers interest paid on debt as an expense item and, therefore, it is deducted from the profits before calculating tax whereas dividends are paid from the profits left after paying taxes. This provides a significant tax advantage to the firms using debt over the equity finance. The financing pattern followed is an internal decision of the firm and is affected by many

19. See, for example, Khan and Jain (2003).

factors, such as attitude of investors, regularity in earnings, nature of firm's business structure, development of finance system, and tax regime.

Until the early 1990s, it was believed that the growth of the firm and its investment decisions are affected by 'real' variables, such as demand for firm's output, productivity of the firm, and technological progress. While firm's financing pattern, with no role to play in its investment decisions, was considered as passive. The empirical studies carried during the 1990s point to the significance of corporate debt structure and suggest that finance is not a veil but financing decisions of the firm have a bearing on its growth. The first systematic research project linked to this area was launched by Singh and Hamid (1992).[20] The main findings of the study were:

1. The corporations in developed countries are far more dependent on internal sources to finance their growth (70 to 100 per cent) than firms in the developing countries i.e., developing countries' firms finance their growth more through external sources.
2. Whatever dependence on external sources for firms in the advanced countries was found, bank loans dominated over the reliance on equity finance[21] i.e., equity finance is the least preferred means of finance in the developed world.
3. For the top corporations of developing countries, 'equity funds dominate over debt finance' i.e., within external source, the reliance on equity is more than that on debt.

For India, during the period covered 1970-1988, dependence on internal finance, equity funds and debts funds was found to be 36, 11, and 46 per cent, respectively. Between the beginning and the end years of the period covered, it was found that dependence on internal finance decreased and that of equity finance increased in the developing countries. Given the

---

20. They examined the corporate financial structure of large corporations during 1970-1985, covering nine countries of the developing and the developed world. They explained the inter-country differences in capital structure and its relation to corporate growth, profitability, stock market valuation, and size.

21. Due to institutional differences, firms from Japan and West Germany are more leveraged than those of the US and UK. The former have bank-dominated financial system and the latter have stock market-dominated financial system.

'standard pecking order theory of finance'[22] and the imperfections in the stock market in the developing countries (e.g., share price volatility, lack of transparency in transactions, and inadequate legal framework), the results were contrary to the expectations. It was observed that the active role of governments of these countries in bringing stock market developments and the world-over rise in interest rates during the period under study discouraged the corporations to resort to debt financing.[23]

In light of the above discussion and the results of the previous chapter, the financing structure of AG and MNAG is considered to examine—whether the difference in sources of funds used for growth explain the acquisition behaviour of firms or not? Four indicators are constructed to find out differences in the sources of funds used to finance net assets. Net assets actually represent value of long-term capital employed by firm that includes funds both owned by shareholders and borrowed from outside. Here, because of the issues relating to the efficiency in the use of corporate capital, net assets that represents the value of long-term capital, is preferred over other measures of size to calculate indicators of financing.

Net assets (NA) = total fixed assets + current assets net of current liabilities.

The four indicators used to represent the pattern of financing are:

a) ratio of internal finance,
b) ratio of external finance,
c) ratio of financing through debt, and
d) ratio of financing through equity.

Each indicator used here is represented as the ratio or proportion of the net assets, created during the year that just precedes the merger. The construction of the indicators is shown in Table 8.4, the definition of each of which is given as below.

---

22. The 'standard pecking order theory of finance' states that firms have a preference for internal over external finance and within the latter, firms prefer to use debt to equity.

23. Also, see Chapter 2.

Net assets = X7 - X2(B1) - X2(C) - X2(D)

Ratio of internal finance (IF/NA) = X1/net assets

= X1(A) +X1(B)/net assets

Internal financing measures the proportion of net assets that is financed from funds collected through retained profits and depreciation.

Ratio of external finance (EF/NA) = X2 - X2(B1) - X2(C) - X2(D)/net assets

= X2(A) +X2(B) - X2(B1)/net assets

External financing measures the proportion of net assets financed from funds collected through fresh capital (excluding bonus issue), share premium and long-term borrowing.

The construction of above two variables is such that,

IF/NA + EF/NA = 1 (1)

Further, the external financing is decomposed between financing through long-term borrowing (i.e., debt) and financing through issue of fresh capital (i.e., equity).

Ratio of Financing through
Debt (LTB/NA) = X2(B) - X2(B1)/net assets

= X2 - X2(B1) - X2(C) - X2(D)/net assets

Ratio of financing through equity (EQ/NA) = X2(A)/net assets

It is again important to specify that construction of the above two variables is such that,

EF/NA = LTB/NA +EQ/NA (2)

We can also write equation (1) as:

IF/NA + LTB/NA +EQ/NA = 1 [using (2)]

All these financing ratios are calculated over one year and as an average of two years before the merger.

8. Size: The importance of size has been widely researched and it is well established that the bigger the size of a firm, the greater the possibility that it will go for a merger. The importance of size was put forward for the first time by Singh (1971), in his pioneering work on the analysis of the economic characteristics of surviving firms. Contrary to neoclassical theory, Singh's work showed that a relatively large and unprofitable company has a better chance of survival compared with a small and profitable firm. It was observed that the main cause of firms that did not survive was either a merger or a takeover.

However, unlike other research studies, the present exercise does not take into consideration the variable, size of a firm. In fact, by considering a sample consisting of all acquiring firms and their similar-sized non-acquiring firms, the present exercise implicitly rules out 'size' as one of the factors affecting the likelihood of a firm going for a merger.

8.5 Regression Results

The analysis presented here is based on two kinds of samples. In the first sample, regression estimates were made using 6 variables (excluding valuation ratio) on 59 firms comprising 32 AG firms and 27 MNAG firms (hereafter sample A). Owing to unavailability of data on valuation ratio on all 59 firms, the second sample (hereafter sample B) included only 51 firms. Thus, regression estimates on the second sample were obtained using 7 variables.

To begin with, the correlation coefficients among all variables under consideration, calculated over one year prior to merger and as an average of two years prior to merger, were calculated. Keeping in view the problem of multicollinearity among variables, the logit estimates are found by considering various subsets of variables. Further, with each subset of variables, estimation is also obtained by considering alternative indicators of variables that in turn are calculated over one or average of two years before merger. In total, there are six variables under consideration and each variable, except age, is calculated over one year or average of two years before merger.

Correlation estimates: The three size indicators have low correlation to D/E and TD/TA, while with LTL/STL it has low positive and non-significant correlation. All the four profitability ratios i.e., PBDIT/sales, PAT/sales, PAT/NA and PAT/NW have low and positive correlation to size indicators. However, correlation is significant only with respect to profit margins (PAT/sales). The three variables i.e., market share, investment in physical assets, and cash flows, are positively and significantly related to all the three indicators of size. It implies that the bigger the firm, the greater is its market share, greater are its cash flows and greater the investment in physical assets. The four ratios showing financing pattern of a firm have very low and not significant correlation to size indicators.

Among the three indicators of leverage ratios (LRs) correlation is positive and significant. It is high between D/E and TD/TA and low with respect to LTL/STL. With few exceptions, LRs have low and negative correlation with profitability ratios based on PAT, implying more geared the firms are, lesser are the profits. The ratio PBDIT/sales has high positive and significant correlation with LTL/STL. This is because PBDIT is calculated before making interest payments arising from total borrowings (short and long-term borrowing) and tax payments. High negative and significant correlation between PAT/sales and TD/TA implies that the firms with greater proportion of total debt in their total assets will be left with lesser profit margins. LR ratios have low negative correlation with respect to market share, investment in physical assets and market share. Financing patterns do not seem to be related to leverage ratios.

All indicators of profitability ratios have high positive and significant correlations between themselves. With respect to market shares, cash flows and investment in physical assets, the profitability ratios have low and positive correlation and the significance level varies from ratio to ratio. Pattern of financing is not correlated to profitability ratio. The age of the firm does not seem to be correlated to any of the variables under consideration. Lastly, internal financing is negatively correlated to both debt financing as well as equity financing, indicating that the greater the dependence on internal financing, the lesser would be obtained from external sources. This is clear from the construction of the variables.

The results regarding correlation largely remain the same in terms of magnitude, sign and significance across the measurement i.e., whether they are calculated from the values of one year preceding the merger or from the averages of two years prior to merger.

Regression Estimates based on Sample A

Regression results, obtained from experimenting with various alternative specifications of explanatory variables, are reported in Tables 8.5 to 8.7.

The regression estimates obtained by using the subset of variables calculated for one year before the merger is shown in Table 8.6 and those obtained from average of two years before merger are in Table 8.5.

In all the regression estimates presented in Tables 8.5 to 8.7, the likelihood ratio is significant at the 1 or 5 per cent level for all specifications,[24] implying that the model used in the analysis provides a statistically significant explanation of a firm's probability of going for an acquisition. Broadly speaking, the results obtained from different specifications, whether performed on records of one year before the merger or average of two years prior to merger, are the same with respect to the signs of most of the coefficients. However, the coefficients vary in magnitude.

All indicators of leverage ratios appear with negative coefficient, however, depending on the subset of variables considered, the significance level varies among them. The highly geared firms are less likely to undertake merger as a preferred strategy to growth. The coefficients of D/E and TD/TA are statistically significant, while that of LTL/TA is not significant. This result is also consistent with Jensen's free cash flow argument since the greater the debt burden, the greater would be the interest burden and accordingly, lesser free cash will be left with the firms to be used for other purposes. The acquisition of Balsara by Dabur[25] for Rs 143 crore, all cash deal, funded largely out of internal accrual, brings out the fact that it is Dabur's relatively debt free balance sheet and large annual cash flows that made it well positioned to use M&As strategy[26] for growth (Vaish, 2005).

---

24. The LR test performs better when estimates are obtained from average of two years prior to merger than from records of one year prior to the merger.

25. Dabur is India's fourth largest FMCG (fast moving consumable goods) company, after Hindustan Lever, ITC and Nestle.

26. Free cash flow is not directly observable. There are several indicators of free cash flow such as, stable cash flow, limited profitable opportunities, low financial leverage, and higher level of diversification (Jensen, 1986).

Table 8.5

Logit Estimates from Sample A
(based on averages of two years prior to merger)

	Specifi:1	Specifi: 2	Specifi: 3	Specifi: 4	Specifi: 5	Specifi: 6	Specifi: 7	Specifi: 8
Explanatory Variable	Estimated Coefficient	Estimated Coefficient	Estimated Coefficient	Estimated Coefficient	Estimated Coefficient	Estimated Coefficient	Estimated Coefficient	Estimated Coefficient
Leverage ratio-D/E	-1.2*** (-2.58)	-.95** (-2.28)			-.57 (-1.51)	-.31 (-.94)	-.6** (-1.99)	
TD/TA			-3.12* (-1.73)	-.12 (-.22)				-1.08 (-1.41)
LTL/STL								
Profitability ratio-PAT/sales								
PBDIT/sales							12.4** (2.33)	
PAT/NA				10.8*** (2.49)	16.7*** (2.88)	13.7*** (2.71)		
PAT/NW	9.44*** (2.79)	9.53*** (2.79)	7.12*** (2.60)					7.6** (2.44)
Market share	146** (2.17)	138.6** (2.26)	122.6** (2.25)	114.1** (2.18)	153.6** (2.25)	137.3** (2.32)	171*** (2.80)	113.2* (1.87)
Age	-.037* (-1.74)	-.04** (-2.12)	-.04** (-2.05)	-.04** (-2.11)	-.04* (-1.82)	-.04** (-2.18)	-.04* (-1.89)	-.03 (-1.51)

contd...

...contd...

Explanatory Variable	Specifi:1 Estimated Coefficient	Specifi: 2 Estimated Coefficient	Specifi: 3 Estimated Coefficient	Specifi: 4 Estimated Coefficient	Specifi: 5 Estimated Coefficient	Specifi: 6 Estimated Coefficient	Specifi: 7 Estimated Coefficient	Specifi: 8 Estimated Coefficient
Investment in physical assets	-.05** (-2.20)	-.04** (-2.19)	-.03** (-2.12)	-.03** (-2.00)	-.05** (-2.32)	-.04** (-2.23)	-.06*** (-2.65)	-.03* (-1.67)
I. Financing IF/NA				.01 (.29)				
E. Financing (debt) LTB/NA		-.03 (-.47)	-.03 (-.53)			-.02 (-.39)	-.05 (-.87)	
E. Financing (equity) EQ/NA	3.25*** (1.78)				3.86** (2.13)			3.47* (1.69)
Constant	-.01 (-.01)	.15 (.19)	1.22 (.97)	-.32 (-.40)	-.94 (-.92)	-.33 (-.37)	-.78 (-.73)	-.57 (-.58)
LR chi² (6)	31.58***	25.65***	21.26***	19.8***	32.9***	24.8***	20***	25.36***
Pseudo R^2	.40	.33	.27	.24	.41	.31	.25	.32
Log likelihood	-23.5	-26.5	-29.3	-30.8	-23.5	-27.7	-30	-27.2
No. of observations	57	57	58	59	58	58	58	58

Notes: Figures in brackets are z-values; * significant at 10 per cent level; ** significant at 5 per cent level; *** significant at 1 per cent level.

Table 8.6

Logit Estimates from Sample A

(based on records of one year prior to merger)

Explanatory Variable	*Specifi: 1* *Estimated Coefficient*	*Specifi: 2* *Estimated Coefficient*	*Specifi: 3* *Estimated Coefficient*	*Specifi: 4* *Estimated Coefficient*	*Specifi: 5* *Estimated Coefficient*	*Specifi: 6* *Estimated Coefficient*
Leverage ratio -D/E	-.9** (-2.37)	-.94** (-2.28)	-.43 (-1.35)	-.99** (-2.42)		
TD/TA					-.57 (-1.28)	-.5 (-1.13)
LTL/STL						
Profitability ratio- PAT/sales						
PBDIT/Sales						
PAT/NA			8.96** (2.06)		8.65** (2.11)	7.4* (1.77)
PAT/NW	6.56** (2.34)	5.5* (1.91)		6.7** (2.34)		
Market share	60.1 (1.52)	74.34 (1.57)	64.18* (1.64)	65.3 (1.58)	54.2 (1.42)	65.3 (1.47)
Age	-.03* (-1.92)	-.04** (-2.11)	-.03* (-1.92)	-.03* (-1.75)	-.03* (-1.91)	-.04** (-2.05)

contd...

...contd...

	Specifi: 1	*Specifi: 2*	*Specifi: 3*	*Specifi: 4*	*Specifi: 5*	*Specifi: 6*
Explanatory Variable	*Estimated Coefficient*	*Estimated Coefficient*	*Estimated Coefficient*	*Estimated Coefficient*	*Estimated Coefficient*	*Estimated Coefficient*
Investment in physical assets	-.013 (-1.50)	-.01 (-1.39)	-.01 (-1.50)	-.01 (-1.53)	-.01 (-.88)	-.01 (-.81)
I. Financing IF/NA.	-.036 (-.16)		-.06 (-.29)		-.12 (-.49)	
E. Financing (debt) LTB/NA		-1.2** (-1.93)				-1.05* (-1.78)
E. Financing (equity) EQ/NA				1.02 (1.12)		
Constant	.62 (.82)	1.08 (1.32)	.3 (.37)	.5 (.65)	.24 (.30)	.41 (.53)
LR chi^2 (6)	14.47**	19.03***	12.98**	16.9***	14.4**	18.01***
Pseudo R^2	.18	.24	.16	.21	.18	.22
Log likelihood	-32.7	-30.4	-33.4	-31.4	-33.5	-31.7
No. of observations	58	58	58	58	59	59

Notes: Figures in brackets are z-values; * significant at 10 per cent level; ** significant at 5 per cent level; *** significant at 1 per cent level.

Profitability ratios consistently appear with positive coefficient signifying, the greater the profitability of a firm, the greater are the chances of the firm adopting merger strategy for its expansion. This is suggestive of the fact that odds are in favour of efficient firms to undertake mergers. Inefficient firms are less likely to go for mergers. The ratio PBDIT/sales, taken as a proxy of cash flows of the firms, also positively affects the probability of a firm going for an acquisition.[27] This implies profits before interest, depreciation and tax payments also acts as an important determinant of acquisition behaviour of firms.

The variable market share appears with a positive sign and is significant at the 5 per cent level (in most of the regressions). It suggests that the greater the market share, the greater is the chance that a firm will acquire other firms. In fact, it has been witnessed that a firm with higher share in the industry's sales is in greater competition to reach at even higher level. Hence, there is a greater probability that the firm will adopt merger strategy to increase its share. This result is consistent with the kind of behavioural responses witnessed in D&P industry. This corroborates our earlier finding that more than 80 per cent of the firms, which are in competition to increase their shares, are also using M&A strategy to increase their size.

The negative sign of the variable age in all the regression estimates suggests that the older the firm, the lesser the likelihood of it going for a merger. As hypothesised, D&P being one of the most knowledge-driven and rapidly growing industries, younger firms being more vibrant and adaptive to changed conditions, *prima facie*, have higher chances of growing through external means.

Further, investments in physical assets also appear with negative sign. Though, it has a low coefficient, it is highly significant. The greater the funds allocated in the form of new investment goods, the lesser is the possibility of a firm using mergers as an expansionary plan. This suggests that internal expansion in the form of investment in physical assets and external expansion through M&As are used as substitutes to each other by

---

27. The coefficient is statistically non-significant in few of the regression estimates, however sign is positive (see specification 2 in Table 8.7)

firms. It could be that due to limited funds, firms are not adopting internal and external expansion plans complementary to each other.

Concerning the financing pattern of firms, on account of their interconnections, the four ratios stated earlier, were considered separately in different regression estimates. The coefficient of variable IF/NA is not significant. Moreover, the direction of its effect is also ambiguous, as the sign of its coefficient changes across different specifications (see Tables 8.5 to 8.7). This illustrates that the internal sources of funds is not a significant factor in explaining the firm's decision to go for a merger. When regression estimates include the variable obtained from decomposing the external financing between long-term debt (LTB/NA) and equity (EQ/NA), it is clearly pointed out that acquiring firms show greater dependence on the issue of fresh capital than reliance on long-term borrowing to finance their net assets. The coefficient of the LTB/NA is found to be negative and significant (see specifications 2 and 6 of Table 8.6), while the EQ/NA appears with a positive sign (see specifications 1, 5, and 8 of Table 8.5). The greater the reliance on equity as an external source of finance, the greater is the likelihood that the firms will adopt the M&A strategy. This is in line with earlier findings with regard to leverage ratios, which appear with a negative coefficient. This implies that a firm with greater dependence on long-term borrowings to finance their net assets has lower probability of it going for a merger. This reinforces our earlier conclusion that dependence on long-term borrowing for financing its net assets seems to be an important binding constraint for a firm going for a merger.

Regression Estimates based on Sample B including Valuation Ratio

Table 8.7 gives the regression estimates of 51 firms, comprising 27 AQ firms and 24 MNAQ firms, which are performed using seven explanatory variables that include valuation ratios. Although valuation ratio always appears with a positive sign, it is not significant in any of the specifications. The sign of the coefficient is in line with our hypothesis that the greater the valuation ratio, the greater is the likelihood that the firm will be guided by merger strategy. It must be mentioned here that the valuation ratios of AD firm matter more in such decisions. If an AD firm is valued at a lower price, it is cheaper to buy such a firm—especially, when bought through share exchange.

Table 8.7

Logit Estimates from Sample B
(based on average of two years prior to merger)

	Specifi: 1	*Specifi: 2*	*Specifi: 3*	*Specifi: 4*	*Specifi: 5*
Explanatory Variable	*Estimated Coefficient*	*Estimated Coefficient*	*Estimated Coefficient*	*Estimated Coefficient*	*Estimated Coefficient*
Leverage ratio - D/E					
TD/TA				-1.26* (-1.80)	-.52 (-.83)
LTL/STL	-4.1** (-2.01)	-3.3* (-1.69)	-4.1** (-2.01)		
Profitability ratio- PAT/sales					
PBDIT/sales		8.65 (1.54)		15.9** (2.26)	
PAT/NA					
PAT/NW	6.59** (2.08)		6.6** (2.08)		5.36* (1.83)
Market share	141.8** (2.04)	155.3** (2.33)	141.8** (2.04)	165.8** (2.26)	123.8* (1.77)
Age	-.03 (-1.51)	-.03 (-1.40)	-.03 (-1.51)	-.03 (-1.40)	-.03 (-1.56)
Investment in physical assets	-.05** (-2.15)	-.05*** (-2.48)	-.05** (-2.15)	-.05** (-2.32)	-.03* (-1.77)
I. Financing IF/NA.	.03 (.70)	.06 (1.09)	.03 (.70)	.05 (.94)	
E. Financing (debt)- LTB/NA					-.03 (-.57)
E. Financing (equity)- EQ/NA					
Valuation ratio (VR)	.20 (.91)	.28 (1.44)	.2 (.91)	.19 (1.32)	.16 (.80)
Constant	1.08 (.84)	.07 (.04)	1.08 (.84)	-1.96 (-1.63)	-.53 (-.61)
LR chi^2 (7)	25.73***	22.02***	25.7***	22.9***	22.07***
Pseudo R^2	.37	.31	.37	.33	.31
Log likelihood ratio	-22.4	-24.3	-22.4	-23.7	-24.2
No. of observations	51	51	51	51	51

Notes: Figures in brackets are z-values; *significant at 10 per cent level; **significant at 5 per cent level; ***significant at 1 per cent level.

Regarding other variables, the signs obtained are consistently the same as in earlier regression estimates. Although all leverage ratios have negative signs, a clear difference in these regressions is that LTL/STL is significant at the 5 per cent level. This is to signify that firms with greater amount of LTL to STL have lower probability of going through merger. Profitability ratios, investment in physical assets and market share all are significant in affecting the probability of a firm going for merger. Further, age and none of the financing ratios are found to be significant in affecting the likelihood of a firm going for merger.

8.6 Conclusion

Using Logit model, this chapter attempts to shed light on variables that determine the probability of a firm going for mergers. The sample considered here consists of a set of AG firms and similarly-sized non-AG firms. Here, the focus is on the firm-specific variables that determine the firm's behaviour to acquire other firms as a part of its growth strategy.

Although the results from the regressions of different subsets of explanatory variables are fairly consistent with respect to the sign of variables, they vary in terms of magnitude and significance of coefficients. The probability of a merger is found to be positively related to profitability. Irrespective of the indicator of profit ratio used, it has an important role in determining the merger probability. The results support the hypothesis regarding cash flow, as it bears the same relationship to merger probability as does the profitability ratio, because both are indicators of the performance of the firm and a firm with greater cash flow is more likely to be the one with greater profit rates as well. The negative coefficient of leverage ratio indicates that the probability of an acquisition is likely to fall for highly geared firms. This result strengthens the finding related to external financing through debt or equity. The coefficient of financing of net assets through debt being significant with negative sign, points to the fact that greater the financing of net assets through debt, lesser the likelihood that the firm would adopt merger strategy for its expansion. Acquiring firms are more dependent on equity issues than on long-term borrowings for financing their net assets.

The variable investment in physical assets is statistically significant and consistently appeared with negative sign. The negative sign suggests that the firms are using internal and external expansionary policies supplementary to each other. Market share is always found to be significant and positive predictor of the probability of an acquisition.

The results concerning age of the firm are new in this work. The coefficient of age of the firm just before the merger appears with a negative sign implying that age is negatively related to the acquisition probability. The young firms, which are expected to be more aggressive, innovative and vibrant, have greater chances of acquiring other firms in a technology-driven drugs and pharmaceutical industry. Depending upon the subset of variables taken, the logit regression estimates successfully predicts the probability of mergers in 65 per cent to 83 per cent of cases.

9 Determinants of Acquisition

Why is a Firm Acquired?

The chapter analyses the determinants of the probability of a firm being acquired. It has already been observed that D&P is one of the most merger-intensive industries. Mergers between firms were considered effective means to restructure, reorganise and consolidate the resources in D&P in the post-reform period. There has been a steep rise in the activity, particularly since the mid-1990s. A large number of firms have disappeared on account of their merger with other firms within the D&P industry. Comparing the acquired (AD) and acquiring (AG) firms in chapter 6, we observed that AG firms bought relatively smaller-sized, less profitable and highly leveraged firms. AG firms are superior in terms of size, profitability and leverage. However, with respect to asset turnover ratio, AD firms performed better than their corresponding AG firms. So far as the distinguishing features between AD and size-matched non-acquired (NAD) firms are concerned, it is identified that both the sets of firms are generally the same with respect to almost all the variables. AD firms performed better only in relation to growth.

This chapter examines the issue of the probability of a firm being acquired. In particular, we are concerned with the question: Why amongst a similarly-sized set of firms, some are acquired and others are not? Or Despite being similar in size, what determines the likelihood of a firm to be a merger target?

To put it simply, the analysis here is concerned with the extent and direction of the independent influence of different variables in the market for corporate control; more specifically, with the probability of firm becoming a merger target. The chapter is organised as follows. Section 9.1 explains the selection of sample considered for the study. Section 9.2 discusses the variables and methodology used. Regression estimates are discussed in Section 9.3. Section 9.4 concludes with a summary of the main findings.

9.1 Selection of the Sample

The point of departure in our study is that it seeks factors that determine the probability of a firm becoming an acquisition target, on the basis of a sample consisting of acquired and size-matched non-acquired firms. Each acquired firm in the sample is paired with its one or more matched non-acquired firms. Matching is done nearest to the size of the AD firms, measured in terms of total assets in the year just before the merger.

Why the control sample includes similarly-sized firms? Empirically, it is well established that large firms are unlikely to be taken over. They are difficult to be acquired because it is expensive and difficult to absorb them. From the comparative study of pre-merger characteristics of AG and AD firms in Chapter 6, we have already observed that AG firms are several times larger than the AD firms. Taking note of this, instead of taking a 'control sample', chosen randomly from the surviving firms[1] in the industry, we have created a specific size-matched control group from a set of firms that are neither acquiring nor acquired. In addition to netting out the effect of size, the matched sample design minimises the possible bias due to aggregation. Moreover, empirical evidence also shows that on the basis of their characteristics, it is easy to distinguish acquired from non-acquired firms in a control sample. However, the null hypothesis that both the sets of firms are drawn from the same population is difficult to be rejected (Singh, 1971).

So our 'control sample' is different from the other empirical studies in two respects.

1. Unlike other studies, the control group is not randomly chosen.[2] Rather, each firm is matched to the given acquired firm. Since AD firms are relatively small firms, it was possible to find, corresponding to each acquired firm considered in the sample, two to three size-matched non-acquired firms from the D&P industry itself.

---

1. Surviving firms include AG, NAG and NAD firms. In such cases, the hypothesised sign of the variable size becomes evident.
2. Schwartz (1982) examined a randomly chosen sample.

2. The other important feature of the control group is that it is chosen from a set of firms that included neither the acquiring nor the acquired firms in the industry.

The selection of control sample was convenient owing to two reasons. Firstly, from the size distribution of firms in the D&P industry in Chapter 5 (see Table 5.8), it was found that more than 80 per cent of the firms are small-sized (less than Rs 200 crore worth of total assets). Secondly, from Chapter 6 [Table 6.2(a) and (c)] we observed that approximately 90 per cent of the AD firms under consideration also lie in this same group. For few AD firms it was possible to find more than two equally-sized companies in the industry, our sample therefore, contains two to three MNAD firms for each AD firm. For this reason, the sample has a greater proportion of MNAD firms than AD firms.[3] No firm is chosen more than once in this sample. Now, it is worthwhile to examine from a large number of small-sized firms, as to why does a particular firm show a greater probability of being chosen as a merger target.

9.2 Variables and Methodology

Variables

In order to find factors that led to the acquisition of a particular firm, when other similarly-sized firms were also present in the industry, we consider 10 variables, each being a certain financial ratio. The choice of variables has been guided by variables that have figured in the debate on M&As.

1. *Profitability:* Empirically, the issue of performance of AD firms has been one of the most essential determinants of its merger likelihood. However, its measurement has varied across research studies.[4] In our study

---

3. If the population from which sample choice is made has a greater proportion of NAD than AD firms, then the sample reflecting the same ratio is a better representative than the one with equal number of AD and NAD firms. For example, Palepu (1986) examined a sample consisting of 156 targets and 256 non-targets during the period 1971-1979 in predicting takeover targets.

4. Martin and McConnell (1991); Palepu (1986); Morck *et al*. (1988) used stock market performance; while, Singh (1971); Kuehn (1975); Powell and Thomas (1994) used different profitability ratios. The study of Powell (1997) used return on capital employed as a measure of performance of AD firms.

four profitability ratios are considered, as proxies for the measure of managerial performance. In several studies, it has been witnessed that inefficient firms have a greater probability of being acquired. It is important to bear in mind that this finding is obtained, when AD firms are put in comparison with all other (surviving) firms present in the industry. Further, the effect of performance also varies by the nature of merger i.e., whether it is hostile or friendly. For the present analysis, we consider four indicators of profitability, *viz.*, PBDIT/sales, PBIT/sales, PAT/sales, PBIT/total assets. The latter most measure has a special significance in the present analysis. The numerator considers profits before making interest and tax payments. If the AD and MNAD firms differ significantly in their long-term debt, this ratio would also differ accordingly between two sets of firms because of the special design of our sample that considers size-matched firms, with size measured in total assets.

2. *Current ratio:* Liquidity is preferred to meet short-run obligations, usually, of one year. Current ratio is the most commonly used measure of liquidity. It is defined as ratio of current assets to current liabilities.

$$\text{Current ratio} = \frac{\text{current assets}}{\text{current liabilitie s}}$$

The numerator includes cash, debtors, marketable security, inventories, loans and advances and prepaid expenses. The denominator includes the liabilities that are expected to be matured in one year's time, such as current liability and provisions and loans (secured and unsecured to be paid in a year). Theoretically, the greater the current liquidities, the shorter is the solvency of a company. In actual practice it has been observed that liquidity of a firm attracts the acquiring firm. Empirically also, it has been observed that the liquidity position of a firm could influence the probability of it being taken over or considered for merger. Therefore, to find out its influence, the current ratio as an indicator of liquidity of a firm has been included as one of the determinants.

3. *Leverage ratio:* Regarding leverage ratio, it is hypothesised that other things being equal, the more leveraged a firm is, the greater is the probability of its acquisition. This is so because it is easy to gain control over a firm with a greater amount of long-term debt compared with the firm that is relatively less geared. The acquiring firm needs to buy out only

some percentage of acquired firm's equity and not the debt. For two firms with same amount of net assets, the one with higher leverage is cheaper to target, as there is no need to buy long-term borrowings. Our analysis considers four indicators[5] of leverage.

a) Total debt/total assets (TD/TA),

b) Long-term liabilities/short-term liabilities (LTL/STL),

c) Long-term liabilities/total assets (LTL/TA), and

d) Short-term liabilities/total assets (STL/TA).

4. Age: The age of the AD firm in our sample is calculated with respect to the observation year. The observation year is defined as the merger year i.e., the year in which it got merged with the other firm and accordingly, for MNAD firm, the year in which it is observed as non-acquired. Schwartz (1982) finds that mature firms are less attractive acquisition targets for growth maximising acquirers.

5. Investment/asset turnover ratio: This is usually not considered as one of the determinants of merger's probability. The justification for its inclusion comes from our analysis performed earlier in Chapter 6. Comparing AG and AD firms, it was observed that AD firms have significantly higher investment or asset turnover ratio (also called productivity of assets). It is defined as,

$$\text{Assets turnover ratio} = \frac{\text{sales}}{\text{net assets}}$$

6. R&D expenditure: The expenditure on R&D has a key role to play in the D&P industry. From the study of the D&P industry in Chapter 5, it was noted that a large percentage of small-sized firms undertake R&D expenditure. Hence, to the acquiring firm, the firm being acquired could be of interest on account of the latter's higher R&D expenditure. This expenditure is expressed as a ratio of sales revenue.

Hall (1988) investigating the attractiveness of R&D intensive firms as takeover targets finds R&D/assets is positively related to the probability of being AD, in other words, successful innovators are preferred as takeover targets. His results suggest that AD firms engaged in R&D expenditure are

5. All indicators are defined in Annexure 1.

valued more highly at the margin by the AG firms that took them over. Controlling for size,[6] his study observed that the firms with large R&D expenditure had high valuation ratio[7] and were more likely to exit from the sample by merging with others. Working on a set of AG and AD firms, he also found that R&D intensity was lower in AG than in AD firms i.e., firms sold on an average had higher R&D intensity than those that bought them.

Three stock market indicators, namely, valuation ratio, price-earning ratio, and earning per share are also considered for the analysis.

7. *Valuation ratio (VR):* It is one of the most commonly used variables to study the probability of getting acquired for a firm. The justification of including valuation ratio is the common observation that firms with lower valuation ratio are more likely to be acquired. Valuation ratio (VR) is taken as an indicator of the future prospects of a firm assessed by the market. Greater the valuation ratio better are the future prospects and thus, lesser is the probability that the firm will be acquired. The price that the raider firm has to pay depends on the market price of the share of the acquired firm in relation to the acquiring firm's share price. It is particularly important if the deal is to be made in terms of shares rather than in cash. The price that the acquirer needs to pay is decided on the basis of the quoted stock price of the AD and AG firms in the market. It is hypothesised that the greater the market price of the share of an AD firm, the higher is the price the acquirer is required to pay for the deal. Therefore, firms with lower profitability (a measure of past performance) and hence lower valuation ratio (market assessment of future prospects of the firm) have greater chances of getting acquired i.e., poor performers with poorer future prospects are more likely to be taken over. Firms with the same profitability could also have different valuation ratios,[8] since the latter depends upon the market assessment of future prospects of a company. The VR is defined[9] as

6. Hall (1988) found negative correlation between size and R&D intensity.
7. High valuation is on account of intangible assets, such as a high R&D programme.
8. With respect to the sample examined in our study, the correlation estimates between valuation ratio and all the indicators of profitability were found to be significantly weak.
9. Its calculation is discussed in detail in Chapter 8.

$$\text{Valuation ratio} = \frac{\text{market value of the share}}{\text{book value of the share}}$$

Empirically, using different methodologies, several research studies (Singh, 1971; Kuehn, 1975; Schwartz, 1982; Powell, 1997) focussed on the variables that help distinguishing between acquired and non-acquired firms. Based on Marris (1964) growth maximising model,[10] Singh (1971) tested whether the valuation ratio, defined as the ratio of market value of a firm's equity to the book value of its net assets, acts as an important discriminator between AD and NAD. Marris argued that, given the same size of two firms, the one with higher VR is less likely to be acquired because the selection process considers both the past profitability (measured by profitability ratio) and the future prospects (measured by VR) of the firm. Singh[11] (1971) found that averages of several variables were statistically different between the two groups of firms. However, it was difficult to reject the hypothesis that both sets of firms belong to the same population. He also suggested the invalidity of the Marris growth model by showing that the valuation ratio alone cannot act as a good discriminator.

Based on a weaker form of the Marris model, Kuehn (1975) tested for factors that affect the firm's likelihood of being acquired. He validated the weaker form of the Marris model. Consistent with Kuehn's and Singh's results, Schwartz (1982) also supported that there is no threshold value of the valuation ratio, above which a firm is certain to remain non-acquired. His study showed that the valuation ratio strongly discriminates between AD and NAD firms and supported the weaker form of the Marris model i.e., valuation ratio is negatively and statistically significantly related.

---

10. Marris (1964) growth maximising model can be expressed in a strong and a weak form of security model. The former states that there is a level of valuation ratio above which the firm's security from acquisition is certain, the latter relates the probability of being acquired inversely to the valuation ratio of the firm, Schwartz (1982).

11. Using discriminant analysis with variables, such as profitability, leverage, size and growth, Singh (1971) found that no variable acted as a good discriminator between AD and NAD firms in the UK, during 1955-1960.

8. Earnings per share (EPS): Analogous to profitability of a firm (PAT/sales), the profitability of a common shareholder's[12] investment is measured in a number of ways. EPS is an important method to measure the latter. It is defined as the ratio of PAT to total number of common ordinary shares outstanding in the market.

$$EPS = \frac{PAT}{\text{total number of ordinary shares outstanding}}$$

9. Price-earning ratio (P/E): It is calculated as the market price of share divided by earning per share.

$$P/E = \frac{\text{market price of shares}}{EPS}$$

10. Size: A large number of studies[13] have consistently found size to be a significant variable affecting the probability of a takeover. It is well established that size decreases the probability of being acquired. Large firms are not only difficult to buy, but are also difficult to absorb in the organisational framework of AG firms. However, size can be considered as an important determinant, if the control sample is chosen randomly from a set of surviving firms. The sample examined in our study comprise acquired and their size-matched non-acquired firms. Hence, size is excluded as one of the determinants of acquisition.

All the above mentioned variables, individually or in conjunction with other variables, can affect the chances of acquisition of a firm. The other variables, such as ratio of tangible fixed assets in total assets (Ambrose and Megginson, 1992), growth-resource imbalance in the firm (Palepu, 1986),

---

12. Share capital is of two types, *viz.*, equity capital (held by ordinary or common shareholder) and preference capital (held by preferred shareholders, usually, promoters and their close friends). The former carries no fixed rate of dividend and in the latter dividend rate payable is fixed. Further, the ordinary shareholders are legal owners of the company and bear the risk of ownership. They receive dividends at the discretion of the board of directors. The preference shareholders have the preference over equity holders, in case of liquidation of the company. See, for example, Chandra (2004) and Pandey (2003).
13. See, for example, Palepu (1986); Levine and Aaronovitch (1981); Powell and Thomas (1994); Singh (1971); Schwartz (1982).

governance structure of AD firms (Weir, 1997),[14] Tobin's q or other industry-specific variables have not been considered; either on account of data non-availability or due to their seemingly unimportant role in explaining the M&A phenomenon in the Indian D&P industry.

Both short-term and long-term records of firms have been used to analyse the behaviour of AD firms. For the former, variables are obtained from the records of one year before the merger and averages of two years before the merger, while averages of three and five years before the merger are computed for long-term comparisons. On account of non-availability of stock market indicators on all the firms included in the sample, the regression estimates had to be made from two samples of different sizes.

Before turning to the regression analysis, it is necessary to point out that several research studies have demonstrated that the features of takeover firms and the effects of takeover vary across the underlying objectives of M&As.[15] The aim behind a takeover could be to discipline the inefficient management of AD firms (Jensen, 1988 and Morck *et al.*, 1988) or to exploit synergistic gains, such as economies of scale and growth (Bradley *et al.*, 1988). The former are generally hostile in nature and accordingly, are referred to as hostile takeovers, while the latter are non-hostile and called synergistic or friendly[16] takeovers (Weir, 1997). M&As also take place with managerial motive i.e., to pursue self-interest of managers, such as their salaries, fame, prestige, resources under their control that in turn are positively related to the size of the company. There is strong evidence that characteristics of hostile and friendly takeovers differ and industry-specific characteristics also play a role in takeover likelihood.

14. In analysing the relationship between the probability of being acquired and governance structures, Weir (1997) found that the proportion of non-executive directors on the board and whether the roles of chief executive officer and chairman are combined, are the two key governance characteristics which differentiated between AD and NAD firms.

15. Details are covered in Chapter 3.

16. Morck *et al.* (1988) observed that it is the motive of the acquirer that determines the mood (hostile or friendly) of acquisition.

Most of the findings[17] show that hostile takeovers are associated with poor performance of AD firms—especially in terms of stock market performance measured through valuation ratio. Powell (1997) observed that the likelihood of hostile takeover is positively associated with size and valuation ratio and negatively with the firm's liquidity and profitability. The chances of going in for friendly takeovers on the other hand are higher, the smaller the firm's size and the greater the firm's leverage. He also suggests that the industry to which target firm belongs can also play an important role in takeover likelihood. Morck *et al.* (1988) showed that friendly targets are better performing and faster growing and have higher market value of their assets. Franks and Mayer (1996), however, observed that hostile bids are not associated with poor performing firms, whether measured through stock market or profitability ratios. Holland and Hodgkinson (1994), on the other hand, found leverage to be the only factor that explains the likelihood of takeover.

Methodology

Using a Logit model, several regressions were run on two samples of different sizes. With the larger sample (hereafter sample A) regression results are obtained using seven variables (excluding stock market indicators) and the smaller sample (hereafter sample B) is run with all 10 variables. The sample is partitioned between acquired and non-acquired firms. Here, the dependent variable:

Y_i = 1, if the firm is acquired, and

= 0, if the firm is not acquired.

Using the same notations as in the earlier chapter, for sample A, we have number of firms, $i = N = 125$, $n_1 = \text{Prob}\ (Y_i=1) = 35$ (acquired firms), $n_2 = \text{Prob}\ (Y_i=0) = 90$ (non-acquired); $n_1 + n_2 = N$ and number of explanatory variables i.e., k is 7. Regressions on sample A were run with two sets of variables. In set 1, only 7 variables were used (Table 9.1), while in set 2, three interactive terms along with 7 variables were used to obtain the estimates (Table 9.2).

17. For details, see Palepu (1986), Morck *et al.* (1988) and Martin and McConnell (1991).

For sample B, i = N = 73, n_1 = Prob(Y_i = 1) = 20, n_2 = Prob(Y_i = 0) = 53, with k =10 explanatory variables, that include three stock market indicators (Table 9.3).

As noted in Chapter 8, the estimating equation is written as,

$$L_i = ln\left(\frac{P_i}{1-P_i}\right) = Z_i = \beta_0 + \beta_1 X_{1i} + \ldots + \beta_k X_{ki} \qquad (1)$$

Maximum Likelihood (ML) estimation is used to obtain the regression results, as ML estimates yield consistent estimates of asymptotic standard errors. The model significance is checked by likelihood ratio (LR) that is distributed as a χ^2 with degrees of freedom equal to the number of parameter in the model. A positive sign before a coefficient indicates that an increase in the corresponding variable increases the probability of being acquired, while a negative value implies the opposite.

9.3 Regression Results

So far as the correlation results are concerned, irrespective of the measurement of records chosen, on an average the correlations between variables are low. Size and profitability are positively related, and the correlation varies between 0.2 to 0.4. Size and leverage ratios are negatively related and the magnitude of correlation is even lower, ranging between 0.1 to 0.3. The correlation of R&D expenditure with all other variables is nearly 0.

Regression Estimates based on Sample A

To begin with, regression estimates were obtained using seven variables, *viz*., profitability, leverage ratio, age, R&D/sales, current ratio, sales/NA, and financing ratios. Firstly, the regression estimates were made using short-term records,[18] calculated as averages of two years before the merger. The likelihood ratio was found to be significant only in two regressions (see specification 1 and 2 in Table 9.1).

---

18. The regression estimates, with regard to the records of firms one year before the merger, are not shown here. In terms of model significance, none of the regressions performed well. However, with respect to significance of individual variables, the estimates were very similar to those obtained by using averages of two years preceding merger.

Considering specification 1 and 2, it is observed that only two variables, *viz.*, profitability and leverage ratio are found to be significantly affecting the probability of being acquired. In contrast with the results established in empirical studies, profitability defined by PBIT/TA appears with a positive sign and is statistically significant at the 5 per cent, implying that the greater the profitability, the greater is the likelihood of a firm being taken over. Although somewhat surprising, the positive sign of PBIT/TA, is consistent with Powell's (1997) findings during 1984-1991 and 1981-1991. Research studies have consistently shown that inefficient firms, defined by low profitability have greater chances of being acquired. It is important to give an explanation to our observation.

The empirical studies have invariably examined this issue by considering a control sample either from the entire surviving firms[19] in the industry or firms selected randomly from the industry. When acquired firms are compared to such samples, there is a greater probability of inefficient firms showing greater likelihood of being acquired. However, our results are drawn from a sample that comprise AD and similarly matched NAD firms, the positive sign imply that among the size-matched firms, better performing firms have greater chances of being targeted. Even in the pre-merger analysis of the AD and AG firms done in Chapter 6, we found a number of small AD firms with good records have been considered for merger. Big firms undertook mergers of both the profitable and unprofitable firms, though smaller in size. (Comparing the average PBIT/TA for the groups of AD and MNAD firms included in the sample under consideration, it is found that the former have significantly greater profitability).

Although profitability measured by returns on capital employed (PAT/NA) is also positively related to the takeover probability, it is not significant. It is important that in our estimates all other indicators of profitability have positive and non-significant influence on takeover likelihood (not shown in Tables). The negative sign of profitability is particularly supported in research studies in the analysis of hostile takeovers that are mostly associated with disciplining the undervalued firms, which is generally on account of inefficient management. There is

---

19. As mentioned earlier, the surviving firms included all the acquiring firms (that are likely to be bigger in size), non-acquiring as well as non-acquired firms.

Table 9.1

Logit Estimates of Regressions on Sample A with Set 1 of Variables

	Specification:1 (based on average of two years before merger)	*Specification:2 (based on average of two years before merger)*	*Specification:3 (based on average of two years before merger)*	*Specification:4 (based on average of three years before merger)*	*Specification:5 (based on average of five years before merger)*
Explanatory Variable	*Estimated Coefficient*	*Estimated Coefficient*	*Estimated Coefficient*	*Estimated Coefficient*	*Estimated Coefficient*
Profitability ratio-PBIT/TA	6.32** (1.99)	6.81** (2.20)	5.81* (1.92)	5.62* (1.77)	5.78* (1.70)
PAT/sales					
PBIT/sales					
PBDIT/sales					
Leverage ratio-LTL/TA	2.88** (2.15)				
TD/TA		1.08** (2.09)		1.08** (2.09)	1.26** (2.17)
LTL/STL			.45* (1.75)		
STL/TA					
Age	.0034 (.29)	-.005 (-.24)	.003 (.67)	-.002 (-.46)	-.002 (-.16)
R&D/sales	9.53 (.95)	-.16 (-.99)		14.29 (1.17)	22.43 (1.43)
CA/CL	.077 (.93)	.12 (.89)	.02 (.83)	.7 (.95)	.3 (.45)
Sales/NA	-.12 (-1.03)	-.11 (-.99)	-.13 (-1.07)	-.08 (-.58)	-.08 (-.58)
I. Financing-IF/NA.	.091 (.95)	.07 (.70)	.09 (.93)	.099 (.82)	.15 (.99)
E. Financing (debt)-LTB/NA					
E. Financing (equity) EQ/NA					
Constant	-2.53 (-3.22)	-2.61 (-3.58)	2.15 (-3.66)	-2.48 (-3.34)	-2.65 (-3.52)
LR chi^2 (7)	12.00*	12.89*	10.30	9.24	9.43
Pseudo R^2	0.09	0.09	0.08	0.07	0.07
Log likelihood	-60.29	-59.35	-60.56	-61.63	-61.38
No. of observations	125	125	125	125	125

Notes: Figures in brackets are z-values; * significant at 10 per cent level; ** significant at 5 per cent level; *** significant at 1 per cent level.

clear evidence that the hostile and friendly targets have different characteristics[20] and argue differently from the takeover point of view.[21]

So far as the nature of M&A activity in our country is concerned, it has already been noted in Chapter 2 that hostile takeovers are not prevalent in India. By and large, the phenomenon of merger and acquisition is friendly in nature and has been undertaken to obtain synergistic gains or as a survival strategy to withstand the competition during the post-liberalisation period. Survival in market, where foreign companies are also competing, is possible only when domestic companies have a global scale of operation. Although there is evidence of competition among acquiring firms in D&P to acquire other firms in the industry, the intentions of firms have largely been to grow bigger, attain cost advantages and to have an edge over the other firms in the market.

The second variable to have significant effect is the leverage ratio. The three indicators, *viz.*, TD/TA, LTL/TA and LTL/STL appear with positive signs and have statistically significant coefficients at the 5 per cent level. This signifies that highly leveraged firms have greater chances of being targeted. The ratio STL/TA was not found to be significant in any of the regressions implying that high leverage is on account of the greater amount of long-term debt in total assets of firms. This is in conformity with the argument that from a set of equally-sized firms in terms of total assets, AG firms are more interested in buying firms, which have greater proportion of long-term debt and relatively lesser amount of equity issue. This allows acquirers to buy firms to be acquired by spending lesser amount of money, as some percentage of equity is to be bought to gain full control over a firm. Further, as whole of the long-term debt of acquired firm is transferred to the acquiring firms, the latter could also obtain tax advantage after the merger. This observation indicates that AG Firms could foresee exploiting financial synergies by merging with debt burdened firms. This finding, however, is not in conformity with Palepu (1986), who found the target firms to be significantly lower leveraged than the non-targets.

Here, it is important to highlight the relation between leverage and profitability. The highly geared firms also need to pay higher amount of

20. For details, see Morck *et al.* (1988).

21. See, for details, Powell (1997) and Weir (1997).

interest payments, which in turn reduces their profit margins. It is on account of this, in our regression estimates, the other profitability indicators perform non-significantly whereas profit ratio computed before interest and tax deductions (PBIT) significantly increases the merger likelihood. In actual practice also, it has been witnessed that debt-saddled companies have restructured themselves through disinvestments or M&As. In fact, the debt-laden companies are also pressured to do so by banks and financial institutions to reduce their debts. Further, our results are consistent with Powell[22] (1997), who found that during 1988-1991, firm's leverage positively affected the takeover probability, if takeover was synergistic in nature. The hostile takeovers, however, were found to be associated negatively to the probability of getting acquired. Weir (1997) in his study for UK also suggests that target or AD firms are not poor performers, when compared to similar-sized firms from the same industry.

Concerning the other variables, R&D/sales and internal financing, appear with positive signs. The sign of the variable current ratio is not uniform across different regressions. However, none have a significant coefficient. Consistent with estimates of Hall (1988), on an average AD firms have higher R&D intensity than the control group. However, it is not significant. The coefficient of age of the firms at the time of merger is 0 and its sign is also not uniform across different regressions. The variable sales/NA, the only variable that appears with a negative sign in all the regressions, is also not significant in explaining the probability of a firm being acquired. Older firms with greater liquidity and R&D/sales ratio and with greater dependence on internal sources to finance net assets are more likely to be targeted for merger.

Regarding the long-term records, several other regressions were also run using averages of the records of three and five years before the merger (two of these are shown in specification 4 and 5 in Table 9.1). However, none of these regressions performed significantly in terms of Likelihood ratio at the conventional significance levels. The signs of the coefficients of all the variables remained the same and only two variables PBIT/TA and leverage ratio were found to be statistically significant.

22. He partitioned the sample examined between hostile and friendly takeovers.

Table 9.2

Logit Estimates of Regressions on Sample A with Set 2 of Variables

	Specification:1 (based on averages of two years pre-merger)	*Specification:2 (based on averages of two years pre-merger)*	*Specification:3 (based on averages of two years pre-merger)*
Explanatory Variable	*Estimated Coefficient*	*Estimated Coefficient*	*Estimated Coefficient*
Profitability ratio- PBIT/TA	5.01 (1.59)	7.87**(2.45)	6.98**(2.20)
PAT/sales			
PBIT/sales			
PBDIT/sales			
Leverage ratio-LTL/TA			
TD/TA	.87 (1.56)	1.08**(2.16)	1.08**(2.16)
LTL/STL			
STL/TA			
Age	-.001(-.1)	-.001(-.13)	-.003(-.29)
R&D/sales	15.4 (1.48)	56.7*(1.62)	10.9(.76)
CA/CL	-.35 (-1.1)	.11(.75)	.09(.82)
Sales/net assets	-.37*(-1.79)	-.15(-1.39)	-.12(-.87)
Sales/NA* CA/CL	.25(1.56)		
R&D/sales* CA/CL		-23.3(-1.27)	
Sales/NA*R&D/sales			1.69(.14)
I. Financing- IF/NA.	.07(.69)	.06(.66)	.06(.65)
E. Financing (debt) LTB/NA			
E. Financing (equity) EQ/NA			
Constant	-1.9(-2.35)	-2.74(-3.12)	-2.6(-334)
LR chi² (8)	16.54**	15.85**	11.9
Pseudo R^2	.126	.12	.10
Log likelihood	-57.5	-57.9	-59.3
No. of observations	125	125	125

Notes: Figures in brackets are z-values; * significant at 10 per cent level; ** significant at 5 per cent level; *** significant at 1 per cent level.

Regression Estimates with Set 2 of Variables (including interactive terms)

Regression estimates were also obtained including three interactive terms, *viz.*,

(i) Sales/NA* CA/CL,

(ii) R&D/sales*CA/CL, and

(iii) Sales/NA*R&D/sales.

Broadly speaking, the regression results obtained along with interactive terms remained the same as those of without the interactive terms. None of the coefficients of interactive terms was significant.

Regression Estimates based on Sample B

The estimates including stock market indicators were obtained from a smaller sample consisting of 20 AD and 53 MNAD firms. Although, the three indicators are interrelated, the correlation between them is very low. Hence regression estimates were obtained using all the 10 variables. The regressions yield interesting insights.

In terms of model significance, logit model applied to regressions with 10 variables performs better than the estimates obtained with seven variables. The Likelihood ratio statistic is significant for all regression estimates shown in Table 9.3, implying that the model provides a statistically significant explanation of a firm's probability of becoming a merger target. Specifications 1 and 2 are significant at the 2 per cent level. The estimates obtained using the records of one year before merger (specification 5 in Table 9.3) have the highest value of LR and are significant at the 1 per cent. Concerning the signs and significance of the coefficients of seven variables used earlier, the results obtained with respect to all but internal financing are reproduced in these regressions. PBIT/TA and TD/TA both positively and significantly affect the probability of a merger. In all regression estimates LTL/TA is statistically significant at the 1 per cent level. This strengthens our earlier observation that the greater the debt burden, the higher the odds that it will be considered as a merger target.

The variables age, R&D/sales and internal financing appear with a positive sign, while sales/NA with a negative sign. But none is significant at 1 or 5 per cent. The coefficient of the ratio IF/NA appears with a positive sign; it significantly affects the probability of a firm being acquired at the 5 per cent level. This implies that the firms that are more dependent on internal financing are more likely to get merged. Similar to the regression in Table 9.2, sign of current ratio is not uniform and non-significant.

The estimates with regard to valuation ratio are not consistent with the earlier empirical studies, which emphasise that the higher the VR, (the greater the future prospects of a firm) the lower the probability that the firm is undertaken for merger. This factor has been considered as the most important variable affecting the takeover likelihood in Marris's (1964) growth maximising model.

In most of the regression estimates shown in Table 9.3, VR is statistically significant and positively affects the takeover likelihood. In fact, it is observed that the VR is positively related to the past performance of the firm. The better the performance of a firm, the higher the market evaluation of the future earnings of the firm as expressed in the form of higher VR. Since, in our regression estimates, both the past profitability (measured by profitability ratio) and the future prospects (measured by VR) of the firm positively affect the takeover likelihood, this clearly implies that among the similarly-sized firms, efficient or better performing with better future prospects, but severely indebted, are more likely to be acquired..

In few specifications (see specification 2), when LTL/TA indicator of the leverage ratio is considered, then sales/NA also becomes statistically significant implying that the higher rate of turning assets into sales (productivity in investment) negatively affects the probability of firms getting acquired.

These regressions were also run with records of one year (see specification 4 and 5 in Table 9.3) and averages of three years before the merger (not shown here). Broadly, the results are consistent across the measurement of the records of the firms.

9.4 Conclusion

The exercise performed in this chapter sought to identify the determinants of a firm becoming a merger target. The design of our sample excluded the role of size and focussed on the other determinants of M&As. The results of our analysis are in conformity with the fact that M&A among the D&P firms have largely been to derive synergies from consolidation and to preserve or increase their market shares.

Profitability ratio—PBIT/TA and leverage ratio especially LTL/TA, have consistently emerged as the two variables that increase the chances of a

Table 9.3

Logit Estimates of Regressions on Sample B

	Specification:1 (based on average of two years pre-merger)	*Specification:2 (based on average of two years pre-merger)*	*Specification:3 (based on average of two years pre-merger)*	*Specification:4 (based on records of one year pre-merger)*	*Specification:5 (based on records of one year pre-merger)*
Explanatory Variable	*Estimated Coefficient*	*Estimated Coefficient*	*Estimated Coefficient*	*Estimated Coefficient*	*Estimated Coefficient*
Profitability ratio- PBIT/TA	11.84* (1.71)	12.62* (1.85)		9.70** (1.94)	12.22** (2.10)
PAT/sales					
PBIT/sales			.0037 (.23)		
PBDIT/sales					
Leverage ratio - LTL/TA		6.96*** (3.07)	5.35*** (2.84)	4.62*** (2.54)	7.41*** (2.92)
TD/TA	7.30*** (2.92)				
LTL/STL					
STL/TA					
Age	.002 (.26)	.016 (.68)	.0211 (.93)	.027 (1.12)	.015 (.62)
R&D/sales	17.17 (1.49)	13.79 (1.14)	12.25 (1.01)	7.47 (1.00)	12.12 (1.51)
CA/CL	.56 (1.02)	-.23 (-.52)	.095 (.25)	-.44 (-1.16)	.39 (.83)
I. Financing- IF/NA.	.27** (2.00)	.32** (2.16)	.31** (2.16)	.11 (1.51)	.14* (1.86)
E. Financing-LTB/NA					
E. Financing-EQ/NA					
Sales/NA	-.43 (-1.16)	-.41 (-2.24)	-.29* (-1.79)	-.38 (-1.51)	-.28 (-.98)
Variable ratio	.34* (1.91)	.32** (1.95)	.32** (1.94)	.20 (1.40)	.31** (1.95)
P/E	.0051 (.5)	.00142 (.14)	.0008 (.10)	.0003 (.06)	.002 (.32)
EPS	-.0061 (-.42)	-.010 (-.57)	-.0039 (-.33)	-.012 (-1.06)	-.009 (-.96)
Constant	-8.17 (-3.16)	-4.29 (-3.14)	-3.53 (-2.98)	-2.72 (-2.69)	-8.15 (-3.16)
LR chi^2 (10)	21.47**	21.78**	17.91*	16.55*	22.44***
Pseudo R^2	0.25	0.25	0.21	0.19	0.26
Log likelihood	-32.12	-31.97	-33.90	-34.58	-31.64
No. of observations	73	73	73	73	73

Notes: Figures in brackets are z-values. * significant at 10 per cent level; ** significant at 5 per cent level; *** significant at 1 per cent level.

firm becoming a merger target. Highly indebted firms have greater chances of getting acquired. Empirically, it has been witnessed that since high leverage is attached to bankruptcy, debt burdened firms—especially small, preferred exiting through merger, which is cheaper than the bankruptcy cost. Seemingly, acquiring firms themselves being less leveraged, preferred merging with these companies to obtain tax advantage on the enhanced value of debt after the merger. This points to the possibility of exploiting financial synergies as one of the key motives of these mergers. Further, increased debt on the part of large firms is also associated with reduced agency cost and positive stock price movements after merger (discussed in Chapter 3).

Among the three stock market indicators, *viz.*, valuation ratio, P/E and EPS, the valuation ratio is the only significant variable that increases the probability of being acquired. The R&D intensity and internal financing affect positively and sales/NA has a negative influence. However, these factors receive no support as significant determinants of merger likelihood. There is no evidence that R&D intensity drives the likelihood of a merger.

Empirically, our results are along the lines of synergistic takeovers. A large proportion of mergers among the group companies also attribute to the fact that the activity is not undertaken to discipline the low profit-earning firms. Rather, attaining synergistic benefits through consolidation seems to be one of the key motives. Prevalence of horizontal mergers in the sample under observation also point to the fact that mergers were primarily synergistic in nature.

10 Concluding Remarks

The post-reform period was a challenging one for the Indian corporate sector. The Indian industry was not only liberalised but was also forced to restructure its businesses to survive in the new competitive environment. In its effort to do so, mergers and acquisitions (M&As), as a means to have quick expansion and as a corrective measure to its pre-reform policies, were adopted in large numbers. While the phenomenon of M&As has accelerated in volume and value—especially over the past 10 years—it has not received adequate attention in research. Envisaging the consequential effects that M&As can have on the economic health of the economy, our study sought to analyse some key issues relating to mergers and acquisitions with special reference to the drugs and pharmaceutical (D&P) industry during the post-reform period. The main objective of our study was to examine the factors that distinguished the participants from non-participants, as well as between acquiring and acquired firms in the former. Towards this objective, the study examined the following issues:

- To evaluate the changes in the macro policy regime and their effects on saving, investment and growth acceleration.
- To analyse the emerging market for 'open offers', following the 'Takeover code'.
- To review the pattern of M&A activity in the post-reform period in India and analyse its trends since the year 2000.
- To analyse trends in cross-border M&As and establish their relation with openness index and income.
- To compare the pre-merger characteristics of acquiring and acquired firms.
- To differentiate the merging from non-merging firms using a specially designed size-matched sample, all pertaining to D&P industry.

- To explore the factors that determine the probability of a firm going for a merger, and
- To assess the factors determining the probability of a firm getting acquired.

This chapter pulls together the central findings of the study. Section 10.1 provides the main findings of our analysis and Section 10.2 draws out some policy implications of the study.

10.1 Summary of the Main Findings

The main results of the analysis are divided into seven parts.

Post-reform Policies and Growth Acceleration

The liberalised policies pursued since 1991-92, had a palpable impact on macroeconomic indicators of the economy. The sectoral growth rates—especially industry and services—and the overall GDP growth of the economy improved substantially. The average annual growth rate during 1980-81 to 2003-04 was 5 per cent with an accelerated trend. The initial pulse for growth acceleration came from the mild reforms initiated in the mid-1980s. Though, limited and mild in coverage, these reforms played a key role in crossing the 5 per cent growth mark. Our econometric analysis corroborates that India experienced a structural break in growth of GDP in 1987-88. This is not to conclude that reforms of 1991-92 did not have much impact. Contrary to other recent views, our analysis also depicts that average annual trend growth rates during 'pre-1991 reform period' i.e., 1980-81 to 1991-92 and 'post-1991 reform' period i.e., 1992-93 to 2003-2004 are statistically different, the latter having significantly higher average growth rate. This suggests that the more comprehensive reforms of 1991 provided a boost to the average growth rate. As regards the issue of growth fragility and variability, our analysis illustrates that these concerns are overstated and sensitive to the data examined.

Regarding the effects of growth in the stock market on gross domestic savings (GDSs), our analysis is based on the period 1980-81 to 2002-03. As against the view that expansion in stock market just led to portfolio substitution from bank deposits to stock market instruments with no increase in savings, our analysis demonstrates a rise in GDSs. Both the households and private corporate sector responded favourably, though at different rates and during different periods. While the former was more responsive from the mid-1980s to the early years of reforms, the latter portrayed a greater response during the post-reform period. Further, a rise in financial instruments of saving until the mid-1990s is a clear sign of increased public confidence in the stock market.

Need for a Takeover Market

The evolution of SEBI's takeover code and consequent development of takeover (open offers) market have been an eye-opener for both the company's managers and its shareholders. On account of benevolent attitude of financial institutions (which were major shareholders, especially in promoter-held companies) and passivity of shareholders, companies in India paid little attention to the objective of maximisation of long-term shareholders' wealth. The development of takeover market was necessary to make realise the companies their duties towards the shareholders of the companies. The analysis of takeover market highlights that 65 per cent of 'open offers' in value and volume made during 1997-2005 aimed at 'change of management', while 24 and 11 per cent were intended at 'stake consolidation' and 'substantial acquisition', respectively. The reforms in this area have made financial institutions more vigilant and shareholders more powerful. However, it may be stated that the experience of western countries with respect to takeover market cannot be generalised to India, as the context varies from country to country.

Trends in M&As: Global

Concerning trends in cross-border M&As, close to 70 per cent of foreign direct investments (FDIs) took place in cross-border M&As to consolidate capacities and attain market dominance in the global market. Similar to the trends in Indian M&As, cross-border M&As witnessed a rising activity up to 1999-2000, a decline from 2000 onwards and a reversal in 2004. The following prominent features emerged from the analysis of cross-border M&As during 1990-2004:

(i) The global trend rate of growth of cross-border M&As was 8 per cent during 1987-2004, whereas during 1990-2000, it was 12 per cent.

(ii) Although this activity is on the rise due to a rise in deals held by both the developed (DDE) and developing economies (DGE), the share of the latter has risen continuously which is counterbalanced by a fall in the proportion of DDE in the total global M&As.

(iii) Decomposing the rise in deals as acquirer and target, it is found that the rise in activity for the DDE is higher as buyer (acquirer), while it is higher as seller (target) for the DGE. As a consequence, the share of the DDE fell from 95 per cent (as both buyer and seller) to 83 per cent as acquirer and to 73 per cent as target, while the share of DGE rose from 5 per cent (as both buyer and seller) to 16 and 24 per cent as buyer and seller, respectively.

(iv) Within the group of DDE, major part of the activity is undertaken by Europe, followed by North America and other developed economies. However, share of the latter two has exhibited a rising trend.

(v) Among the DGE economies, Asia and Oceania have maintained the highest and a rising share especially since the mid-1990s, followed by Latin America and Africa (both with a falling trend).

Analysis of cross-border M&As broadly reflects similar movements in value terms. However, relative shares of different groups exhibit greater year-to-year fluctuations than reflected in the total number of deals. This is due to the large-sized cross-border M&A deals (called mega deals-M&A worth more than US $1billion), which despite being a small proportion of total number of deals, bring large changes in the value of transactions.

(vi) Further, relative shares of DGE as acquirer (8 per cent) and target (13 per cent) are lower in total value of cross-border M&As. This points to the fact that these economies entered in a greater number of smaller deals whereas developed countries entered into lesser number of bigger deals. From the negligible share in cross-border M&As, transitional economies started participating as targets from the early 1990s, with only 2 per cent of share. However, from 2000 onwards, their participation as acquirer has also become apparent with 1 to 2 per cent of the total deals.

(vii) From an individual country point of view, the UK and US held the top two positions, with Germany, Canada and France as the main competitors for the next three places. A noticeable change since

2003 is that a few of the Asian countries, such as China and Hong Kong (China) are emerging as important destinations for cross-border M&As, however, their positions as purchasers (acquirer) are quite low.

(viii) With the primary sector maintaining an average of 2-3 per cent during 1990-2003, the manufacturing and service sectors are exhibiting opposing trends, with the latter moving in an upward direction. On account of worldwide liberalisation of services, its share in total cross-border M&As activity increased from 33 per cent in the late 1980s to 55 per cent in the mid-1990s and climbed to roughly 65 per cent in the year 2000.

In an exploratory attempt to find the determinants of cross-border M&As, our analysis showed that institutional quality index played an important role in determining the investments received through cross-border M&As. In conformity with the Rybczynski Theorem, it clearly emerged that cross-border M&As (investments received) and openness of an economy (measured in trade shares of GDP) are negatively and significantly related to each other. This is due to the dominance of horizontal mergers, which are essentially market-seeking and in such cases, both production and sales take place in the host country. In other words, the export-promoting investments are weaker than the import-replacing resources that give rise to a negative relation between trade volumes and cross-border M&As sales and purchases.

Trends in M&As: India

On account of the erstwhile restrictive policy regime adopted in India, the Indian companies diversified their businesses and grew into big conglomerates. With greater exposure to more competitive world and to take advantage of the liberalised policies in the post-reform period, Indian firms resorted to M&As as a means of internal restructuring at a rapid pace. The essential features observed are:

(i) Dominance of mergers in manufacturing—especially in the private manufacturing industry;

(ii) A majority of mergers between firms from the same management, called 'within group' mergers;

(iii) Predominance of horizontal mergers (or intra-industry);

(iv) All-sized companies (not necessarily large or MRTP companies), undertaking mergers;

(v) Predominance of intra-industry mergers relative to inter-industry mergers;

(vi) Prevalence of mergers in few industries such as, drugs and pharmaceutical, textile, electrical machinery, and food and beverages i.e., exhibiting occurrence of industrial clustering;

(vii) Active participation of MNCs to strengthen their control, primarily through acquisitions (and not through mergers). Moreover, these companies invested in consumer goods industries which were sensitive to brand loyalties and also preferred to acquire companies that had well-established marketing and distribution network; and

(viii) After a slowdown in the M&A activity during 2000-2004, both mergers and acquisition touched new heights in 2005.

The pattern of mergers observed during the early years of post-reform period clearly points to the fact that through the mergers, firms consolidated in similar businesses, corrected for their early over-diversified businesses, avoided competition 'within' or intra-group companies, and hence protected themselves from the takeover threat. However, after the mid-1990s, firms largely undertook mergers as a means of external growth to have quick expansion and attain larger market shares.

Pre-merger Characteristics of Acquiring (AG) and Acquired (AD) Firms

In order to examine the nature of the selection mechanism in M&A activity, our study analyses the distinguishing features of the participants or merging firms and non-participants or non-merging firms in the M&As activity. The analysis is based on horizontal mergers that took place in the Indian D&P industry during the period 1992-93 to 2005-06.

Analysis of pre-merger characteristics of participants i.e., acquiring and acquired firms, based on five variables, *viz.*, size, profitability, leverage, productivity of investment and growth, measured through several indicators, yield the following results:

(i) AG firms are three to four times larger than AD firms.

(ii) For all indicators of profitability, AG firms are significantly more profitable. The main cause of lower profitability of AD firms seems to be higher interest payments arising from their higher debt burden, while tax payments have a stronger effect on AG firms.

(iii) The difference between AD and AG firms with regard to various indicators, is higher in the short-term, before merger.

(iv) The distribution of AG and AD firms by total assets and profit margins (PAT/sales) suggest that a large proportion of AD firms are less profitable and not all AG firms have high profitability.

(v) AD firms generate higher sales out of their net assets than their corresponding AG firms. Hence, a part of higher profit margins (PAT/sales) of AG firms is offset by lower productivity of net assets (sales/NA) that reduces their return on capital employed (PAT/NA).

(vi) AD firms are more debt burdened on account of both higher short-term liabilities and long-term liabilities, though none of them is statistically significant.

(vii) In terms of net assets AG firms grow at a higher rate, while AD firms have quantitatively higher growth in terms of sales.

On an average, it can be observed that bigger, less leveraged, and more profitable firms are acquiring smaller and less profitable firms. However, this is not to suggest that AD (AG) firms are inferior (superior) in all respects. AD firms in fact are more productive and exhibit higher growth of sales than AG firms.

Pre-merger Characteristics of Merging and Size-matched Non-merging Firms

To examine how the firms that participated in the merger activity differed from those that did not, the analysis was further extended to include the non-merging firms. To rule out the effect of size and to focus better on other factors, the analysis was carried out using a size-matched control sample of non-merging firms corresponding to each merging firm. Accordingly, two sets of control firms were created, one corresponding to the AG firms, called matched non-acquiring (MNAG) firms, and the other corresponding to AD firms, called matched non-acquired (MNAD) firms. Comparing AG and MNAG firms, the following observations are noted:

(i) The MNAG are found to be significantly less profitable—especially in terms of measures calculated before deducting interest payments.

(ii) In terms of generating sale out of net assets, MNAG firms are significantly less productive.

(iii) MNAG firms are more debt-burdened—especially on account of higher proportion of long-term liabilities in total assets.

(iv) Regarding growth measured in terms of both sales and net assets, AG firms do not differ from the MNAG firms, and

(v) Despite being similar in size, MNAG firms are inferior in terms of productivity of investment, leverage and profitability levels. From these investigations, it follows that long-term borrowings are a constraint on MNAG firms in acquiring other firms and thus, for participating in the merger activity.

Concerning the other set of AD and MNAD firms, there is little to distinguish one group from the other. The firms that are made merger targets, though less efficient than their corresponding AG firms, are very similar to other size-matched non-AD firms in terms of all variables. Accordingly, it is difficult to answer why a particular firm is taken as a merger target.

Factors affecting the Likelihood of a Merger

Why do all firms not participate in the merger process? One reason could be size. However, when size-matched AG firms are taken, then the question is different: why among similarly-sized firms, some acquire and others do not? Or why amongst similarly-sized firms, some are acquired and others are not? The objective is to highlight inter-firm differences among similarly-sized firms to ascertain, why do firms acquire? And why are firms acquired? In other words, the aim is to search for the factors that increase the probability of a firm entering into a merger. For a clearer exposition, the econometric analysis was divided in two parts:

(i) Factors affecting the probability of a firm going for an acquisition; and

(ii) Factors affecting the probability of a firm becoming a merger target.

Our analysis on the first part shows:

(i) Firms with higher profitability (measured as return on capital employed i.e., PAT/NA or return on equity i.e., PAT/NW) have greater probability of adopting merger as a growth strategy. Inefficient firms are less likely to go for mergers as their preferred growth strategy.

(ii) Firms with higher investments in physical assets are less likely to go for an acquisition strategy, implying that internal and external means of growth are used as substitutes for each other.

(iii) Firms with higher market shares have a greater tendency to go for mergers. This has also been witnessed in practice. Firms competing with each other to grab higher market sales, are also the ones that fully exploited the opportunity of adopting M&As means to grow.

(iv) Further, in conformity with our hypothesis, age of the firm negatively affects the likelihood of going for a merger. In D&P industry, younger firms are more dynamic and vibrant, and therefore have greater chances of going for an acquisition.

(v) Regarding financing patterns of firms, our results demonstrate that internal financing has no significant role to play, while within external finance, firms that have greater dependence on equity finance, are more likely to go for mergers. This clearly implies that firms with greater exposure to stock market have higher probability of going for mergers.

(vi) In accordance with these findings, the probability of more leveraged firms is inversely related to the possibility of undertaking a merger. This result is in line with our earlier finding that long-term borrowing for financing net assets seems to be an important binding constraint for a firm seeking to adopt a merger strategy.

Concerning the factors determining a firm's probability of getting acquired, from a sample of AD and similarly-matched NAD firms, the main results obtained are:

(i) Although somewhat surprising, the regression estimates show that the better performing firms (measured by PBIT/TA) have greater chances of becoming merger targets.

(ii) LTL/TA is found to be positively and significantly affecting the likelihood of takeover. This signifies that companies on account of high leverage and consequently, high interest payments make better targets for the acquirers that are less burdened by debt. Acquiring highly leveraged firms is doubly advantageous; first, it is cheaper to buy a debt-burdened firm, and, second, there is a possibility of exploiting financial synergies.

(iii) The probability of becoming a merger target is also found to be positively related to internal financing, current ratio and R&D intensity but this finding is not robust.

(iv) The age of the firm at the time of merger does not seem to matter. Its coefficient is negligibly small and non-significant.

(v) Regarding valuation ratio of a firm, our results suggest that it plays a positive role in determining the odds in favour of a firm becoming a merger target. This again points to the fact that firms with better future prospects (as evaluated by the market) are preferred as merger targets. Empirically, it has been witnessed that, hostile takeovers have been aimed at firms with low valuation ratios and not friendly acquisitions.

(vi) In actual practice also, it has been found that companies weighed down by debt have restructured themselves either by disinvesting a part of their businesses or by merging with other firms. In fact, debt encumbered companies are also pressured to do so by banks and financial institutions to reduce their debts.

(vii) Our findings are more in agreement with the studies that examined only friendly M&As i.e., the takeovers, which are undertaken to attain synergistic benefits.

To conclude, the result that finally emerges from our analysis of merging and non-merging firms is that in the post-reform period, larger, more profitable and less leveraged firms were more likely to use acquisition strategy to grow and face greater competition from the domestic and foreign firms. In their effort to do so, acquiring firms chose to merge with smaller and debt-saddled firms i.e., the companies, which are not able to earn reasonable profits on account of heavy interest payments. The acquired companies however, are not the most inefficient firms in the industry.

Rather, they are better than their similarly-sized matched non-acquired firms. They are also found to have higher asset turnover ratio than their corresponding acquiring firms and relatively higher profits—especially before deducting interest payments—than their matched non-acquired firms. This points to the fact that, apart from attaining economies of scale, faster growth, bigger size, and higher market share through consolidation, acquiring firms also sought to exploit financial synergies.

Although our analysis is carried out on D&P industry, the results regarding size and profitability can be generalised for other industries as well. The observations concerning variables, such as leverage ratio, age and valuation ratio, however, require more specific analysis.

10.2 Policy Implications

International experiences suggest that the market that allows mergers, acquisitions and takeovers (also called, market for corporate control or MCC) is an important vehicle through which the efficiency of utilisation of assets in the economy is enhanced. However, on the basis of evidence available from western countries, specific conditions prevailing in the Indian markets and given its present stage of development, it is argued that such reforms are likely to harm the economy and should therefore be discouraged (Singh, 1998).

The development of MCC is still in its initial stage in India. It has given much required boost to the corporate sector that has helped it to withstand the intense competition in the global market. Moreover experience show that Indian corporates always weighed down the importance of meeting shareholders' interests. The latter, despite holding a large percentage of equity, had no say in removing inept management. It was the development of 'Takeover code' that made shareholders realise their powers and stimulated the existing management to perform better.

From a review of the available evidence on the MCC, it is suggested that there are certain imperfections in such markets that lower its potential. The imperfections highlighted in research studies are based on the experience of the US, UK and other European countries. These limitations do merit attention in developing economies like ours. However, it must be kept in mind that they are more applicable to developed markets. On the basis of our analysis, the following observations are made.

Firstly, the selection in the MCC occurs more on the basis of size rather than that of profitability or efficiency or firm's stock market valuation. Several studies identified size to be the most important factor for the takeover. It is asserted that this consideration is particularly important for a country like ours, where there are large potentially predatory conglomerate groups, which could easily take over smaller and more profitable firms and as a consequence, reduce potential competition to the detriment of the real economy (Singh, 1998).

After the initiation of economic reforms the firms had to face increasing competitive pressure from the domestic as well as world market. M&As were used as a route to efficiency. Firms—especially, conglomerate groups—restructured their businesses to correct for their initial diversified strategies followed during restrictive regime. Through M&As, these firms focussed on core competencies to reduce cost and survive in the new business environment. As far as takeover of small by big firms is concerned, we have the following comments.

From the analysis of M&As in D&P industry, the first observation is that not all acquiring firms are large-sized firms. Close to 50 per cent of firms belong to small and medium size classes. This suggests that a firm may not necessarily be a large-sized firm to be an acquiring firm. Further, if it is asserted that a relatively large size is sufficient for a firm to adopt M&A strategy, the obvious question is: why all large-sized firms do not adopt this strategy to grow? To put it differently, if a firm is large-sized, will it necessarily go for a merger to grow? Comparison of all AG and their matched non-acquiring firms demonstrates that AG firms are significantly more productive, profitable and less leveraged. By implication, along with size, a firm needs to be more efficient as well. This signifies that bigness is neither a necessary nor a sufficient condition for a firm in adopting a merger strategy to grow externally.

Recent experience in India as well as in other developed countries suggests that even small companies are instrumental in taking over companies, larger than their own size. Due to the emergence of 'innovative financing techniques' during the late 1980s and early 1990s in the US, many smaller and profitable firms took over large corporations by issuing claims on the value of assets of the firm being targeted. This means the large and unprofitable firms that are supposed to be insulated from takeovers are not so due to their big size, rather it is the unavailability of finance that constrained the smaller firms in acquiring other firms.

Secondly, regarding AD firms, it is contended that small and profitable firms are more likely to be acquired. It is easily discerned that more than 90 per cent are small-sized and close to 70 per cent of AD firms are unprofitable (either negative or very low profit margins). However, comparison with other matched small-sized acquired firms shows that if profitability is compared before interest and tax deductions, AD firms perform significantly better than their other size-matched firms. This suggests that despite being burdened by heavy interest payments, AD firms are more efficient than their size-matched firms. In addition to this, our analysis shows that AD firms' higher debt burden increases the probability of their acquisition. All this corroborates that AD firms are chosen over their other size-matched firms on account of their high leverage ratio and efficiency i.e., those small AD firms have been targeted, which are under pressure for lack of funds, however have the potential to grow.

Further, when it is put along with the fact that AG firms are less leveraged, this also brings in the possibility of obtaining financial synergistic gains that AG firms could foresee in making these acquisitions. First, it is cheaper to buy a debt-saddled firm; second, there is a possibility of getting a tax advantage on the enhanced amount of debt after merger. What finally comes out from the analysis is that despite AD firms being small, unprofitable and highly leveraged, they are attractive targets for AG companies. All this resonates with the objective of exploiting mutual synergies, as opposed to taking advantage of low stock market valuations. On account of this most of the acquisitions were friendly in nature. The contention that efficiency has no role to play is not supported by our analysis.

Third, concerning the contention that M&As increase concentration, it must be noted that in drugs and pharmaceutical industry, the industrial concentration fell till 2000. In fact this is owing to the fact that entry of firms outstripped the exit. Evidence of mergers increasing concentration exists only during 2000-2004. Even the evidence in the western world is uncertain. Further, so long as increasing concentration is not associated with any entry deterring effects, it is not considered to have adverse effects on the economy. However, an issue of greater importance is the effect of concentration on competition. The preliminary results from D&P indicate an increase in competition in the industry. Changing ranking pattern of firms and their respective shares are indicators of vigour of competitive forces prevalent in D&P industry post-M&As. Ranbaxy Laboratories Ltd. is the only firm, which maintained its first position in the industry since 1993, however its share has changed from 8 to almost 12 per cent during 2000-2004. Even if a rise in concentration leads to emergence of a few dominant firms, this is not a sufficient ground for a case against the development of market for mergers, acquisitions and takeovers. Rather, this calls for an effective regulation of the Competition Law. The law clearly states that it is not dominance *per se* but the abuse of dominance that is bad. If Competition Commission of India (CCI) is effective enough to prevent misuse of dominance, there is a case for MCC to evolve.

Although it matters whether a big firm is taking over the smaller ones or whether it is the other way around, the more important question is: what are the benefits to the society at large?, i.e., whether the mergers have been wealth reducing or wealth enhancing. This necessitates post-merger analysis of the entities that adopted M&A strategy to grow. Although the post-merger performance is outside the scope of our study, few observations may be helpful. A report of ET intelligence group's analysis on M&As over the past 10 years (*The Economic Times*, 26th October, 2005) reports a rise in sales and PAT synergies of the merged entities. Assuming the pre-merger growth of individual companies would have continued in the absence of M&As, the sales and PAT synergies are calculated on the basis of gains made by the combined entities in relation to the net sales and PAT projections of individual companies. It is observed that with few exceptions, most of the companies investigated obtained higher PAT synergies than sales synergies. Calculated as a per cent of the actual net sales/net profits, on an average, the PAT synergy accounted for more than 50 per cent and the sales synergy ranged between 20 to 35 per cent for most of the companies. The report spells out that, while the pharmaceutical and cement industries were able to capture the sales synergies immediately after the merger, the auto ancillary took two to three years to deliver the results.

In addition to this, in India it is witnessed that with few exceptions, M&As took place with the mutual interest of those who sold and of those who acquired i.e., the activity was friendly and synergistic in nature. So long as economies of scale and other synergies are exploited, cost is reduced, efficiency is improved and consumers are benefited in terms of lowered prices, MCC will continue to benefit the society.

To sum up, this analysis is an exploratory attempt on the issue of selection mechanism and is just a preliminary step in this direction. To find whether the evolution of such a market has been conducive to Indian industrialisation and faster economic growth, a fuller analysis of the area requires extensions to other industries and to other aspects of M&As activity, such as post-merger effects, effects on the managements of merged firms, effects on competition and effects on employment levels of the merged entity.

Annexures

Annexure I

Definitions of the Variables Used

1. *Sales/operating income:* Sales/operating income is defined as the revenue generated by a firm from its main business activities. It excludes other income and income from non-recurring transactions, income of extraordinary nature and prior period income. The distinction between sales, other income and non-recurring income is explained below.

   Sales and other income are distinguished on the basis of a firm's economic activities from which such income is earned e.g., income earned by way of dividends, interest, rent and other similar non-operating income of industrial and trading companies is classified as other income.

   Non-recurring income such as profit on sale of investments, insurance claims, tax refunds, prior period incomes, provisions written back, etc., are classified separately under extraordinary income. While calculating any profitability ratio other income is included and non-recurring income is excluded.
2. *Net Assets:* Total Assets–short-term liability.
3. *Short-term liability*: All obligations maturing within an accounting year (usually, one year) are included in it. It comprises current liabilities and provision, short-term bank borrowing, commercial paper and deferred tax liability.
4. *Deferred tax liability*: Taxable income is calculated in accordance with the tax laws. In some cases the requirements of these laws to compute taxable income differ from the accounting policies applied to determine accounting income. It is this tax effect of difference in the taxable income and accounting income that results in a 'deferred tax or deferred tax liability'.

5. *Total debt*: It includes, total borrowing + current liability and provisions + deferred tax liability.
6. *Total borrowing*: It includes all forms of debt (interest bearing or otherwise)—debt from bank (short-term as well as long-term) and financial institutions, inter-corporate loans, fixed deposits from public and directors, foreign loans, loans from government Funds raised from capital market through debt (e.g. debentures) and commercial paper are included.
7. *Long-term borrowing*: These include all the obligations or debts payable in a period of time more than an accounting period (usually, one year). It is defined as: total borrowing – short-term borrowing (i.e., short-term bank borrowing +commercial paper)
8. *Net worth*: This represents the share capital and retained earning of a company. It includes equity capital, preference capital, reserves and surplus (revaluation reserves and miscellaneous expenses not written off, are excluded from it).
9. *Debt-equity ratio:* This is a measure of the financial leverage of a company. This ratio is calculated using the following formula, total borrowings/net worth.
10. *Current liabilities and provisions:* This includes all liabilities that are due within twelve months. Sundry creditors, bills payables/ acceptances, interest accrued and due, form part of current liabilities. It also includes provisions for taxation and provision for dividend, provision for diminution in investment, etc. Current liabilities also include share suspense account and share application amount. Only those provisions for dividends are included which are proposed but not yet paid. If an interim dividend was paid during the year, it will not be a part of this provision.

    There are two types of profitability ratios: (i) profit margin ratios, (ii) rate of return ratio. The former are expressed as a ratio of sales, and the latter as a ratio of investment. Since profit can be measured at different stages, there are five measures of profit margin ratios.
11. *PBDIT (NNRT) as ratio of sales:* This is the profitability margin ratio derived considering the profits before depreciation, interest and tax,

which are net of the non-recurring item (NNRT) as percentage of sales.

12. *PBIT (NNRT) as a ratio of sales:* This is the profitability margin ratio derived considering the profits before interest and tax which is net of non-recurring item as percentage of sales.
13. *PBDT (NNRT) as ratio of sales:* This is the profitability margin ratio derived considering the profits before depreciation and tax which is net of non-recurring item as percentage of sales.
14. *PBT (NNRT) as ratio of sales:* This is the profitability margin ratio derived considering the profits before tax which is net of non-recurring item as percentage of sales.
15. *PAT (NNRT) as a ratio of sales:* This is the profitability margin ratio derived, considering the profit after tax which is net of non-recurring item, as percentage of sales.

    Depending on the measure of investment, the two commonly used ratios are:
16. *Rate of Return on net worth (PAT/NW):* This is a measure of the profitability of a company. It is a calculated data field and is arrived at using the following formula: PAT (NNRT)/net worth.
17. *Rate of return on net assets or capital employed (PAT/NA)*: This represents the return on capital employed, it is calculated using the following formula: PAT (NNRT)/net assets or capital employed.
18. *Current ratio:* This is a measure of the short-term liquidity position of a company. This ratio is calculated using the following formula: current assets/current liabilities and provisions.
19. *Earnings per share (EPS):* It is defined as the ratio of the profit after tax of the company in the most recent 12-month period to the number of shares outstanding as on that date.
20. *Price to earnings ratio (P/E):* Using the definition of EPS given above, the P/E ratio is defined as P/E = closing price of shares/EPS.
21. *Book value per share:* The book value per share of the company is defined as the sum of the equity capital and reserves divided by outstanding number of shares.

Annexure II

List of Acquiring and Acquired Companies Selected for the Sample

S. No.	*Name of the Acquiring Company*	*Name of the Acquired Company*	*Year of Merger*
1	Max India Ltd.	Max India Ltd. [merged]	1992-93
2	SOL Pharmaceuticals Ltd.	Standard Organics Ltd. [merged]	1993-94
3	Core Healthcare Ltd.	Core Laboratories Ltd. [merged]	1993-94
4	Novartis India Ltd.	Sandoz (India) Ltd. [amalgamated]	1995-96
5	Nicholas Piramal India Ltd.	Boehringer Mannheim India Ltd. [merged]	1996-97
6	Ranbaxy Laboratories Ltd.	Croslands Research Laboratories Ltd. [merged]	1996-97
7	Wyeth Ltd.	Wyeth Laboratories Ltd. [merged]	1996-97
8	Wyeth Ltd.	John Wyeth (India) Ltd. [erstwhile]	1997-98
9	Aventis Pharma Ltd.	Roussel India Ltd. [merged]	1997-98
10	Sun Pharmaceutical Inds. Ltd.	Tamil Nadu Dadha Pharmaceuticals Ltd. [Merged]	1997-98
11	TTK Healthcare Ltd.	TTK Biomed Ltd. [merged]	1999-2000
12	Dr. Reddy'S Laboratories Ltd.	American Remedies Ltd. [merged]	2000-01
13	Dr. Reddy'S Laboratories Ltd.	Cheminor Drugs Ltd. [merged]	2000-01
14	Novartis India Ltd.	Ciba CKD Biochem Ltd. [merged]	2000-01
15	Lupin Ltd.	Lupin Laboratories Ltd. [merged]	2000-01
16	Aurobindo Pharma Ltd.	Sri Chakra Remedies Ltd. [merged]	2000-01
17	Sun Pharmaceutical Inds. Ltd.	Pradeep Drug Co. Ltd. [merged]	2000-01
18	Sun Pharmaceutical Inds. Ltd.	MJ Pharmaceuticals Ltd. [merged]	2001-02
19	Strides Arcolab Ltd.	Bombay Drugs & Pharmas Ltd. [merged]	2001-02
20	Nicholas Piramal India Ltd.	Rhone-Poulenc (India) Ltd. [merged]	2001-02
21	Glaxosmithkline Pharmaceuticals Ltd.	Smithkline Beecham Pharmaceuticals (India) Ltd. [amalgamated]	2001-02
22	TTK Healthcare Ltd.	TTK Medical Devices Ltd. [merged]	2001-02
23	Cadila Healthcare Ltd.	Zydus Pathline Ltd. [merged]	2001-02
24	Glaxosmithkline Pharmaceuticals Ltd.	Croydon Chemical Works Ltd. [merged]	2002-03
25	Wyeth Ltd.	Geoffrey Manners & Co. Ltd. [merged]	2002-03
26	Cadila Healthcare Ltd.	German Remedies Ltd. [merged]	2002-03
27	Matrix Laboratories Ltd.	Medicorp Technologies India Ltd. [merged]	2002-03
28	Pfizer Ltd.	Parke-Davis (India) Ltd. [merged]	2002-03
29	Matrix Laboratories Ltd.	Vorin Laboratories Ltd. [merged]	2002-03
30	Matrix Laboratories Ltd.	Fine Drugs and Chemicals[merged]	2003-04
31	Pfizer Ltd.	Pharmacia Healthcare Ltd. [merged]	2004-05
32	Matrix Laboratories Ltd.	Vera Laboratories[merged]	2004-05
33	Punjab Chemicals and Crop Protection Ltd.	Alpha Drug India Ltd. [merged]	2005-06

Source: Compiled from Prowess database (CMIE).

Annexure III

Logit and Probit Models

Logit Model

The Logit model is based on cumulative logistic probability function, which is specified as,

$$P_i = F = (Z_i) = F(\beta_1 + \beta_2 X_i) = \frac{1}{1+e^{-zi}} = \frac{1}{1+e^{-(\beta_1+\beta_2 X_i)}} \quad (1)$$

Here, Z_i ranges from $-\alpha \text{ to} + \alpha$, P_i ranges between 0 and 1, and P_i is non-linearly related to Z_i (X_i). In order to estimate the model, we proceed in the following manner. If P_i is the probability of going for an acquisition then $(1 - P_i)$ is the probability of not going for an acquisition.

$$1 - P_i = 1 - \frac{1}{1+e^{-zi}} = \frac{1+e^{-zi}-1}{1+e^{-zi}} = \frac{e^{-zi}}{1+e^{-zi}}$$

$$= \frac{\frac{1}{e^{zi}}}{1+\frac{1}{e^{zi}}} = \frac{1}{1+e^{zi}}$$

$$\therefore \quad \frac{P_i}{1-P_i} = \frac{\frac{1}{1+e^{-zi}}}{\frac{1}{1+e^{zi}}} = \frac{1+e^{zi}}{1+e^{-zi}} = \frac{1+e^{zi}}{\frac{e^{zi}+1}{e^{zi}}}$$

$$\frac{P_i}{1-P_i} = e^{zi} \quad (2)$$

Now, $P_i/1\text{-}P_i$ is odds ratio in favour of a firm going for an acquisition i.e., if $P_i = 0.8$, then $0.8/0.2 = 4$. It means odds in favour of the firm going for an acquisition is 4:1. Taking log on both the sides of equation (2)

$$L_i = ln\left(\frac{P_i}{1-P_i}\right) = Z_i = \beta_1 + \beta_2 X_i \quad (3)$$

The L, the log of odds ratio is linear in X and is called the logit and hence, the name of this model is Logit model. For estimation purposes we write our model as,

$$L_i = \beta_1 + \beta_2 X_i + u_i \quad (4)$$

As far the interpretation of Logit model is concerned, β_2, measures the change in L for a unit change is X i.e., how the log-odds in favour of a firm going for an acquisition or merger change, as X changes by a unit.

$$\frac{\partial}{\partial X_i}\left(ln \frac{P_i}{1 - P_i} \right) = \frac{\partial L_i}{\partial X_i} = \frac{\partial (\beta_1 + \beta_2 X_i)}{\partial X_i} = \beta_2 \quad (5)$$

$$\frac{\partial P_i}{\partial X_i} = \beta_2 P_i (1 - P_i) \quad (6)$$

If we want to estimate the probability of a firm going for an acquisition at a certain level of X, this can be done using equation (4), after estimating β_1 and β_2 coefficients. Further, the change in the probability of a firm going for an acquisition for a unit change in X depends on the estimated β_2 and also on the level of X, at which the probability is being computed [equation (6)].

Probit Model

If instead of logistic CDF, the normal CDF is used, then the estimating model is known as the Probit model i.e.,

$$P_i = F(Z_i) = \int_{-\infty}^{Z_i} \frac{1}{\sqrt{2\pi}} e^{-t^2/2} dt \quad (7)$$

$$P_i = F(Z_i) = \frac{1}{\sqrt{2\pi}} \int_{-\infty}^{\beta_1 + \beta_2 X_i} e^{-t^2/2} dt \quad (8)$$

Where t is a random variable which is normally distributed with zero mean and unit variance and Z_i is a continuous index which is determined by an explanatory variable X. Thus, the index:

$$Z_i = \beta_1 + \beta_2 X_i.$$

To obtain an estimate of the index Z_i we apply the inverse of the cumulative normal function to (8).

$$Z_i = F^{-1}(P_i) = \beta_1 + \beta_2 X_i$$

In case of more than one variable, the model can be written as:

$$Z_i = \beta_1 + \beta_2 X_{2i} + \dots \beta_k X_{ki} + u_i,$$

Here, the objective is to predict the likelihood that a firm with certain attributes, such as size, profitability, financing ratios and leverage ratios, will go for a merger/get acquired, or not. The estimation of Logit or Probit model depends upon the availability of data. The estimates of P_i are obtained either from grouped data or by using maximum likelihood method (in case of individual data).

Annexure IV

Sources of Data

To carry out the analysis, the following data sources were used:

1. The data on both the merging and non-merging firms from D&P were mainly drawn from the Prowess database (CMIE). It is considered to be the most reliable corporate database. All financial ratios, stock market indicators and sources and uses of funds were calculated using the 'balance sheets', 'profit and loss accounts' and 'sources and uses of funds' statements. Data on few companies were also obtained from the *Bombay Stock Exchange Directory*.
2. The trends in mergers and acquisitions in India, since 2000, were analysed using data from Mergers and Acquisitions—a monthly bulletin published by CMIE.
3. Information regarding number of takeovers (open offers) along with their objectives, was extracted from SEBI's website <*www.sebi.gov.in*>.
4. Data regarding the global trends in cross-border M&As (in number and value of deals) from both the sellers' and purchasers point of view were collected from UNCTAD's cross-border M&A database, available at its website <*www.unctad.org/fdistatistics*>, while the income and regional classification of various countries was obtained from the World Bank's website <*www.worldbank.org*>.
5. Various sources were used to compile a list of mergers and acquisitions in D&P industry since 1990-91, such as *Monthly Review of Indian Economy*-CMIE, *Company News and Notes* (Monthly publication of Department of Company Affairs), website of Bombay Stock Exchange <*www.bseindia.com*> and data on mergers compiled by National Informatics Centre (NIC)—a division of the Department of Company Affairs.
6. Information on the performance measures, such as output, exports, imports and R&D expenditure of D&P industry, was collected from the Organisation of Pharmaceutical Producers of India (OPPI) publications and its website <*www.indiaoppi.com*>.
7. Debate on growth acceleration was analysed using data provided in *Economic Survey,* GOI publication, various issues.

References

Aaronovitch, S. and M.C. Sawyer (1975). *Big Business*. London: Macmillan.

Acharya, S. (2004). "India's Growth Prospects Revisited", *Economic and Political Weekly*: 4537-4542. October 9.

Agarwal, M. (2002). "Analysis of Mergers in India", Unpublished M.Phil dissertation, Delhi School of Economics, University of Delhi.

——. (2005). "Mergers and Acquisitions in India: Implications for Competition", in Pradeep S. Mehta (ed.), *Towards A Functional Competition Policy For India: An Overview*. New Delhi: Academic Foundation; (CUTS International).

Agarwal, M. and H. Singh (2002). "Merger Announcements and Insider Trading Activity in India: An Empirical Investigation", *National Stock Exchange (NSE) Research Paper 48*, February.

Aggarwal, A. (2004). "Strategic Approach to Strengthening the International Competitiveness in Knowledge Based Industries: The Indian Pharmaceutical Industry", *Discussion Paper, Research and Information System for Developing Countries* (RIS- DP # 80/ 2004), September.

Ahluwalia, I.J. (1991). *Productivity and Growth in Indian Manufacturing*. New Delhi: Oxford University Press.

——. (1995). *Industrial Growth in Indian Manufacturing*. New Delhi: Oxford University Press.

Ahluwalia, M.S. (1999). "India's Economic Reform: An Appraisal", in J. Sachs, A. Varshney and N. Bajpai (eds.), *India in the Era of Economic Reforms*. New Delhi: Oxford University Press.

——. (2002). "Economic Reforms in India Since 1991: Has Gradualism Worked?", *Journal of Economic Perspective* 16(3): 67-88.

——. (2002). "Indian Economic Reform: An Appraisal", in Jeffrey Sachs, Ashutosh Varshney and Nirupam Bajpai (eds.), *India in the Era of Economic Reforms*. New Delhi: Oxford University Press. pp. 26-80.

Ambrose, B.W. and W.L. Megginson (1992). "The Role of Asset Structure, Ownership Structure, and Takeover Defences in Determining Acquisition Likelihood", *Journal of Financial and Quantitative Analysis* 27(4): 575-89.

Amihud, Y. and B. Lev (1981). "Risk Reduction as a Managerial Motive for Conglomerate Mergers", *Bell Journal of Economics* 12: 605-617, Autumn.

Aminian, N., S. Campart and E. Pfister (2005). "Macro Determinants of Cross-Border Mergers and Acquisitions: European and Asian Evidence", A paper presented at European and East Asian Experiences International Conference on *International Trade and Logistic Corporate Strategies and the Global Economy*, 28-29 February 2005.

Andrade, G. and Erik Stafford (1999). "Investigating the Economic Role of Mergers", *Harvard Business Chool Working Paper*, August.

Andrade, G., Mark Mitchell and Erik Stafford (2001). "New Evidence and Perspectives on Mergers", *Journal of Economic Perspectives* 15(2): 103-120. Spring.

Asquith, P. (1983). "Mergers Bids, Uncertainty and Stockholders Returns", *Journal of Financial Economics*: 51-83.

Auerbach, A.J. (ed.) (1988). *Corporate Takeovers: Causes and Consequences*. National Bureau of Economic Research. Chicago: University of Chicago Press.

Balakrishnan, P. (2005). "Macroeconomic Policy and Economic Growth in the 1990s", *Economic and Political Weekly*: 3969-3977. September 3.

Baldwin, J. (1991). *The Dynamics of the Competitive Process*. Queen's University. (mimeo).

Banerjee, A. (2000). "Hostile Takeover", *The Economic Times*, November 10.

Bardhan, P. (2003). "Disjuncture in the Indian Reform Process: Some Reflection", in K. Basu (ed.), *India's Emerging Economy: Performance and Prospects*. New Delhi: Oxford University Press.

Barnes, P., I. Davidson and M. Wright (1996). "The Changing Nature of Corporate Control and Ownership Structure", *Journal of Business Finance & Accountancy* 23 (5&6), July.

Barua, S.K. (2000). "Fine-tuning the code", *The Economic Times*, November 21.

Basant, R. (2000). "Corporate Response to Economic Reforms", *Economic and Political Weekly*: 812-822. March 4.

Baumol, W.J. (1965). *The Stock Market and Economic Efficiency*. New York.

Beena, P.L. (1998). "Merger and Amalgamations: An Analysis of the Changing Structure of Indian Oligopoly", Doctoral Dissertation. New Delhi: Centre for Economic Studies and Planning, JNU.

———. (2000). "An Analysis of Merger in Private Corporate Sector in India", *Working Paper* No. 301, Kerala: Centre for Development Studies.

Belkoul, A. (1978). "Financial Ratios as Predictors of Canadian Takeovers", *Journal of Business Finance and Accounting:* 93-107. Spring.

Bertrand, O. and Habib Zitouna (2006). "Trade Liberalisation and Industrial Dynamics: Firm Survival, Exit or Cross-Border M&A", ms, Paris 1 Pantheon-Sorbonne University and CNRS, February.

Bhagat, S., A. Shleifer and Rober W. Vishny (1990). "Hostile Takeovers in the 1980s: The Return to Corporate Specialization", *Brookings Papers on Economic Activity: Microeconomics*, (Special issue). pp. 1-84.

Bhagwati, J.N. (1982). "Directly Unproductive, Profit-seeking (DUP) Activities", *Journal of Political Economy* 90(5): 988-1002.

Bhagwati, J.N. and T.N. Srinivasan (1980). "Revenue Seeking: A Generalization of the Theory of Tariffs", *Journal of Political Economy* 88(61): 1067-1087.

Bhattacharya, H.K. (1987): "Amalgamations and Takeovers", *Company News and Notes* 25 (4).

Bhaumik, S.K. (2002). "Does Concentration of Ownership Alleviate Agency problem? Some Evidence from the Market for Corporate control in India", UK: Centre for New and Emerging markets, London Business School. October.

Bhoi, B.K. (2000). "Mergers and Acquisitions: An Indian Experience", *Reserve Bank of India Occasional Papers* 21, Summer.

Bittlingmayer, G. (1996). "Merger and the Returns to Labour and Investment", *Applied Economic Letters* 3: 145-148.

Boudreaux, K.J. (1973). "Managerialism' and Risk return Performance", *Southern Economic Journal*: 366-372. January.

Bradley, M., A. Desai and E.H. Kim (1988). "Synergistic Gains from Corporate Acquisitions and their Division between the Stockholders of Target and Acquiring Firms", *Journal of Financial Economics* 21: 3-40.

Buckley, A. (1972). "A Profile of Industrial Acquisitions in 1971", *Accounting and Business Research:* 243-252. Autumn.

Carr, D.L., J.R. Markusen and K.E. Maskus (2001). "Estimating the Knowledge-Capital Model of the Multinational Enterprises", *American Economic Review* 9(3): 693-708, June.

Carroll, C.A. (2002). "A Century of Mergers and Acquisition", in B.E. Gup (ed.), *Megamergers in a Global Economy: Causes and Consequences*. USA: Greenwood Publishing Group.

Carter J. (1977). "In Search of Synergy: A Structure Performance Test", *Review of Economic and Statistics* 61(2): 292-296.

Chakravarthy, S. (2004). "Competition Act, 2002: The Approach", in Pradeep S. Mehta (ed.), *Towards A Functional Competition Policy For India: An Overview*. New Delhi: Academic Foundation, (CUTS International).

Chandra, N.K. (1977). "Monopoly Legislation & Policy in Indian Business Houses", *Economic Political Weekly* 12 (33-34): 1405-1418. August.

Chandra, Prasanna (2004). *Financial Management: Theory and Practice*. New Delhi: Tata McGraw-Hill Publishing Company Limited.

Chandrasekhar, C.P. (1999). "Firms, Markets and the State: An Analysis of Indian Oligopoly", in Amiya Kumar Bagchi (ed.), *Economy and Organisation- Indian Institutions under Neo Liberalized Regime*. Sage Publications.

Chatterjee, R. and G. Meeks (1996). "The Financial Effects of Takeover: Accounting Rates of Return and Accounting Regulation", *Journal of Business, Finance and Accounting* 23 (5&6), July.

CMIE[1]. *Corporate Sector*, various issues.

CMIE[2]. *Industry: Financial Aggregates & Ratios*, various issues.

CMIE[3]. *Industry: Market Size & Shares*, various issues.

CMIE[4]. *Mergers and Acquisition*, various issues.

Cobham, D. and R. Subramaniam (1995). "Corporate Finance in Developing Countries: New Evidence for India", *CRIEFF Discussion Papers Series*. No. 9512. Scotland: University of St. Andrews.

Cooke, Terrence (1980). *Mergers and Acquisitions*. UK: Basil Blackwell Ltd.

Cosh, A., A. Hughes and A. Singh (1980). "The Causes and Effect of Takeover in United Kingdom: An Empirical Investigation of the Late 1960s at the Micro-Economic Level", in D.C. Mueller (ed.), *Determinants and Effects of Mergers*. pp. 227-270.

Cosh, A., A. Hughes, K. Lee and A. Singh, (1998). "Takeovers Institutional Investment and the Persistence of Profits", in Iain Begg and S.G.B. Henry, (eds.), *Applied Economics and Public Policy*. UK: Department of Applied Economics, Cambridge University Press. pp. 107-144.

CSO (2006). National Accounts Statistics, GOI.

D'Souza, Errol (2000). "Structure of Corporate Finance and Corporate Governance in India", *Economic and Political Weekly:* 4196-4205. November 25.

Das, Nandita (2000). "A Study of the Corporate Restructuring of Indian Industries in the Post-New Industrial Policy Regime–The Issue of Amalgamations/Mergers", Unpublished Ph.D. thesis submitted to the University of Calcutta, Calcutta.

Davis, G.F. and S.K. Stout (1992). "Organisation Theory and the Market for Corporate Control: A Dynamic Analysis of the Characteristics of Large Takeover Targets, 1980-90", *Administrative Science Quarterly* 37(4): 605-33.

DeAngelo, H., L. DeAngelo and E. Rice (1984). "Going Private: Minority Freezeouts and Stockholder Wealth", *Journal of Law and Economics* 27: 367-402.

Delong, J.B. (2004). "India since Independence: An Analytic Growth Narrative", in D. Rodrik (ed.), *Modern Economic Growth: Analytical Country Studies*, Chapter 7. pp. 184-204.

Desai, A. (1999). "The Economics and Politics of Transition to an Open Market Economy: India", *OECD Working Paper* V11(100).

Desai, A.V. (1981). "Factor Underlying the Slow Growth of Indian Industry", *Economic and Political Weekly* XVI(10-12): 381-392.

Devine, M. (2003). *Successful Mergers: Getting the People Issues Right*. London: Profile Books Limited.

Dietrich, J.K. and E. Sorensen(1984). "An Application of Logit Analysis to Prediction of Merger Targets", *Journal of Business Research* 12: 393-402.

Dodd, P. and R. Ruback (1977). "Tender Offers and Stockholders Returns", *Journal of Financial Economics* 5, December.

Eckbo, B.E. (1983). "Horizontal Mergers, Collusion and Stockholder Wealth", *Journal of Financial Economics* 11(1-4): 241-73. April.

Fama, E.F. and M.C. Jensen (1983). "Separation of Ownership and Control", *Journal of Law and Economics* 26: 301-325.

Firth, M.A. (1976). "Synergy in British Results", *Journal of Finance* 33, May.

Frankel, J.A. and D. Romer (1999). "Does Trade Cause Growth?", *The American Economic Review* 89(3): 379-399. June.

Franks, J. and C. Mayer (1996). "Hostile Takeovers and the Correction of Managerial Failures", *Journal of Financial Economics* 40: 163-81.

Gaiha, R. and Katsushi Imai (2005). "Do Institutions Matter in Poverty Reduction?: Prospects of Achieving the MDG of Poverty Reduction in Asia", *Economics Discussion Paper*, EDP-0506, The University of Manchester. February.

Gaiha, R., K. Imai and A. Nandhi (2005). "Millennium Development Goal of Halving Poverty in Asia and the Pacific Region: Progress, Prospects and Priorities", *Discussion Paper*, January.

Gaughan, Patrick (ed.) (1994). *Readings in Mergers and Acquisition*. UK: Basil Blackwell Ltd.

Gibbs, P.A. (1993). "Determinants of Corporate Restructuring: The Relative Importance of Corporate Governance, Takeover Threat and Free Cash Flow", *Strategic Management Journal* 14: 51-68.

GOI (Government of India): *Economic Survey*. New Delhi: Ministry of Finance, (various issues).

Golbe, D.L. and L.J. White (1988). "A Time Series Analysis of Mergers and Acquisition in the US Economy", in A.J. Auerbach (ed.), *Corporate Takeovers: Causes and Consequences*. NBER, Chicago: University of Chicago Press. pp. 265-309.

Goldar, B. and V.S. Reganathan (1991). "Capacity Utilization in Indian Industries", *Indian Economic Journal* 32(2): 82-92. (October-December).

Goldberg, L.G. (1973). "The Effect of Conglomerate Mergers on Competition", *Journal of Law and Economics* 16: 137-58.

Gort, M. (1969). "An Economic Disturbance Theory of Mergers", *Quarterly Journal of Economics* 83: 624-642. November.

Gould Jr., J.P. and E.P. Lazear (1996). *Microeconomic Theory*. USA: Richard D. Irwin, INC, Homewood, (6th edition).

Gregory, A. (1997). "An Examination of the Long Run Performance of UK Acquiring Firms", *Journal of Business Finance and Accounting* 24 (7&8), September.

Grossman, S. and O.D. Hart (1980). "Takeovers Bids, the Free Rider Problem and the Theory of the Corporation", *Bell Journal of Economics* 11: 42-64.

Gujarati, D.N. (2003). *Basic Econometrics*. Singapore: McGraw-Hill.

Gup, B.E. (ed.) (2002). *Megamergers in a Global Economy: Causes and Consequences*. USA: Greenwood Publishing Group.

Gupta, L.C. (1989). *Corporate Boards and Nominee Directors*. Delhi: Oxford University Press.

Hall, Browyn (1988). "The Effect of Takeover Activity on Corporate Research and Development", in A.J. Auerbach (ed.), *Corporate Takeovers: Causes and Consequences*. National Bureau of Economic Research. Chicago: University of Chicago Press. pp. 69-94.

Hannah, L. and J.A. Kay (1977). *Concentration in Modern Industry*. London: Macmillan.

Hay and Untiet (1981). "Statistical Measurement of the Conglomerate Problem", in Roger D. Blair and R.F. Lanzillotti (eds.), *The Conglomerate Corporation*. Cambridge, Mass.: Oelgeschlager, Gunn and Hain. pp. 163-91.

Hay, D.A. and G.S. Liu (1998). "When do Firms go in for Growth by Acquisition", *Oxford Bulletin of Economics and Statistics* 60(2): 143-164.

Hay, Donald A. and D.J. Morris (1991). *Industrial Economics and Organization: Theory and Practice*. Oxford: Oxford University Press.

Hazari, R.K. (1966). *The Structure of the Corporate Private Sector: A Study of Concentration, Ownership and Control*. London: Asia Publishing House.

Healy, Paul M., K.G. Palepu and R.S. Ruback (1992). "Does Corporate Performance Improve After Mergers?", *Journal of Financial Economics* 31(2): 135-175.

Holl, P. (1975). "Effect of Control Type on the Performance of the Firm in the UK", *Journal of Industrial Economics:* 257-271.

Holl, P. and D. Kyriazis (1997). "Agency, Bid Resistance and the Market for Corporate Control", *Journal of Business Finance & Accountancy* 24 (7&8), September.

Holland, K.M. and L. Hodgkinson (1994). "The Pre-Announcement Share Price Behaviour of UK Takeover Targets", *Journal of Business Finance & Accounting* 21(4): 467-489. (June).

Hughes, Allan, D. Mueller and A. Singh (1980). "Hypotheses about Mergers", in D.C. Mueller (ed.), *The Determinants and Effect of Mergers: An International Comparison*. Cambridge, MA: Gunn & Hain Publishers. pp. 27-65.

Hughes, A. (1993). "Mergers and Economic Performance in UK: A Survey of Empirical Evidence (1950-90)", in M. Bishop and J. Kay (eds.), *European Mergers and Merger Policy*. Oxford University Press.

ICRA (1999; 2002; 2004): *Industry Watch Series, The Indian Pharmaceutical Industry.*

———. (2005a): *Indian Pharmaceutical Industry: Impact of Product Patent* (ICRA Rating Features).

———. (2005b): *Industry Comment: Pharmaceuticals: Indian Pharmaceutical Industry'*, INGRES - a division of ICRA Ltd., February.

———. (2005c): *Industry Watch Series, The Indian Pharmaceutical Industry.*

Jacquemin, A. and H. de Jong (1977). *European Industrial Organisation*. London: Macmillan.

Jalan, B. (1992). "Balance of Payments, 1956-1991", in Bimal Jalan (ed.), *Indian Economy: Problems and Prospects.* New Delhi: Penguin. pp.1623-94.

Jarrell, G.A. and A.B. Poulsen (1987). "Bidder Returns", *Working Paper*.

Jarrell, G.A. and Annette B. Poulsen (1989). "The Return to Acquiring Firms in Tender Offers: Evidence from Three Decades", *Financial Management* 18(3): 12-19. Autumn. Also in P. Gaughan (ed.), *Readings in Mergers and Acquisition*, 1994. UK: Basil Blackwell Ltd.. pp. 284-295.

Jarrell, G.A., J. Brickley and J.M. Netter (1988). "The Market for Corporate Control: The Empirical Evidence since 1980", *Journal of Economic Perspective*: 49-68. Winter. Also in P. Gaughan (ed.), *Readings in Mergers and Acquisition*, 1994. UK: Basil Blackwell Publishers.

Jenny, F. and A-P Weber (1980). "France, 1962-72", in D.C. Mueller (ed.), *Determinants and Effects of Mergers*. pp. 133-162.

Jensen, M.C. (1988). "Takeovers: Their Causes and Consequences", *Journal of Economic Perspectives* 3(2): 21-48. Winter. Also in P.A. Gaughan (ed.), *Readings in Mergers and Acquisition*. pp. 15-43. UK: Basil Blackwell Publishers, 1994.

———. (1993). "The Modern Industrial Revolution and the Challenge to Internal Control Systems", *Journal of Finance* 48: 831-880.

Jensen, M.C and C.W. Smith Jr. (1985). "Stockholder, Manager and Creditor Interests: Applications of Agency Theory", in E. Altman and M. Subramanyam (eds.), *Recent Advances in Corporate Finance.* Homewood: Richard Irwin. pp. 93-131.

Jensen, M.C. and R. Ruback (1983). "The Market for Corporate Control: The Scientific Evidence", *Journal of Financial Economics* 11: 5-50. April.

———. (1990). "Performance Pay and Top Management Incentives", *Journal of Political Economy* 98(2): 225-64. April.

Jensen, Michael C. (1986a). "Agency Cost and Ownership Structure", *Journal of Financial Economics* 3(4): 305-360.

———. (1986b). "Agency Costs of Free Cash Flow, Corporate Finance and Takeovers", *American Economic Review* 76(2): 323-29.

Joshi, V. and I.M. Little (1994). *India: Macroeconomics and Political Economy: 1961-91*. Washington, DC. World Bank.

———. (1996). *India's Economic Reforms 1991-2001*. Oxford: Clarendon Press.

Kapila, Uma (ed.) (2003). *Indian Economy Since Independence: A Comprehensive and Critical Analysis of the Indian Economy since Independence*. New Delhi: Academic Foundation.

Kaplan, Steven N. (ed.) (2000). *Mergers and Productivity*. The University of Chicago Press.

Kaufmann, D., A. Kraay and M. Mastruzzi (2003). "Governance Matters III: Governance Indicators for 1996-2002", *World Bank Policy Research Working Paper* 3106. Washington DC: World Bank.

Kaur, Gurminder (2005). *Corporate Mergers in India*. New Delhi: Deep & Deep Publication.

Kaveri, V.S. (1986). *Financial Analysis of Company Mergers in India*. Bombay: Himalaya Publishing House. April 1983. pp. 5-50.

Khan, M.Y. and P.K. Jain (2003). *Financial Management: Text and Problems*, (Third edition). New Delhi: Tata McGraw-Hill Publishing Company Limited.

Khanna, Sushil (1999). "Financial Reforms and Industrial Sector in India", *Economic and Political Weekly* 3231-3241. November 6.

Kindleberger, C.P. (1996). *International Economics*. Illinois: RDI Publishers.

Krueger, A.O. (1974). "The Political Economy of the Rent-Seeking Society", *American Economic Review* 64(3): 291-303.

Kuehn, D. (1975). *Takeovers and the Theory of the Firm*. Macmillan.

Kumar, Nagesh (2000). "Mergers and Acquisition by MNEs: Patterns and Implications", *Economic and Political Weekly*. 2851-2858. August 5-11.

Kumps, A.M. and R. Witterwulghe (1980). "Belgium, 1962-1974", in D.C. Mueller (ed.), *Determinants and Effects of Mergers*. pp. 67-97.

Lehn, K. and A.B. Poulsen (1987). "Sources of Value in Leveraged Buyouts", in *Public Policy Towards Corporate Takeovers*. New Brunswick, NJ: Transaction Publishers.

Lev, B. and G. Mandelkar (1972). "The Microeconomic Consequences of Corporate Mergers", *Journal of Business* 45: 85-104.

Levin, R.I. and D.S. Rubin (1995). *Statistics and Management*. New Delhi: Prentice-Hall of India Private Limited.

Levine, P. and S. Aaronovitch (1981). "The Financial Characteristics of Firms and Theories of Merger Activity", *The Journal of Industrial Economics* 30(2): 149-72.

Lichtenberg, F.R. and D. Siegel (1987). "Productivity and Changes in Ownership of Manufacturing Plants", *Brookings Papers on Economic Activity* 3: 643-73.

Lipsey, R.G. and K.A. Chrystal (1995). *An Introduction to Positive Economics*. Oxford University Press.

Lynch, H.H. (1971). *Financial Performance of Conglomerates*. Boston, MA: Harvard Graduate School of Business Administration.

Mani, S. and Bhaskar M.V. (1998). "A Curmudgeon's Guide to Economic Reforms in India's Manufacturing Sector", *Economic and Political Weekly*: 3257-3272. December 19.

Manne, H.G. (1965). "Mergers and Market for Corporate Control", *Journal of Political Economy* 73: 110-20.

Markham, J.W. (1955). "Survey of the Evidence and Findings on Mergers", in *Business Concentration and Price Policy*, NBER. NY: Princeton University Press.

———. (1973). *Conglomerate Enterprises and Public Policy*. Boston, MA: Harvard Graduate School of Business Administration.

Marris, R. (1964). *The Economic theory of Managerial Capitalism*. London: Macmillan.

Martin, K. and J. McConnell (1991). "Corporate Performance, Corporate Takeovers and Management Turnover", *The Journal of Finance* 46: 671-87.

Matsusaka, J.G. (1993). "Takeover Motives during the Conglomerate Merger Wave", *RAND Journal of Economics* 24(3): 357-79.

McConnell, J. and C.J. Muscarella (1985). "Corporate Capital Expenditure Decisions and the Market Value of the Firm", *Journal of Financial Economics*: 399-422. September.

McDougall, F.M. and D.K. Round (1986). *The Determinants and Effects of Corporate Takeovers in Australia, 1970-81*. Victoria: Australian Institute of Management.

McGowan, J.J. (1980). "The Effect of Alternative Antimerger Policies on the Size Distribution of Firms", *Yale Economic Essays* 5: 423-474.

McGuckin, R.H. and S.V. Nguyen (1995). "On Productivity and Plant Ownership Change: New Evidence from the Longitudinal Research Database", *RAND Journal of Economics* 26(2): 257-276. Summer.

Meeks, G. (1977). *Disappointing Marriage: A Study of the Gains from Merger*. Cambridge, Mass.: Oelgeschlager, Gunn and Hain.

Mikkelson, W. and R.S. Ruback (1985). "An Empirical Analysis of the Interfirm Equity Investment Process", *Journal of Financial Economics* 14: 523-53.

Mitchell, Mark L. and J. Harold Mulherin (1996). "The Impact of Industry Shocks on Takeover and Restructuring Activity", *Journal of Financial Economics* 41: 193-229.

Mitchell, Mark L. and K. Lehn (1990). "Do Bad Bidder Become Good Targets", *Journal of Political Economy* 98(2): 372-98.

Mittal, A. (2003). *Economic Reforms and Capital Market in India*. New Delhi: Galgotia Publishing House.

Modigliani, H. and M.H. Miller (1958). "The Cost of Capital, Corporation Finance and the Theory of Investment", *American Economic Review* 48: 261-297. June.

Mohammad, S. and J. Whalley (1984). "Rent Seeking in India: Its Cost and Policy Significance", *Kyklos* 37(3): 387-413.

Morck, R., A. Schleifer and R. Vishny (1988). "Characteristics of Targets of Hostile and Friendly Takeovers", in A.J. Auerbach (ed.), *Corporate Takeovers: Causes and Consequences*. Chicago: University of Chicago Press. pp. 101-29.

Mueller, D.C. (1969). "A Theory of Conglomerate Mergers", *Quarterly Journal of Economics* 83: 643-659.

———. (1980a). "A Cross-National Comparison of the Results", in D.C. Mueller (ed.), *Determinants and Effects of Mergers*. pp. 299-314.

———. (1980b). "The United States, 1962-72", in D.C. Mueller (ed.), *Determinants and Effects of Mergers*. pp. 271-298.

———. (ed.) (1980c). *The Determinants and Effects of Mergers: An International Comparison*. Cambridge, Massachusetts: Oelgeschlager, Gunn & Hain, Publishers, Inc.

———. (1985). "Mergers and Market Share", *The Review of Economics and Statistics* 47: 259-67.

———. (1986). *Profits in the Long Run*. Cambridge: Cambridge University Press.

——. (1995). "Mergers: Theory and Evidence", in G. Mussati (ed.), *Mergers, Markets, and Public Policy.* Dordrecht, The Netherlands: Kluwer Academic. pp. 9-43.

Mueller, D.C. and H.G. Grabowski (1972). "Managerial and Stockholder Welfare Models of Firm Expenditure", *Review of Economics and Statistics*. November.

Muller, J. (1976). "The Impact of Mergers on Concentration: A Study of 11 West German Industries", *Journal of Industrial Economics* 25: 113-132.

Nagaraj, R. (1996). "India's Capital Market Growth: Trends, Explanations and Evidence", *Economic and Political Weekly* 31 (35, 36, 37): 2553-2563. Special Issue, September.

Newbound, G.D. (1970). *Management and Merger Activity*. UK: Guthstead Ltd.

OPPI (2001, 2004): *Pharmaceutical Compendium, Organisation of Pharmaceutical Producers of India*.

Palepu, K.G. (1985). "The Determinants of Acquisition Likelihood", *Working Paper*, Cambridge: Harvard University, Mass.

——. (1986). "Predicting Takeover Targets: A Methodological and Empirical Analysis", *Journal of Accounting and Economics* 8: 3-35.

Panagariya, A. (2003). "Miracles and Debacles: Do Free Trade Sceptics Have a Case?", *http://www.bsos.umd.edu/econ/panagariya/apecon/polpaper.htm.*

——. (2004). "Growth and Reforms during 1980s and 1990s", *Economic and Political Weekly* 36: 2581-94.

Panandiker, D.H.P. (2000). "The Takeover Game", *The Hindustan Times*, November 27.

Pandey, I.M. (2003). *Financial Management*. New Delhi: Vikas Publishing House.

Peer, Henk (1980). "The Nether lands, 1962-1973", in D.C. Mueller (ed.), *Determinants and Effects of Mergers*. pp. 163-191.

Pindyck, R.S. and D.L. Rubinfeld (1998). *Econometric Models and Economic Forecasts.* Singapore: McGraw-Hill.

Powell, R.G. (1997). "Modelling Takeover Likelihood", *Journal of Business Finance & Accountancy* 24 (7&8), September.

Powell, R.G. and H.M. Thomas (1994). "Corporate Control and Takeover Predictions", *Working Paper* 94/07. UK: Department of Accounting and Financial Management, University of Essex.

Pradhan, J.P. (2003). "Liberalisation, Firm Size and R&D performance: A Firm Level Study of Indain Pharmaceutical Industry", *Discussion Paper, Research and Information System for Developing Countries* (RIS- DP # 40/2003), January.

Pursell, G. (1992). "Trade Policy in India", in Dominick Salvatore (ed.), *National Trade Policies.* New York: Greenwood Press. pp. 423-58.

Rakshit, M. (2003). "Some Macroeconomics of India's Reform Experience", in K. Basu (ed.), *India's Emerging Economy: Performance and Prospects.* New Delhi: Oxford University Press.

Ramu, S. (1996). *Corporate Growth through Mergers and Acquisitions*. New Delhi: Response Books.

Rao, N.V. and P.V. Krishna Rao (1987). "Regulations of Mergers under MRTP Act 1969: A Critical Study", *Company News and Notes* 25(6).

Ravenscraft, D.J. and F.M. Scherer (1987). "The Long Run Performance of Mergers and Takeovers", in M.L. Weidenbaum and Kenneth W. Chilton (eds.), *Public Policy Towards Corporate Takeovers*. US: Transaction Publishers.

RBI[1]. (Reserve Bank of India). *Reserve Bank of India Bulletin*, various issues.

RBI[2]. (Reserve Bank of India). *Report on Currency and Finance*, Vol. I and II, Bombay: RBI, various issues.

Rodriguez, F. and Dani Rodrik (2000). "Trade Policy and Economic Growth: A Skeptic Guide to the Cross-National Evidence", Revised version of *NBER Working Paper* 7081, April 1999.

Rodrik, D. (2004). "Institutions, Integration and Geography: In Search of the Deep Determinants of Economic Growth", in Dani Rodrick (ed.), *Modern Economic Growth: Analytical Country Studies*.

Rodrik, D. and A. Subramanian (2004). "From 'Hindu Growth' to Productivity Surge: The Mystery of the Indian Growth Transition", *NBER Working Paper* No. 10376, March.

———. (2004). "Why India Can Grow at 7 per cent a Year or More, Projections and Reflections", *Economic and Political Weekly*: 1591-1597. April 17.

Rodrik, D., A. Subramanian and F. Trebbi (2004). "Institutions Rule: The Primacy of Institutions over Integration and Geography in Development", *Journal of Economic Growth* 9: 131-165.

Roll, R. (1986). "The Hubris Hypothesis of Corporate Takeovers", *Journal of Business* 59(2): 197-216.

Roy, Malabika (1999). "Mergers and Takeovers: The Indian Scene during 1990s", in Amiya Kumar Bagchi (ed.), *Economy and Organisation- Indian Institutions under Neo Liberalized Regime*. New Delhi: Sage Publications.

Sachs, J. and W.A. Warner (1995). "Economic Reforms and the Process of Global Integration", *Brookings Papers on Economic Activity* 1: 1-118.

Salvatore, Dominick (1996). *Managerial Economics in a Global Economy*. McGraw Hill: Irwin McGraw Hill, III Edition.

Sankar, K.R. and K.V. Rao (1999). "Takeover and Turnaround", *Charted Secretary*, February. pp. 149-154.

Saple, V. (2000). "Diversification, Merger and their Effect on Firm Performance: A Study of the Indian Corporate Sector", Unpublished Ph.D thesis submitted to Indira Gandhi Institute of Development Research, Mumbai, May.

Schoar, A. (2000). "Effects of Corporate Diversification on Productivity", *Working Paper*, MIT Sloan School.

Schwarz, S. (1982). "Factors Affecting the Probability of Being Acquired: Evidence for the United States", *Economic Journal* 92, June.

SEC (1985). "Institutional Ownership, Tender Offers, and Long-Term Investments", SEC study (Security and Exchange Commission), Office of the Chief Economist. Washington DC: GPO, April.

Servaes, Henry (1991). "Tobins q and Gains from Takeovers", *Journal of Finance* 66. March.

Sharma, D.S. and J. Ho (2002). "The Impact of Acquisition on Operating Performance: Some Australian Evidence", *Journal of Business, Finance & Accounting*. 29(1&2), January-March.

Shinde, S.R. (1995). "Takeovers and Mergers-as Means of Industrial Restructuring", *The Management Accountant*, July.

Shleifer, A. and W. Vishny (1991). "Takeovers in the '60s and the '80s: Evidence and Implications", *Strategic Management Journal* 12: 51-9.

Simkowitz, M. and R.J. Monroe (1971). "A Discriminant Analysis Function for Conglomerate Targets", *Southern Journal of Business* 1-16. November.

Singh, Sampat P. and S. Singh (2004). *Financial Analysis for Bank Lending in Liberalised Economy*. Delhi: Himalaya Publishing.

Singh, A. and G. Whittington (1975). "The Size and Growth of firms", *Review of Economic Studies* 42: 15-26. January.

———. (1968). *Growth, Profitability and Valuation*. London: Cambridge, University Press.

Singh, A. (1971). *Takeovers: Their Relevance to the Stock Market and the Theory of the Firm*. Cambridge: Cambridge University Press.

———. (1975). "Takeovers, Economic Natural Selection, and the Theory of the Firm: Evidence from the Post-War United Kingdom Experience", *The Economic Journal* 85: 497-515. September.

———. (1995). "Corporate Financial Patterns in Industrialising Economies: A Comparative International Study", *IFC Technical Paper* No. 2. Washington, DC: The World Bank.

———. (1998). "Liberalisation, the Stock Market, and the Market for Corporate Control; A Bridge too far for the Indian Economy?", in I.J. Ahluwalia and I.M.D. Little (eds.), *India's Economic Reforms and Development: Essays for Manmohan Singh*. New Delhi: Oxford University Press.

Singh, A. and J. Hamid (1992). "Corporate Financial Structures in Developing Countries", *IFC Technical Paper No*. 1. Washington, DC: The World Bank.

Singh, N. (1986). "Foreign Ownership, Size and Performance of a Firm: A Case Study of Indian Pharmaceutical Industry", Ph.D Dissertation, University of Delhi.

Singh, S.R. and V. Kumar (1994). *Corporate Rehabilitation and BIFR*. New Delhi: Shipra Publication.

Smith, C.W. (1986). "Investment Banking and the Capital Acquisition Process", *Journal of Financial Economics* 1-2, 15.

Sodersten, Bo (1979). *International Economics*, Second edition. The Macmillan Press.

Sood, G.S. and S. Kaur (2004). "Predicting Corporate Takeovers in India: An Empirical Analysis", *Vision: The Journal of Business Perspective* 8(2): 57-67, July-December.

Sorensen, Donald E. (2000). "Characteristics of Merging Firms", *Journal of Economics and Business* 52: 423-33.

Sridharan, R. (2005). "Indian Pharma's Mid-Life Crisis", *Business Today*: 50-55, February 27.

Srinivasan, T.N. (1987). "Economic Liberalisation in China and India: Issues and an Analytical Framework", *Journal of Comparative Economics* 11: 427-443.

Srinivasan, T.N. and S. Tendulkar (2003). *Reintegrating India with the World Economy*. Washington, DC.: Institute for International Economics.

Stevens, D.L. (1973). "Financial Characteristics of Merged Firms: A Multivariate Analysis", *Journal of Financial and Quantitative Analysis* 8: 149-165. March.

Stigler, G.J. (1966). "The Economic Effects of the Antitrust Laws", *Journal of Law and Economics* 9: 225-258. October.

Stillman, Robert (1983). "Examining Antitrust Policy Towards Horizontal Mergers", *Journal of Financial Economics* 11: 225-240.

Sudarsanam, S., P. Holl and A. Salami (1996). "Shareholder Wealth Gains in Mergers: Effect of Synergy and Ownership Structure", *Journal of Business Finance & Accountancy* 23(5); 7(6), July.

The Economics Times, various issues.

Tobin, J. (1984). "On the Efficiency of the Financial System", *Lloyds Bank Annual Review:* 1-15. July.

Trahan, E.A. (1994). "Industry Effects on the Abnormal Returns to Acquiring Firms", *Journal of Applied Business Research* 19(3): 10-16.

Trahan, E.A. and H.A. Shawky (1992). "Financial Characteristics of Acquiring Firms: An Industry Specific Approach", *Review of Financial Economics* 48(7): 81-94.

Tyabji, N. (1999): "Globalisation in a Unipolar World: Five Case Studies of the Corporate Sector in India under Deregulation", in Amiya Kumar Bagchi (ed.), *Economy and Organisation- Indian Institutions under Neo Liberalized Regime*. New Delhi: Sage Publications.

Tzoannos, J. and J.M. Samuels (1972). "Mergers and Takeovers: The Financial Characteristics of Companies Merged", *Journal of Business Finance* 4(3): 5-16. Autumn.

UNCTAD (1999, 2000a, 2004, 2005). *World Investment Report*, UNCTAD (United Nations Conference on Trade and Development), United Nations: New York and Geneva.

———. (2000b). "Impact of Cross-Border Mergers and Acquisitions on Development and Policy Issues for Consideration", Trade and Development Board (TD), UNCTAD, UN. June.

Vaish, Nandini (2005). "Dabur on Chyawanaprash", *Business World*: 33-35. March 28.

Van Horne, J.C. and J.M. Wachowicz Jr. (1996, 2001). *Fundamentals of Financial Management*. New Delhi: Prentice Hall of India.

Virmani, A. (1997). "Economic Development and Transition in India", Paper presented at the Tokyo Dialogue on *Alternatives to the World Bank- IMF Approach to Reforms and Growth*. Tokyo, Japan: Economic Planning Agency, November 7.

Vu, Khuong (2004). "ICT and Global Economic Growth", Paper presented at *Program on Technology and Economic Policy*, Harvard Kennedy School of Government. November.

Weir, Charles (1997). "Corporate Governance, Performance and Takeovers: An Empirical Analysis of UK Mergers", *Applied Economics* 29: 1465-1475.

Weston, J. Fred, Chung Kwant S. and Hoag Susan E. (1998). *Mergers, Restructuring and Corporate Control,* New Delhi: Prentice Hall of India Pvt Ltd.

———. (1990). *Mergers, Restructuring, and Corporate Control*. New Jersey, USA.: Prentice-Hall Englewood Cliffs.

Weston, J.F. and S.K. Mansinghka (1971). "Tests of Efficiency Performance of Conglomerate Firms", *Journal of Finance* 26(4): 919-36. September.

White, L.J. (1982). "Mergers and Aggregate Concentration", in K. Michael and J.W. Lawrence, (eds.), *Mergers and Acquisitions*. Lexington, Mass: Lexington Books. pp. 97-111.

Williamson, O.E. (1964). *The Economics of Discretionary Behaviour: Managerial Objectives in a Theory of the Firm*. Englewood Cliff, NJ: Prentice Hall.

World Bank (2005). *World Development Indicators*. Washington DC: Oxford University Press.

World Economic Forum (2005). *Global Competitiveness Report, 2005-06*.

Yadav, S., P.K. Jain and N. Jain (1994). "Profitability of Mergers: Some Selected Cases", *Management Accountant* 34(7). July.

Yanikkaya, H. (2003). "Trade Openness and Economic Growth: A Cross-Country Empirical Investigation", *Journal of Development Economics* 72: 57-89.